Theologies and Practices of Inclusion

Theologies and Practices of Inclusion

Insights From a Faith-based Relief,
Development and Advocacy
Organization

Edited by

Nina Kurlberg and
Madleina Daehnhardt

scm press

© The Editor and Contributors 2021

Published in 2021 by SCM Press
Editorial office
3rd Floor, Invicta House,
108–114 Golden Lane,
London EC1Y OTG, UK
www.scmpress.co.uk

SCM Press is an imprint of Hymns Ancient & Modern Ltd
(a registered charity)

Hymns Ancient & Modern® is a registered trademark of
Hymns Ancient & Modern Ltd
13A Hellesdon Park Road, Norwich,
Norfolk NR6 5DR, UK

British Library Cataloguing in Publication data
A catalogue record for this book is available
from the British Library

ISBN 978 0 33406 057 4

Typeset by Regent Typesetting
Printed and bound by
CPI Group (UK) Ltd

Contents

Contributors

Barnabé Anzuruni Msabah

Barnabé is Tearfund's Church and Community Transformation (CCT) Lead for East and Central Africa. He holds a PhD in Theology and Development, and is Research Associate at the University of Stellenbosch, South Africa, and at the Adjunct Faculty at Pan Africa Christian University in Nairobi, Kenya. He has published several articles in international journals and is the author of *The Wayfarer: Perspectives on forced migration and transformational development* (HippoBooks, 2021). Barnabé is a member of international societies including the International Society for the Research and Study of Diaconia and Christian Social Practice (ReDI), and the International Fellowship for Mission as Transformation (INFEMIT).

Catriona Dejean

Catriona is the Strategy and Impact Director for Tearfund, based in the UK. She leads on strategy, impact assessment and research. She has worked on strategy and development programmes for World Vision, as a social enterprise consultant, and as an environmental consultant in the private sector. She is a board member of the Joint Learning Initiative on Local Faith Communities, and International Research Network on Transitions to Adulthood from Care (INTRAC). She is a Fellow of the Royal Society of Arts, Manufactures and Commerce (RSA), and of the Society of Leadership Fellows.

Emmanuel Murangira

Emmanuel is Tearfund's Country Director for Rwanda. He is co-editor of *Jubilee: God's answer to poverty* (Regnum 2020) and co-author of *Ageing in Rwanda, Challenges and opportunities for the church, state and nation* (Tearfund and University of

Birmingham, 2019). Emmanuel is a PhD candidate in Trans-formational Theology through the Oxford Centre for Religion and Public Life. His thesis is titled 'Theology and Practice, in ministry and pastoral care for older people in Protestant churches in Rwanda'. Emmanuel is an ordained minister and an itinerant preacher.

Jessie Fubara-Manuel

Jessie is a final-year PhD student in the University of Edinburgh's School of Divinity. Her research examines the role of Christian faith for women who are living with disability and HIV in Nigeria. She is a resource person and facilitator for the World Council of Churches (WCC) programmes on HIV and disability. She is also a member of the Circle of Concerned African Women Theologians and has published several articles and book chapters on gender, disability and HIV. She is the author of *Giver of Life, Hear Our Cries!* (WCC, 2014) and *Beside the Water Brooks: Poetic reflections from the heart* (Presby Press, 2006, 2008).

Jocabed Reina Solano Miselis

Jocabed is Panamanian and originally from the Gunadule nation (an indigenous people in Panama). She holds an undergraduate degree in Business Administration and a Masters in Interdisci-plinary Theology. Her areas of expertise include issues related to indigenous theology, Guna identity, multiculturalism and youth. Jocabed is Director of Memoria Indígena, which seeks to make visible the stories of indigenous women and men who seek to impact their communities through their commitment to the kingdom of God and pursuit of justice. She is on the board of Fraternidad Teológica Latinoamericana.

Jonas Kurlberg

Jonas is Deputy Director of the Centre for Digital Theology at Durham University, Convenor of the Global Network for Digital Theology, and Programme Director of the MA in Digital Theology at Spurgeon's College. He is the author of *Christian Modernism in an Age of Totalitarianism: T. S. Eliot, Karl Mannheim and the Moot* (Bloomsbury, 2019) and co-editor of *Missio Dei in a Digital Age* (SCM Press, 2020).

Juana Luiza Condori Quispe

Juana is Aymara, born in Chirapaca, La Paz, Bolivia. She studied Anthropology and Cultural Studies at the Universidad Mayor de San Andrés in La Paz, and the University of Arizona. She is the Coordinator of Memoria Indígena in Bolivia. Juana also studied intercultural theology at the Andean Ecumenical Institute for Theology (ISEAT). She seeks to practise and add value to theology from the context of the Aymara woman in her home, community, field, weaving and language.

Liz Muir

Liz is Tearfund's Head of Diversity and Inclusion, with responsibility for embedding effective change management and inclusion across the organization globally. She is a qualified probation officer and an accredited governance practitioner. Liz previously worked as a governance manager supporting organizations across the public, private and third sectors with governance compliance and delivering modules on the accredited Effective Board Member Programmes. Liz is a trustee at Conciliation Resources. She is also the editor of a number of books written by international governance consultant Dr Karl George MBE.

Loida Carriel Espinoza

Loida is Tearfund´s Regional Advocacy Advisor in Latin America and the Caribbean (LAC). She is an Ecuadorian journalist, development and advocacy specialist with 23 years' experience working in development and human rights organizations where she has been advocating and mobilizing Christian churches in favour of women, children and migrants' rights. She has authored booklets, manuals, guides and articles about how to support and advocate for vulnerable people. Loida is President of the LAC Children and Youth Movement's board, and one of the leaders of Tearfund's migration campaign 'As born among us'.

Madleina Daehnhardt

Madleina is Impact and Research Advisor for Tearfund where she sits in the Strategy and Impact Group. She holds a PhD from the Centre of Development Studies, University of Cambridge, and is a Panel Tutor in International Development at the Institute of Continuing Education, Madingley Hall. Madleina is the author of a book on *Migration, Development and Social Change* (Routledge Studies in Development, Mobilities and Migration, 2019).

María Alejandre Andrade Vinueza

María leads Tearfund's Theology and Network Engagement team and has more than 15 years' experience accompanying Christian communities on issues related to faith, justice and development. In recent years, she has focused particularly on environmental justice, migration, gender, spirituality and decolonial theologies. She has published articles in the *International Journal for Children's Spirituality* and *Journal of Latin American Theology*, among others. She serves as a board member of Bible Societies Ecuador, the Evangelical Community of Interdisciplinary Studies (CETI) and Memoria Indígena (Native American Memory).

Mariam Tadros

A graduate in Theology and Religious Studies, Mariam also has a postgraduate degree in Conflict Regulation in Divided Societies (King's College, London). Mariam has previously worked with Tearfund in its operational response in the Kurdish region of Iraq as well as on the West and Central Africa desk. At the time of writing, Mariam was leading the Fragile States Unit and was the Technical Specialist for Peacebuilding at Tearfund. She is Coptic Orthodox by baptism and an alumna of the St Anselm Ecumenical Community.

Nam-Chen Chan

Nam-Chen is the Executive Director of AsiaCMS, a trans-denominational missions agency serving South Asia and South-East Asia. AsiaCMS is associated with the global Church Mission Society (CMS) network. Nam-Chen holds a PhD in Intercultural Studies and his research interests lie in the intersections of leadership, church, culture, migration and God's mission.

Nina Kurlberg

Nina is Tearfund's Theology Development Officer, with a focus on diversity and inclusion. She is in the final year of a PhD at the University of Edinburgh's Schools of Divinity and Business, where she has also worked as a Senior Tutor in research methods at the School of Social and Political Science. Through her research, she is examining the practice of faith-based development organizations using the lens of institutional logics.

Oenone Chadburn

Oenone is Head of Tearfund's Humanitarian and Resilience team. She has been working with Tearfund since 2004 in various roles and, prior to this, was working with UNDP in conflict-affected areas of Sri Lanka, and then later on the Sri Lankan peace process. An advocate for locally led disaster management and the role of local organizations in humanitarian response, Oenone has commissioned several prominent research pieces, including *Characteristics of a Disaster-Resilient Community* (Twigg, 2007). Oenone has overseen the launch of several emergency responses by Tearfund, including the Indian Ocean tsunami, the Syria conflict and, most recently, its Covid-19 response.

Prabu Deepan

Prabu is Head of Tearfund's Thematic Support team, based in Colombo, Sri Lanka. He is the architect of Tearfund's evidence-based Transforming Masculinities intervention, a faith-based approach on gender equality and positive masculinities, which is being implemented in 12 countries. Prabu has co-authored several academic papers on gender equality, men and masculinities, including a chapter on the Transforming Masculinities intervention in *Global Masculinities: Interrogations and reconstructions* (Routledge, 2018). Prabu holds an MBA from Cardiff Metropolitan University.

Rei Lemuel Crizaldo

Rei is Tearfund's Theological Education Network Coordinator for East and South-East Asia. In the Philippines, he serves on the faculty of the Asian Seminary of Christian Ministries and as the Advocacy Coordinator for Integral Mission of Micah Philippines. He is also a local author, with several books published in the vernacular by OMF Literature, including *Boring Ba Ang Bible Mo?* (*Is Your Bible Boring?*), which won a Filipino Readers' Choice Award.

Ruth Valerio

Ruth is Global Advocacy and Influencing Director at Tearfund. An environmentalist, theologian and social activist, Ruth holds a doctorate from King's College, London, and honorary doctorates from the Universities of Winchester and Chichester. She is Canon Theologian at Rochester Cathedral and the author of *L is for Lifestyle: Christian living that doesn't cost the earth* (Inter-Varsity Press, 2004) and *Just Living: Faith and community in an age of consumerism* (Hodder & Stoughton, 2016). She wrote the Archbishop of Canterbury's 2020 Lent book, *Saying Yes to Life* (SPCK, 2019). Ruth is a regular contributor to BBC Radio 4 and BBC World Service.

Selina Palm

Selina is a researcher with the Unit for Religion and Development Research at Stellenbosch University in South Africa. She delivers consultancy work for organizations around the world on the roles of faith actors in violence prevention and social justice. Selina holds a PhD in Theology and Human Rights and is a lay faith leader in her local church congregation in Cape Town. She has authored numerous book chapters and accredited journal articles on developing liberating theologies for social transformation.

Sisay Mammo Sime

Sisay is Tearfund in Ethiopia's Lead for Disability Inclusion. Sisay, who is living with a visual impairment, is a historian and has a postgraduate degree in Leadership and Management from the Ethiopian Graduate School of Theology (Master of Arts in Leadership and Management). He spent much of his career in teaching, but has been engaged in disability inclusion activities since 2016, working with the Ethiopian National Association of the Blind, the consortium Civic Engagement Alliances, The Ethiopian Centre for Disability and Development, and the Australian-based research firm Includovate.

Acknowledgements

The process of editing this book has in many ways been transformative. It has challenged our thinking, not only academically but also personally, as we have read and engaged with each chapter and contributor. We would like to thank each and every one for what they have brought to the book – for their time, experiences and passion, but also for their dedication and willingness to continue with the process during what has been a very difficult year for many. Writing has taken place almost entirely in lockdown, and many of the chapters went through several rounds of editing and copy-editing, a process that has required patience and commitment on all sides.

We would like to acknowledge those who have taken the time to review each chapter, some of whom have been named in the pages that follow, others of whom remain anonymous. The views expressed in this volume are those of individual contributors, and chapters have not been written on behalf of Tearfund. We are grateful to Tearfund for allowing us to embark on the journey of this book, and have greatly appreciated the time and insight of Ruth Valerio and Catriona Dejean. Kate Moreton and Ellie Hall have provided project management support with grace, patience and diligence, and for this we are thankful. We would also like to thank SCM Press, and David Shervington in particular, without whom the book would not have come into being. Finally, we would not have achieved the desired level of quality without Seren Boyd, who has been most skilful and meticulous in addressing the language aspects of each chapter, copy-editing every page in painstaking detail. We are most grateful for her tremendous work, and encouraging and gracious nature.

As co-editors, we have learnt a great deal from walking through the editing process together, growing not only in our understanding and experience of how to bring together diverse theological and social science perspectives on the topic, but also in mutual admiration and friendship.

In closing, Nina Kurlberg would like to dedicate this book to her uncle, Deepak Mahtani (1960–2020), whose inclusive nature and passion for releasing dreams in others touched the lives of many, including her own.

Nina Kurlberg and Madleina Daehnhardt

Foreword

Diversity and inclusion are 'on trend' words. Nearly every day something arrives in my inbox telling me about a webinar, podcast, blog post or conference looking at these issues from a variety of perspectives. The danger is that we become so used to these words that we forget not only what lies within the topics, but also – more crucially – *who*. Diversity and inclusion are not theory: they relate to people and their lived experiences, in all their beauty and struggle.

And it's not only *their* lived experiences: it's *ours* and *mine*. Diversity and inclusion are not issues that lie 'over there' somewhere: they are a part of us. As we dive into the depths of this book, we do so knowing that we bring to the conversation who we are and the many experiences and relationships that have formed us.

I think, for example, of the male Christian leaders committed to equality and to seeing me grow in my ministry as a young woman. But I also think of the one who kept his hand on my knee under the table at a meeting and the other who touched more than my knee at a social occasion. I think of the local government official who told me to 'ignore Mr Potatohead' when a man with withered arms and legs was brought into his office in a wheelbarrow. I think of my next-door neighbour who likes to start her sentences with, 'I'm not being racist but …' And I reflect on my own upbringing, with one side of the family carrying deep wounds from the Holocaust and anti-Semitism, and my childhood spent with people from across the world in an international Bible college.

All of these personal experiences – and many more besides – shape me and how I relate to the themes we will be exploring in the coming chapters. And similarly they will shape how you as a reader approach and think about the topics discussed in this book.

For my part, I am constantly learning. And this, I believe, is the right attitude in which to approach topics on inclusion, those we can naturally relate to and those we need to listen to first, in order to learn.

I now stop my next-door neighbour and say to her, 'Before you go any further, please be aware that starting a sentence with those words means you probably *are* about to say something racist.' I'm learning through my sassy, articulate teenage daughter who holds strong opinions on all issues around diversity and inclusion and likes to push and test my own thoughts and actions. I am constantly learning how privileged I am that my primary experiences are of inclusion rather than exclusion and that I therefore need to think carefully and act courageously on issues of power and privilege.

I am learning through the inspiring people I meet through my work at Tearfund, and the incredible work we are privileged to support, being done by churches around the world. What becomes so clear is how closely linked all of these issues are with the poverty and injustice that we are working to overcome.

It is shocking to realize that, in my own country, the UK, nearly half of Black, Asian and minority ethnic (BAME) households are living in poverty (Social Metrics Commission, 2020). People in minority ethnic groups are twice as likely to be unemployed as people of White British descent, and social security and tax benefits make up 25 per cent of the gross income of Pakistani and Bangladeshi households in the UK (Valerio, 2019). Around the world, of course, it is people of colour who suffer most from the effects of environmental destruction and climate change.

Globally, women earn 24 per cent less than men and at the current rate of progress, it will take 170 years to close the gap (Oxfam). There is a lack of decent work for women: '75 per cent of women in developing regions are in the informal economy … where they are less likely to have employment contracts, legal rights or social protection, and are often not paid enough to escape poverty' (Oxfam). One in three women have no say about major household purchases (United Nations, 2015) and 'women do at least twice as much unpaid care work, such as childcare and housework, as men – sometimes 10 times as much, often on top of their paid work' (Oxfam).

The links between poverty and disability are also stark, both as a cause and a consequence of each other. In the UK, nearly half the people living in poverty are living with a disability or live with someone who has a disability, and poverty is especially high among families where there is an adult living with a disability. People living with disabilities are more likely than others to face barriers to paid work. In 2017–18, 50 per cent of working-age people living with a disability were not working, compared with 18 per cent of others (Disability Rights UK, 2020).

But as we will see throughout this book, all that can change.

I think of people such as Huawa from Nigeria, who has faced trauma and violence at the hands of her husband and her relatives. She also lives with HIV. Huawa (whose name has been changed here) was able to take part in a trauma-healing programme run by Tearfund, where she was able not only to meet with other survivors and share about her trauma, but also benefit from training on entrepreneurship, become part of a self-help group (SHG) and access financial support to start up a small business (Tearfund, 2020).

In the Amhara region of Ethiopia, the self-help groups and churches that Tearfund supports have been integrating disability awareness and inclusion into their programmes and identifying where there are particular people who are falling through the net as a result of their disability. This has led to more children with learning difficulties actively engaging in school and more people with disabilities participating in local churches and in income-generating schemes, seeing their income improve as a result (see Chapter 11).

This book comes from the recognition that issues of inclusion are vitally important in working to help people lift themselves out of poverty. It also recognizes that inclusion is a learning process and we do not have all the answers. This book is offered from a place of humility and a desire both to stimulate a dialogue and also to learn from it.

So let us learn together, rooted in the triune God who calls us to model ourselves on the divine pattern of inclusivity, equality and self-giving love.

Dr Ruth Valerio, Director of Global Advocacy and Influencing, Tearfund

References

Disability Rights UK, 2020, 'Nearly half of everyone in poverty is either a disabled person or lives with a disabled person', *Disability Rights UK*, www.disabilityrightsuk.org/news/2020/february/nearly-half-every-one-poverty-either-disabled-person-or-lives-disabled-person, accessed 22.03.2021.

Oxfam (no date), 'Why the majority of the world's poor are women', *Oxfam International*, www.oxfam.org/en/why-majority-worlds-poor-are-women, accessed 22.03.2021.

Social Metrics Commission, 2020, *Measuring Poverty 2020: A report of the Social Metrics Commission*, London: Legatum Institute, https://socialmetricscommission.org.uk/measuring-poverty-2020/, accessed 22.03.2021.

Tearfund, 2020, *16 days of activism against gender-based violence: A Tearfund resource for prayer, reflection and action*, Teddington, UK: Tearfund, www.tearfund.org/-/media/tearfund/files/get-involved/resources/16daysprayeractivity.pdf, accessed 22.03.2021.

United Nations (UN), 2015, 'Poverty', in UN, *The World's Women 2015*, New York: UN, https://unstats.un.org/unsd/gender/chapter8/chapter8.html, accessed 22.03.2021.

Valerio, R., 2019, *L is for Lifestyle: Christian living that doesn't cost the earth*, 2nd edn, London: InterVarsity Press.

PART I

Inclusion and Faith-based Organizations

Introduction

NINA KURLBERG AND
MADLEINA DAEHNHARDT

When the Covid-19 outbreak was declared a pandemic by the World Health Organization in March 2020, there were those who claimed that the virus was a 'great leveller' (see, for example, Kapadia and Sirsikar, 2020). In other words, it was assumed that the virus would affect everyone in the same way without discrimination, and have an equalizing effect on society. Yet, it soon became apparent that this was far from the case, and that Covid-19 had instead exacerbated existing inequalities – on the basis of race, ethnicity, sex, disability, age and class. UN Women (2020), for example, highlighted that across 'every sphere, from health to the economy, security to social protection, the impacts of COVID-19 are exacerbated for women and girls simply by virtue of their sex'. The UK's international development network, Bond, drew attention to the fate of older people, who 'suffer doubly in crises: not only are they disproportionately impacted, but they are also neglected and discriminated [against] in the response' (Lilly, 2020). Vaccine nationalism began to surface across the globe, excluding many majority world populations from receiving protection from the virus. In the UK, ethnic minorities were also disproportionately impacted by the virus, and a Public Health England report noted that racism and discrimination may have been a contributing factor (Razai et al., 2021, p. 1). Thus, these groups of people – women and girls, older populations, economically poorer nations and ethnic minorities – experienced discrimination and marginalization in the global response to Covid-19 on account of their diversity: they were excluded.

In their article on ethnic disparities and Covid-19, Mohammad Razai et al. cite a powerful phrase from Alexandre Dumas' 1844 novel *The Count of Monte Cristo*, 'moral wounds', using it to refer to the racism underlying the plight of minority groups.

Dumas wrote: 'Moral wounds have this peculiarity – they may be hidden, but they never close; always painful, always ready to bleed when touched, they remain fresh and open in the heart' (quoted in Razai et al., 2021, p. 1). These same words could be used to describe the impact of the injustice and discrimination that prevail around diversity. Yet, such moral wounds – although painful – are fertile ground for creative and constructive theological thinking, as practical theologian Mary McClintock Fulkerson argues:

> Theologies that matter arise out of dilemmas – out of situations that matter ... [T]heological thinking is generated by a sometimes inchoate sense that something must be addressed. Such a process itself is defined by an a priori logic of transformation. More precisely, transformation is inherent in the image of the wound, for it invokes a sense of something wrong – of a fracture in things that should be joined or whole. The very sense of harm implies an impulse toward remedy – a kind of longing for it to be otherwise. (McClintock Fulkerson, 2007, pp. 13–14)

Herein lies the purpose of the present volume. As the title suggests, its focus is on theologies and practices related to the topic of inclusion within faith-based organizations (FBOs). Inclusion is a broad concept that evades easy definition and one that will be unpacked throughout the book. The word 'inclusion' may sit uncomfortably with some readers: it could be perceived as seeking to erase all value judgements, ending in value-free chaos, or, by contrast, as implicitly imposing norms. Yet, at the same time, there is also a sense of excitement around inclusion, since its recent prominence within the public sphere provides organizations with the opportunity to put in place change processes that have the potential to bring life and joy to the whole, not just to previously excluded groups. As will become apparent to readers, although exclusion, diversity and equality are not explicit within the title, they are implicit throughout the book. The emphasis has been placed on inclusion to signal the questions at the heart of the book: What is inclusion, theologically and practically? How can it heal the wounds of exclusion? What should organizations and communities that desire to be inclusive be aiming towards? In addressing these questions, the book seeks to inspire readers to revisit their own theologies and practices towards inclusion: a process that has the potential to be transformative.

The book draws in part on the experience of Tearfund as an FBO that intentionally seeks to prioritize diversity and inclusion. Tearfund was established by the Evangelical Alliance in 1968, yet, even today, theological reflection is a foundational element of its life and work. The organization embarked on its diversity and inclusion journey in 2017, setting out to create an inclusive and diverse workforce, decentralizing its leadership structure and initiating organization-wide workstreams that imbues all aspects from human resources to communications, programming and theology. It should be pointed out, however, that the chapter contributors bring their own voices and perspectives, which are not necessarily those of Tearfund, though many are employed by Tearfund.

In this introduction, the editors first review inclusion as it is currently discussed across the wider development sector, and then faith-based organizations in particular. This sectoral overview is followed by a theological positioning of the topic: insights on inclusion are drawn from several works across the theological literature. Lastly, the structure of the book is introduced in its four parts.

Inclusion and the development sector

The topic of inclusion is a contemporary and fast-emerging one in the international development sector. Predecessors of the inclusion agenda were concerned with 'marginalized groups' in the UN Millennium Development Goals (MDGs), when the term 'marginalization' was in wider use. According to the UN, the MDGs were 'specifically designed to address the needs of the world's poorest citizens and the world's most *marginalized* populations' (UN, 2015, emphasis added). Post-2015, with the 'Leave no one behind' 2030 agenda, there has been a shift towards addressing the root causes of persisting inequalities and towards inclusion. Now, inclusion often refers to the 'meaningful participation' of previously excluded groups, such as people with disabilities (Guterres, 2020; Rattray and Lako, 2018). Here, inclusion – understood as a comprehensive structural approach – is seen as key to achieving the UN's Sustainable Development Goals (SDGs).

This shift towards inclusion is reflected in the recent use of language appropriated by international organizations. Here, the term inclusion is often used with reference to *representation* in both development programmes and in internal organizational cultures and systems. For example, Bond's 'News and views' webpage shows several blogs, events and podcasts in 2020–21 making the case for fostering diversity and inclusion in the UK NGO workforce, for diversifying racial representation, and for the use of ethical and inclusive language, as well as for promoting inclusion of people with disabilities in programming (Bond, 2021). However, when we compare different INGOs (international NGOs), it appears that what exactly is understood by inclusion, and which groups of people are included in this drive, is far from homogenous. The difference in uses of the term 'inclusion' is evident in a search exercise we conducted on external-facing NGO websites, as part of a comparison of organizational priorities.[1]

We selected a total of 17 INGOs and FBOs in this screening exercise.[2] The main themes that emerged from the review of mainstream INGO reports in relation to inclusion were: education, disability, gender and LGBTQI+ inclusion. A similar emphasis on gender and LGBTQI+ exclusion is reflected in the latest annual *State of Civil Society* report, which identifies the main trends impacting civil society each year (Civicus, 2020). Linkages to financial inclusion, sustainability, social protection and human rights were made across organizations. The link between socio-economic vulnerability and socio-economic exclusion was highlighted in particular, whereby economic and social reasons for exclusion are deeply intertwined (Morgan, 2016; Stewart and Khurshid, 2019). Intersectionality has become prominent in more recent publications across the sector, explicitly linking age, gender and diversity (AGD) inclusion to the principle of 'leave no one behind' and the SDGs. The AGD approach emphasizes the way in which individuals can experience differing levels of vulnerability and exclusion depending on intersecting identity factors, for example, displaced older women or economically poorer girl children (Beales, 2000; Plan International, 2020). An AGD approach enables programmatic and humanitarian responses to be adapted inclusively to different needs through 'meaningful participation'. The need for inclusion and meaningful participation of older people and people with disabilities in humanitarian action has gained traction across the sector more recently (CBM et al., 2018; Elrha, 2020; HelpAge, 2018; Plan International, 2020).

Our screening exercise showed that exclusion of different groups from services and programmes is extensively discussed. For example, Plan International primarily understands inclusion in terms of 'tackling exclusion'; inclusion is discussed as relating to both an approach to programme development – reaching excluded groups – and a principle within the organization's set-up and culture (Plan International, 2015, p. 3). In response to the growth in 2020 of the Black Lives Matter (BLM) movement, organizations have written statements outlining their stance on building inclusive anti-racist organizations (Save the Children, 2020). Gender equality and inclusion are often discussed in combination, since sharing power, achieving non-discrimination and gender equality, promoting gender justice and realizing girls' rights are seen as a fundamental part of an inclusive society (Plan International, 2017; ActionAid, 2020). Child-centred organizations, such as UNICEF, Plan International and Save the Children logically focus on inclusion themes relevant to children in lower- and middle-income countries, mainly targeting barriers to inclusion in education, such as poverty, geographic location, gender, ethnicity, disability and HIV status (Stewart and Khurshid, 2019; UNICEF, 2019; Verma, 2018). Consequently, an abundance of reports and policy briefs on access to education for the poorest children, girls' education and disability inclusion in schooling and curriculum development has emerged across the sector (ActionAid et al., 2020; Jones, 1999; Lee-Rife et al., 2019; Wang, 2016; UNICEF, 2017). Inclusive education is linked to SDG 4 'Quality education', which is seen as a vital tool for achieving other SDGs, such as SDG 1 'No poverty'. This is because inclusive quality education provides young people with 'the skills, knowledge, competences and values to help them to break cycles of poverty, discrimination, social and gender inequality' (Plan International, 2019, p. 2).

Inclusion and the faith-based NGO sector

Faith-based international relief, development and advocacy organizations operate both theologically and programmatically in the broader sectoral context discussed above. Here, for all the organizations screened alike, inclusion has a direct link to the creation of a just and fair world in socio-economic terms, since poverty, inequality and exclusion are systemically interlinked.

Inclusion therefore plays a key role in social protection in low-and middle-income countries (UNICEF, 2019), thus being pivotal in achieving SDG 1 'No poverty'. By extension, in the context of the Catholic Church's social teaching and the SDGs, faith-based actors promote the SDG agenda of 'Leave no one behind' on multiple levels, including individuals, communities, social groups, as well as states and nations on the international stage (Fidelus et al., 2021, p. 154). FBOs engage with and appropriate the 'Leave no one behind' agenda in a similar vein to other NGOs, linking their take on inclusion with the SDGs and a general human rights framework (CAFOD, 2015; Clark and Grant, 2017; Dennis, 2015). Many organizations, in their approach to inclusion, also recognize the importance of intersectional vulnerabilities such as gender, age, ethnicity and disability (Christian Aid, 2015; Baden and Mohun, 2016; Ogega et al., 2020).[3] Four of the five Joint Learning Initiative's learning hubs are interlinked with inclusion themes: refugees and forced migration, gender-based violence and faith, ending violence against children and anti-human trafficking and modern slavery (JLI, 2021).

More specifically, the search of inclusion-related themes on FBO websites shows that predominant inclusion areas publicly discussed are disability and gender. Gender refers specifically to addressing gender inequality, that is, the multiple disadvantages women experience in a number of spheres, contrary to 'theological understandings that all people are of equal and unique value and worth' (Christian Aid, 2017, p. 7). World Vision's gender equality and social inclusion approach focuses on women as 'agents of change', by working towards overcoming exclusionary social norms and systems alongside increasing equal and inclusive access (Ogega et al., 2020, p. 6). CBM is a strong advocate for disability inclusion, both in programmatic work as well as in organizational participation, linking inclusion with overcoming social exclusion, stigma and discrimination (CBM, 2021a; CBM, 2021b). World Vision too highlights the need to engage faith leaders and wider communities in order to achieve disability inclusion (DeNap, 2018; World Vision, 2017). A study of World Vision's socially inclusive principles also found that challenging staff and community attitudes was the key first step to achieving inclusion of people with disabilities in development work (Coe and Wapling, 2010). Drawing particular attention to the 'economic costs' of disability exclusion, CBM links inclusion to the 'Leave no one behind' agenda, making an economic case for inclusion, in addition to human rights and value-based inclusion approaches (CBM, 2016). While its focus is specifically on inclusion in relation to disability, CBM does also highlight how disability links to other intersections of marginalization (Aston, 2018; CBM, 2016; CBM, 2017). What is more, the Black Lives Matter movement has prompted Christian organizations to examine their own corporate cultures, to affirm with their staff and supporters that Black Lives Matter, and to take an anti-racism stand linked to the biblical foundations of racial and ethnic diversity in the global Church (BMS, 2020; Christian Aid, 2020; World Vision, 2020).[4] Our scan of FBO websites showed that LGBTQI+ inclusion was not widely discussed, possibly due to divergent theological views on sexuality within FBOs themselves.

Theologies of inclusion in FBOs

The screening exercise showed that only some of the FBOs reviewed link inclusion in programmatic approaches to an over-arching theological commitment to equality and human dignity (CAFOD, 2020a; Clark and Grant, 2017). For example, Christian Aid links its faith base to a long heritage of working to challenge social norms that reinforce inequalities (Clark and Grant, 2017, p. 3). The organization views inclusion in light of power and structural inequality and has a strong historic and present organizational focus on inclusion, in terms of both programmatic and operational systems. This de-centres Christian Aid in its work, moving towards 'inclusive programming', defined as 'the process of ensuring that everyone, regardless of gender, age or other dimension of diversity is treated equitably and given fair and free opportunity to participate and have influence in activities, decisions and structures which affect their life' (Clark and Grant, 2017, p. 7).

Strikingly, theologies of inclusion have not been made explicit by most FBOs that we reviewed. There could be numerous reasons for this: for example, organizations may have developed thinking internally which may not be publicly available, or their faith-based approach, and theologies of inclusion, may be more intrinsic and less explicit. Christian Aid and CAFOD were the only FBOs that stood out in our screening exercise for having publicly articulated some sort of theology of inclusion. Catherine

Loy's study of Christian Aid identifies 'inclusivity' as one of four pillars of Christian Aid's distinctive identity, and finds inclusivity shaping Christian Aid's theology both implicitly and explicitly (Loy, 2010). Half of the Christian Aid staff Loy interviews see the organization's 'inclusive approach as guiding *implicit theology*' (Loy, 2010, p. 62, emphasis added). Loy's review of Christian Aid's explicit documents shows that inclusivity stems from a 'belief that all people are created in the image of God and are therefore equal in dignity and worth', which is so frequently articulated across documents that it attains an 'unprecedented degree of organisational consensus' (Loy, 2010, p. 65). In line with the concern of inclusion noted above being perceived as 'value free', the study notices an ongoing underlying tension among Christian Aid staff regarding this 'open and inclusive approach', that is, 'how to be inclusive and loving of all while retaining a Christian identity' (Loy, 2010, p. 64).

CAFOD is one of the few FBOs that makes explicit linkages between inclusion and specific theologies, linking inclusion primarily to a theological commitment to 'the dignity of every human person as set out in Catholic Social Teaching' (CAFOD, 2020a).[5] Like other organizations, CAFOD relates its commitment to diversity and inclusion to both how it works in the world and how it structures the organization (CAFOD, 2020a). Inclusion and interconnectedness are central to its vision for 'Our Common Home', 'where all people, communities and the earth may flourish, and no one is beyond reach' (CAFOD, 2020c, p. 7).[6] This links to Pope Francis' Encyclical *Laudato Si'* and preferential option for the poor (Pope Francis, 2015).[7]

It is in this context of different FBO approaches to inclusion that this volume sits, as a 'live' study of Tearfund's emerging inclusion work, taking an explicitly theological approach to programmatic work.

Towards theologies and practices of inclusion

The majority of the academic theological literature tends to focus on thematic areas related to diversity, such as race or disability, rather than on inclusion. There are several possible reasons for this limited explicit engagement, such as the relatively recent focus on inclusion within the public sphere. However, it might also stem from a concern that inclusion either leads to 'a chaos without boundaries', that in effect erodes plurality, or 'oppression with them' (Volf, 1996, pp. 63–4), where inclusion is seen as negative in so far as to include is simply to provide access to a fixed group or structure.

Writing in the context of disability, Christopher Newell notes the difference between 'mere inclusion' and 'embrace' (2009, p. 313), while John Swinton argues that there is a need to 'shift our thinking from inclusion to belonging' (2012, p. 172). Meanwhile, Erin Raffety refers to the 'pitfalls of inclusion' (2020, p. 198), issuing a call to nurture those living with disabilities 'beyond inclusion, and into dynamic leadership' (2020, p. 209). Raffety's argument emphasizes the 'ideology of normalcy' (2020, p. 198), which she sees as prevalent yet hidden within congregational ministry, and the consequent ways in which inclusion can then 'maintain rather than disrupt power dynamics' (2020, p. 202).

Here, it is worth noting Hannah Bacon and Wayne Morris's volume, *Transforming Exclusion: Engaging Faith Perspectives*. Bacon and Morris also associate inclusion with a 'process of "normalization"' (2011, p. 4) and speak of the 'normative' centre that '"includes" by trying to make that which is different the same' (2011, p. 3). Thus, in their view, inclusion is problematic since it sustains the logic of exclusion by erasing otherness. An additional challenge they bring is that inherent within the very word 'inclusion' is the assumption that no person or group is excluded (2011, p. 3).

In this volume, the editors seek to move beyond theologies and practices of inclusion that are solely access-oriented or that seek to erase either value judgements or difference. The aim is to transform dominant conceptualizations of inclusion using the voices and perspectives of a diverse group of 18 individuals – 11 women and 7 men – spanning almost as many countries, with a range of first languages. The structure of this book developed organically, as the editors began receiving chapters from contributors. As themes emerged across the various chapters, so also our understanding of inclusion deepened. What is pioneering about the book, then, is its approach, as well as the bringing together of a range of theologians, practitioners, and those who bridge the two. Contrary to books written *about* Tearfund, which are built around outsider perspectives (Freeman, 2019; Dejean and Kurlberg, 2021), the approach this edited volume takes is to work from the inside out, giving space to a broad range of voices from within the organization and beyond. Contributors span Tearfund staff members, consultants and friends, who reflect on topics related to their expertise from their particular standpoint. This too adds diversity, as does the variety of methods employed by contributors, ranging from literature reviews and case studies to reflections from internal learning and empirical research. Thus, the book seeks to embody the very theology it advances.

The book's structure represents different aspects of inclusion that have emerged as common themes through the editing process: inclusion as journey, inclusion as requiring change, and inclusion as belonging. Rather than inclusion being about either eliminating all value judgements or opening access to a normative centre, inclusion is about the centre being reconfigured in the light of difference. To use Bacon and Morris's framing, the 'legitimacy of the centre' must be challenged (see Chapter 2). Further, inclusion is as much about external dynamics as it is about internal dynamics; that is, as well as encompassing organizational culture, inclusion is also a posture or attitude towards the other, and towards difference in general (see Chapter 7).

It is important to reflect on how theology and practice are understood in the context of this volume, given the variety of possible definitions and associations. The book is located in a broad field of theology that encompasses both theory and practice: practical theology. In line with Pete Ward's understanding of the field, it conceives of practical theology 'as any way of thinking that takes both practice and theology seriously' (Ward, 2017, p. 5). Practical theology has many different approaches and methods, but the theme that unites the discipline is 'its beginning-point within human experience' and desire to reflect theologically on such experience (Swinton and Mowat, 2016, p. 6). As Bonnie Miller-McLemore notes, the distinctive contribution of practical theology as a discipline is that it places emphasis on 'mediating and integrating knowledge ... between seminary, congregation, and wider society' (2012, p. 6).

The chapters note and draw on theology in differing ways and to varying degrees, since the editors were not prescriptive in this regard. Individual contributors were also free to choose their focus, resulting in some chapters being more explicitly theological than others. As editors, we have also tried hard to avoid creating clear-cut dichotomies between theologies and practices in the context of faith-based development work. In fact, for FBOs to shape their faith-based identity and retain their vitality, it is important to develop theological thinking and programming in parallel, and not in isolation. This volume makes a strong case for such mutuality. It is further reflected in the choice of structure, according to which chapters are arranged by theme rather than by whether they sit under theologies or practices. This emerged as crucial during the editing process, when it became apparent that most chapters draw from theological thinking embedded in practice to a certain degree. Separating themes into distinct chapters (such as race, ethnicity, gender, disability and age) should not be misinterpreted. As editors, we recognize the intersectionality of inclusion and exclusion, and this is a prominent inherent feature in several chapters; for example, Chapter 11 and Chapter 12 cover disability and gender, and Chapter 10 covers age and gender.

Structure of the book

The book opens with Selina Palm's literature review on diversity and inclusion that focuses on theological perspectives and emerging voices in the majority world. This work was commissioned by Tearfund in 2019 and played a key role in its development of a theological framework for inclusion, introduced by Nina Kurlberg in Chapter 2. This second chapter's theological starting point is Volf's theology of embrace, which has had a significant impact on the organization to date, and this is developed into a framework in dialogue with the organization's socio-cultural location. Inclusion is seen as the process of embrace in the margins, but emphasis is placed on the role of the Spirit through this journey as a reconciliatory and decolonizing force. Liz Muir then presents a case study based on Tearfund's response to racial injustice in light of George Floyd's death in police custody in the US in Chapter 3. Muir intertwines key aspects of the organizational response with personal insights as a Black British Caribbean staff member.

The second part of the book explores further inclusion as a journey towards embrace. Mariam Tadros begins the section by drawing on Tearfund's peacebuilding work, highlighting lessons learnt and introducing the theological framework for peacebuilding developed as part of this (Chapter 4). Tadros notes that rather than being a straight path, the journey towards reconciliation can best be understood as a 'cyclical dance'. Nam-Chen

Chan then employs a biblical-theological approach in Chapter 5 to propose that embracing what he terms a 'pilgrim identity' alters the way we view both migrants and the socio-cultural 'other', and is a foundational component of what it means to be inclusive. This section closes with a case study written by Loida Carriel Espinoza and María Alejandre Andrade Vinueza on including the foreign-other (Chapter 6). This is based on Tearfund's advocacy response in a migration campaign launched by faith-based actors in several countries in Latin America and the Caribbean in June 2019, titled 'As Born Among Us' and live at the time of writing.

Part 3 focuses on the change that inclusion necessitates. Change is conceived of within the book in various ways: as systemic, organizational and cultural. In Chapter 7, Jonas Kurlberg and Rei Lemuel Crizaldo explore how digitality provides conceptual language that can enhance inclusion, both theologically and practically. They argue that beyond the metaphor of the network it provides, digital communication technology is a means by which inclusion can be achieved. Bringing a different perspective to systemic change, Prabu Deepan and Nina Kurlberg focus on gender norms. They present key learning from Tearfund's pioneering Transforming Masculinities approach, arguing that inclusion requires the 'active interrogation' and transformation of gender norms in order to achieve gender justice (Chapter 8). The section concludes with a case study written by Oenone Chadburn on localization in relation to the international humanitarian system (Chapter 9). Chadburn argues that in order to be truly inclusive, international organizations such as Tearfund must prioritize the voices and perspectives of local partners and faith actors, building capacity for locally led responses.

In Part 4, Madleina Daehnhardt and Emmanuel Murangira present the findings emerging from an empirical study conducted with older Rwandans drawing from their lived experiences (Chapter 10). The chapter discusses how churches can be places of belonging, since inclusive communities are those where everyone can belong, and this experience of belonging is therefore understood as a key component of inclusion. In Chapter 11, Jessie Fubara-Manuel also uses an empirically grounded approach, which is in itself inclusive and intersectional: rather than drawing on the theology of academic theologians, she draws on the lived theologies of a group of women in Nigeria living with disability and HIV, and these women's voices shape her argument. Fubara-Manuel argues that inclusion goes beyond access: it is also about a sense of belonging experienced in transformed identities and holistic healing. In Chapter 12, Sisay Mammo Sime and Barnabé Anzuruni Msabah review lessons learnt from more than a decade of Tearfund in Ethiopia working towards disability-inclusive self-help groups. People living with disability often do not find belonging in development programming or faith-based initiatives, and this chapter shares insights for disability inclusion in practice.

Finally, in Chapter 13, Jocabed Reina Solano Miselis and Juana Luiza Condori Quispe, through an earthed narrative approach, explore the potential of narratives and ancient stories in the context of Abya Yala. They demonstrate that the particularities of different social and cultural practices 'both feed our sense of belonging and differentiate us from others'. The authors leave us with a challenge: do indigenous voices find their belonging within the body of Christ? And if not, is the body of Christ lacking something by not welcoming such difference?

The chapters in Part 4 are not the only ones where belonging appears as an (implicit) concept. The theme of belonging is influential and interwoven throughout the book. As Tadros writes in Chapter 4, belonging is humanity's 'most common calling', 'that liminal space, where we have a longing to belong and the fear that we will not or do not, is the space where ... transformation and reconciliation takes place'. This book invites the reader to step into this space, and to explore the potential and possibilities that inclusion opens up.

Acknowledgements

The editors would like to thank Roisin Jackson for her help with relevant literature reviews. We are also grateful to colleagues and friends who reviewed the draft and provided feedback.

Bibliography

Action Aid, Education International and Light for the World, 2020, *The Bedrock of Inclusion: Why investing in the education workforce is critical to the delivery of SDG4. Lessons from five African countries*, Toronto: International Centre for Disability and Rehabilitation.

ActionAid UK, 2020, 'How We Practise Feminism at Work', *ActionAid*, www.actionaid.org.uk/about-us/how-we-practise-feminism-at-work, accessed 9.03.2021.

Aston, R., 2018, 'Global Disability Summit: 4 actions to further inclusion', 5 September, *CBM*, www.cbmuk.org.uk/blog/global-disability-summit-4-actions-inclusion, accessed 9.03.2021.

Bacon H., W. Morris and S. Knowles (eds), 2011, *Transforming Exclusion: Engaging faith perspectives*, London: Bloomsbury Publishing.

Baden, S. and R. Mohun, 2016, *Integrating Gender into Inclusive Markets Development Programmes*, London: Christian Aid.

Baptist Union (no date), 'Five Core Values', *Baptists Together*, www.baptist.org.uk/Publisher/File.aspx?ID=117271, accessed 25.03.2021.

Beales, S., 2000, 'Why We Should Invest in Old Women and Men: The experience of HelpAge International', *Gender and Development* 8(2), pp. 9–18.

BMS World Mission, 2020, 'Black Lives Matter', 8 June, *BMS World Mission*, www.bmsworldmission.org/news/black-lives-matter/, accessed 11.03.2021.

Bond, 2021, 'New and Views', *Bond*, www.bond.org.uk/news, accessed 23.03.2021.

CAFOD, 2015, *Sustainable Development Goals: Action towards 2030*, London: CAFOD.

CAFOD, 2020a, 'Diversity and Inclusivity', *CAFOD*, https://cafod.org.uk/About-us/How-we-work/Diversity-and-inclusivity, accessed 10.03.2021.

CAFOD, 2020b, 'Seven Catholic Social Teaching Principles', *CAFOD*, https://cafod.org.uk/Pray/Catholic-social-teaching, accessed 10.03.2021.

CAFOD, 2020c, *Our Common Home: Dare to be different: Our vision of progress, our agenda for change*, London: CAFOD.

CAFOD, 2021, *The Distinctive Role of the Catholic Church in Development and Humanitarian Response*, London: CAFOD.

CBM, 2016, *Inclusion Counts: The economic case for disability-inclusive development*, Bensheim: CBM.

CBM, 2017, 'New CBM survey concludes disability-inclusion urgent priority in Guatemala', 22 March, *CBM*, www.cbmuk.org.uk/news/new-cbm-survey-concludes-disability-inclusion-urgent-priority-guatemala, accessed 9.03.2021.

CBM, 2021a, 'Disability & development', *CBM*, www.cbmuk.org.uk/policy-practice/disability-development/, accessed 9.03.2021.

CBM, 2021b, 'Inclusion & rights', *CBM*, www.cbmuk.org.uk/what-we-do/inclusions-rights/, accessed 9.03.2021.

CBM, HelpAge and Handicap International, 2018, *Humanitarian Inclusion Standards for Older People and People with Disabilities*, Bensheim, London and Lyon: CBM International, HelpAge International and Handicap International.

Christian Aid, 2015, *Equal Citizens, Equality in Disasters: Ensuring inclusive disaster recovery and rebuilding in Nepal*, London: Christian Aid.

Christian Aid, 2017, *Gender Justice: Achieving just and equitable power relations for all*, London: Christian Aid.

Christian Aid, 2020, *Black Lives Matter Everywhere: A study of public attitudes towards race and climate change*, London: Christian Aid.

Cichos, K., J. A. Sobkowiak, R. Zenderowski, R. F. Sadowski, B. Zbarachewicz and S. Dziekoński (eds), 2021 *Sustainable Development Goals and the Catholic Church: Catholic social teaching and the UN's Agenda 2030*, London: Routledge.

Civicus, 2020, *State of Civil Society Report 2020*, Johannesburg: Civicus.

Clark, D. and C. Grant, 2017, *Christian Aid and the Leave No One Behind Agenda*, London: Christian Aid.

Coe, S. and L. Wapling, 2010, 'Practical Lessons from Four Projects on Disability-inclusive Development Programming', *Development in Practice* 20(7), pp. 879–86.

Dejean, C. and N. Kurlberg, 2021, 'Book Review: Tearfund and the Quest for Faith-Based Development', *Christian Relief, Development, and Advocacy* 2(2), pp. 85–7.

DeNap, C., 2018, *A Holistic Approach to Disability Inclusion*, Washington DC: World Vision.

Dennis, H., 2015, *Leave No One Behind: From goals to implementation*, London: Christian Aid.

Elrha, 2020, *Gap Analysis on the Inclusion of People with Disability and Older People in Humanitarian Response – Literature review*, London: Elrha.

Fidelus, A., E. H. Morawska and A. Wysocki, 2021, 'Reducing inequality (social inclusion, social capital and protection of migrants in the context of Catholic social teaching)', in K. Katarzyna et al. (eds), *Sustainable Development Goals and the Catholic Church: Catholic social teaching and the UN's agenda 2030*, London: Routledge.

Freeman, D., 2019, *Tearfund and the Quest for Faith-based Development*, London: Routledge.

Guterres, A., 2020, *Report of the Secretary-General: Disability Inclusion in the United Nations system*, New York: United Nations.

HelpAge, 2018, 'Age and Disability Capacity Programme (ADCAP)', *HelpAge International*, www.helpage.org/what-we-do/emergencies/adcap-age-and-disability-capacity-building-programme, accessed 9.03.2021.

JLI, 2021, 'About JLI Learning Hubs', *Joint Learning Initiative on Faith and Local Communities*, https://jliflc.com/about/learning-hubs/, accessed 23.03.2021.

Jones, H., 1999, 'Integrating a Disability Perspective into Mainstream Development Programmes: The experience of Save the Children (UK) in East Asia', in E. Stone (ed.), *Disability and Development: Learning from action and research on disability in the majority world*, Leeds: The Disability Press, pp. 54–73.

Kapadia, J. and A. Sirsikar, 2020, 'Covid-19 – The Great Leveller', *Ipsos*, 24 April, www.ipsos.com/en-in/covid-19-great-leveller, accessed 14.03.2021.

Lee-Rife, S., S. Tanner and Y. Nestel, 2019, *Planning for Inclusion: How education budgets and plans target the most marginalized*, London: Plan International.

Lilly, D., 2020, 'Older People are Being Left Behind in Humanitarian Action', 27 November, *Bond*, www.bond.org.uk/news/2020/11/older-people-are-being-left-behind-in-humanitarian-action, accessed 1.02.2021.

Loy, C., 2010, *Development Beyond the Secular: Theological approaches to inequality*, London: SCM Press.

McClintock Fulkerson, M., 2007, *Places of Redemption: Theology for a worldly church*, Oxford: Oxford University Press.

Miller-McLemore, B. J., 2012, 'Introduction: The contributions of practical theology', in B. J. Miller-McLemore (ed.), *The Wiley-Blackwell Companion to Practical Theology*, London: Blackwell Publishing, pp. 1–20.

Morgan, R., 2016, 'Addressing the Poverty Barriers so We Can Reach Every Last Child', *Save the Children*, www.savethechildren.net/news/addressing-poverty-barriers-so-we-can-reach-every-last-child, accessed 9.01.2021.

Newell, C., 2009, 'Inclusion or Embrace: Communion and a theology of embrace', *Journal of Religion, Disability & Health* 13, pp. 311–13.

Ogega, J., Z. Douglas and E. Winter, 2020, *Gender Equality and Social Inclusion: The World Vision approach and theory of change*, Washington DC: World Vision.

Plan International, 2015, *Strategic Review of Inclusion, Plan International Programme Briefing*, London: Plan International.

Plan International, 2017, *Global Policy on Gender Equality and Inclusion*, London: Plan International.

Plan International, 2019, *Area of Global Distinctiveness: Inclusive quality education*, London: Plan International.

Plan International, 2020, *Leaving No One Behind: Ensuring an age, gender and diversity (AGD) inclusive approach to internal displacement*, London: Plan International/Joint Submission to the High-Level Panel on Internal Displacement.

Pope Francis, 2015, *Laudato Si': On care for our common home*, London: Catholic Truth Society.

Raffety, E., 2020, 'From Inclusion to Leadership: Disabled "misfitting" in congregational ministry', *Theology Today* 77(2), pp. 198–209.

Rattray, S. and E. Lako, 2018, *Disability Inclusive Development in UNDP: Guidance and entry points*, New York: UNDP.

Razai, M. S., H. K. N. Kankam, A. Majeed, A. Esmail and D. Williams, 2021, 'Mitigating Ethnic Disparities in Covid-19 and Beyond', *British Medical Journal* 372.

Save the Children International, 2020, 'Building an Anti-racist Organis- ation', *Save the Children*, www.savethechildren.net/building-anti- racist-organisation, accessed 9.01.2021.

Stewart, D. and A. Khurshid, 2019, *UNICEF's Global Social Protection Programme Framework*, New York: UNICEF.

Swinton, J., 2012, 'From Inclusion to Belonging: A practical theology of community, disability and humanness', *Journal of Religion, Disability & Health* 16, pp. 172–90.

Swinton, J. and H. Mowat, 2016, *Practical Theology and Qualitative Research*, 2nd edn, London: SCM Press.

Tomalin, E. (ed.), 2015, *The Routledge Handbook of Religions and Global Development*, London: Routledge.

UN Women, 2020, 'UN Secretary-General's Policy Brief: The impact of COVID-19 on women', *UN Women*, www.unwomen.org/en/digital- library/publications/2020/04/policy-brief-the-impact-of-covid-19-on- women, accessed 14.03.2021.

UNICEF, 2017, *Inclusive Education – Including children with disabilities in quality learning: what needs to be done?* New York: UNICEF.

UNICEF, 2019, *Every Child Learns: UNICEF education strategy 2019– 2030*, New York: UNICEF.

United Nations, 2015, 'The Millennium Development Goals (MDGs) and Disability', *United Nations*, www.un.org/development/desa/disabilities/ issues/the-millennium-development-goals-mdgs-and-disability.html, accessed 4.03.2021.

USAID, 2021, *Social Norms Lexicon*, Washington, DC: Institute for Reproductive Health, Georgetown University for the US Agency for International Development (USAID).

Verma, T., 2018, 'There Are No Accidents in Who Learns and Who Doesn't', 31 January, *Save the Children*, www.savethechildren.net/news/ there-are-no-accidents-who-learns-and-who-doesn%E2%80%99t, accessed 9.03.2021.

Volf, M., 1996, *Exclusion and Embrace: A theological exploration of identity, otherness, and reconciliation*, Nashville, TN: Abingdon Press.

Wang, C., 2016, 'An Inclusive Society Starts from an Inclusive Education', 2 December, *Save the Children International*, www.savethechildren.net/ news/inclusive-society-starts-inclusive-education, accessed 15.07.2021.

Ward, P., 2017, *Introducing Practical Theology*, Grand Rapids, MI: Baker Academic.

World Vision, 2017, *Best Practices in Disability Inclusion*, Washington, DC: World Vision.

World Vision, 2020, '3 Ways World Vision is Fighting Racial Bias and Injustice', 22 October, *World Vision*, www.worldvision.org/christian- faith-news-stories/3-ways-world-vision-fighting-racial-bias-injustice.

Notes

1 For NGO websites, searches began by examining the 'About us' and 'Vision' pages, before moving on to using the search functions. The terms searched for were 'inclusion', 'exclusion', 'social exclusion', 'leave no one behind' and any other agency-specific terms that came up as relevant during this scan. In addition, on academic databases, the search terms were 'NGO inclusion', 'development inclusion', 'inclusion' plus each of the inclusion themes covered in this volume, and 'inclusion' plus each of the INGOs and FBOs highlighted in previous searches.

2 The reviewed organizations were: Bond, UNDP, UNICEF, HelpAge, Plan International, ActionAid, Save the Children, Christian Aid, CAFOD, CARE International, CBM, BMS World Mission, CMS, Anglican Alliance, World Vision USA, World Vision UK and the Joint Learning Initiative (JLI).

3 The term 'intersectionality' refers to how individuals or groups have multiple, interdependent social identities, including different factors such as race, class, religion, age, disability, sexuality and gender. As described in the entry under 'intersectionality' in the *Social Norms Lexicon*, 'these identities create interconnected systems of discrimination, disadvantage, or relative privilege and affect each person's lived experience, health, and behavioral outcomes' (USAID, 2021, p. 24).

4 Christian Aid's recently commissioned research study on public attitudes towards race and climate change is highly relevant here. The study found that climate change, although affecting everyone, is a deeply racialized phenomenon (Christian Aid, 2020).

5 The seven Catholic social teaching principles according to CAFOD are 'rooted in Scripture, formed by the wisdom of Church leaders, and influenced by grassroots movements' (CAFOD, 2020b). They are: dignity, solidarity, the common good, the option for the poor, peace, care for creation and the dignity of work and participation (CAFOD, 2020b). CAFOD views the option for the poor as paying 'particular attention to those on the margins of society, those people and communities that others may have overlooked, those who suffer discrimination, injustice or oppression' (CAFOD, 2021, p. 5).

6 CAFOD's mission statement in its ten-year vision for change states that 'inspired by gospel values … we come together in partnership with others, locally and globally: … to challenge and transform the structures and behaviours that drive poverty, vulnerability, inequality, injustice and exclusion and harm the natural world' (CAFOD, 2020c).

7 Pope Francis made a case for inclusion in *Laudato Si'*: 'We are faced not with two separate crises, one environmental and the other social, but rather with one complex crisis which is both social and environmental. Strategies for a solution demand an integrated approach to combating poverty, *restoring dignity to the excluded*, and at the same time protecting nature' (Pope Francis, 2015, p. 70, emphasis added).

I

One Body, Many Voices: Theological Perspectives on Inclusion and Diversity from the Global South

SELINA PALM

Introduction

This chapter showcases selected themes around inclusion and diversity seen as emerging from evangelical[1] theologians from the Global South. It does not claim that these voices are representative of Christianity in these regions but it seeks to amplify certain voices that can offer important correctives to a West-centric narrative alone on inclusion and diversity. Christianity and its missions were often historically entangled in the colonial, capitalist and civilizing projects of the West in ways that linger in inherited belief patterns within many communities who often encountered Christianity as part of a weaponized approach. South African theologian Anthony Balcomb (2016) notes the dangers of importing a Western evangelical propositionalism that was often shaped by raced, classed and gendered assumptions into African contexts. He urges that more attention be paid to the praxis-oriented, orality and lived-out modes of faith in the Global South. Perspectives on inclusion and diversity from a range of Global South contexts can offer pointers towards more open evangelical theologies that reimagine mission not merely to the margins but primarily from, and with, marginalized voices (George, 2011).

Christianity has been marked from its inception by an evangelistic commitment that has inspired many of its followers to take the 'good news' into diverse contexts as part of a missionary imperative. South African minister and theologian Dion Forster avoids defining 'evangelical' as a single type and notes instead the reality of 'plural evangelicalisms' with shared traits and important differences that are shaped by their various contexts (2019, p. 6). Christian belief therefore intersects with other aspects of social identity in diverse ways in different places. This chapter reinforces Forster's claim that emerging cross-cultural evangelicalisms can be, and are, engaging differently with contextual liberational theologies from the South than much Western evangelism has historically done. This helps to decolonize missionary Christianity and resonates with Latin American calls (George, 2002; Padilla, 2004) for forms of liberating evangelism:

> This different perspective will surely bring many unexpected consequences for those of the old representative Western Christianity, including upside-down scriptural interpretations, radical unlearning, self-emptying, disturbing challenges, surprising partnerships, mission-in-reverse, renewal, new evangelization, continuing conversion, mutual transformation, and hope. (George, 2002, p. 108)

Evangelical Christians have strong roots in the primacy of Scripture and conversion, an emphasis on the good news of the gospel, and the unique salvific role of the cross. In the West, this has often taken the form of rigid liberal/conservative binaries (Forster, 2019). However, forms of social evangelicalism, often influenced by liberation theologies (Bedford, 2012), have taken strong root in many Southern contexts and offer contributions towards a more inclusive evangelical approach that takes human diversity seriously as created by God. This chapter surfaces some contributions from the Global South and indigenous voices on inclusion and diversity from which those in Western contexts also need to learn. Historical patterns of dominating power may need to be unlearned, including the forced assimilation of 'them' by 'us' as a form of distorted inclusion. Sri Lankan theologian Vinoth Ramachandra (1996) offers a reminder that, as the axis of the Christian church shifts southwards to Latin America, Africa and Asia, there is a need to 'embrace each other's concerns and stretch to each other's horizons'.

Methodology

This chapter is based on an extensive literature review commissioned by Tearfund (Palm, 2019). It explored academic theological literature across eight regions of Tearfund's work in the Global South that focused on inclusion and diversity. It used an inductive qualitative approach to surface key themes to contribute towards Tearfund's theological framework for inclusion. The study focused on written contributions from scholars within each region from the year 2000 onwards, with more than 2,000 documents identified and 240 of these receiving in-depth engagement. Primary search criteria were theologies of inclusion and diversity. Evangelical contributions were prioritized. The variety in each region militated against developing one universal theology. A search for diverse and inclusive theologies must pay attention to the many different 'vernaculars' emerging from each region to avoid theological generalizations about what is typical of 'the Asian mind' or the 'African world view', or it runs the risk of essentializing different regions. A targeted approach listened in to themes as regionally prioritized by local scholars. For example, in the Middle East, questions of migration and peace dominated. Prioritizing written, academic literature limited access to important modes of oral theologizing through traditions, stories, songs and prayers that need to be explored further, as do the voices of Tearfund staff in these regions.

Exploring inclusion and diversity: a theological task

The study suggests that the linguistic concepts of diversity and inclusion can be hard to translate, or may have specific local histories attached. For example, in South Africa these words can be associated primarily with racial transformation (Forster, 2019), while in Latin American churches they are often seen negatively as 'codewords' for gender and sexuality issues. Theologically, the theme of inclusion seeks to relate traditional faith tenets to the modern world in new ways, but it can also be attached to problematic forms of Western assimilation (Ford and Muers, 2005). Diversity seeks to avoid assimilation but has also at times been interpreted in damaging ways to support a lack of equality, including the separation of racial groups in apartheid South Africa or the religious divisions in Nigeria. Decolonizing these terms requires understanding their resonances in different contexts. Questions of religious diversity are contested within Christianity regarding whether other religions are to be seen as equal partners (Azumah, 2007). Christianity has often been accompanied by Western cultural forms and is challenged by voices who seek cultural plurality.

Global Christian movements such as the World Council of Churches and the Micah Network have helped churches reflect more on inclusion and diversity, often in the light of questions raised by participants from Southern contexts.[2] More attention is being given to vernacular, contextual Bible interpretations from outside the West. Seeking inclusion and diversity is seen as a theological task, shaped by a faith that emerged from the margins as a religion of oppressed peoples. A commitment to the good news must refuse to allow God to become a justification for historical systems of existing power and authority but reclaim its concrete liberating dimensions as good news for the marginalized. Christianity's strong presence in the South today raises important questions about its liberating contextuality. In some parts of the world, denominational divisions are negligible. In other places, evangelical theology is still seen as foreign or imported and is often associated with White outsiders. Humility is required if the export of Western Christian historical divides is to be avoided:

[O]ur primary attitude should be humility when it comes to doing mission and theology in the global context. The diversity, range, and subtlety of contexts, history, issues, and challenges is breath-taking. Global theology demands particularity ... given the wonder and mystery of human beings who bear the *imago dei*. Human existence, including global theology, involves paying attention to God and paying attention to the world in God's name ... part of how our diversity of gifts enable the body of Christ to attend to God and the world. (Dumitrescu, 2019, p. 150)

With this in mind, this chapter explores key insights that emerged from each region in the wider study to showcase the breadth available. The themes under each region offer a brief summary of the issues surfaced in that wider study. Its qualitative, inductive analysis identified key themes emerging from scholars from these contexts as prominent across each specific region. It forms an overarching contribution to inform the specific subtopics explored in later chapters. It is attentive to, but does not impose, those subtopics but seeks to 'listen in' to what emerges from them.

Latin America and Caribbean region

Integral mission

In the Latin American and Caribbean region, the theme of integral mission, often under the influence of liberation theology, has shaped decades of concern with socio-economic injustice (Padilla, 2004). Evangelical churches have been invited to embrace a prophetic human rights-oriented task in the public realm (Pérez, 2017). Orthopraxis is viewed here by many as a biblical mandate and reconciliation tied not only to God but also to other humans and to wider creation. In this way, justification and justice creation, human rights and prophetic citizenship are reconnected into a holistic system of faith and life:

> An increasing number of Christians ... have become convinced that in their life and mission they are called to keep Jesus' Great Commission and Great Commandment together. No longer are they inclined to accept that the mission of the Church can be reduced to proclaiming the Gospel for the sake of saving souls and planting churches ... God's mission, in which the Church is summoned to participate, is integral mission ... Justice and justification by faith, worship and political action, the spiritual and the material, personal change and structural change belong together. As in the life of Jesus, being, doing and saying are at the heart of our integral task. (Padilla, 2004, n.p.)

The image of God

New interpretive paradigms have given birth to liberation theologies from this region, which emphasize the centrality of the image of God in poor, socially oppressed and excluded people (Leer-Helgesen, 2016). This image of God theme has since been applied elsewhere to many aspects of diversity and inclusion, including that of disability (Danforth, 2005). Theologians such as Orlando Costas from Puerto Rico and Leonardo Boff from

Brazil have applied this creational goodness to the plight of excluded peoples and to wider creation, with implications for rethinking sin, salvation and reconciliation through a cosmic Christology lens (Book, 2007). New ways of reading Scriptures have also been contextually developed here to open up biblical mandates for inclusive social engagement with sacred texts by lay people (Bedford, 2012).

Spirit ecumenism

Much of this region remains Catholic. However, an upsurge has been noted in recent years in Pentecostal churches (Bedford, 2012). Pentecost offers possibilities for grass-roots churches here to connect the Spirit with social activism. Theologians here show that the book of Acts offers a Spirit-filled challenge to all social divisions. Baptism in the Holy Spirit becomes an inclusive ritual that levels these diverse social discriminations (Peterson, 2009). An emphasis on Service ecumenism invites churches to work together to secure abundant life for all through a Spirit-filled unity and hope for righteous justice:

> The Spirit who gives, sustains, and promotes all life, calls us as people and cultures to be part of God's work ... [and] lead[s] us to a clearly defined mission in society. The Spirit does not exclude or discriminate: we are all invited. The Spirit constantly surprises us and calls us to unity, reconciliation, and forgiveness. It makes unity possible within diversity, the holistic union of all parts of Christ's body, since Pentecostalness includes recognizing others without fear. (Bedford, 2012, p. 107)

Some evangelicals in Latin America are finding new ways to be part of a dialogue between Catholics, Pentecostals and Protestants, finding common ground on creative forms of liberating missiology (Nacho, 2018). Peruvian theologian Rolando Pérez (2017) calls evangelicals to engage in dialogue with political stakeholders around the shared themes of citizenship for the common good, and human rights is seen as part of a commitment to a system of life, rather than as a secular ideology to be resisted by the church.

Religious hybridity

This region also has a history of indigenous religions. Afro-Caribbean theologians such as Roderick Hewitt (2012) call for an embrace of hybridity to celebrate these traditions. This refutes any forms of exclusivity or assumed Christian superiority, to offer what are seen as being more hospitable forms of inclusive religious rituals. This same theme is picked up by Puerto Rican theologian Wilmer Estrada-Carrasquillo who notes:

> The table must be approachable for those who are part of the broader community and not just the Christian ... an open table! ... The Eucharistic event can be a salvific moment for a non-Christian ... we can gain more by being inclusive than exclusive ... By opening the table, Pentecostals bear witness to the generous oneness of the church and the radical hospitality of the church's Lord. (2013, p. 113)

However, gender and sexuality remain contested issues. Feminist and queer theological scholars such as Ivone Gebara (2010) from Brazil, Elsa Támez (2010) from Mexico and Marcella Althaus-Reid from Argentina (2003) have all raised the issue of the dominance of hetero-patriarchy within Christianity in this region and offer new upside-down readings of the Bible. Some churches see inclusion and diversity as code words for these issues alone. Maria Jose Rosado-Nunes (2010) notes from a Catholic context that conservative denominational alliances often reinforce patriarchal systems as God-ordained and some may then resist any engagement with themes of diversity and inclusion.

South-East Asia region

Non-dual methodologies

In South-East Asia, religious and cultural pluralism form an entry point for reflections on inclusion and diversity. Fluid identities of hybridity challenge Western binary ways of thinking. Non-dual thinking can place relationality and unity at the centre of Asian Christian faith rather than the need for salvation and create commitment to two-way dialogue. Singaporean theologian Michael Poon notes that:

Asian evangelicals must articulate common evangelical concerns in a distinctively Asian way in order to address distinctively Asian problems. Methodological issues focus on the non-dualistic, concrete ways of doing theology here using stories, parables, and songs, as opposed to the Cartesian, abstract, or 'Greek' way of the West. (2010, p. 26)

Liberation from poverty

Many people in this region remain very poor and spiritual engagement with people's material social-economic conditions is critical. The Pentecostal Spirit has been connected in places such as South Korea to liberation for oppressed peoples from both colonization and poverty (Yun, 2009). Malaysian theologian Amos Yong (2007) has helped to develop a liberating and inclusive Asian evangelical theology that pays more attention to the material, social and economic dimensions of the gospel.

Disability and cultures of shame

Shame is a key issue in many Asian contexts and can shape how Christian themes around social marginalization are interpreted. Religious and cultural ideas about holiness become intertwined. A Christology of inclusion and diversity can offer theological ways to remap shame around issues such as disability. Amanda Shao-Tan (2018) addresses this concept of shame through the book of Hebrews to point to an empathetic, empowering Jesus whose own response to shame can be emulated by his followers. She argues that Tsinoys like her, who have shame about their disability, can relate to Jesus' personal shame experiences to nurture their own spirituality. People with disabilities may in fact be able to point people without disabilities towards new ways of facing their own struggles with shame.

Yong (2011) also gives suggestions for how Asian churches can engage disability theology to tackle this entrenched culture of shame. He interrogates a biblical holiness tradition on disability which sees blemishes as a curse (Deut. 28). He calls instead for a disability hermeneutic if the Bible is to be read redemptively and suggests churches still often adopt the ecclesiology of Corinth over a Pauline theology of weakness.

Gender and the family

Communal values of the family and filial piety are highly valued across much of Asia and are often seen as contrasting with individualistic ideas still associated with the West (Chan, 2014). This can open up promising Trinitarian relational models of engagement but can mean that issues of gender and sexuality, if seen to threaten the family, remain taboo. Much of the evangelical church here still views women as needing to be submitted to male leadership but this is being contested by Asian feminist scholars such as Kwok Pui-lan (2010). Vietnamese scholar Le Ngoc Bich Ly notes that progressive approaches to gender shaped by communism have often been rejected by the church and that 'an inherited missionary patriarchal gender perspective has been shielded by this church's self-isolation from wider society' (2019, p. 117). The importance attached to the family here also extends to family ancestor rites which can sometimes be dismissed by Christianity. However, feminist scholars emerging here point to alternative, integrative, holistic approaches (Bong, 2010). They use the Holy Spirit not to reinforce binary separations between body and spirit, which often become gendered, but to point to theologies of embodiment.

Incarnational engagement

In much of Asia, Christianity forms a tiny minority perspective alongside multiple other religions and cultures. A respectful theology of other religions and cultures is essential. Binary questions around salvation can sit at odds with a more syncretic approach or a respectful dialogue (Tan, 2010). Questions of dual identity and religious hybridization are complex and may not fit into the neat pre- and post-conversion categories often imposed by Western evangelism. A dual-allegiance Christianity is prevalent as evangelical Filipino theologian Melba Maggay (2008) notes. This often internalizes colonial ideas that 'the West is best' and can inherit a body–soul dichotomy that fails to speak holistically to deep-rooted Asian concerns around health and healing. Yong suggests instead that Asian body thinking that is shaped by Daoism can form an affinity with 'the Christian understanding of truth embodied in the life of Jesus and in the biblical narratives' (2007, p. 376). It offers an incarnational hermeneutic for reading the Bible that may resonate more with existing Asian religious traditions and perspectives.

Divine Spirit healing

South-East Asia is also experiencing a rise in Pentecostal churches. Many of these offer new forms of interreligious dialogue around the Spirit and issues of healing. They can open inclusive spaces for rituals and active participation by all, especially those who are illiterate, as they are often less focused on a word-based tradition. Scriptures that emphasize Pentecost and the ongoing work of the Spirit and the Great Commission are popular (Yun, 2009). However, Scriptures that may reinforce shame or an emphasis on perfection may need deconstruction and challenge in the light of disability stigma in this region that can lead to damaging theologies of healing becoming abusive for vulnerable people (Shao-Tan, 2018; Yong, 2011).

Southern Asia

An inclusive gospel

Christian mission in this region is typically oriented towards society, with a focus on Jesus as both liberator and healer (Jayakumar, 2009; George, 2011). Historically, in the Indian subcontinent, it has often been those on the margins of society who have been most likely to turn to Christianity. Scriptures here often emphasize the gospel's connections to the poor and oppressed, and the good news of Jesus where the poor are included and where healing and freedom from caste restrictions are offered. A reconciliation motif emphasizes that all can be children of God and that no one is excluded. This ties the image of God with human rights, going beyond the exclusions of an entrenched religious caste system. Indian scholars emphasize that in the Bible 'the poor and oppressed are not deserted by God but loved through Jesus Christ whose preaching begins by quoting Isaiah in Luke 4.18–19' (Jayakumar, 2009, p. 155). However, disability and poverty remain stigmatized and exclusive theologies and practices need challenge.

Religion meets religion

Christianity forms a very small religious minority across most of southern Asia. Religion and culture are also entangled within wider communal and kinship identities and seek holistic integration. Christianity has also been shaped by a colonial missionary history that needs post-colonial interrogation. Respectful inter-religious dialogues are therefore essential and may offer new insights on multiple religious belonging where individuals may decide, for example, to identify as a Hindu Christian or a *Yesu Bhakta* (Bhakiaraj, 2010). Jesus opened the net of salvation beyond the Jewish people only in his time. In the Indian context, this extends to Scheduled Castes – so-called Untouchables or Dalits – who form a large proportion of Christians in India who are excluded from other religious frameworks. As a result, Christianity could help to create space for a more inclusive conversation around integrative faith frameworks that transcend culture and caste boundaries as a sign of fidelity to their own tradition (Jayakumar, 2016).

Holistic mission

Social oppression is often related to caste, ethnicity, disability and poverty – and is to be found in their intersections – with religious justifications often used to exclude certain groups. Dalit theology has a unique voice to offer Christianity around issues of inclusion. Christianity in the Indian subcontinent has also focused on social concerns and challenging oppressive cultural practices for women and children. The Christian story was connected to hopes for a new society and was seen to be a battle against 'bad' religion that harms people. However, this story was also misshaped by colonial, civilizing assumptions that pitted Christianity against all other religions rather than them working together to build a shared commitment to the marginalized. Church authorities tied to existing colonial power structures often failed to recognize the existing ancient Pentecostal Christian presence in this region that predates modern mission (Pulikottil, 2009).

Gender and sexuality

Women's subordination in this region has led to a critical engagement by many women scholars on patriarchal sacred texts and religious rituals. Many women in South Asia bear the brunt of poverty, illiteracy and cultural oppression, and women's movements here have often seen religions as oppressive. In response to this, a rise in post-colonial feminist Christian scholarship (Pui-lan, 2010) offers a hermeneutic of suspicion on how sexuality and gender texts have been read. Yet the complex entanglement of religion and culture to reinforce patriarchy remains. Indian feminist scholar Monica Melanchthon notes, 'Indian Christian women need to be liberated from a twofold bondage, the patriarchal hermeneutic of the Bible ... and scriptures of other faiths ... All scripture in India has patriarchal assumptions' (2010, p. 114). For example, while women's ordination has received increased attention, many Indian women especially are still expected to be humble, and to sacrifice and suffer as part of their faith in ways that prioritize family well-being over their own. The critical engagement of evangelical theology with these framing faith narratives, their entanglement with patriarchy and their damaging social impact on the lives of women is key. Diverse sexualities are also being increasingly discussed in this region, as recent work by the Indian National Council of Churches shows (Gaikwad and Ninan, 2017; Kuruvilla, 2017). Non-binary frames of reference are seen by these scholars to offer new theological possibilities for an embrace of LGBTIQ+ inclusion and diversity that does not rely on Western gender binary categories.

Disability and a theology of access

Disability is a significant issue of concern in this region and is often related to caste, gender and religious identities (Engage Disability, 2016). The motif of the church as the one body of Christ enables disability theologians here to insist that the Christian God is committed to inclusion, offering a theology of access to God for all who live on the margins (George, 2011). Indian theologian Samuel George, who lives with a disability himself, insists that the gospel of Jesus Christ is a gospel of inclusion and access, and that it creates access for those on the margins as a central Christian mandate:

God is not incompatible with disability and God is for and on the side of people with disabilities. The Exodus God is the God who is on the side of the marginalized ... [churches] should attend to this issue as an issue of justice, that people with disability, too, are part and parcel of the church. Unity and mission without the inclusion of their voices and visions is not only a truncated mission endeavour, but is also impossible, because God is not a partner to such an endeavour. (2011, p. 103)

Eurasia, Central Asia and China

Religious freedom

The communist history in much of this region has shaped difficult church–state relationships. Religion was forced 'underground' for decades and also experienced political repression by the state in unique ways. As a result, religious freedom forms a key issue here for inclusion and diversity. In post-communist times, parts of this region have now been heavily influenced by new evangelical movements that are often connected to Western modernity (Bays, 2003). Evangelical groups in China often emphasize autonomous house churches, dramatic conversion experiences, personal experience of God and literal readings of the Bible, but also suffer from a lack of formally trained preachers. At the same time, religion remains policed by secular authorities in the case of China or by Orthodox religious authorities in Russia.

Peaceful coexistence

This region also sits as a meeting point between the East and the West. Romans 12.18 is often used to support the Christian imperative to live at peace with everyone and also the need for Christian apology, humility and repentance for past religious violence in the region (Nickel, 2016, p. 355). Theologians here have also pointed to a 'complex unity' at the heart of God. This offers means to engage with Islamic and Christian ways of understanding God so as to promote a plural respectful interfaith dialogue:

Conflicts between European Christians resolved by the use of violence and the wars started by Christians against Muslim nations make a mockery of the Gospel message of peace and bring the credibility and the missionary efforts of the churches into disrepute. (Wietzke, 1994, p. 66)

Ecumenical unity in diversity

Wietzke (1994) also points to the need for a creative fragmentation of Christianity in order to relate it more authentically to different cultures and to appreciate their diversity. Eastern Orthodox traditions focus on relational personhood, as does Confucianism, which emphasizes the non-binary oneness of all reality, the need to live in harmony with 'the way' (Dao), and the interrelation of humans and nature. In 2018 in Turkey, seven church denominations published a book on Christianity, as the result of ten years of ecumenical work together (Schirrmacher, 2018). A rising urban Pentecostalism in places such as the Ukraine and Poland is often shaped by African diasporas and looks beyond North American theologies only to engage with Eastern Orthodoxy, contextual and African theologies (Cosden, 2002).

Disability

This issue is often associated with religious discrimination and exclusion in this region, with spiritually infused ideas of blessings and curses from God often stigmatizing those living with disabilities. Nathan Hoppe, who worked as a missionary with the Orthodox Church in Albania, notes that this framing of disability needs to urgently change and that 'disability ... needs to be reflected as a problem of the health of the church. In a healthy church all members pray and work together, they do not condescend toward other members' (2015, n.p.).

Patriarchal traditions

Some of these regions historically have a religiously infused patriarchal influence. Cultures shaped by filial piety may have remained quite fixed for centuries, and religious frameworks that went underground can have failed to evolve gradually alongside modernization. In recent decades, however, alongside socialist values, there have been changes, with women playing more active roles in society and the church. New biblical interpretations by women here are also being seen, partly due to the positive influence of gender equality promoted through socialism in China. For example, Meng Yanling in China (2010) points to women in the Bible, such as the stigmatized bleeding woman who approaches Jesus, as offering alternative religious images that can model female strength and independence. A history of socialism in this region has had a positive impact on women taking up leadership roles in the church in China especially.

Middle East and North Africa

Politicized religion

In this region, which is characterized by multiple conflicts, religion is highly politicized. Christianity can become dangerously entangled in this politicization due to rising religious extremisms and must avoid being co-opted into violent conflations of religious and political identity (Younan, 2007). As a result, peacebuilding and migration themes here offer important insights for theologies of peaceful hospitality to enable the monotheistic religions of Judaism, Christianity and Islam to coexist peacefully.

Diakonical hospitality

The themes of hospitality to the stranger and those at the margins takes on new forms in the light of mass migrations in this region. A Christian commitment to incarnational diakonical ministry to poor or needy neighbours becomes critical (Hamd, 2013). For example, research shows that Lebanese Christians are offering hospitality to Syrian refugees despite historical tensions between the two nations (Gourlay et al., 2019). This points to the importance of reconciliation across differences. For example, Ethiopian Evangelical Church Mekane Yesus is the largest Lutheran church on the African continent and emphasizes church practices of reconciliation across many aspects of diversity that move beyond homogeneity to heterogeneous community across race, gender, ethnicity and socio-economic make-up as a practice of hospitality (Bulaka, 2015).

Respectful interfaith engagement

Scriptural engagement in this region emphasizes shared sacred stories that can enable sensitive interfaith dialogue, as well as promote shared values such as the Golden Rule and justice. Religious inclusion and diversity have concrete practical implications, such as reconceptualizing key religious sites in non-exclusive ways. Using sacred texts in ways that focus on Jerusalem as a city of importance to God across many religious traditions can offer a concrete theological example of this approach (Younan, 2007; Ateek, 2017). Jesus' life and ministry witness to a holistic mission on the margins, as found in Matthew 15.21–28. Bible verses that are agnostic regarding who is to receive salvation, such as Revelation 7.10, can avoid further inflaming wider political conflicts. The Middle East is seen to make potentially a unique contribution to Christian–Muslim dialogue by insisting on the urgent need for a genuine encounter with the 'other's' tradition as equally valuable as one's own (Avakian, 2015).

Land, conflict and justice

The question of land and its religious symbolism remains highly contested in much of this region, for example in the decades of political conflict around the State of Palestine. Zionist ideologies draw highly contested connections between modern Israel and biblical religious promises. However, Christian theologians from the State of Palestine such as Naim Ateek (2017) have engaged with liberating Christian themes of peacebuilding held together with justice, reconciliation and non-violence as central tenets, to prevent the politicization of religion and distortion of any Scriptures to justify exclusive ideologies.

Female leadership

Gender issues here are seen to require a post-colonial feminist lens on historical and current-day intersecting hierarchies of domination, as is seen in the work of Palestinian theologian Jean Zaru (2010) on biblical hermeneutics. Some shifts in churches here are being seen, however, regarding entrenched patterns of patriarchy, especially around the issue of ordaining women. For example, Algeria, Egypt, Lebanon and Syria all have examples within their evangelical churches of women teaching, preaching and establishing churches. Feminine metaphors for God are also often being used in this region, such as the scriptural image of the eagle mother from Deuteronomy 32.11 and from Psalm 17.8 (Sara, 2018). However, despite some movement on gender, sexuality often remains a taboo topic here, with conservative religious attitudes on female modesty and dress codes.

Francophone Africa

Liturgy and ritual

Historically, French-speaking regions were often dominated by Catholic missionaries and a focus on sacraments, liturgy and rituals (Bujo and Muya, 2005). Since the 1970s, a strong drive towards developing African ecclesiologies has emerged on the continent. An emphasis on oral, participatory modes of engagement is also noted by Cameroonian theologian Jean-Marc Ela who calls for an oral theology of the people that live 'under the tree' (Bujo and Muya, 2005, p. 186). Central African Republic theologian Kalemba Mwambazambi (2011) notes that many African churches prioritize manifestations of the Holy Spirit over abstract or written doctrines and focus on a positive transformation towards autonomy from old colonial missions. This transformation affirms African identity with songs, uniforms, marching and rituals. African ecclesiologies often use a Spirit-centred hermeneutic for their biblical interpretations of sickness, poverty and evil spirits, which also leads to a wider embrace of Pentecostalism, sometimes shaped by new forms of American importation of Pentecostal prosperity gospel models. However, African indigenous churches form a rapidly growing movement in this region in particular (Mwambazambi, 2011).

Culture and religion

Many parts of West and Central Africa experienced violent forms of colonization and slavery at the hands of Western nations. Missionary forms of Christianity were brought in from outside, with complex historic interlinkages with colonialism. As a result, liberation from racist and cultural dominance remains a key concern. Christianity's relationship to African cultural forms and traditional religions has been a long-term focus. Political and cultural themes of inculturation and liberation predominate but often remain male-dominated, while gender and sexuality are still underexplored issues. The colonial misuse of Scripture to legitimize slavery and colonization here requires new contextual African readings of the Bible as advocated early on by scholars such as Bimweni Kweshi from the Democratic Republic of Congo (Bujo, 2003). Strong connections are often made between culture and religion by, for example, seeing Jesus as an ancestor. A number of West African scholars rethink missionary ideas of 'conversion by opposition', which requires a radical rupture with culture, to embrace alternative indigenous approaches of 'conversion by composition', which remain more open to reconciling culture and religion (Bujo, 2003, p. 73). This can extend to interfaith engagement where Africans may inhabit a dual religious identity with Muslim and Christian ancestry or ongoing connections to African traditional religion. Many African scholars offer different hybrid approaches to ongoing questions around this multiple religious heritage (Bujo, 2013).

Holistic reconstruction and reconciliation

Congolese theologian Kä Mana has developed a theology of reconstruction that directly connects spiritual and social transformation (Mwambazambi, 2013; Dedji, 2001). This ties conversion and the re-establishment of a relationship with God to relationships with neighbours, the environment and with self. It focuses on the concreteness of sins against others and the ongoing consequences of these for the social fabric. Kä Mana calls for a re-evangelization of communities, institutions and structures in places characterized by fragile states and conflict (Bujo, 2013). Social reconstruction, reconciliation and human rights are essential for those often excluded from the benefits of globalization. These require religious rituals of lament as explored by Ugandan theologian Emmanuel Katongole (2017).

A theology of life

Ela draws on John's Gospel to offer a 'theology of life' with the cross seen as an instrument of liberation. Affirming African culture then becomes a protest against colonialism (Bujo and Muya, 2005). For Ela, African theologies must focus on the poor, tackle socio-economic issues and reclaim forms of oral dialogue 'under the tree' as mentioned above. The church can exercise a ministry of reconciliation within small communities where lay members are valued and equipped to share the sacraments in ways that reject a narrow hierarchy of clerical power. The doctrine of the Trinity, for Ela, offers a way to see each other as adopted kin. Congolese ethicist Bénézet Bujo (2003) emphasizes traditional African practices such as the important role of community *palavar* dialogues as an inclusive alternative to hierarchical modes of church authority. However, other African theologians such as Nigerian theologian Agbonkhianmeghe Orobator (2011) point to latent forms of exclusion that often remain present in these traditional modes of participation, which need to be avoided. He suggests that these approaches may resonate more with an older, rural generation than with a younger African urban elite.

Sexuality, gender and disability

These issues have received far less theological attention in this region to date. Laurent Mpongo from Cameroon has explored liturgies of marriage and family in ways that engage the diversity of forms of these institutions that exist across Africa, which were often rejected by missionaries (Bujo and Muya, 2005). Patrick Awondo, Peter Geschiere and Graeme Reid (2012) explore the contested topic of religion and homosexuality across Cameroon and Senegal in ways that contest oversimplified stereotypes. Finally, up until her death in 2020 Micheline Kamba (2019) from the Democratic Republic of Congo focused on challenging disability exclusion and its complex connections to sin and healing.

Anglophone Africa

Gender and sexuality

The HIV pandemic in this region has generated a range of more inclusive theologies around sexuality and gender. African women theologians have played a prominent role here, often as part of the Circle of Concerned African Women Theologians (Tarus, 2014). While conservative African voices still reject much engagement on gender and sexuality as 'unAfrican', other African female and queer voices contest this (Dube, 2010; Hinga et al., 2008). One approach is the Tamar Campaign, a contextual Bible study and materials that have been developed by scholars in this region to help faith communities discuss gendered sexual violence (West and Zondi-Mabizela, 2004). Contributions have also been made by diverse theologians around LGBTIQ+ inclusion, especially within Southern Africa (West et al., 2016).

The Bible and culture

The Bible is highly respected in this region. Questions of inculturation and contextual Bible readings are therefore essential, especially where the Bible has been used, such as in South Africa, to underpin exclusive racist theologies. Liberating the Bible requires a hermeneutic of social transformation. Contextual Bible study methods (West, 2004) can open space for a plurality of engagement where, for example, Galatians 3.28 is used to point to a new freedom in Christ, with baptism as a socially inclusive ritual. Acts 15 shows that Christianity can be at home in a range of cultures, and a ministry of reconciliation focuses on restoring relationships (1 Cor. 5.18–19). African scholars such as Musa Dube (2010) have worked to decolonize the Bible and to dialogue respectfully with African traditional religion. African independent churches (AICs) are fast growing hybrid paradigms that connect African culture and religion with Christianity. A range of scholars have explored promising connections here, such as Jesus as ancestor (Bediako, 1990). However, these theologies and practices need critical engagement, as without care they can misuse the Bible to defend harmful practices (Hinga et al., 2008).

Liberation, reconstruction and reconciliation

A liberational approach here has historically drawn on insights from Black and Latin American theology to challenge colonial and apartheid practices. In emerging African democracies often fraught with challenges, reconciliation and reconstruction theologies emerge to point to a pluralistic nation-building task that goes beyond tribal or ethnic rivalries (Mugambi, 1995). Patterns of adopted kinship, family and fraternity are drawn on. Many churches have been called to make a shift from providing 'mission to the margins' to doing 'mission from the margins' (Knoetze, 2016, p. 5) and to emphasize practising justice as a focus of all mission.

Spirit of prosperity and healing

A rising wave of neo-Pentecostal churches across the African continent draw on the Spirit to offer solutions to practical human needs and to connect body and soul holistically. Health and healing are key concerns. However, issues of corruption and financial abuse have dogged many of these churches, with a lack of training and accountability for their leaders. Zionist churches have a long powerful history, and many take a strongly triumphalist approach to hope, healing and prosperity. They attract, but at times also exclude, those who are poor, struggling or living with disabilities, who are often seen as failing to manifest God's blessing. This prosperity gospel has limits in creating inclusive communities.

Inclusive communities

In this region, Christianity has an accepted role in many public spaces and often sits alongside other religions without conflict. All are seen as God's children, as brothers and sisters (1 John 3.1–2). Unity is important, with diversity not leading to divisiveness (Rom. 12.5). This region emphasizes the need to nurture hospitable, inclusive and peaceful communities in the light of regional migration and xenophobia. Ghanaian theologian John Azumah (2007) points to the African proverb, 'Truth is like a baobab tree; one person's arms cannot embrace it', to show that truth is too big for one faith tradition to monopolize. Christian inclusivism can become paternalistic. For Azumah, a willingness to 'not know' on salvation is a premise of interfaith dialogue (1 Cor. 13.9), to avoid becoming 'visa officials for heaven' (2007, p. 298).

Disability

Problematic theological connections between disability and sin, curses, witchcraft and demonology shape much of this region (Ishola-Esan, 2016) and need urgent engagement to prevent exclusion and harm. In recent years, South African scholars such as Louise Kretschmar (2019), and theological institutions across Africa, have begun to develop promising, inclusive theologies on disability as well as listening in to the voices of people living with disability and the stigma they encounter. The Bible and cultural beliefs remain entangled in damaging ways, especially around issues of albinism and mental health (Mugeere et al., 2020).

Cross-regional indigenous voices

Indigenous peoples exist in multiple parts of the globe.[3] They do not speak with one voice. However, they have collaborated in theological settings to raise their voices on questions of diversity and inclusion, in the light of their collective exclusion and marginalization from a nation-state framework, and from much theologizing. Although they do not form one geographic region, they offer unique contributions to Christian spirituality and have even been termed the 'fourth world' by Asian theologian Kwok Pui-lan (2010, p. 2). Violent displacement of their ways of life by colonizers, often accompanied by Christian doctrine, means there is an urgent need to listen attentively to these voices today (Skye, 2010). Below are five themes on inclusion identified as emerging from selected indigenous literature.

Eco-reconciliation and restoration

Many indigenous Christian voices connect the God of abundant life to the earth and to the land, which is seen as sacred, to offer an earth-incarnation approach. They reclaim scriptural insights regarding the wisdom of all creation, the incarnational restoration of all things and a cosmic Christology. Terry LeBlanc, an evangelical Christian within the Canadian indigenous tradition of the Acadia people, notes:

> Our history as indigenous people, and our general disposition toward life suggests that all creation is of a spiritual nature, not just human beings. We see this clearly expressed in Scripture (Gen 1.28, Job 12.1, Rom 8.22). This has implications for how we view the work of Jesus and the cross, not simply as providing soul salvation, but rather ensuring the restoration of all things to the plan and intent of God. (2018, n.p.)

Peace in one body

Indigenous voices seek to reconnect humans to each other and to wider creation, seeing them as interdependent. Unia Kaise Api (2018) from Papua New Guinea notes that in the light of the endemic patterns of violence against and between indigenous tribes, themes of peace and shalom need to emphasize inclusion as a place where different groups with histories of exclusion and conflict can come together into a shared house and build new patterns of reconciliation, connection and reciprocity. This is tied to Pentecost (Mani, 2013) and a metaphor of the one body of Christ, where Christ suffers in solidarity with all who still suffer today due to many forms of exclusion. Indigenous Christians call the church to move from an anatomy of exclusion to one of inclusion and hope where the Christ-centred theme of inclusion of different peoples of the earth is seen to be biblical, with implications for the cross and the church. The *La Paz* report, which placed indigenous and marginalized people's voices at the centre of its theological approach, suggests that 'such a pluralistic understanding of Christ enables the church – the body of Christ – to be an inclusive community' (WCC, 2007, n.p.).

Plurality of voices

Theologies of inclusion require solidarity with the many different intersections of human identity that are embedded within a relational cosmos. Indigenous people have often borne the brunt of colonial missionary-imported prejudices. As a result, they insist on a 'home-grown wholeness' of faith (Vargas, 2010, p. 96). Their lived experiences of forced assimilation offer unique perspectives on the dangers of prioritizing one religious voice or one truth. Indigenous Christian theologians claim that diverse contributions should remain as unique threads in a plural tapestry of beliefs (WCC, 2012).

Gender inclusion

An emphasis on God as Spirit is an important part of Christian tradition and texts, providing openness to the idea of the feminine side of God. Indigenous women theologians from Oceania such as Moeawa Callaghan (2013) and Lee Miena Skye (2010) contribute to reimagining the cosmic Christ figure in ways that have direct implications for gender exclusion. The cross is connected to Christ's solidarity with those who suffer today, and not only to a vertical reconciliation with God. Indigenous voices on gender, sexuality and disability issues are also emerging and emphasize the need for respectful dialogue and encounter between diverse peoples and religions on these issues. Queer people sometimes play important roles in indigenous rituals, offering positive gifts to the community and this may offer alternative ways to reimagine LGBTIQ+ belonging within churches also.

Rereading the Bible

Indigenous people recognize the Bible as a communally written text with many diverse voices. Participatory, oral, experiential and cyclical methodologies reread Scripture to centre historically excluded perspectives. Scriptures that emphasize the wisdom and inclusion of all creation, a prophetic commitment to deliver justice for the excluded, a gospel-centred anatomy of inclusion and the social dimensions of abundant life are emphasized. The book of Acts then becomes the cornerstone for a church where all cultures are welcomed and filled with the Spirit of life and where hospitable friendship replaces exclusion. This also opens up space to belong for people with disabilities, as Samoan Christian Manuele Teofilo (2016), who lives with a disability himself, notes. Rereading the Bible through indigenous eyes offers a post-colonial lens for ordinary readers; for example, retelling the story of Ruth and Orpah as Laura Donaldson (2010) does can help decolonize Christian mission in practice, not just in theory.

Learnings across the eight regions

Six cross-cutting themes were identified across the different regions that speak to the theological questions of inclusion and diversity across their different dimensions. These are briefly summarized below.

Deconstructing ethnic superiority

The reality of excluded peoples and the development of exclusive theologies within Christian traditions has shaped many harmful interactions between diverse ethnicities. Western Christianity, often imported by missionaries, has frequently been accompanied by racism and theological justifications of practices such as taking land, separating ethnic groups, slavery and the demonization of indigenous religions. Deconstructing these harmful theologies is an urgent task if churches are not to perpetuate racism or treat other cultural frameworks as either superior or inferior. Theologians from the Global South can take a more communal approach to humans as relationally embedded and emphasize harmony, dialogue and reconciliation to hold multiple social identities together.

Upturning socio-economic divides and caste systems

Despite Christianity's origins among the poor and marginalized, it has often become a religion of the educated, rich and powerful, and many of its theologies and practices have come to discriminate against the poor. A focus on the soul, after-life and individual salvation can turn attention away from concrete structures of injustice and oppression that have perpetuated poverty for those trapped within them. Rediscovering a missional approach that prioritizes life characterizes much Southern engagement with poverty, caste, disability and class distinctions. A Jesus-centred commitment to the marginalized can shape a holistic Pentecostal mission around embodied praxis. Theologies grounded in a Spirit of inclusive justice can enable prophetic roles in inclusion and diversity.

Gender and sexuality

These remain areas of debate within global Christianity, with female theological contributions contesting male-dominated leadership, religious patriarchy and its condemnation of various sexual practices. This issue has often been framed as a disunity between Northern and Southern voices. However, by listening to many Southern female voices that speak out on these issues, this binary framing can be challenged. Women's voices and gendered concerns here – in home and church – are challenging historical Christian claims, inculturation approaches and Western assumptions.

Disability

Questions around disability have emerged from many Southern settings where the majority of people with disabilities live. In many of these, however, harmful theologies still connect sin and disability in ways that exclude and even demonize people with disabilities. As a result, problematic Pentecostal theologies of healing and exorcism often remain in place, and Christian sacred texts and stories of healing can be misused to exclude and to shame. Southern theologians are developing promising alternative approaches that place friendship, hospitality and the voices of people living with disabilities at their heart.

Other religions

Missionary Christianity has a complex and contested history around a theology of religions and has often exported the religious wars and divisions of European history. Its close association with the 'civilizing' projects of colonialism created binaries that labelled many other faith traditions as barbaric, uncivilized, heretical and unsalvific. Christianity was often imposed hegemonically on to other religious traditions in the name of one truth. Southern scholars insist that more attention be paid to respectful interfaith engagement, mutual dialogue, and decolonizing mission and ecclesiology. This requires dialogues that break with old mission paradigms to find new patterns of dialogue and mutual power-sharing models.

An ecological lens

Inclusion and diversity have typically focused only on human interactions. Across many Southern voices, and especially among indigenous ones, this is expanded theologically to insist that in God's eyes all creation is included in the Christian story. This opens space to explore land as sacred and resources as shared. Doctrines of Christology, soteriology, reconciliation and restoration can recover their holistic cosmic dimensions where the sacred and secular are intertwined. These spiritual connections include the treatment of land, its resources and its most vulnerable people, as well as an ethos of hospitality to migrating strangers through a culture of inclusive welcome. In the light of climate challenges, recovering a theological lens on creation within inclusion and diversity is urgently needed.

Conclusions: a theological way forward on inclusion and diversity

In many contexts of the Global South, theologies of inclusion and diversity have life-and-death implications in practice. How Christians relate to their Jewish or Muslim neighbours in the Middle East shapes violent conflicts in which religion is entangled. How communal, cultural and family rituals relate to the practices of Christian faith in Asia can tear apart families. Whether holiness is interpreted through a lens of social shame and stigma or through a lens of the inclusion of diversity shapes who is welcomed in churches in practice and who is still turned away. What beliefs are held about the Holy Spirit's Pentecostal power in Africa can determine whether people take their HIV medication or whether they are seen as demon–possessed due to their disabilities. The female half of the human race have also historically been excluded from playing material roles in shaping religious traditions across multiple regions. Prophetic voices within the South are being raised in protest in response to all these forms of exclusion and assimilation. Their imperative to engage emerges from a theological commitment to an inclusive, reconciling God and an incarnational faith rooted in the unique contexts of exclusion within which many people still live.

Critical interpretive methodologies place the Bible in constructive conversation with ordinary people's lived experiences, diverse faith traditions, and the ongoing role of the Spirit within communities. They can nurture decolonizing theological insights that include diverse voices and centre those who have been historically marginalized. Songs, prayers, rituals and action can nurture theological forms of embodied knowledge for religious followers in which they can all participate, moving beyond the rationalized binaries inherited from Western modernity. They can explore a dynamic, holistic engagement with sacred texts, traditions, rituals and current realities based on a commitment to ensure no one is left out. Participatory ecclesiologies can help Christians explore what it means to be church in new ways in their various contexts. Dialogues around being united within diversity can also enable creative grassroots engagement between Evangelicals, Catholics, Pentecostals and liberation scholars in ways that can enable shared responses to social challenges – despite different theological views held. Such dialogues can also open a way for more diverse voices in leadership.

Five ongoing tensions emerged from the wider study. First, Christianity's complex relationship to other religions around salvation and conversion remains an ongoing challenge. Second, questions about how theological truths are to be known can be complicated by the colonial imposition of certain epistemologies and the historical denigration of others. Binary, oppositional understandings of truth inherited from Western philosophy can conflict with other ways of knowing that may prioritize harmony, inclusion and dialogue as equally important truths. Third, the concepts of inclusion and diversity often have plural meanings in different cultural contexts. Fourth, the South's negative experiences at the hands of the West and Christianity's entanglement in this create a legacy of power dynamics that has to be engaged with and overturned. Finally, inclusion and diversity often form a complex nexus. In some regions, one aspect of inclusion (for example, gender) may appear to sit at odds with another (for example, culture). A holistic theological approach must grapple intersectionally with all these interconnected issues and avoid focusing on just one issue alone.

However, the study also identifies some powerful metaphors to develop further. Celebrating a plurality of theological views is pictured as a tapestry or basket of many strands woven together. The image of hospitality is used in the welcome of others who are strangers or different, to connect our relationship with God to our relationships with others. The call to be ministers of reconciliation promotes inclusive communities of embrace as one body. The social reconstruction task of building together as citizens of the household of God connects justification and justice creation. An eco-vision focuses on restoring all creation. Finally, the role of the dynamic Spirit of life and its hopeful, holistic mission promote inclusion and diversity:

> The Spirit of God supports life and resists life-destroying acts and attitudes as well as supports an inclusive vision of salvation and liberation. It does not suffice to speak of 'new birth' as a personal experience alone; it also has to do with the hope for the 'rebirth' and renewal of the whole cosmos. Justification is not only about forgiveness of sins but also about walking justly in newness of life. Sanctification is not merely abstaining from sin but also about sanctity and honoring of life ... Liberation, inclusivity, and human flourishing ... are key values. (Asamoah-Gyadu, 2013, p. 36)

If inclusion and diversity are to take root as shared theological imperatives in today's world, all geographic regions must learn from each other's different contexts and seek common themes, intersectional approaches and address interconnected questions together. These should reflect the specific contexts within which they are generated and remain cognisant of the historical power dynamics that have determined whose voices have been seen to count most. Engaging religious diversity with mutuality and respect is a critical step for faiths to be able to learn from one another and to help people engage dynamically with multiple belongings. There is still much for the Christian church to 'confess' in relation to its historical failure to live up to its vision of inclusive love and justice. Entrenched ideologies of exclusion and assimilation remain explicit or latent in many Christian doctrines, traditions and texts, and need radical reinterpretation. Yet, there is reason to hope. Inclusion and diversity can be explored theologically in productive ways across their intersections. Many Southern voices are taking the lead in this to reimagine Christianity's classic doctrines of creational equality, sin, Pentecost, a boundary-crossing Jesus, a theology of life and healing, conversion and the shared task of building God's just household.

Bibliography

Althaus-Reid, M., 2003, *The Queer God*, London and New York: Routledge.

Api, U. K., 2018, 'Towards a Biblical Theology of Gutpela Sindaun ("highest value") in The Kamea Context', Intercultural Studies unpublished PhD dissertation at Fuller Theological Seminary, https://digitalcommons.fuller.edu/dmiss/, accessed 29.03.2021.

Asamoah-Gyadu, K., 2013, 'Spirit and Spirits in African Religious Traditions', in V. M. Kärkkäinen, K. Kim and A. Yong (eds), *Interdisciplinary and Religio-Cultural Discourses on a Spirit-Filled World*, New York: Palgrave Macmillan, pp. 41–53.

Ateek, N. S., 2017, *A Palestinian Theology of Liberation: The Bible, Justice, and the Palestine–Israel Conflict*, New York: Orbis Books.

Avakian, S., 2015, 'The turn to the Other: Reflections on contemporary Middle Eastern theological contributions to Christian–Muslim dialogue', *Theology Today* 72(1), pp. 77–83.

Awondo, P., P. Geschiere and G. Reid, 2012, 'Homophobic Africa? Toward a more nuanced view', *African Studies Review* 55(3), pp. 145–68.

Azumah, J., 2007, 'Following Jesus as Unique Lord and Saviour in a Broken Pluralistic World', *Evangelical Review of Theology* 31(4), pp. 294–305.

Balcomb, A., 2016, 'Evangelicalism in Africa – what it is and what it does', *Missionalia* 44(2), pp. 117–28.

Bays, D. H., 2003, 'Chinese Protestant Christianity Today', *The China Quarterly* 174, pp. 488–504.

Bedford, N. E. (ed.), 2012, 'Following Jesus in God's Kingdom of Life', *Participant's Guide for the Fifth Latin American Congress on Evangelization (CLADE V)*.

Bediako, K., 1990, *Jesus in African Culture: A Ghanaian Perspective*, Asempa, Accra, Ghana.

Bhakiaraj, P. J., 2010, 'New Faces of the Church: An Indian case study', *Evangelical Review of Theology* 34(1), pp. 79–83.

Bong, S., 2010, 'The Suffering Christ and the Asian Body', in K. Pui-lan (ed.), *Hope Abundant: Third world theology and indigenous women's theology*, New York: Orbis Books, pp. 186–93.

Book, C. W., 2007, 'The Continuing Relevance of Orlando Costas' Ecclesiology', *Mission Studies* 24, pp. 47–78.

Bujo, B. (ed.), 2003, *African Theology: The contribution of the Pioneers, Vol. 1*, Nairobi: Pauline Press.

Bujo, B. (ed.), 2013, *African Theology: The contribution of the Pioneers, Vol. 3*, Nairobi: Pauline Press.

Bujo, B and J. Muya (eds), 2005, *African Theology: The contribution of the Pioneers, Vol. 2*, Nairobi: Pauline Press.

Bulaka, H. Y., 2015, 'Theology of Holy Spirit: Experiences of the Ethiopian Evangelical Church Mekane Yesus', *Missio Apostolica* 23(1), pp. 126–39.

Callaghan, M., 2013, 'Indigenous Women and Christ in Pacific Contexts', *Seachanges* 6, pp. 1–22.

Chan, S., 2014, *Grassroots Asian Theology: Thinking the faith from the ground up*, Downers Grove, IL: InterVarsity Press Academic.

Cosden, D., 2002, 'Coming of Age: The future of a post-Soviet evangelical theology', *Evangelical Review of Theology* 26(4), pp. 319–36.

Danforth, S., 2005, 'Liberation Theology of Disability and the Option for the Poor', *Disability Studies Quarterly* 25(3).

Dedji, V., 2001, 'The Ethical Redemption of African Imaginaire: Kä Mana's theology of reconstruction', *Journal of Religion in Africa* 31(3), pp. 254–74.

Donaldson, L., 2010, 'The Sign of Orpah: Reading Ruth through native eyes', in K. Pui-lan (ed.), *Hope Abundant: Third world theology and indigenous women's theology*, New York: Orbis Books, pp. 138–51.

Dube, M. W., 2010, 'Towards a Post-colonial Feminist Interpretation of the Bible', in K. Pui-lan (ed.), *Hope Abundant: Third world theology and indigenous women's theology*, New York: Orbis Books, pp. 89–102.

Dumitrescu, C., 2019, 'The Impact of Globalized Immigration on Mission and Missiology', *Asbury Theological Journal* 157, pp. 138–52.

Engage Disability Toolkit, 2016, *Engaging Disability in the Church*, Delhi: Engage Disability and National Council of Churches India.

Estrada-Carrasquillo, W., 2013, 'Constructing Latino Pentecostal Communities: A response to the Mcdonaldization process', *Latin American Theology* 9(1), pp. 97–114.

Ford, D. and R. Muers (eds), 2005, *The Modern Theologians*, 2nd edn, London: Blackwell Publishing.

Forster, D., 2019, 'New Directions in Evangelical Christianities', *Theology*, pp. 1–9.

Gaikwad, R. and T. Ninan, 2017, *A Theological Reader on Human Sexuality and Gender Diversities: Envisioning inclusivity*, India: SPCK.

Gebara, I., 2010, 'A Feminist Theology of Liberation: A Latin America perspective with a view towards the future', in Kwok Pui-lan (ed.), *Hope Abundant: Third world theology and indigenous women's theology*, New York: Orbis Books, pp. 51–71.

George, S. K., 2002, 'Brazil: An "Evangelized" Giant Calling for Liberating Evangelism', *International Bulletin of Missionary Research* 26 (3), pp. 104–9.

George, S., 2011, 'Voices and Visions from the Margins on Mission and Unity: A disability informed reading of the Pauline metaphor of the church as the body of Christ', Geneva: World Council of Churches.

Gourlay, M., M. Swamy and M. Daehnhardt, 2019, *How the Church Contributes to Well-being in Conflict-affected Fragile States – Voices from the local church*, Cambridge and Teddington: Cambridge Centre of Christianity Worldwide and Tearfund.

Hamd, R., 2013, 'A Theology of Diakonia: The role of diakonia praxis in the context of the churches of the Middle East', *Theological Review* 34, pp. 95–124.

Hewitt, R., 2012, *Church and Culture: An Anglo-Caribbean Experience of Hybridity and Contradiction*, Pietermaritzburg: Cluster Publications.

Hinga, T. M., A. Kubai, P. Mwaura and H. Ayanga (eds), 2008, *Women, Religion and HIV/AIDS in Africa*, Pietermaritzburg: Cluster Publications.

Hoppe, N., 2015, 'Orthodox Theological Perspectives on Disability Urge Churches to be More Inclusive', 14 October, *Orthodox Church in America*, www.oca.org/news/headline-news/orthodox-perspectives-on-disability-focus-of-international-consultation, accessed 5.07.2021.

Ishola-Esan, H. O., 2016, 'Impact of the Remnants of African Worldviews on Perception of Pastors Towards Ministering to Persons with Disabilities in Nigeria', *Journal of Disability & Religion* 20(1–2), pp. 103–18.

Jayakumar, S., 2009, 'Transforming the Indian Culture of Poverty and Oppression', *Evangelical Review of Theology* 33(2), pp. 139–57.

Jayakumar, S., 2016, 'Towards a Theology of Human Identity: Competing identities: Imagining and inventing new identities', *Evangelical Review of Theology* 40(3), pp. 232–46.

Kamba, M., 2019, 'Mission to Persons with Disabilities: A transforming love for justice in 1 Samuel 9:1–11', *International Review of Mission* 108:1, Geneva: John Wiley and Sons.

Katongole, E., 2017, *Born from Lament: The theology and politics of hope in Africa*, Grand Rapids, MI: Eerdmans.

Knoetze, J., 2016, 'Welcoming Africa's Children: The nature and implications of being a missional church', *Verbum et Ecclesia* 37(1), pp. 1–9.

Kretschmar, L., 2019, *The Church and Disability*, Pietermaritzburg: Cluster Publications.

Kuruvilla, P., 2017, *Christian Responses to Issues of Human Sexuality and Gender Diversity: A guide to the churches in India*, London: SPCK.

LeBlanc, T., 2018, 'Indigenous Theology: Changing the ministry landscape', *Mission Central*, www.missioncentral.ca/articles/indigenous-theology-changing-the-ministry-landscape, accessed 20.06.2021.

Leer-Helgesen, A., 2016, 'Transformative Theology: An ecumenical approach to transformation in Guatemala', *Mission Studies* 33, pp. 187–208.

Ly, L. N. B., 2019, 'The Impact of State Religious Policies on Christian Women's Leadership Status in Vietnam: The case of the Evangelical

Church of Vietnam since 1975', *Journal of International Women's Studies* 20(2), pp. 106–19.

Maggay, M, 2008, 'The Persistence of the Old Gods: Some inter-cultural dimensions', *Journal of African Christian Thought* 11, pp. 20–9.

Mani, M., 2013, 'Towards a Theological Perspective on the Mystery of Suffering in the Midst of Prosperity Theology within the Pentecostal and Evangelical Churches in Papua New Guinea, Particularly Yangoru', *Melanesian Journal of Theology* 29(2), pp. 5–78.

Melanchthon, M. J., 2010, 'Dalit Women and the Bible: Hermeneutical and methodological reflections', in Kwok Pui-lan (ed.), *Hope Abundant: Third world theology and indigenous women's theology*, New York: Orbis Books, pp. 103–22.

Mugambi, J. N. K., 1995, *From Liberation to Reconstruction*, Kenya: East African Educational Publishers.

Mugeere, A. B., J. Omona, A. E. State and T. Shakespeare, 2020, 'Oh God! Why Did You Let Me have this Disability? Religion, spirituality and disability in three African countries', *Journal of Disability & Religion* 24:1, pp. 64–81.

Mwambazambi, K., 2011, 'A missiological Reflection on African Ecclesiology', *Verbum et Ecclesia* 32(1), pp. 1–8.

Mwambazambi, K., 2013, 'Kä Mana; Champion on the Theology of Reconstruction', in B. Bujo (ed.), *African Theology: The contribution of the Pioneers, Vol. 3*, Nairobi: Pauline Press.

Nacho, D., 2018, 'Progressive Evangelicalism and the Development of Liberation Theology', *Religion and its Publics*, http://relpubs.as.virginia.edu/progressive-evangelicalism-and-the-development-of-liberation-theology-by-david-nacho/ accessed 29.03.2021.

Nickel, G., 2016, 'The Use of Sura 3:64 in Interfaith Appeals: Dialogue or da'wa?', *Evangelical Review of Theology* 40:4, pp. 346–55.

Orobator, A. E., 2011, 'Ethics Brewed in an African Pot', *Journal of the Society of Christian Ethics* 31 (1), pp. 3–16.

Padilla, R. C., 2004, 'The Local Church: Local change and global impact', London: Micah Network.

Palm, S., 2019, *Weaving a Tapestry of Many Strands: Theological contributions on diversity and inclusion from Southern contexts*, internal research report for Tearfund by Unit for Religion and Development Research, Stellenbosch University.

Pérez, R., 2017, 'From Prophetic Witness to Public Policy: Rethinking faith-based engagement in Peru', London: Micah Network.

Peterson, D., 2009, 'A Moral Imagination: Pentecostals and social concerns in Latin America', in V. M. Kärkkäinen (ed.), *The Spirit in the World: Emerging Pentecostal theologies in global contexts*, Grand Rapids, MI: Eerdmans, pp. 53–68.

Poon, M. N. C. (ed.), 2010, *Christian Movements in Southeast Asia: A theological exploration*, Singapore: Genesis Books.

Pui-lan, K. (ed.), 2010, 'Introduction', in *Hope Abundant: Third world theology and indigenous women's theology*, New York: Orbis Books, pp. 1–16.

Pulikottil, P., 2009, 'One God, One Spirit. Two Memories: A postcolonial reading of the encounter between Western Pentecostalism and Native Pentecostalism in Kerala', in V. M. Kärkkäinen (ed.), *The Spirit in the World: Emerging Pentecostal theologies in global contexts*, Grand Rapids, MI: Eerdmans, pp. 69–88.

Ramachandra, V., 1996, *The Recovery of Mission: Beyond the pluralist paradigm*, Grand Rapids, MI: Eerdmans.

Rosado-Nunes, M. J., 2010, 'Catholicism and Women's Rights as Human Rights', in K. Pui-lan (ed.), *Hope Abundant: Third world theology and indigenous women's theology*, New York: Orbis Books, pp. 241–54.

Sara, M., 2018, 'Towards Women Leaders in the Palestinian Evangelical Church', *Doctor of Ministry*, p. 249, http://digitalcommons.georgefox.edu/dmin/249, accessed 29.03.2021.

Schirrmacher, T., 2018, 'In Honour of the Release of Christianity: Fundamental teachings in Turkey', *Evangelical Review of Theology* 42(3), pp. 280–3.

Shao-Tan, A., 2018, 'Spirituality for the Shamed Tsinoys with Disabilities: The shamed Jesus in the book of Hebrews', *Asian Journal of Pentecostal Studies*, pp. 5–31.

Skye, L. M., 2010, 'Australian Aboriginal Women's Christologies', in K. Pui-lan (ed.), *Hope Abundant: Third world theology and indigenous women's theology*, New York: Orbis Books, pp. 194–202.

Támez, E., 2010, 'The Patriarchal Household and Power Relations between Genders', in K. Pui-lan (ed.), *Hope Abundant: Third world theology and indigenous women's theology*, New York: Orbis Books, pp. 152–64.

Tan, K. S., 2010, 'Can Christians Belong to More than One Religious Tradition?', *Evangelical Review of Theology* 34(3), pp. 250–64.

Tarus, D. K., 2014, 'Social Transformation in The Circle of Concerned African Women Theologians', *Africa Journal of Evangelical Theology* 33(1), pp. 3–22.

Teofilo, M., 2016, '"He's my Mate." Cerebral Palsy, Church and the Gift of Friendship', in A. Picard and M. Habets (eds), *Theology and the Experience of Disability: Interdisciplinary perspectives from voices down under*, New York: Routledge, pp. 78–85.

Vargas, M., 2010, 'A NeoPentecostal Experience of Aimara people', *Evangelical Review of Theology* 34(1), pp. 92–6.

West, G. O. and P. Zondi-Mabizela, 2004, 'The Bible Story that Became a Campaign: the Tamar Campaign in South Africa (and beyond)', *Ministerial Formation* 103, pp. 4–12.

West, G., C. Van der Walt and J. K. Kapya, 2016, 'When Faith Does Violence: Reimagining engagement between churches and LGBTI groups on homophobia in Africa', *HTS Teologiese Studies/Theological Studies* 72(1), pp. 1–8.

Wietzke, J., 1994, 'Christian Witness in Eastern Europe and Central Asia', *Mission Studies* XI(1), pp. 43–75.

World Council of Churches (WCC), 2007, 'Report of Theological Consultation. La Paz Report, Bolivia, 2007', *Oikoumene World Council of Churches*, www.oikoumene.org/en/resources/documents/wcc-programmes/unity-mission-evangelism-and-spirituality/just-and-inclusive-communities/la-paz-report-just-and-inclusive-communities, accessed 5.06.2021.

World Council of Churches (WCC), 2012, 'Indigenous Theologians' Reflections on the WCC 10th Assembly Theme', *Oikoumene World Council of Churches*, www.oikoumene.org/en/resources/documents/wcc-programmes/unity-mission-evangelism-and-spirituality/just-and-inclusive-communities/indigenous-people/wcc-10th-assembly-theme, accessed 5.06.2021.

Yanling, M., 2010, 'A Feminist Looks at the Challenges for Women', in K. Pui-lan (ed.), *Hope Abundant: Third world theology and indigenous women's theology*, New York: Orbis Books, pp. 229–40.

Yong, A., 2007, 'The Future of Evangelical Theology: Asian & Asian American Interrogations', *Asia Journal of Theology* 21(2), pp. 371–97.

Yong, A., 2011, *The Bible, Disability, and the Church*, Grand Rapids, MI: Eerdmans.

Younan, M., 2007, 'The Future of Palestinian Christianity and Prospects for Justice, Peace, and Reconciliation', *Currents in Theology and Mission* 34(5), pp. 338–45.

Yun, K. D., 2009, 'Pentecostalism from Below: Minjung liberation and Asian Pentecostal theology', in M. Kärkkäinen, K. Kim and A. Yong (eds), *Interdisciplinary and Religio-Cultural Discourses on a Spirit-Filled World*, New York: Palgrave Macmillan, pp. 89–114.

Zaru, J., 2010, 'Biblical Teachings and the Hard Realities of Life', in K. Pui-lan (ed.), *Hope Abundant: Third world theology and indigenous women's theology*, New York: Orbis Books, pp. 123–37.

Notes

1 This chapter focuses primarily on voices from within evangelical Christianity due to Tearfund's theological persuasion, and its partners being primarily located on this spectrum.

2 See, for example, the Third Lausanne Movement Congress in 2010. See www.lausanne.org/gatherings/congress/cape-town-2010-3.

3 For the purposes of this study, contributions were explored within Papua New Guinea, Fiji, Solomon Islands, Micronesia, Vanuatu, Samoa, Polynesia, Kiribati, Tonga, Marshall Islands, Palau, Tuvalu, Nauru and from indigenous cultures within nations.

2

Embrace in the Margins: A Theological Framework for Inclusion

NINA KURLBERG

Introduction: the wider context

The challenge to the international development sector to address diversity and inclusion has been growing in volume and urgency. Its safeguarding scandals of 2018, George Floyd's death in 2020 and the Black Lives Matter movement, and the disproportionate impact of Covid-19 on racial and ethnic minorities, all these have highlighted vulnerabilities and inequalities the sector needs to address. Some point the finger at the sector as a whole 'for being deeply imbued by its colonial past and structural racism' (Nwajiaku-Dahou and Leon-Himmelstine, 2020; see also Bruce-Raeburn, 2019). Others are more specific in their criticism, urging radical improvements within the sector's workforces and cultures which they see as neither diverse nor representative of the communities with which organizations work (Bheeroo et al., 2020). The focus of this chapter is on inclusion within faith-based organizations (FBOs) in the sector, but it is helpful first to situate these within a wider context.

A brief scan of articles published by the UK network for organizations working within the sector, Bond, and other similar networks, highlights the nature and content of the discussions taking place. Whether they focus on racism, ageism or other forms of prejudice and exclusion, these conversations have at their core a concern about the inequality and power dynamics perceived to imbue and impact all aspects of work within the sector. This can range from recruitment and organizational cultures to externally facing programmatic work. There are calls for the 2030 Agenda for Sustainable Development's commitment to 'leave no one behind' to be evidenced internally, for power dynamics and structures to be addressed, and for the margin-alized to be 'centred' (see, for example: Lilly, 2020; Schwarz, 2020; Cole-Hamilton, 2020).

However, while there might be agreement on the sector's track record in relation to diversity, the way forward is far from appar-ent. There is clearly a need to address systemic injustice and inequality, but there is no straightforward answer to the question of what precisely inclusion looks like within an organizational context and how it can be actualized. This is particularly the case when it comes to organizational cultures, systems and processes, and systemic forms of discrimination such as ableism, classism or even racism that often remain hidden. As noted in the Intro-duction to this volume, within the sector inclusion is primarily understood either as 'access' or 'meaningful participation'. Yet, if inequality is ingrained within systems and processes, simply increasing diversity – that is, enabling 'inclusion as access' – or even intentionally celebrating diversity and ensuring equal par-ticipation, is no guarantee that an organization will be inclusive.

A further challenge relates to the difficulty of identifying exactly who has been excluded or marginalized, and therefore who it is that needs to be included. Within the sector the focus to date has been on minorities and those under-represented, those who typically are identified on the basis of certain categories such as ethnicity or disability. Yet this approach is reliant on these factors being disclosed and excludes groups who are not visible, such as those with undisclosed or hidden disabilities. Depending on the context of specific debates and discussions, many might plausibly claim to be marginalized. So, on what basis can an organization discern which of the marginalized it should centre, and when? Although the answer to this question might be easier to discern in relation to the sector's program-matic work – where it is clear that an organization's focus should be on the communities it has been established to serve – the ques-tion arguably still holds relevance. In a recent opinion piece on older people, for example, one commentator noted that, while aid agencies often focus on women and children, '[t]here is an emerging agenda to promote more inclusive humanitarian action and older people must be at the centre of this. The humanitarian system is facing unprecedented challenges, but it would be unjust to neglect the rights of older people' (Lilly, 2020). Intersection-ality and the multifaceted nature of diversity further complicate the discussion.

It is questions such as these that I seek to address in the current chapter. While its specific focus is on FBOs within the sector, questions concerning inclusion and diversity are arguably more widely applicable and of relevance to, for example, churches and parachurch organizations. In seeking to articulate a theological framework for inclusion, this chapter is at its heart concerned with the inequality and discrimination that arise within such organizations on account of diversity – on the basis of race, ethnicity, age and so forth – whether visible or hidden. As the discussion within the sector illustrates, the problem is not only that inequality prevails within the world at large, but that inequality is a persistent feature of our own communities, ingrained in our societal systems and processes. Therefore, inequality and exclusion are systemic as well as interpersonal, and any theology of inclusion must take this into account.

The point of departure for the construction of such a 'situated' framework must be our current position. This chapter has begun with a brief assessment of where the sector is positioned in this regard. The following section homes in on the organizational context. In response to a perceived need for theological reflection on diversity and inclusion, Tearfund commissioned a literature review in 2019 to explore theological perspectives from the majority world (see Chapter 1). To complement this research, which focused on perspectives within the academic literature, further conversations were carried out with staff members in different contexts. The findings from these two processes are briefly summarized in the section that follows. I then explore two different theological conceptualizations of inclusion that have resources with the potential to contribute to a theological framework for inclusion in this context: inclusion as embrace (Volf, 1996) and inclusion as shalom justice through the power of the Spirit (Kim, 2015). Bringing these ideas into conversation with one another, a theological framework for inclusion is developed.

The argument that emerges through the chapter is that inclusion must go beyond access or meaningful participation to include systemic transformation. It can most helpfully be seen as embrace, but this is conditional upon justice. The need for liberation from systemic injustice cannot be ignored and intentional steps must be taken in this regard. At a practical level, this means that inclusion requires the centre to move to the margins through the power of the Spirit of God. In this process, the centre is reconfigured; in other words, there is systemic change, the nature of which must remain open-ended. Yet liberation must operate within a reconciliatory framework so that a new centre of colonizing power is not established in the margins. It is the Spirit of God that enables this – a decolonizing force since, by its very nature, it is never centred.

Inclusion: perspectives from diverse contexts

In 2019, Tearfund commissioned a literature review within the eight regions in which the organization operates in order to gain a deeper understanding of different academic perspectives on diversity and inclusion. This was carried out by Selina Palm (2019) and the findings have been included within this volume (Chapter 1). Several points are worth emphasizing. The review highlights the need for a theological approach to diversity and inclusion that is holistic and takes into account the intersectionality between the various thematic areas. It encourages a move away from '[b]inary, oppositional understandings of truth inherited from Western philosophy' to prioritize ways of knowing that emphasize 'harmony, inclusion and dialogue' (p. 48). It also underscores the necessity of addressing power dynamics. Lastly, it brings to light 'the role of the dynamic Spirit of life and its hopeful, holistic mission' (p. 49).

Following on from Palm's review, I carried out a series of conversations with Tearfund staff members based within different countries. The focus of these discussions was more broadly on inclusion and diversity, both at an individual level and in relation to the organization. Their purpose was to better understand perspectives from a range of individuals themselves representative of diversity.[1] The hope was that this would lead not only to a deeper understanding of how staff perceive inclusion and diversity, and therefore to what end the framework should be pointing, but also to greater insight into key differences between contexts that might be important to consider in its construction. Since Palm's review focuses solely on academic literature, it was important to consider lived experience as well. Individuals were asked how they would describe 'diversity' and 'inclusion', what words are used for these in their languages, and how these words would translate into English. They were also asked about practices within their churches and communities, and what elements they would expect a theological framework for inclusion for the organization to encompass.

The insights emerging from these conversations can be used to create the definition of inclusion to which the organization's theological framework should aim. First, interpretational nuances between the languages expressed across the organization have a bearing on how the word 'inclusion' is understood. In Spanish, for example, 'inclusion' has an added sense of acceptance, and in some parts of Asia it can be interpreted as a net or blanket that covers people. These two interpretations bring a different dimension to complement those that predominantly view inclusion as access or participation, however meaningful that participation is. Further, the image of the net or blanket contains the sense of structural change in accordance with those who are included within it. In addition to the image of the blanket or net, other images mentioned include: a puzzle or jigsaw, where everyone is a piece that is essential for keeping the organization's work going; a playground or arena, where there is room, space and opportunity for everyone; and a table, where all have a seat, including those previously neglected or who have not had a voice.

Bringing these insights together with those noted in the introduction to this chapter, it is clear that the inclusion to which the framework should aim must go beyond access and meaningful participation. While both are implied by the images of inclusion noted above (for example, net, jigsaw) – there is still a primary space where activity takes place and to which more people need to be given access and the freedom to participate fully – the images also imply relational and systemic equality. The idea that those previously without a voice should have a seat at the table could be seen as compatible with interpretations of 'inclusion as access' that aim to bring those from the margins to the centre. Yet, the images of inclusion as a puzzle or blanket that covers everyone bring a challenge to such centre-focused interpretations. Instead, inclusion implies structural change in the same way that the structure of a net or blanket adapts according to those it covers. Finally, inclusion carries a sense of acceptance, implying that the person being included is seen and valued.

Exploring theological models for inclusion

There are important reasons to construct a theological framework for inclusion for this context. One of the assumptions underlying the chapter is that organizations such as Tearfund will have an organizational theology, whether explicit or implicit. Making organizational theology explicit affords organizations the opportunity to be more intentional in their practice. The purpose of a framework such as the one developed within this chapter is to provide a theologically informed approach to address a specific question or theme. In this case, the theme is inclusion; more specifically, the framework seeks to articulate how FBOs can be inclusive bearing in mind the context in which they are situated. At a practical level, a theological framework has the potential not only to guide action, but also to help an organization assess and evaluate its work.

Here, I draw upon two different models that contain theological resources that can help in the construction of a theological framework for inclusion. The first – inclusion as embrace – has been selected because it has historically been influential within Tearfund. The second – inclusion as shalom justice through the power of the Spirit – has been chosen because it emphasizes systemic dynamics. Thus, the framework is formed by combining these two models.[2]

Inclusion as embrace

Although the theme of inclusion as defined above is not explicit within Miroslav Volf's *Exclusion and Embrace* (1996), it is present throughout the book, which explores reconciliation in the light of 'otherness'. The premise upon which Volf's theology of reconciliation is based is that although we live in the hope of 'final reconciliation', this is not something that will be experienced in this lifetime, but in the age to come. Thus, he holds that a 'responsible theology' is one that is constructed to enable 'nonfinal reconciliation in the midst of the struggle against oppression' (1996, pp. 9–10); in other words, it must address the question of how we can live peaceably with others within our present circumstances. There is an underlying tension within the sector on account of the historical context of colonialism that some would argue permeates it, alluded to above. The debate on inclusion speaks into this history of oppression, and therefore Volf's thought on reconciliation is highly applicable for the present discussion. Although Volf understands the word 'inclusion' solely in terms of access and therefore does not employ the term to describe embrace, inclusion as defined within this chapter relates very closely with his understanding of reconciliation.[3]

Thus, inclusion could be envisaged as embrace, which resonates with the notion of relational equality that emerged above. One of the key features of Volf's theology is that 'exclusion' and 'embrace' are seen in relational terms. Exclusion, at its core, is about the infraction of the boundaries between self and other that have their roots in the act of creation, where God brings order to chaos by 'separating and binding together' (1996, pp. 65–6). In an ideal world, human relationships would be dynamic, characterized by interdependency and genuine, mutual openness brought about by the porous boundaries that exist between self and other. This is what Volf envisions when he speaks of embrace. Within such relationships, each person's identity is shaped through their encounter with others: a genuine encounter will not leave either party unchanged. Exclusion occurs when these boundaries are not respected. Relationships are then characterized by domination, elimination, assimilation or abandonment (1996, p. 75).

The concept of 'inclusion as embrace' can be transferred to an organizational or group context. For example, it could be argued that exclusion occurs when one culture dominates organizational culture and seeks – consciously or not – either to erase other cultural expressions within the organization or to absorb them without allowing itself to be shaped through engagement with them. While it can be easy to see when exclusion occurs within such a context, it also operates in more subtle and subconscious ways, such as through unconscious bias. Another example of exclusion in action is what some have referred to as the 'White gaze' of the sector: that is, when 'Whiteness' or 'Northernness' is used – often unconsciously – as the ideal against which all are measured (Bheeroo et al., 2020; Pailey, 2019). Systemic expressions of exclusion such as these tend to be much more difficult to counter, and this is particularly relevant in relation to those that are hidden from view: for example, when invisible boundaries exist within an organization that prevent some people from moving into certain roles or positions on the basis of gender, race, ethnicity or a disability.

Volf's work clearly contains theological resources that can be helpful in constructing a theological framework for inclusion as defined in Section 1. With the ultimate aim of reconciliation, his theology of embrace allows room for difference and encourages acceptance of and engagement with the other in their diversity. It works towards an inclusion that goes beyond access to make space both for the other and for being shaped by the presence of the other. Nevertheless, for an organizational context, several adjustments need to be made. Leaving aside for a moment more specific operational questions related to appropriating Volf's theology for such a context, one adjustment concerns the operation of power within the act of embrace, which arguably needs to be made more explicit so as not to be overlooked.

The operation of power is implicit within the process of embrace: indeed, its initial steps entail the act of opening one's arms and the act of waiting, the latter symbolizing the power 'of signalled desire, of created space, and opened boundary of the self, not the power that breaks the boundaries of the other and forces the fulfilment of desire' (Volf, 1996, p. 143). Yet, without an analysis of power dynamics and structures before embarking on this process, there is a risk that embrace might perpetuate the status quo in the name of unity, whether intentionally or not. Writing on liberation and reconciliation as a Black liberation theologian, James Cone notes in *God of the Oppressed* that 'in black history, reconciliation and liberation on white terms have always meant death for black people' (1997, p. 244). Put differently, without acknowledging, identifying and confronting the power dynamics in operation within organizational systems and norms, there is a risk that calls for reconciliation might enable exclusion to operate under the guise of embrace.

A brief exploration of Volf's positioning of liberation in relation to reconciliation is in order at this point. When it comes to calls for reconciliation in the face of injustice, one of the main lines of contention often concerns the relationship between reconciliation and liberation, and which takes primacy. Volf would agree that for reconciliation to be possible, it is essential that injustice is acknowledged and confronted. All are not starting from a place of equality and this needs to be addressed before a point of reconciliation can be reached. Nevertheless, Volf holds that the 'project of liberation' needs to be situated within the framework of embrace (1996, p. 105). He disputes the argument that liberation must precede reconciliation. Just as reconciliation without liberation re-entrenches exclusion, so also liberation without reconciliation will lead to the continuation of oppression under a different oppressor, as one power or bias is substituted for another: that is, it will lead to a new form of exclusion. Volf responds to this dilemma with the concept of grace. As he argues in 'The Social Meaning of Reconciliation', the overarching message of the life, death and resurrection of Jesus Christ 'stands and falls with the idea that grace has priority over justice (grace, again, which does not negate justice but which affirms justice in the act of transcending it)' (1999, p. 11). What is non-negotiable within Volf's theology of embrace is therefore not embrace but rather the 'will to embrace'. This correlates with his view of reconciliation as being always provisional.

A further argument put forward against the insistence that liberation must precede reconciliation is that such a position requires a clear victim and perpetrator and therefore would be 'suited only to situations of manifest evil in which one side is only the victim and the other only the perpetrator. Most social conflicts are, however, not so clean' (Volf, 1999, p. 9). On the latter point, feminist liberation theologian Mary Grey (2012) takes a similar view. On account of 'the myth of female innocence', she notes that 'women can remain in denial about a certain essentializing and reifying of gender polarity, blind to their own misuse of power, and to new ways in which they are guilty of collusion in oppressive structures' (2012, p. 227). People have 'multiple, overlapping identities' and this adds complexity to the discussion, echoing the challenges posed in the introduction to this chapter that touch on the difficulties an organization might face in discerning not only who is marginalized but also which of the marginalized it should centre and when. In Grey's opinion, however, this fact does not sound the death knell for feminist liberation theology, but is nevertheless one of the reasons why she advocates aiming for reconciliation rather than liberation, which she believes 'does not take us far enough' (2012, p. 228).

Returning to Volf's theology of embrace, it is the will to embrace, depicted within the metaphor in the act of opening one's arms towards the other, that addresses both of these dilemmas. A will to embrace does not guarantee that an embrace will occur. While the invitation is non-negotiable, whether or not an embrace takes place is contingent upon 'certain conditions [being] fulfilled' (1996, p. 142). This seems promising for the quest for liberation in the face of systemic injustice. However, although Volf considers systemic in addition to interpersonal dynamics, the emphasis he places on the former is arguably insufficient for a theological framework for an organizational context. The focus of his theology of embrace is on 'social agents' and, more specifically, on the question of 'what kind of selves we need to be in order to live in harmony with others' (1996, p. 21). He does not deny the existence of systemic exclusion (1996, p. 87) – indeed, he writes with the context of the war in the Balkans in mind – but his starting point for countering systemic exclusion is addressing interpersonal exclusion. In his view, the 'system' is reliant on 'persons to make it "breathe" with the spirit of evil. If people acquiesce, it is not because they are forced to acquiesce, but because there is something in the texture of their selves that resonates with the logic of exclusion' (1996, p. 90). Volf's response to exclusion lies in the Spirit, through whose power the self generates the will to 're-adjust' its identity in order to embrace the other (1996, p. 110). The Spirit enables the will to embrace by 'de-centring' and moulding the self so that it embodies the 'self-giving Christ'. He writes:

> Central to the Christian faith is the belief that the Spirit of the crucified Messiah is capable of creating the promised land out of the very territory the Pharaoh has beleaguered. The Spirit enters the citadel of the self, de-centers the self by fashioning it in the image of the self-giving Christ, and frees its will so it can resist the power of exclusion in the power of the Spirit of embrace ... It is by this seemingly powerless power of the Spirit – the Spirit who blows even outside the walls of the church – that selves are freed from powerlessness in order to fight the system of exclusion everywhere – in the structures, in the culture, and in the self (1996, p. 92).

While one might agree that systemic exclusion is rooted in inter-personal exclusion – after all, systems are created by people – and that the Spirit empowers the self to counter systemic exclusion by imbuing it with the will to embrace, Volf's theology of embrace arguably needs to be supplemented to address systemic exclusion within an organizational context. As has been shown, embrace is conditional on systemic justice. Yet, one aspect of systemic injustice that enables it to flourish is the fact that it is often deeply ingrained within systems and processes. People can create systems that discriminate, which are then inherited by others. Systemic exclusion is so pervasive and enduring precisely because it is so often hidden, and thus all the more insidious. Within Volf's theology of embrace, the onus appears to be placed on self and other – in other words, on the individual or group

– to overcome systemic exclusion through the will to embrace the other. Yet while systemic injustices can be softened by a will to embrace, they cannot be corrected or overcome by that will alone. Volf's focus on interpersonal relationships, while valuable in relation to organizational culture, is arguably inadequate on its own to address systemic exclusion within this specific context. It is for this reason that I turn to a second work that can complement Volf's by drawing out aspects that operate within his theology of embrace in a less prominent way.

Inclusion as shalom justice through the power of the Spirit of God

The second model that will be examined can be found in Grace Ji-Sun Kim's book *Embracing the Other* (2015), which is a theological exploration of racism and sexism rooted in her experience of growing up as a Korean immigrant in America in the 1970s. Again, Kim does not speak in terms of diversity and inclusion, but the theme is present within the book. She notes the prevalence of institutional forms of racism and sexism, highlighting the ways in which their legacies continue into the present. Placing more emphasis from the outset on systemic injustice than Volf, Kim speaks of the need to challenge the boundaries that maintain the separation between the centre and the margins.[4] Her work brings a critique to approaches that focus on bringing those at the margins to the centre. These mirror interpretations of inclusion as access, where power remains in the centre. Kim notes bell hooks'[5] argument that the 'centre needs to move to the margins' (Kim, 2015, p. 74), but challenges this on the basis that within such an approach '[p]ower still derives from a central source' (2015, p. 74). Ultimately, Kim emphasizes the role of Spirit God, who has the power to erode the boundaries between the centre and the margins (2015, p. 157).

While in agreement with Kim on this latter point regarding the need for the boundaries that hold power in the centre to be broken through the power of the Spirit, the argument put forward in this section is that within an organizational context, the intentional move to the margins is an essential first step in the process of embrace and thus a critical aspect of the theological framework. This act, occurring through the power of the Spirit, signals the will to embrace. It implies a relinquishing of power as space is created for the marginalized other. It demonstrates awareness that decolonization is necessary – if this is understood as the undoing of all forms of colonial rule – and that power can no longer remain solely in the centre. This resonates with Volf's conceptualization of the role of the Spirit in his exegesis of Acts 2. Regarding the Tower of Babel and Pentecost, he writes: 'Whereas the tower ... sucks the energies out of the margins in order to stabilize and aggrandise the center, the Spirit pours energies into the margins' (1996, p. 228). As the centre moves to the margins, it is necessarily reconfigured, responding to the need for systemic change noted earlier. This approach, then, addresses systemic injustice by challenging the status quo and moving to prioritize voices and perspectives previously sidelined. According to Volf, the move entails a shift in perspective; here, I argue that it must also entail structural change.

Nevertheless, this move requires something of all community members. As Kim rightly highlights, the danger in the centre moving to the margins is that instead of the boundaries between centre and margins being dismantled, a new centre is established in the margins. This could take the form either of the move being a colonizing move on the part of power-holders or, inversely, of it leading to their domination or elimination by those previously marginalized. It is at this juncture that the two works can helpfully be combined. Although they are not radically different, their emphasis is, with Kim's work drawing out the role of the Spirit and the hidden nature of systemic exclusion. The move to the margins that I propose not only demands structural change as the boundaries between centre and margins are broken, but also a response from all community members so that embrace rather than exclusion is enabled. From the power-holders located in the centre, the move requires vulnerability in relation to power, demonstrated in the act of opening one's arms, and also the act of waiting, not forcing a response; from those located in the margins, it requires the ability – when ready – to choose grace over vengeance. The structural move initiated from the centre is essential, since the process in many ways asks more of those at the margins than at the centre. The Spirit has a crucial role to play throughout the process.

As Kim notes in her introduction, while her theology is Trinitarian, 'its focus is away from Christology and toward the Spirit' (2015, p. 9). Borrowing from Peter Hetzel's concept of 'shalom justice' (Hetzel, 2012), Kim argues that it is the Spirit that '[embodies] shalom in and for the whole community of creation' (2015, p. 115). She writes:

> How do we eliminate this oppression and achieve justice and shalom for all humanity and all creation? How can we join in deep solidarity with the freedom struggles of women and people of color? How do we work towards healing, reconciliation, and justice among people, regardless of their race or gender? I suggest it is through the power of the Spirit. (2015, p. 4)

This focus on the Spirit is helpful for the present discussion and deserves further reflection. Both Volf and Kim place emphasis on the role of the Spirit in enabling the process of reconciliation to occur. For both, the Spirit is a way to counter 'centring': it counters the centring of the self within Volf's theology of embrace, and the centring of societal systems within Kim's theology. By its very nature, the Spirit is never centred. In Hans Urs von Balthasar's words: 'The Spirit is breath, not a full outline, and therefore [it] wishes only to breathe through us, not to present [itself] to us as an object' (1993, p. 111).

The Spirit enables both liberation and reconciliation. It is reconciliatory because, as Michael Welker writes, the Spirit of God 'does not bear witness to the Spirit but makes present the self-withdrawing and self-giving Crucified One. Characteristic of the Spirit of God is a self-giving nature and self-withdrawing, even selflessness. The Spirit is a turning to others' (1994, cited in Kärkkäinen, 2002, p. 138). Central to Volf's theology of embrace is the cross of Christ, and the belief that Christ's act of self-giving love on the cross – his willingness to embrace humanity despite humanity's broken relationship with God – is rooted in the self-giving love of the triune God, and provides the model for us to follow (1996). Yet, the Spirit of God plays a critical role here. In *The Spirit at the Cross*, Carolyn Tan argues that the Spirit plays four principal roles at the cross: 'divine power', as seen in the incarnation and life, death and resurrection of Jesus; 'divine unifier' between God and humanity; 'consuming fire' that executes God's judgement; and 'life-giver' through whom humanity is reborn (2019, pp. 256–68). This is worth noting since it provides a more nuanced account of how the Spirit enables both liberation and reconciliation. The Spirit judges, but the Spirit also unites. Tan writes: '[I]t is clear that divine judgment must occur if reconciliation is to succeed, and if humanity is to be reborn. It is also clear that it is God who is the Judge' (2019, p. 260).

Drawing these concepts together to form a theological framework for inclusion, two challenges come to the fore. The first concerns the difficulty of locating the margins – a recurring theme within this chapter – and in relation to this, the difficulty of unearthing invisible boundaries and hidden margins. Second, the challenge posed by this framework concerns how the centre can move to the margins without establishing a new centre there. If our aim is decolonization, this must refer to all colonizing power. Both Kim and Volf are sensitive to this risk and would argue that this is enabled by the Spirit, which cannot be contained in one place. However, what might this look like at a practical level within an organizational context?

Practical implications

The basic structure of the theological framework developed above envisions inclusion as the process of embrace in the margins through the power of the Spirit of God. The first step in this process is for power-holders at the centre to 'move to the margins'. Through this move, the centre must be reconfigured, thereby enabling systemic change. In an organizational context, this is more than simply readjusting identities to make space for the other, although this is an essential aspect of the process: it necessitates practical and intentional steps that must lead to structural change. Yet the precise outcome of the process must remain open-ended.

However, two challenges were brought to this framework: first, the difficulty of locating the margins; and second, once the margins have been identified, ensuring that a new centre of colonizing power is not established there. At this stage it is helpful to return to where I began – with practical insights from the sector.

The first tool that can be used in conjunction with the theological framework is power analysis.[6] As employed within the sector, power analysis 'seeks to identify and understand overt, hidden, and invisible power dynamics that can perpetuate inequality' (Cole-Hamilton, 2020). Tools such as this can enable organizations to discern rather than assume internal structures of power. At present, they tend to be used to analyse power externally, but if used internally they can play a role in bringing about the move to the margins described above:

There is an irony that while INGOs apply power analysis to highlight inequality elsewhere, they rarely apply it to themselves to expose their own inequalities or the ones that they might cause. Thankfully, a much-needed shift has started to emerge. Diversity and inclusion, safeguarding, 'shifting the power', and organisational culture are being prioritised by the sector. Power analysis is key to actually making this happen … By being honest about where power sits, how it is used, and which imbalances need to be addressed, deep organisation-wide change can happen. (Cole-Hamilton, 2020)

Nevertheless, in order to guard against the move to the margins being a colonizing move, a critical aspect of the process of analysing internal power dynamics and structures is intentional listening. Further, rather than power analysis being conducted by power-holders, it should be an organization-wide activity that seeks to prioritize those voices and perspectives least often heard (see Chapter 3 for a further discussion on power). Lastly, power analysis should be applied not only to an organization's systems and processes, but also to its epistemologies (see Chapter 13 for a discussion on epistemicide in relation to indigenous voices). Along with power analysis, the concepts of 'access' and 'meaningful participation' remain important; the latter, for example, can be used to direct the focus of power analysis towards those affected by certain decisions, to ensure their participation in decision-making processes. Practices that increase diversity in relation to recruitment also remain important.

A focus on organizational culture is another essential aspect of the journey towards embrace, especially given the existence of invisible or hidden boundaries. The comments that emerged through the internal conversations can provide pointers to aspects of organizational culture that are important to staff members. The additional interpretations of the word 'inclusion' emerging through the internal conversations resonate with the idea of 'belonging', as do the images of the playground, puzzle and table. Writing in relation to disability, theologian John Swinton (2012) highlights the importance of 'belonging' within community. He argues that 'the idea of including people with disabilities does not go far enough in overcoming the alienation, stigmatization, and exclusion of those whom we choose to name "disabled." We need to move from ideas of inclusion to the practices of belonging' (2012, p. 172). Whether or not one agrees with Swinton's centre-focused interpretation of the word 'inclusion', the point he makes regarding the role of belonging in community is an essential one. An inclusive organizational culture is one in which all feel that they truly belong and know that its nature is shaped by their presence. It is worth recalling here the image of the net or blanket whose shape changes according to those it covers. However, belonging requires something of all community members – not least a willingness to make space for others to belong, and a commitment to unearth and challenge exclusion. (Chapter 10 develops this concept of belonging further in the context of inter-generational interdependence.) Inclusive community is reliant on its members to retain its inclusive character.

Within a faith-based organizational context, the process of embrace requires something from all community members: an openness to the Spirit, regardless of where this might lead; relinquishing power and claims to innocence; vulnerability and grace; a commitment to decolonization; a commitment to the process even though it holds the potential for tension as differences of opinion emerge. As Cecilia Clegg notes in 'Between Embrace and Exclusion', 'conflict and struggle can be both necessary and positive' aspects of the process of embrace (2004, p. 88). Thus, in addition to power analysis and fostering belonging, it is also important to create spaces both where the will to embrace can be enabled and where staff can engage with those whose perspectives and approaches might differ from their own in order to listen and imagine new ways of thinking and being. Tearfund has been running diversity and inclusion 'hearts and minds' drop-in sessions since 2018. These are safe and confidential spaces where topics such as neurodiversity in the workplace can be discussed (see Chapter 3 for more on the internal spaces that have been provided).

Finally, in applying the theological framework to an organizational context, it is important to underscore that some concentration of power is inevitable and necessary. What must be eradicated is colonizing power – interpersonal and systemic – rather than the concentration of power. Perhaps what is needed to achieve this is greater recognition of the legitimacy of difference, and how this might play out in practice. Paul's image of the body could be helpful here (1 Corinthians 12). It is the Spirit who brings life to the body and through whom each part, though distinct, is connected and interdependent. The Spirit is God and cannot be contained in one place only, yet the Spirit is also present within our everyday, concrete and specific realities. An additional image that could be explored is that of the digital network, in which although diverse centres persist there is reciprocity as information flows between its different nodes (see Chapter 7). Combining these images of the body and network together in a powerful way, Guillermo Hansen writes: 'the body (of Christ) does not appear as a homogenous space, or even a hierarchical system of differences, but as a network of differences that makes a difference' (2012, p. 33).

Conclusion

In this chapter, I have developed a theological framework for inclusion for a Christian faith-based relief, development and advocacy organization based on a definition of inclusion developed through research within the organization and wider sector. Although developed for a specific organization, the framework potentially has broader relevance, not only within the sector, but also to churches and parachurch organizations. Without negating the importance of either access or meaningful participation, I have argued that inclusion must go beyond these to include decolonization that leads to systemic change. Theologically, inclusion can be conceived of as reconciliation, or embrace, through the power of the Spirit of God. Nevertheless, this is dependent on relational and systemic justice. Due to power dynamics in operation within the sector that have historically tended to prioritize certain voices and perspectives at the expense of others, the first step towards inclusion must be for power-holders at the centre – through the power of the Spirit – to yield their power and move to the margins to listen intently to and amplify those voices and perspectives less often heard, allowing them to change the shape and nature of the organization. This move is a first step towards addressing systemic injustice, whether to do with racism, classism or ableism, and so forth. Through the process of intentional listening and responding to diverse perspectives, there is the possibility for systemic change, the precise nature of which must remain open-ended.

Through the approach taken in this chapter, I have sought to demonstrate what a decolonizing move towards the margins might look like by listening to different voices and perspectives and allowing them to adjust the shape and nature of my argument. Yet, at the same time I am conscious that my method is 'centred' since the framework developed within this chapter is still situated, constructed predominantly on the basis of my own positionality as a researcher at a Western academic institution and FBO, albeit as a second-generation British Asian operating within this space. This leads me back to the metaphors of the body and network, which embody the notion of reciprocity and interconnection between distinct parts, hubs or nodes. Perhaps before embarking on the move to the margins, practising the will to embrace must begin with an awareness of one's own positionality and place in the wider system as simply one, among many, interconnected parts.

Acknowledgements

I would like to thank Rei Lemuel Crizaldo, Madleina Daehnhardt, Jonas Kurlberg, Nomi Pritz-Bennett and Joshua Ralston for reviewing this chapter and providing helpful comments and suggestions. My thanks also to Tearfund staff members Loida Carriel, Romnal Colas, Marcela Guzman, Alberto Lins, Jennipher Sakala and Dino Touthang, who graciously shared their thoughts on diversity and inclusion with me.

Bibliography

Bheeroo, L., L. Billing, E. Ampomah, P. Mafethe and A. Lally-Francis, 2020, 'Time to Dismantle Racism in International Development', 17 June, *Bond*, www.bond.org.uk/news/2020/06/time-to-dismantle-racism-in-international-development, accessed 1.02.2021.

Bruce-Raeburn, A., 2019, 'Opinion: International development has a race problem', 17 May, *Devex*, www.devex.com/news/opinion-international-development-has-a-race-problem-94840, accessed 1.02.2021.

Clegg, C., 2004, 'Between Embrace and Exclusion', *New Blackfriars* 85(995), pp. 83–96.

Cole-Hamilton, A., 2020, 'Why INGOs Need to Put Power Analysis at the Heart of Governance', 15 December, *Bond*, www.bond.org.uk/news/2020/12/why-ingos-need-to-put-power-analysis-at-the-heart-of-governance, accessed 1.02.2021.

Cone, J., 1997, *God of the Oppressed*, Maryknoll, NY: Orbis Books.

Grey, M., 2012, 'It All Began with Miriam … Feminist Theology's Journey from Liberation to Reconciliation', *Feminist Theology* 20(3), pp. 222–9.

Hansen, G., 2012, 'The Networking of Differences that Makes a Difference: Theology and the unity of the church', *Dialog: A Journal of Theology* 51(1), pp. 31–42.

Hetzel, P., 2012, *Resurrection City*, Grand Rapids, MI: Eerdmans.

Kärkkäinen, V., 2002, *Pneumatology: The Holy Spirit in ecumenical, international, and contextual perspective*, Grand Rapids, MI: Baker Academic.

Kim, G. J., 2015, *Embracing the Other: The transformative Spirit of love*, Grand Rapids, MI: Eerdmans.

Lilly, D., 2020 'Older People are Being Left Behind in Humanitarian Action', 27 November, *Bond*, www.bond.org.uk/news/2020/11/older-people-are-being-left-behind-in-humanitarian-action, accessed 1.02.2021.

Nwajiaku-Dahou, K. and C. Leon-Himmelstine, 2020, 'How to Confront Race and Racism in International Development', 5 October, *Overseas Development Institute (ODI)*, www.odi.org/blogs/17407-how-to-confront-race-and-racism-international-development, accessed 1.02.2021.

Pailey, R., 2019, 'Decentering the "White Gaze" of Development', keynote speech from the Development Studies Association Annual Conference 2019, www.open.ac.uk/ikd/dsa2019, accessed 1.02.2021.

Palm, S., 2019, *Weaving a Tapestry of Many Strands: Theological contributions on diversity and inclusion from Southern contexts*, internal research report for Tearfund by Unit for Religion and Development Research, Stellenbosch University.

Schwarz, F., 2020, 'NGOs have Improved Safeguarding, but the Aid Sector Needs Systemic Change to be Safer', 30 September, *Bond*, www.bond.org.uk/news/2020/09/ngos-have-improved-safeguarding-but-the-aid-sector-needs-systemic-change-to-be-safer, accessed 1.02.2021.

Swinton, J., 2012, 'From Inclusion to Belonging: A practical theology of community, disability and humanness', *Journal of Religion, Disability & Health* 16, pp. 172–90.

Tan, C., 2019, *The Spirit at the Cross: Exploring a cruciform pneumatology*, Eugene, OR: Wipf & Stock.

Volf, M., 1996, *Exclusion and Embrace: A theological exploration of identity, otherness, and reconciliation*, Nashville, TN: Abingdon Press.

Volf, M., 1999, 'The Social Meaning of Reconciliation', *Transformation* 16(1), pp. 7–12.

von Balthasar, H. U., 1993, *Explorations in Theology Vol. 3: Creator Spirit*, San Francisco, CA: Ignatius Press.

Notes

1 Initial conversations were held in 2019 with a range of staff members based in India, Zambia, Haiti, Brazil, Honduras and Ecuador (see Acknowledgements).

2 It is necessary to note researcher positionality from the outset. Although intended for a global organization, being a UK-based researcher, the framework I establish, like any framework, is a situated one. While effort has been made to listen intently to diverse voices, and to represent them, this starting point must be acknowledged.

3 Referring to Foucault's thought, Volf writes, '*A consistent pursuit of inclusion places one before the impossible choice between a chaos without boundaries and oppression with them*' (Volf, 1996, pp. 63–4, italics original).

4 'Centre' and 'margins' are used within this chapter to refer to colonization broadly conceived to encompass all forms of domination. As Kim writes: 'The boundary between the colonizer and the colonized separates the dominant from the dominated' (2015, p. 73).

5 bell hooks is the pen name of Gloria Jean Watkins.

6 Kim also highlights the importance of power analysis (2015, p. 152).

3

Case Study: Racial Justice

LIZ MUIR

Poverty and racial injustice are inextricably linked. An article by the United Nations states that 'poverty, underdevelopment, marginalization, social exclusion and economic disparities are closely associated with racism, and contribute to the persistence of racist attitudes and practices which in turn generate more poverty' (United Nations, n.d.). For decades, INGOs have operated in the majority world where populations are largely people of colour or those with other non-White identities. Because of this racial dynamic, an understanding of the causes and impact of racial injustice should have always been firmly at the centre of how this work was delivered. Unfortunately, the historical model of aid is rooted in colonialism which birthed a somewhat misguided mantra, mindset and mandate for how we work with these communities.

The year 2020 brought racial disparities into sharper focus. What was previously a stream of thought is becoming a tidal wave of resistance to racial injustice in INGOs, encapsulated by the challenge to bring about the 'decolonization of aid'. On 25 May, George Floyd, a Black man, was murdered in Minnesota, in the US, after a White police officer knelt on his neck for 9 minutes and 29 seconds. This defining event became the crest of this tidal wave and these three words echoed the world over: #BlackLivesMatter.

My own experience during and up to the time of writing has been life-changing in many ways. I have been privileged to help Tearfund navigate its response to racial injustice. A summary of some of the key elements of that response forms the basis of this case study. It also includes some personal reflections of growing up Black British Caribbean during the years that the profile of aid became raised, especially in response to famine in Ethiopia and the HIV and AIDs epidemic.

My journey into the development world

Growing up, there was a story the world around me told me about poverty. It was the story a generation was told about poverty. It was a story told in pictures, words and music. Those stories taught me that poverty was synonymous with race. Living in poverty was the experience of Black people. Black people *were* poverty.

As I became more conscious of popular culture and the world around me, I was drawn to what I now know to be the concept of justice. Songs such as 'Do they know it's Christmas?'[1] and its memorable chorus of 'feed the world', 'Heal the World'[2] and 'Earth Song'[3] became the deeply affecting soundtrack to pre-teen and teenage consciousness. I remember at about 11 years old being taught in school about the hole in the ozone layer and the impact of CFC gasses – both of which led to arguments with my mum about closing the fridge door. My consciousness was being awakened to the injustice in the world around me.

I was bombarded with images of malnourished Black children with bloated stomachs, flies in tow, usually parentless. Images of those delivering aid appeared, in the main, to be White people. This was the way I was educated about aid. It was the standard marketing material, designed to evoke pity, sympathy or similar emotions in order to generate donations to 'feed the world'. In a world where the White gaze has governed how we see anyone who is non-White, the aid sector capitalized on the romanticized heroism of saving 'those poor people' across the seas.

Despite this, or maybe because of this, I was drawn to a career in this world.

Being racialized as Black, born and raised in a White major-ity country, I have become accustomed to the burden and sense of obscurity that this carries. Being in the minority is normal. Not being able to access the things I need or am familiar with, being educated and working in environments where I have had to censor myself or 'code-switch' (see McCluney et al., 2019) are the norm. Not seeing people like me in positions of leadership who have decision-making power is the norm. While this is the case across nearly all sectors in the UK, and the charity sector is no exception,[4] the development sector always struck me as being inaccessible. It was a place where job opportunities were limited to those who had the socio-economic and class freedom to intern or gain experience abroad during a gap or post-degree year, those with the means to travel and live in places that afforded the experience the sector demanded. And in my experience, those people were White.

In 2019, I did what I thought impossible. I got a job with an INGO – and a Christian one at that. It was (and is) the stuff of dreams. I recall preparing for my interview, my background in governance habitually directing my attention to the 'About us' section of the website to see who was leading this INGO, working in the majority world and based in London where the percentage of people from communities of colour is significantly higher than other parts of the UK. Both disappointingly but unsurprisingly to me, I found that the senior leadership team was not reflective of the location in which the office was based or those whom the organization served. The social apathy attached to this is so normal that I just fused my disappointment with my excitement about the opportunity I was being presented with to shepherd the organization towards becoming more diverse and inclusive.

A racial reckoning – the murder of George Floyd

The murder of George Floyd took place about six months into my role. On the surface, it wasn't an event that seemed linked to the INGO sector. It was one in a string of fatal police brutality encounters between White police officers and Black people. However, this time, something changed. Earlier in 2020, as the Covid-19 pandemic unfolded, large populations were placed in lockdown. Increased screen time, the opportunity to access constant news feeds, footage of the abhorrent and traumatic way in which George Floyd was murdered going viral – the haunting cries for his dead mother, his pleas to the officer of 'I can't breathe' – resonated differently this time.

Racial injustice had reared its ugly head … again. For the first time in my living memory, the response seeped into every place in society. There was a reckoning. Many organizations across the world began speaking out against racial injustice. #BlackLivesMatter protests took place across the world, social media was awash with #BlackLivesMatter graphics and black squares for Black Out Tuesday. Some institutions reflected on how racism had been left unaddressed and ignored in their policies. Conversations emerged between leaders and employees in many development organizations. Black people were feeling simultaneously vulnerable, seen and heard.

The movement shone a light not just on the injustice that centuries of oppression had inflicted on Black people but also on the injustice experienced by other marginalized ethnic groups. The experiences of people of colour were suddenly and finally being acknowledged. Across the INGO sector, the devastating consequences of colonialism were being recognized as the tributary that had flowed into the river of the colonial aid delivery model. It was like the perfect cataclysmic storm.

Catalysing Tearfund's ongoing journey towards inclusion

While posting #BlackLivesMatter on social media was the start for many (and end for some), I was fortunate to find myself working for an organization during this time where that call for systemic change was just the beginning. Tearfund started a review of the way it operated in 2017 – decentralizing leadership and humanitarian roles and establishing teams in clusters covering East and Central Africa, Eurasia and North Africa, Southern and East Africa, Asia, and Latin and Central America.[5] A diversity and inclusion plan had introduced and facilitated dialogue spaces to enable sharing and learning on topics linked to diversity and inclusion. Monitored objectives in technical areas (human resources, recruitment, staff and leadership development, communications, theology, programming and advocacy) were already helping to shift the organization towards more inclusive policies, practices and culture.

Despite this, the pivotal moment caused Tearfund to realize that when it came to race and ethnicity, this was very much just the beginning of the journey towards required change.

Responding to racial injustice

In order for any significant change to take place in an organization, it is important for the leadership to recognize and support the change process.

Even with several previous high-profile instances of police brutality against Black people in the US, and the resonance of this in the UK and across the world, there was no precedent for

Tearfund speaking out in solidarity with the #BlackLivesMatter movement. It was therefore important to provide the leadership with the information necessary to help them see that, while this tragic event took place outside the development context, it was inextricably linked to Tearfund's global work. It was important to amplify the why.

There was no doubt that this was not just a problem in the US: it had resonated and caused trauma and outrage worldwide. To make the case, Tearfund's leadership was asked to consider that racism is one of the root causes of extreme poverty, so issues of racism cannot be separated from Tearfund's call to end the injustice of extreme poverty.

Lawyer Bryan Stevenson says, 'We are all implicated when we allow other people to be mistreated' (2014, p. 18). As a global organization that was also Christian (which added its own complexities) and that was working in many communities of colour around the world, being cognizant of the impact and history of colonialism and seeing that the outcry was more than just Black and White, it was clear that silence was not an option.

It was also important that there was synergy with Tearfund USA – part of the Tearfund family. On 29 May, they shared a simple three-word post that provided the catalyst needed for Tearfund in the UK, as a minimum, to repurpose content and make clear to its staff and supporters that racism, just like poverty, is caused by broken relationships. Those words were: Black Lives Matter.

Consequently, Tearfund's ensuing response was centred in three main areas.

Well-being

While speaking out as an organization was necessary, ensuring the well-being and psychological safety of people of colour within Tearfund was imminently important. A distinction to be noted here is that for people of colour living and working in majority White spaces and countries, the consequences of racial injustice are part of daily, lived experience which represses their identity and causes trauma. As a global organization, Tearfund recognizes that racial injustice manifests in different ways between people of colour who live and work in majority contexts and those who do this while being in the minority. In the former, the nuance is manifested in ways such as tribalism and ethnic tension. This meant that the impact of the murder of George Floyd and trauma that resurfaced as a result was expressed more openly by people of colour living and working in White majority contexts.

A decision to hold a listening circle for people of colour working in the UK only was made. The purpose of the space was to provide a safe, non-judgemental environment in which people would not feel they had to justify their experiences or hurt, to hold a space for collective worship and pastoral support. In circumstances such as these, spaces for people of colour only are essential for their well-being. As one commentator advocating for Black-only spaces wrote following opposition to a Black feminist festival in Paris, 'Safe spaces for Black folks are not negotiable; they are necessary and vital to protect the mental health and support the multi-faceted well-being of Black people' (Wear Your Voice, 2017). The listening circle was held in an attempt to minimize the impact of further trauma caused by triggering. It demonstrated to colleagues that their feelings, experiences, pain and trauma were acknowledged and that Tearfund wanted to recognize, listen and offer support.

A memorable personal reflection to interject here is that some people suggested that this was a harmfully segregated space. The connotation, especially in the midst of dealing with my own trauma, was deeply painful and made me question my approach. Nevertheless, I proceeded. As an Organization Development Practitioner, I have been taught to use self as an instrument in the process of participatory change. As a follower of Jesus, I am called to apprenticeship under him. Jesus often made choices that seemed unpopular in a bid to show compassion to those in the minority and on the fringes of society, and was judged for doing so. As a leader, despite the negativity, I would do the same thing again.

Colleagues who attended the listening circle were asked for feedback. One of the questions was: Do you think it was important that the listening circle was only for people of colour? Asking this question was probably as a direct response to being made to feel like a segregationist, an act of justifying why Black people and other people of colour should ever need to have a space where they don't need to be the educators. But I asked it anyway, consciously and subconsciously as a means of having proof – a symptom of the Black experience. One of the respondents replied:

Yes. It was attending to a wound first ... It was like a 'first responder's response' or a 'first aid response', it attended to the wounded ones. At first I wasn't fully convinced I was worried about leaving others out but the intention and spirit was to hear the pain of those 'wounded' first and then speak to everyone afterwards. After being in the session, I realised afterwards how important it was to just have this group first so that people could feel safe to speak and express [themselves].

To the question: 'How did the listening circle help you?', one respondent replied:

[It] created a space where I didn't have to work so hard to be understood. People got it. There was shared pain, shared experience and without the exhaustion of having to explain.

That was the impact of 90 minutes. Ninety-four per cent of the attendees reported finding the listening circle useful, with the remaining 6 per cent saying they found it partially useful. No attendees said it wasn't useful.

What the listening circle made clear was that there was more work to do. Tearfund's diversity and inclusion work already consisted of spaces where the complexities of race and ethnicity had been explored, but we had further to go. The racial injustice reckoning of the summer of 2020 exposed the cracks – not just for us, but globally. There was a lot that had been left unsaid and undone, but a large part of the legacy of George Floyd's tragic and untimely death will be that it awakened a sleeping giant.

This event triggered a whirlwind of conversations but also manifested pain and discomfort and resurfaced trauma that needed to be addressed, confronted and understood. Globally, all teams within Tearfund were encouraged to facilitate listening circles. These conversations helped to push back the tide of discomfort and unease, and allowed awareness and understanding to pave the way for a more inclusive culture where depth and not duty became the foundation for the acknowledgement, shared understanding and respect non-White people are overdue.

As conversations ensued, what became clear is that despite the #BlackLivesMatter movement being born out of police brutality by White people against Black people, there was a resonance that sat with and between other racial groups. Colleagues in Asia shared stories of caste discrimination, those in Africa spoke of biased hiring practices that overlooked individuals from tribal groups who are judged as being beneath others. In Latin America and the Caribbean, the legacy of colonialism and colourism formed the basis for many discussions. What also emerged was the fact that, even among these groups, there exists widespread discrimination and racism towards Black people.

During Tearfund's annual staff conference in 2020, intentional space was created for lament and reflection. The opening statement in this section refers to the importance of leadership when responding to crisis. It was not comfortable, but in this space Tearfund's leaders showed up to lead. Reflections from some colleagues on how they had been feeling since the events began and more generally were shared. Two of these reflections were:

I feel anger and rage at the Church for dragging its feet and being among the last to awaken to this moment, even though it remains a part of the structural injustice.

A deep engulfing sadness over the perceived threat and the lack of value that this world has for my heritage and skin colour. There is even deeper pain for having to learn (from a very early age) how to navigate this world cautiously because I am Black.

After hearing reflections, staff were asked to share how they felt about racial injustice. One response read: 'I'm sorry when I haven't taken time to listen or respond. This is on me. I will do better.'

The next thing the organization focused on helped make 'doing better' possible.

Education

When asked the question, 'What is Tearfund going to do?', we decided the answer would be: 'Education *is* action.' In the global bestseller *Start with Why*, Simon Sinek emphasizes that '*you have to know why you do what you do*' (Sinek, 2009, emphasis added). This was not the first high-profile case of police brutality in the US; it was not the first time there had been an issue of injustice related to race and ethnicity that was highlighted at a national or global level. So it was clear that previous approaches were not working. In fact, many previous reactions focused on 'fixing' the problem and neglected to hold people to account, encourage curiosity or truly recognize the physical, mental and emotional impact racial injustice has on people from marginalized racial and ethnic groups.

And so education was where Tearfund set its focus to undo and uproot, to create dialogue and to help those in the mainstream begin to understand the reality of what it means to be in the margins.

Since its inception in 2018, Tearfund's 'heart and minds' diversity and inclusion work has encouraged conversations that address individual attitudes and beliefs, inviting people to confront their own stereotypes and assumptions about others. This process was accelerated after the death of George Floyd. Deep-dive sessions were hosted where, for 90 minutes, colleagues from across the world came together to learn, share and discuss topics such as allyship, theology and racial justice, and White privilege. The #BlackLivesMatter Book Club was formed. Initially, to foster widespread participation, colleagues were encouraged to share their views on whatever they had been reading, watching or listening to related to racial injustice. As the space became more settled, specific books were chosen. Colleagues from across the world engage in these spaces, which creates a rich and full discussion covering the spectrum of experiences of racial injustice. The organization recognizes that while global conversations are important, there is nuance in the way in which racial injustice is played out in different geographical contexts. Consequently, context-specific spaces are being established to explore this topic locally.

Much of Tearfund's work since the summer of 2020 has been the work of providing the space for education and learning. One of Tearfund's 'Characteristics', which define the people we want to be, is a desire to 'learn and grow'. A toolkit was designed to help colleagues access resources to do just that in developing their understanding or beginning the journey to advocating against racial injustice. It comprised advocacy guidance, resources including podcasts, books, articles, movies and short videos, guidance on hosting listening circles, Bible studies and a prayer. Later in the year, Tearfund released a version of the toolkit to supporters to help them also pursue this journey (Tearfund, 2020).

In his 2019 book *We need to talk about race*, author, pastor and activist Ben Lindsay quotes a Black woman's thoughts on the minority reality:

'Too often minority groups have shied away from expressing the reality of their experiences because they do not want to come across as victims. They do not want to be defined by those experiences and they tire of defending themselves to majority groups who accuse them of self-indulgent navel gazing, and question whether their views, experiences or struggles are real.' (Lindsay, 2019, p. xxv)

Staying in the education space is helping Tearfund begin to rewrite this narrative. Dialogue became the tool with which the process of putting down deeper, wider roots of understanding is being grounded. This is helping the organization move forward to create a more inclusive culture, one where there is a shared understanding of the impact of injustice, one that fosters brave communication and one that extends an invitation for people to feel they belong.

Rebalancing power and creating an inclusive culture

'We acknowledge that we have not done enough in the past to dismantle the systems, policies and processes that keep systemic racism alive.' This was one of the recognitions in Tearfund's anti-racism statement (Tearfund, 2020). Dismantling unjust systems, policies and processes, ensuring they are anti-racist, is the 'how' by which we will continue to move forward as an organization. Here, there are many things to be considered, including who Tearfund is (recruitment), where decision-making lies (culture and power), and what Tearfund says (how we talk about the links between racial injustice and poverty, what stories we are telling, and the words and images that are used).

There is a famous quote associated with management consultant Peter Drucker that says, 'Culture eats strategy for breakfast.' The inference is that, regardless of how good your strategy might be, it is the culture that determines an organization's success. Who leads an organization contributes to the culture that is created. It becomes richer because of the diversity, not just of background but also of thought.

The humanitarian sector has been largely led by those from the minority world. At the heart of Tearfund's work is the acknowledgement that no one knows what is needed better than the people who are impacted by the issues around them. One of Tearfund's corporate priorities is Church and Community Transformation (CCT) (see Chapter 12), an approach wherein humanitarian work is being led by those who understand the communities in which they work. This fosters inclusion, diversity of background, experience and thought, and puts people in communities of colour at the centre of the work. Yet it is only one of many pieces of the puzzle that needs to be completed in pursuit of true inclusion.

As Tearfund's response to racial injustice continues, the organization is becoming more intentional in its practices, such as diversifying where jobs are advertised in order to attract more diverse candidates. Tearfund is also in the process of setting recruitment targets and establishing a Diversity and Inclusion Committee at Board level to create greater accountability and oversight of the work.

Conclusion

Responses to high-profile, race-related events have a tendency to be reactive. Often this results in the writing of a plan, new standard or report. All of these things have their place. But if the approach remains reactive and societies do not do the work to understand the causes and impact of centuries of systemic racism, can those societies ever move forward effectively?

Growing up Black British, there were seminal moments that framed my perception of my value and status in society and, more widely, of how racism plays out across the world, leading to conflict, inequality, displacement and poverty. Once such moment was the racist murder of Stephen Lawrence in 1991. The response to this tragedy did not create enough of an awakening to racial injustice in the UK to prevent 18-year-old Anthony Walker or 10-year-old Damilola Taylor being murdered in racist attacks in 2000 and 2005. The Stephen Lawrence Inquiry, widely known as the Macpherson Report, commissioned by the UK government to determine if there was institutional racism in the Metropolitan Police Force, was a seminal piece of work in relation to race relations, with 70 recommendations made (see Macpherson, 1999). As an 'institution' in the UK, it does not seem that the INGO sector has heeded its learnings on how to address institutional racism.

Society has not yet woken from the sleep that allows ethnic

tension to seep into world governments who exist to create fair societies and the police and armed forces whose supposed mandate is to protect and serve citizens. Otherwise, would we have seen thousands of Rohingya Muslims flee to Bangladesh from Myanmar to avoid being slaughtered en masse because of xenophobia? Should we not have the benefit of hindsight and learning from the 800,000 people who died in the Rwandan genocide of 1994 – arguably the result of a colonial legacy? The causal links between racism, xenophobia and broken relationships are clear.

My question is this: historically, has the global response been enough? My answer: evidently not.

We (the global we) have done just enough to give the outward appearance that we care about racial equity, that our choices empower, enable and equip those on the margins to be full participants in society. But we have not completed the deep soul work needed to move forward to a world where justice is the thread and not the pop-up shop.

Tearfund has been working in the majority world for over half a century. For all of this time, it has been focused on relieving poverty. Poverty has always been perpetuated by injustice. Tearfund's Theory of Poverty (Ling and Swithinbank, 2019) points us towards the restoration of broken relationships as a way to end poverty. Racism is caused by broken or 'unjust' relationships between people. This breakdown in relationships is described in our Theory of Poverty as 'leading to problems such as power imbalances' (Ling and Swithinbank, 2019). It is these structural imbalances that have allowed racial injustice to be perpetuated for centuries.

This is evidenced by the fact that the majority world is the economic minority, and in the ways that White supremacy and the White gaze have shaped societal standards of beauty, attainment and success. White saviourism is deeply rooted in the foundation of the INGO sector, where communities of colour have been seen in need of rescue, despite the immense level of natural resource wealth, the creativity, innovation, beauty, talent and intelligence that is attributed to the majority world.

This is a deep-rooted issue that will take time to undo. There are things as individuals and as a sector we can and must do. We must recognize and give priority to education as an imperative in addressing individual attitudes and beliefs. We must dismantle systemic racism by improving policies and processes and creating more diverse workforces to enable a shift in culture and practice.

My prayer following the events of 2020 is that the walls of racial injustice come tumbling down, bringing poverty down with them.

Acknowledgements

The author would like to thank the friends that have walked this journey with her – some of whom have reviewed this chapter – and the leaders who gave her space to grow.

Bibliography

ACEVO, 2018, *Racial Diversity in the Charity Sector*, London: ACEVO.

BBC News, 2020, 'George Floyd: What happened in the final moments of his life', 16 July, *BBC News*, www.bbc.co.uk/news/world-us-canada-52861726, accessed 29.03.2021.

Lindsay, B., 2019, *We Need to Talk about Race: Understanding the Black experience in a White majority church*, London: SPCK.

Ling, A. and H. Swithinbank, 2019, *Understanding Poverty. Restoring broken relationships*, Teddington: Tearfund.

Macpherson, W., 1999, *Report of the Stephen Lawrence Inquiry*, London: UK Home Office.

McCluney, C. L., K. Robotham, S. Lee, R. Smith and M. Durkee, 2019, 'The Costs of Code-Switching', *Harvard Business Review*, 15 November, https://hbr.org/2019/11/the-costs-of-codeswitching, accessed 15.07.2021.

Sinek, S., 2009, *Start with Why: How great leaders inspire everyone to take action*, London: Penguin Books.

Stevenson, B., 2014, *Just Mercy: A story of justice and redemption*, New York: Spiegel & Grau.

Tearfund, 2020, 'Black Lives Matter: A guide to help you respond to racial injustice', Teddington: Tearfund.

United Nations (n.d.), 'Let's Fight Racism', *United Nations*, www.un.org/en/letsfightracism/poor.shtml, accessed 15.07.2021.

Wear Your Voice, 2017, 'No, Black Only Spaces Are Not Racist', 31 May, https://wearyourvoicemag.com/tag/black-only-spaces/, accessed 14.03.2021.

Notes

1 Song written in 1984 by Bob Geldof and Midge Ure to raise funds for the 1983–85 famine in Ethiopia.

2 Song released in 1991 by Michael Jackson.

3 Song released in 1995 by Michael Jackson.

4 According to ACEVO's 2018 report, *Racial Diversity in the Charity Sector*, the charity sector 'is failing to reflect the racial diversity' of the people and places it serves. For example: 'Fewer than one in 10 voluntary sector employees (9%) are from Black, Asian and minority ethnic groups (BAME), a lower proportion than both the public and private sectors (both at 11%) and a lower proportion than the UK as a whole (14%)' (ACEVO 2018, where many other such statistics can be found).

5 At the time of writing, four out of six Cluster Leads and all Country Directors are from their respective regions.

PART 2

Inclusion as a Journey

4

Between Longing and Fear: Peacebuilding and Religious Diversity

MARIAM TADROS

According to a recent report by the World Bank (2020), up to two-thirds of the world's extreme poor will live in fragile and conflict-affected countries by 2030, making it evident that without intensified action – including peacebuilding efforts – international development goals will not be met. In this context, reflections on peacebuilding and religious diversity are vital. The year 2020 marked 110 years since the start of the modern ecumenical movement and 127 years since the first 'Parliament of the World's Religions', both of which have sought to prioritize dialogue in order to address religious divisions and bring unity. While much progress has been made, it has often remained predominantly at the leadership level rather than at the congregant, day-to-day level (where openness and willingness for cohesion is often more organic). In the wider context, this also sits against the backdrop of an increase in intra-state and proxy wars, often along sectarian lines. In addition, there seems to be a gap between academic analysis and research on political theory, sectarianism and conflict on the one hand, and, on the other hand, theologies and practices of peacebuilding in religious communities. This gap perhaps has meant that analysis, theory and theology have sat apart from each other, creating siloed approaches to addressing sectarianism at different levels and hampering the cause of peacebuilding in religiously diverse communities.

How can this deep need for healing divisions be married with a movement for unity and cohesion? Tearfund has been working alongside peacebuilders from across different faiths for several years now, to build relationship and friendship as an antidote to division and as an added dimension to interfaith dialogue and Christian ecumenism. Research on ecumenical peacebuilding commissioned by Tearfund has been grounded in both a theological framework, which emphasizes the ability to imagine, to offer hospitality and to embrace in relationship, and research on ecumenism in peacebuilding and cross-faith programming (Eaves, 2018). A central lesson has been that issues pertaining to all faiths can be addressed through bridge-building models, from which we can derive common ground.

In this chapter I outline several key aspects that all play into one another: I begin with my own lived experience of and in places where sectarianism shapes the context. I then provide a theological framing that uses the metaphor of a journey to emphasize the importance of progressing towards one another for the sake of peacebuilding in the light of religious diversity. This is followed by an academic analysis of how this is played out on the global stage (with a focus on the Middle East), and, finally, I look at two programmes that Tearfund has implemented at the grass-roots level to address sectarianism by focusing on interreligious peacebuilding.

Lived experience

I started my journey into interreligious peacebuilding early on, just as I was coming out of university. Two sequential experiences led me to question interreligious and cross-identity peacebuilding, yet also persuaded me of their value. The first was when, having just completed my Masters in Theology and focused on Palestinian Liberation Theology, I took up an internship in Israel/Palestine based with a non-violent action NGO. While in the West Bank, living under Israeli occupation, I witnessed separation barriers, house demolitions, restrictions on access and basic services, all along sectarian lines. I also attended listening circles[1] and gatherings between Israelis and Palestinians. All this left me facing that age-old dichotomy of justice and peace. A number of questions arose: How do you build peace in the midst of injustice? How do you reduce the separation and segregation of people groups in order to move towards understanding and peace, and yet not just normalize the status quo? Is it really possible for there to be friendship between people who are literal enemies in the eyes of the state and according to the facts on the ground?

The second experience after returning from Israel/Palestine was a Young Leaders Council (YLC) in Dublin under the International Committee for Christians and Jews (ICCJ) that I was sponsored to attend. It was my first real experience of sharing heart-and-mind space with others from different religious backgrounds (while seriously questioning the purpose of dialogue, facilitation and interfaith spaces). Most participants were under the age of 25, and with about 30 delegates from Iran, Saudi Arabia, Israel, the US, Canada, the UK, Ireland, Slovakia and Germany, the conference was certainly 'multi-everything'. Our time together was guided by both veterans and emerging leaders in the interfaith world who deeply believed that encountering one another through relationship was the way to break down divisions. Attending the YLC challenged me in my own resistance and reminded me of our basic connection as humanity and how much encounter, relationship and dialogue break barriers. My experience in that space made me realize some of the ingrained assumptions and assertions I had about the 'other' and how much mistrust I carried towards people of other faiths. In that space, where openness and vulnerability were key to being able to create a shared experience, I found myself holding back and conscious of my wariness towards those I had been subtly taught to mistrust, particularly our Muslim delegates. (Coming from a background of a persecuted church, I had not realized the Islamophobia that had grown in me.) Noticing this and being able to voice it meant I could begin to face my own prejudice as well as acknowledge the pain I carried for 'my people' and begin to get to know those delegates from a place of honesty.

My time in the Holy Land and at the YLC gathering still leaves a mark on me, even a decade later, as an entry point into the topic of peacebuilding and diversity. This is mostly because I still enjoy deep and lasting friendship with some of those I encountered there, and none of us has ever thought, or felt the need, to change our identities or religions as a result of these interactions. We have managed to fumble our way through, evolving together and spurring each other on in who we each are.

Yet it is not an easy road to walk, or to stay on. The key question that I believe we – as faith-based institutions and organizations – have to live in is: how are we willing to be transformed by our encounter with 'the other'?

Since those two personal events, and having travelled to Nigeria, Central African Republic, DRC, Côte d'Ivoire, South Africa, Iraq, Lebanon and Colombia and seen countries in the midst of and in the aftermath of religious and ethnic conflict, I have become all the more certain that the way we do peacebuilding and the way we seek to be more diverse and inclusive has to be fundamentally rooted in relationships. Yet, more than this, we have to have a genuine desire for change. My observations have led me to the conclusion that we have spent decades paying lip service to interfaith work and to inclusion work, kept it at a high, dialogue level and been fearful for the transformation that has to ensue, should we actually learn to love our 'enemies'.

This does not just exist in the polarization of religion but also in the political, ethnic sphere. I explore this in greater depth below, in looking at sectarianism as a method by which we have organized ourselves and which has also become a weapon to 'divide and conquer'.

At national and global levels of development and humanitarian interventions, what I have experienced in my role as Peacebuilding Specialist for Tearfund is that institutions (political, societal and religious) are sometimes so entrenched in power struggles and fear of a loss of identity that they end up in deadlock. They become stuck and entrenched, longing perhaps for a better way but unable to break through. This is the space where I have found hope: the liminal space between longing and fear.

For me, the most sacred spaces I have encountered have been spaces where individuals are invited to come as they are, where they can bring every aspect of their identity and define for themselves who that makes them. These are spaces where, acknowledging the realities of nationality, race, ethnicity, gender and geography but creating openness for all that lies between those labels, hearts and souls can find commonality in the human experience that transcends the borders we find ourselves born into.

I was born with a multiplicity of identities, having Middle Eastern parents and being born in the UK. I was baptized into a minority-Christian denomination, straddling Western society with Middle Eastern values as an olive-skinned woman, attending Catholic schools and now finding myself working in an evangelical INGO. What I have come to learn of myself is applicable to what I have learnt in wider society: that we are often at war within ourselves and between our identities, because our deepest desire and perhaps the most common calling we all have is to belong. And so that liminal space, where we long to belong but fear we will not or do not, is the space where transformation and reconciliation can take place. Through the work of restorative justice and peacebuilding, I have seen the gap between people slowly narrow. Yet, the fundamental challenge remains, that in order to narrow that gap we must be willing and open to change.

This is especially true (and also hard) when it comes to religious diversity and interreligious activity because the added dimension of doctrine and creed has further embedded the narrative of separation, between and across faiths. From my observation, this has been where interreligious dialogue has found its ceiling, in that often there are limits to the conversation and to the 'what's on the table'. Over the centuries, doctrine and creed have been created and fought over, as we struggle to find language and form to understand the sacred and divine. They set boundaries to tell people how and to what they belong; veering from them risks being outside and no longer belonging. Perhaps this moment in history is calling us to transcend that which blocks out the potential for relationship, dialogue and collaboration. I believe we need to acknowledge that there is very little doctrine that has not been the product of conflict, grappling and division; likewise, there is very little doctrine that is not a cause of division (particularly between denominations). And so in order to come closer to one another, we need to ground our understanding of doctrine and belief in a deeper understanding of the history and context from which they came, in order to grapple with how they are used to divide and exclude. Spaces of hospitality and collaboration then must be found where there is opportunity to transcend or transform those divides.

To love our enemies, we have to be willing for them to cease to be enemies and become friends (friends who can still disagree, but in love and with a desire to grow into better versions of themselves). We have to want to share in something with veracity and commonality. Our religious diversity, if we are courageous enough to explore it, should begin to look like a belonging to one another. I believe this is where our differences are no longer divisive and schismatic but different aspects of God that move us towards a more holistic vision of his creation and purpose in humanity. That being the 'utopia', the steps along the way will require us to address injustice, to highlight our separation where it marginalizes, to remain in the liminal, grappling with our identities until we forge through with mercy, justice, peace and love towards one another.

In order to ground some of these personal reflections in a wider context, I employ two frames – a theological frame of peacebuilding, and a contextual frame through the lens of sectarianism – that are helpful for understanding both the reality of division and how it might be addressed. First, exploring the theological framing at Tearfund, a core component of its peacebuilding strategy has been to articulate and frame its role specifically as a Christian organization in this space. Part of this has been the production of Tearfund's own comprehensive theological framework (Swithinbank, 2016), contextual Bible studies, podcasts and videos reflecting on key theological themes: moral imagination, hospitality and embrace. This work has given Tearfund the foundation to understand its theological imperative and framing in the practice of peacebuilding. What follows here is a concise unpacking of some of the core tenets that make up this theological framework and how they work together to inform organizational peacebuilding practice.

Theology and the journey to peacebuilding

Tearfund's theological framework for peacebuilding is foundational to the way in which Tearfund approaches programming and should be a lens through which all its peacebuilding programmes are viewed. The three theological themes (moral imagination, hospitality and embrace) work together as a journey towards peacebuilding. The following three sections follow this framework, developed by Hannah Swithinbank (2016). In understanding the three elements first, we can then look at how they interweave.

Moral imagination[2]

John Paul Lederach describes moral imagination as having a quality of transcendence in its ability to break out of what seem to be pre-determined structures, situations and dead ends. Doing this requires what he refers to as 'paradoxical curiosity' – the desire to seek to understand, holding things in tension without reducing complexity to binary options (Lederach, 2010, p. 5). It also requires a willingness to embrace risk, setting out without necessarily knowing all the steps on the journey. Lederach sees Romans 8.22[3] as a metaphor for the birth pangs of something that is longed for and possible but does not yet exist, and one that may be used to describe the possibility for peace to be born out of conflict, given a vision and a catalyst – just as the death, resurrection and hope of Christ make possible the new creation:

> The north of peacebuilding is best articulated as finding our way toward becoming and being local and global human communities characterized by respect, dignity, fairness, cooperation, and the nonviolent resolution of conflict. To understand this north, to read such a compass, requires that we recognize and develop our moral imagination far more intentionally. (Lederach, 2010, p. 24)

The moral, or Spirit-led, imagination is what brings into being the very creation of the earth out of the chaos below, as the Spirit hovers over the water and speaks into existence a new form. We see this potential throughout Scripture and in particular throughout the Exodus story (Ex. 20) and the prophets (Jer. 29.1–14; Isa. 61; Micah 4.1–5). They paint a picture, during exile or oppression, of what justice, equity and freedom could look like and what needs to be loosed, changed and undone in order to move towards peace.

Hospitality[4]

Swithinbank (2016, pp. 29–40) guides us in exploring what it means to live a life in the spirit of Jesus Christ. Henri Nouwen (1998) describes three journeys that Christians take as they mature: from loneliness to solitude, from illusion to prayer, and from hostility to hospitality. It is this last that makes disciples peacemakers. According to Nouwen, a hospitable space is one in which change can happen, where strangers can become friends, building relationships across differences. It is also a space where people are present, not absent. It is a space where the host allows the stranger to display and develop their own self-confidence, ideas and talents, and their own ability to love others rather than fearing them. In a hospitable space, people are received as they are, not offered love or welcome under conditions. At the same time, however, it must be a space where the stranger respects the identity, experiences and beliefs of the host who does not surrender or compromise their beliefs in order to welcome the guest.

It is in this kind of space that people will be able to share their experiences of conflict and oppression, and to hear and recognize the stories of others. Here, approaches and processes for peacebuilding, such as those proposed by Lederach and Volf, may be able to take place. It is a space in which the active nature of giving and receiving hospitality, in which all participants are aware that there are behavioural expectations and etiquette, can enable and safeguard communication and relationship building:

> Our world is full of strangers, estranged from their past, culture, country, friends, neighbours, God, and themselves – searching for a hospitable place where life can be lived without fear and where community can be found. Society is growing more fearful of the stranger and the harm they may do. It is obligatory for Christians to offer an open and hospitable space where strangers cast off strangeness. We need to convert the hostis into a hospes.[5] (Nouwen, 1998, p. 43)

René August (2018) reminds us that this invitation of hospitality recalls that God is a community, one-in-three and three-in-one. He holds community together. Hospitality is inherent in his repeated commandments to love our neighbour as ourselves, and to care for the orphan, the widow and the refugee. In August's words (2018), the parable Jesus tells in Luke 14 is one such example. Guests are invited to a great dinner. After the invited guests decline the invitation, the master opens up the invitation to everyone from the streets and lanes of their town, bringing in those who are socially marginalized, excluded and on the fringes of society. So too it is with the kin-dom of God. The invitation is for us to bring even the parts of ourselves that are kept hidden, that limit us or put a question mark on our inclusion, so that we can be welcomed by God and find our place of belonging.

Embrace[6]

Volf explores exclusion and reconciliation within and between communities. The peacebuilding framework looks particularly at his use of the metaphor of embrace as a process for reconciliation and peacebuilding. The willingness to embrace is both a moment of union or reunion, and an attitude or orientation towards other people that can be developed (Swithinbank, 2016, p. 43). It also has four stages or moments:

- opening the arms to the other person
- waiting for the other person to respond to the offer of embrace
- closing the arms, with each party holding and being held. The embrace must be gentle so that both sides remain identifiably themselves
- opening the arms again. Each must let go of the other so that they can remain themselves and yet be enriched by the traces of the other after an embrace

The movement towards the embrace is a journey that both sides of a conflict need to make. They can journey on their own, as part of their own healing process – moving towards repentance or forgiveness. But ideally, they will undertake these journeys in sight of the other, coming to hear what the other has experienced and understand their perspective on a situation.

> The answer, I hope, would be that at the core of the Christian faith lies the persuasion that the 'others' need not be perceived as innocent in order to be loved, but ought to be embraced even when they are perceived as wrongdoers. (Volf, 1996, p. 85)

As August (2018) highlights, it needs to be said, very clearly and without reservation, that the movement towards embrace does not mean the following:

- putting oneself in harm's way when relationships with 'the other' have been violent or abusive
- trusting everyone
- remaining in relationships with people who have repeatedly abused power.

August (2018, p. 73) draws on Lisa Sharon Harper's (2016) book, *The Very Good Gospel*, in which she explains that 'goodness' is not inherently in anything, but lies between things – between people, between relationships and between ideas of 'the other'. So, in thinking about this movement towards an embrace, the transformative power lives between those moving towards each other. Repentance, forgiveness, making space in oneself for others and healing of memories are not to be seen as four steps to fixing what is wrong. They do, however, provide milestones on the journey towards righteousness. While the trajectory is forward, we also sometimes circle back, revisiting the same places with different perspectives and new insights. The embrace here, then, is a sacred, complex movement towards one another, allowing the very nature of relationship to become and to change with every movement towards and away from each other.

The journey towards peacebuilding

These concepts of moral imagination, hospitality and embrace provide the framework for a 'journey towards building peace': the guiding frame by which we act, programme and relate to others in the field of peacebuilding. It begins by creating space in the chaos and conflict to imagine a reality different from the current one. Similar to the way that the Spirit hovered over the face of chaos in Genesis – and from it creates newness and life – so too must we in our chaos allow the Spirit of peace to give us creative, moral imagination to reimagine, rebuild and bring newness to that which is broken. This open creative space then invites us to step in, with all we are, to be fully present and to turn from hostility towards hospitality, where we are received and receive the other. Finally, we edge towards an active embrace of one another that fundamentally changes the nature of our relationships by creating a new way of being through belonging to one another.

This journey is by no means a straight trajectory towards reconciliation and peace, but rather a consistent and cyclical dance that we must continuously infuse into all our efforts in pursuit of peacebuilding. These concepts also emphasize that effective peacebuilding comes as much from the character and values of the peacebuilder as from the nature and spirit of the spaces created for peacebuilding to take place. In the next section, I show how these have worked in practice, rooted in an understanding of sectarianism and through Tearfund's programmes in Iraq and Egypt.

Sectarianism

The second imperative in developing work on peacebuilding and religious diversity considers the roots of conflict and sectarianism. Sectarianism can provide a helpful contextual frame for theological reflection on inclusion and its applicability in conflict-affected states and states of fragility. Here, sectarianism focuses on politics arranged in a manner that separates and sometimes segregates populations from each other along (religious) identity lines. In looking for a theology of inclusion that calls for reflection on what 'more inclusive' might look like, exclusionary constructs (sectarianism) must be understood.

Ussama Makdisi, writing on the Middle East, unpacks the value of the term 'sectarianism'. He insists that 'sectarianism as an idea and as a practice belongs to the realm of the modern' (Makdisi, 2000, p. 166). He asserts that the story being told must be a modern one, not a medieval one rooted in orientalist fantasies of the Middle East that confuses ideology with history and as a result conveniently ignores the crucial role that Western imperialism had in shaping the political context within which modern periods of sectarianism have occurred (Makdisi, 2008, p. 559).

Suad Joseph (2008) outlines the vast importance and complexity of looking at sectarianism. She eloquently frames the task of scholars and analysts responding to the question of why sectarianism is so enduring in the Middle East as an entire region:

> We must learn how to think 'sectarianism' while thinking of all that it is not, how to deploy categories of analysis while asserting their instability, how to capture the materiality of the moment while historicizing it, and how to grasp the power of religion while demystifying it. (Joseph, 2008, p. 553)

Analysing this subject has arguably never been more relevant then at this moment in the Middle East's history. 'Revolutionary' governments and long-standing state powers in countries such as Tunisia, Egypt, Libya, Syria, Iraq, Lebanon, Israel/Palestine, Yemen and as far as the Saharan Gulf countries are having to confront the problem of sectarianism now more than ever. This is a problem that has endured for centuries but has been exacerbated since the fall of colonial powers and more recently in the aftermath (and continuance) of the Arab uprisings since 2010.

To look at the form that many of these countries are taking we can see how years of unrepresentative politics has resulted in an eruption of sectarian tension – with those previously suppressed seeking power to right years of injustice, often resulting in a cycle of sectarian tension.[7]

There are two issues to highlight here. First, religious sectarianism across the Middle East is an enduring phenomenon because of post-colonial policy, which had political and state systems drawn up along sectarian lines. Second, and as a result, the enduring collective memory and post-war memory of suppressed or minority factions fuel sectarian tensions until justice and/or equality comes about.[8]

Politics organized along sectarian lines

In the early twentieth century, as Ussama Makdisi and Paul Silverstein record, 'European post-colonialism undeniably created the physical borders of almost all the area's nation-states through treaties that partitioned the defeated Ottoman Empire. Colonialism has also precipitated several ongoing conflicts' (Makdisi and Silverstein, 2006, p. 1). The somewhat arbitrary drawing-up of states by former colonizers has no doubt contributed greatly to the inability of post-colonial leaders to create space for diversity, equality and freedom for people to live out their identities fully. We can draw upon so many examples of this over the last century, from the Arab-Israeli war (it being the longest-standing), to the plight of the Kurds, the Armenians, Shi'a Muslims in Iraq, the domination of the Alawites in Syria, the ongoing persecution of Copts in Egypt, the constant simmering tensions in Lebanon – none of which suggests that a road to coexistence has yet been found in their respective contexts. What this seems to illustrate is that the various players in this sectarian Middle East have been trapped inside a power struggle ever since gaining 'independence'.

What seems to have been a major driving force behind the organizing of politics along sectarian lines is the orientalist paradigm of sectarianism reducing the tensions in the region to age-old religious struggles (Makdisi, 2008, p. 559). Post-9/11, the colonial mindset developed into an orientalist highlighting of what was considered the inherent discriminatory nature of Islamic rule in the Middle East. Makdisi suggests an alternative: 'Rather than emphasizing the religious aspect of sectarianism, and thus encouraging distorted and historically untenable comparisons, we ought to put politics first in order to think of sectarianism as what it is: politics organised along sectarian lines' (2008, p. 559).

Collective and post-war memory

A second possible reason for the continued sectarian divisions and conflict in the Middle East considers the effects of collective and post-war memory. Fanar Haddad names one of the drivers of sectarian identity as 'competing myth-symbol complexes'. She suggests that a group's myths and symbols are crucial to understanding sectarian identity and that they have the power to 'sustain group identity providing a sense of uniqueness and purpose for members' (Haddad, 2011, p. 17). She outlines three levels at which myths and symbols can be venerated: sectarian/religious, national and ethnic. One example of this in the sectarian conflict between Sunnis and Shi'as in Iraq, she says, is the veneration of Abbas, Ali ibn abi Talib's son and step-brother to Hussein, the Prophet Muhammad's grandson.[9] Abbas' centrality to Shi'a identity cannot be overstated: he is venerated as a saint for his role in the seventh-century Battle of Karbala.[10] Saddam Hussein, a Sunni leader, had forbidden Shi'a congregations from commemorating Abbas' death, so when the regime fell in 2003, Shi'as took to the streets to mark Abbas' death: their ritual became a mark of protest against those who disapproved of them, and a mark of their struggle for equal recognition. Yet, Haddad asserts, embodying collective memory in symbol and myth is 'inherently problematic in that they always carry the potential to antagonize the other' (2011, p. 19).

The bigger picture

The two dimensions of sectarian conflict in the Middle East put forward here are not the definitive reasons for why it is such an enduring phenomenon. They do, however, provide a framework for considering other contexts and dynamics. Whether tensions are ethnic, religious, tribal, political or historic, the current sectarian state of the Middle East can be understood as an intersection of all of these dimensions. Differences have been legitimized and exacerbated through the post-colonial sectarian political set-up across the region. By institutionalizing divide and disparity, this has locked societies into seeking justice and equality for their own identity group, and therefore holding on to past hurts and wounds as the lens through which they perceive justice.

Considering the unavoidable reality of these divisions along religious lines and taking into account my opening call to find a way to transcend these, the need to include a theological dimension is ever more urgent. As much as we like to believe that political sectarianism remains in that political realm, the reality is that we have deepened our theological differences even further because of how we have organized ourselves along religious lines. This is where we begin in our peacebuilding programmes:

- rooted in our theological framing and journey, and
- informed by the contextual, geo-political realities on the ground.

These two dimensions also give us entry points for programming, to address division by bringing peacebuilders together and to address memory and trauma through storytelling and restorative justice.

For international faith-based organizations (FBOs) to be relevant and for them to truly pursue peace, there is the need to build on a commitment to working not only in an ecumenical way, across church denominations, but also across religions and faiths. This means giving equal space and investment to all peacebuilders and intentionally seeking to build communities of peacebuilders that reflect the fabric of society. Therefore, Tearfund's peacebuilding work, as and where relevant, is inter-religious. The necessity and impact of this way of working has been evaluated and observed in projects implemented in Iraq, Egypt, Myanmar, South Sudan, Lebanon, Syria and Nigeria. The creation of communities of peacebuilders across divided lines is in itself an outcome as well as a vehicle by which to implement peacebuilding programmes in the community. In order to explore this work, it is essential to be rooted in an informed, contextual understanding of what is meant by sectarianism. What follows is an exploration of sectarianism as a linguistic framework for talking about division. This will be examined through the context of the Middle East as a case study.

Practice of intra- and interreligious peacebuilding

Tearfund's interreligious peacebuilding programmes have been rooted in an approach that seeks to achieve three things:

- **Nurture** peacebuilders in their well-being and sustainability.
- **Equip** them with the tools and resources needed to programme.
- **Connect** them horizontally and vertically to enable communities of peacebuilders and influence those with power.

This NEC approach was born out of programmes in Iraq, Egypt and several countries in West Africa and interweaves the journey to peacebuilding (Tearfund, 2020). It is integral to the way we set up and work out our programmes. They always begin with an initial space, curated to allow for storytelling and relationship building, which opens up the potential to imagine possibilities together. This is where the approach focuses on nurture, commitment and an understanding that the vocation of peacebuilding takes a heavy toll on heart and soul. Only when we are nurtured can we allow space for the imagination. Only then can we work together, being equipped to carry out those visions and open up space (hospitality) for the 'other', both among peacebuilders and in their communities, in the hope this will lead to restored relationships (embrace).

Tearfund's interreligious programmes in Iraq and Egypt were both born out of an initial regional gathering of peacebuilders. This was a first step in a strategic process for Tearfund in developing its peacebuilding strategy for the Middle East. A four-day gathering was facilitated in Egypt in May 2015 for key individuals with a vision for peacebuilding, from the countries where Tearfund is currently working (Jordan, Lebanon, Egypt, Kurdish Region of Iraq, Syria and Yemen). Thirty-five men and women participated, spanning different faiths, age groups and denominations. The main purpose was to create an environment where relationships could be developed among those who had gathered. The core outcome was to birth a nascent community of refreshed, connected peacebuilders, willing to explore shared stories and experiences by journeying together, so that they could collectively transform sectarianism in their communities. Tearfund facilitated a safe, creative space so that people could envision a different future and begin taking first steps towards what they had reimagined.

The gathering was an investment of time and space for building relationships across the community. This was helped by the physical space of a retreat centre, time built in for people to rest together outside of sessions, going on a tour together one morning and having cultural/entertainment evenings. The depth of friendships and relationships that developed was manifest in the strong desire from participants to continue connecting. The gathering showed that bringing people together like this can begin to create a supportive and empowering community and strengthen and equip peacebuilders within a region. By taking an approach that allows participants to formulate and envision the shape and outputs of such a community, their ownership increased. The role of the facilitating organization – Tearfund – was shaped by those who took part.

Iraq

Given the context of sectarianism highlighted above, the focus here will be on Tearfund's pilot peacebuilding programme implemented in northern Iraq. It has focused on local activists, with the following assumed theory of change: *If individuals are nurtured, equipped and connected with each other, with other peacebuilders and with sectoral experts, then they will drive efforts within their communities and more widely across the country to build peace across sectarian divides.* The following reflections are drawn from the management of the programme and two separate evaluations conducted over the course of the four-year pilot (Garred, 2018; Refai, 2019).

The activists Tearfund is working through represent diverse ethnic and religious traditions, reflecting local demographics and highlighting the reality that religion plays a role in many inter-group conflicts in the region. Northern Iraq is known for sectarian patterns of violence, culminating in the Islamic State (IS) occupation of 2014–17, notwithstanding the already existing, ongoing struggle for autonomy in the Kurdish region. At the beginning of the pilot, Tearfund only had access to the Kurdish region and so all the activities and workshops were held there; since the fall of IS, it has been possible to expand and even focus on the Ninewa Governorate, as it attempts to recover from the devastation of insurgency.

Following the initial regional gathering, Tearfund held a

workshop on 'healing the wounds of war' and strategy planning, leading to two initiatives in the education sector over six months. Following a Training-of-Trainers[11] for eight activists on peace-building and social cohesion, Duhok-based activists trained 84 school teachers (in four sessions). Erbil-based activists trained 36 Salahaddin University students (in two sessions); ten of those students went on to assist four social cohesion needs assessments in Erbil. In early 2018, four new activists were recruited in Ninewa, and were joined by two from Erbil and Duhok. Following another Training-of-Trainers, activists selected two women's groups and four parent–teacher associations in the diverse minority communities of Hamdaniya and Bashiqa. Activists provided training and then coaching on conflict transformation, the role of women and youth in civil society, and minority rights, with a view to those groups going on to implement local follow-up activities involving cross-faith interaction. Tearfund also conducted Ninewa conflict mapping with activists' support.

One of the key findings from the primary evaluation by Michelle Garred (2018) was that repeated instances of 'coming together' across identity lines are primary positive outcomes. Identity refers primarily to faith affiliation, and secondarily to the other complex interwoven factors of ethnicity, region, displacement status, and so on. This coming together is highly unusual and difficult in the context. An activist interviewed during the evaluation explains: 'To gather teachers and people from different faiths and ethnic groups is by itself an achievement. Especially after IS, these groups do not often come together. Especially between Yazidis and Christians with Sunni Muslims as a result of the conflict' (Garred, 2018, p. 3). Joint activities represent legitimate 'outcomes' when they occur in settings where such relational contact has never existed, or where it has been significantly disrupted. These outcomes have multiple causes, including changes in activists' lives, such as the expansion of their existing skills or roles, and ground-breaking cross-faith relationships with other activists. They describe the latter as a shift from being acquaintances to co-labourers, to friends who communicate outside of project activities. The activists were consistently surprised by their trainees' receptivity to the cross-faith approach, identifying underlying success factors, such as a sense of initiative and responsibility, due to perceiving the needs of the context and a spirit of collaboration and teamwork among both activists and trainees. Tearfund support, including training, staff accompaniment, financial backing and freedom for activists to choose their own strategies and activities were also listed as success factors (Garred, 2018). Even so, there remains a need to interrogate the future scope, scale and sustainability of these interactions.

The pilot affirmed both the interreligious strategy as well as the 'nurture, equip and connect' approach outlined above. The programme evaluation highlighted that the cross-faith approach is a priority in the Iraqi context, and this relevance will extend to other contexts in which identity-based conflict has a significant religious aspect (Garred, 2018).

Egypt

Similarly, the programme in Egypt was born out of that initial gathering but took a very different form. It was built on the vision of a husband-and-wife team who had been engaged in development and education work for decades. The area of Egypt where they lived and worked has some of the highest rates of sectarian violence as well as poverty. The violence and conflict in these areas is predominantly between Muslims and Christians and has increased over the last decade or so and in particular conjunction with political upheaval in the country.

In more rural areas such as these, there is very little interaction between Muslims and Christians beyond the necessities of life, as anthropologist Samuli Schielke observed: 'Since the Islamic revival of the 1970s, rigid religious moralism has become a leading tone of the debates in Egypt on norms and values' (Schielke, 2009, p. 25).

Since the 1970s there have been ongoing sectarian tensions between Islamic revivalists and other factions of the faith in Egypt (such as the Sufis), the state, minority groups (such as the Copts and Baha'is) as well as an increasing analysis of the region through a religious lens – especially in Western media and foreign policy (Schielke, 2009). As a result, the constant and intense focus on religious sectarianism may in itself be a cause of looking from a misleading reductive perspective.

The intensity of this focus has perhaps driven a deeper wedge between religious communities, and the longevity of these issues has been passed down through generations, resulting in a millennial generation who have inherited these divisions.

Tearfund's programme, named Barah (roughly translated from Arabic as 'open/liberating space'), is a pilot peacebuilding project that aims to build a culture of peace and non-violence by engaging local Muslim and Christian youth (aged 18–30) throughout the selected governorate. Because of the sensitivities locally, initially the young people were invited to apply to attend through known contacts and channels. By bringing together male and female, Muslim and Christian youth to engage in workshops that introduce various peace, non-violence and conflict-resolution concepts and methods, the youth are able to learn and build relationships with one another.

After exploring the vision of the team of peacebuilders, which was to create a space for peaceful coexistence, Tearfund supported them in putting the dream into words, and turning the words into action. An evaluation that focused on behavioural and attitudinal change found that some of the outcomes achieved were far-reaching, as documented in the following selection of evaluation findings, including participant statements narrated by the evaluator:

> At the start of the Barah training sessions, both male and female, Muslim and Christian participants would physically keep to themselves which was observed by their crossing of arms or keeping [hands] up their sleeves. By the end … participants would share physical space by keeping their arms open, shaking hands, hugging, and leaning a head on a shoulder while watching a film … [The significance of this was that] 'within Egyptian society hugging and physical contact is not observed much between different genders so to go from not touching at all to male/female, Muslim/Christian hugging indicates a high level of comfort and intimacy … Barah provided a space where participants learned together and got to know one another to the point where there was great familiarity among the group.' (Refai, 2019, p. 10)

Another significant outcome was that 'participants of both faiths engage in public social activities outside of the Barah space together'. This was in a society where 'opportunities for youth of different faiths to meet are extremely limited' (Refai, 2019, p. 11). Another noteworthy outcome was participants of different faiths sharing 'in a guided meditation that included verses from both the Qur'an and the Bible together for the first time':

In Egypt, different faiths rarely visit different places of worship, let alone share words from both their holy books in a shared space. Congregations of different faiths are very much kept separate when worshipping – even Catholic and Orthodox are not seen praying together. (Refai, 2019, p. 12)

Movingly, one Muslim participant had for the first time entered a church – as uncommon an experience for a Muslim in Egypt as it would be for a Christian to enter a mosque. 'Barah is allowing a space for Muslims and Christians to really get to know one another' (Refai, 2019, p. 13).

Throughout the programme, several attitude changes were observed to be linked with this behaviour change. They include a feeling of belonging to a group, family, cohesion within Barah, a change in views/perceptions towards people who are different ('other'), a broadened awareness of spirituality and increased trust towards people who are different, within Barah and its network of relationships.

Conclusion

Tearfund has been working alongside peacebuilders from across faith communities to build relationship and friendship as an antidote to division and as an added dimension to ecumenism and interfaith dialogue. This has been grounded in a theological framework that emphasizes imagination, hospitality and embrace, as well as in research conducted on ecumenism in peacebuilding and cross-faith programming. We have learnt that there are issues of division, doctrine, sectarianism, exclusion that pertain to all faiths, from which we can build common ground.

The impact of the small-scale projects in such complex and difficult contexts as Iraq and Egypt was surprising. All of us who envisioned and entered these spaces were cautious and very conscious of the risks to our peacebuilders, to the organization, to the cohesion of the community, but deeply convinced that the barriers created between people on religious lines needed to be dismantled.

There is a desire in many individuals to break down those divisions and to find our common humanity, and to find relationships. This has been hampered by multiple factors as outlined in the chapter: sectarian conflict, colonial legacies, religious fundamentalisms, demography along the lines of identity, and a lack of balance and cohesion between exclusionary doctrine and praxis. Also, the very dichotomy between the exponential growth in interreligious dialogue alongside growth in sectarian conflict globally shows that there is something broken in the way we have sought to address building peace.

Key learnings from programmes implemented in Iraq, Egypt and elsewhere have shown that there is an urgent need for communities of faith, FBOs and religious actors to work intentionally and actively to create and build common ground – beyond dialogue, and beyond doctrine that seeks to restore and build relationships for the sake of peace and fullness of life. The grief, trauma and generational violence that have been endured for so long by so many because of sectarian conflict, within and across faiths, should not be underestimated, nor should it be dismissed. There is a call on religious actors to enter into a new way of being together, that really questions how we can live together as humanity beyond our identity divisions. This questioning could and should be applied to so many current (and age-old) conflicts: from racial injustice to post-colonial reparations, to the freedom of religion and belief; to equitable flourishing of humanity. There is an urgent need to learn from experiences like those that we have had in our programmes and to look at how we can grow them, replicate them and take them to scale.

The questions that linger for me are these: Can we truly move towards a common humanity and human flourishing as long as we continue to organize ourselves (countries, states, religions, tribes and clans, even organizations) along our divided identities? If what makes us different is how we separate ourselves, can we ever truly, with integrity and wholeness, build lasting peace?

This chapter has shown that in coming together on the journey to peacebuilding through imagination, hospitality and embrace, by being intentional in grounding ourselves in deep contextual and historical analysis, and by committing to the nurture, equipping and connecting of agents of change, we can see significant and meaningful change to identity-based conflict. By engaging our hearts, souls, minds, as well as lived experiences, we open ourselves up to possibilities of existing with others in new, restorative ways, something that is so desperately needed in this time.

Bibliography

August, R., 2018, *Seeking Peace Pilgrimage through God's Word in God's World with God's People*, Teddington: Tearfund.

Davies, E., 2008, 'A Sectarian Middle East?', *International Journal of Middle East Studies* 40, pp. 555–8.

Eaves, J., 2018, 'Building Peace, Ecumenically: A research brief', Tearfund: Teddington.

Garred, M., 2018, *Iraq Cross-Faith Peacebuilding Pilot: Evaluation report*, Teddington: Tearfund.

Haddad, F., 2011, *Sectarianism in Iraq: Antagonistic visions of unity*, London: Hurst.

Harper, L. S., 2016, *The Very Good Gospel*, WaterBrook.

Joseph, S., 2008, 'Sectarianism as Imagined Sociological Concept and as Imagined Social Formation', *International Journal of Middle East Studies* 40, pp. 553–4.

Larkin, C., 2012, *Memory and Conflict in Lebanon: Remembering and forgetting the past*, New York: Routledge.

Lederach, J. P., 2010, *The Moral Imagination: The art and soul of building peace*, Oxford: Oxford University Press.

Makdisi, U., 2000, *The Culture of Sectarianism: Community, history and violence in nineteenth-century Ottoman Lebanon*, Berkeley, CA: University of California Press.

Makdisi, U., 2008, 'Moving Beyond Orientalist Fantasy, Sectarian Polemic, and Nationalist Denial', *International Journal of Middle East Studies* 40(4), pp. 559–60.

Makdisi, U., and P. Silverstein (eds), 2006, *Memory and Violence in the Middle East and North Africa*, Bloomington, IN: Indiana University Press.

Nouwen, H. J. M., 1998, *Reaching Out*, Grand Rapids, MI: Zondervan.

Peteet, J., 2008, 'Imagining the "New Middle East"', *International Journal of Middle East Studies* 40(4), pp. 550–2.

Refai, M., 2019, *Barah Evaluation: Outcome harvesting approach to evaluate peacebuilding pilot project in Minya, Egypt*, Teddington: Tearfund.

Reilly, B., 2012, 'Centripetalism: Cooperation, accommodation and integration', in S. Woolf and C. Yakinthou (eds), *Conflict Management in Divided Societies*, New York: Routledge.

Schielke, S., 2009, 'Being Good in Ramadan: Ambivalence, fragmentation, and the moral self in the lives of young Egyptians', *Journal of the Anthropological Institute* 15, S25.

Swithinbank, H. J., 2016, *Theological Framework: Peacebuilding*, Teddington: Tearfund.

Tearfund, 2020, 'Peacebuilding Approach Paper', Teddington: Tearfund, unpublished internal document.

Volf, M., 1996, *Exclusion and Embrace: A Theological exploration of identity, otherness and reconciliation*, Nashville, TN: Abingdon Press.

World Bank, 2020, 'Fragility and Conflict: On the front lines of the fight against poverty', Washington DC: World Bank, available from www.worldbank.org/en/topic/poverty/publication/fragility-conflict-on-the-front-lines-fight-against-poverty, accessed 29.03.2021.

Notes

1 'Listening circles' are a structured but informal way for groups to process personal experiences, thoughts and feelings with each other.

2 This section has been taken and adapted from Tearfund's theological peacebuilding framework (Swithinbank, 2016).

3 'We know that the whole creation has been groaning as in the pains of childbirth right up to the present time' (NIV).

4 This section has been taken and adapted from Tearfund's theological peacebuilding framework (Swithinbank, 2016).

5 *Hospes* is the Latin word for guest or stranger, and *hostis* is Latin for enemy. 'Hospitality' and 'hostility' are derived from these words, respectively.

6 This section has been taken and adapted from Tearfund's theological peacebuilding framework (Swithinbank, 2016).

7 This could be seen, for example, with the rise of sectarian attacks on Coptic Christians in Egypt with the short-lived rise to power of the Muslim Brotherhood.

8 It is important to recognize, however, that each case study and country must be set in proper historical context when studying them at a greater depth than space here allows. (Failure to do so is often a reason contexts are misunderstood and interventions fall short.) These are complex, multifaceted contexts and what is offered here is a snapshot in relation to the topic at hand.

9 The Battle of Karbala took place on Muharram 10, in the year 61 of the Islamic calendar (10 October 680) in Karbala, in present-day Iraq.

10 It should be noted that Abbas is a key figure in both Sunni and Shi'a myth and symbol. He is venerated as a direct relation to the house of the Prophet and both take pride in the fact that he is buried on Iraqi soil.

11 This was a five-day training, equipping our peacebuilders with tools that they could then use in their communities.

5

The Pilgrim Identity: A Biblical Basis and Motivation for Inclusiveness

NAM-CHEN CHAN

Introduction

Migration has shaped my family for at least five generations. My great-grandfather and grandfather spent decades in British-controlled 'Malaya' at the turn of the 1900s before resettling in the ancestral village in China. My father and my mother made their way to Malaya just before World War Two, among the thousands from the southern parts of China who came as poor migrant labour for the plantations, tin mines and other parts of the colonial economy. They met and got married in Malaya during the war years. With the 1949 Communist takeover of China, they soon gave up hopes of ever resettling back 'home'. When Malaya gained independence in 1957 and later formed Malaysia in 1963, my parents took on citizenship in this fledgling nation. My siblings and I were raised in this highly diverse nation of Malaysia.

I grew up in a largely Chinese-speaking neighbourhood, but my early education was in a Roman Catholic mission school. There I had Malay, Chinese and Indian classmates from across a range of faiths – Muslim, Hindu, Sikh, Buddhist-Taoist and Christian. Friendships and interactions in that rich diverse environment shaped my sense of identity beyond the boundaries of my immediate family. Into adult life, I remain very much a Malaysian, but I lived for extended periods elsewhere, in Singapore, the Philippines and the United States. Into the next generation, some of my nephews and nieces, two from inter-ethnic marriages, are now residents or citizens in Australia and the United Kingdom.

Individuals and families were similarly shaped, even deeply impacted by global migrations – there are probably many parallels in today's globalized world. Pertinent to this chapter, migrations set the stage for encounters between peoples from highly disparate cultures, world views and socio-economic backgrounds. Sadly, many of these encounters are not benign, but often toxic and oppressive where entire groups of people are marginalized, especially those involving migrants from the lower end of the socio-economic ladder, refugees and those lacking legal documents. In recent years, rhetoric about migrants and refugees has intensified. Threats of verbal and physical abuse are real dangers for minorities and migrants. In Malaysia, the plight of Rohingya refugees and the exploitation of the millions of migrant workers from Bangladesh and other Asian countries are ongoing concerns. In the Western world, Brexit and ex-President Trump's 'build the wall' are but reflections of the deeper sentiments of many.

What does the Bible have to say about migration? It is quickly apparent that many of the major events in the Bible occur in, and through, migration. Although not labelled as such in the Bible, many of the biblical characters were in fact migrants and they naturally developed what we may call migrant identities. However, it does not stop there. Embedded in the biblical narratives is a distinctive 'pilgrim identity' – an inner spiritual posture that, realizing the impermanence of this earthly life, converts its uncertainties into an inner journey with God. It is a spirituality consciously embraced and a life lived as a pilgrimage. The pilgrim identity is not synonymous with the migrant identity which reflects the natural socio-psychological changes in people who migrate. This will be explained further, but in its essence, the pilgrim identity is a spirituality that becomes a lens through which we live life and frames how we view others. It is a biblical corrective to practices of exclusion.

This chapter argues that embracing the pilgrim identity changes our perspectives about migrants and the socio-cultural 'other' in ways that lead to authentic inclusiveness when combined with the biblical concept of hospitality. It starts by briefly describing the wider landscapes of global migrations and Christian thought on migration. These landscapes make relevant the main part – a biblical exploration of the role of migration, the migrant identity and, specifically, the pilgrim identity, hospitality and inclusiveness. The pilgrim identity and connotations of inclusiveness are woven into the concept of the 'alien' in the Old Testament, its liturgies and narratives. The New Testament authors then assumed the pilgrim identity and its attached themes. It became a spiritual resource that provided dignity, perspective and purpose for the early church. It was what enabled them to welcome the outsider and the marginalized, living as an inclusive community of God's people.

Global migrations: the wider landscape

According to the *World Migration Report 2020*, an estimated 272 million people do not reside in their countries of birth. If combined with the estimated 740 million internal migrants, it makes for a global total of more than 1 billion migrants (IOM, 2019, p. 19). People movements are not a new phenomenon, but what makes today's migrations vastly different from those of the past is not just the scale, but also the nature of these migrations and their multi-level impacts in a modern globalized world. The processes in globalization involve multiple factors of which migration is a central dynamic and both are now mutually accelerated by modern transport and communication technologies (Castles et al., 2014, pp. 2–7).

Cross-border migrations can drastically change the ethno-cultural landscapes, native-migrant ratios and socio-economic structures of cities and even entire countries (Chan, 2018, pp. 49–50). International migrations may involve only 3.5 per cent of the global population, but the impact is far-reaching. For example, most economic sectors in the Gulf countries would come to a virtual standstill if not for their migrant workforce. Foreign migrants now outnumber their native population or constitute a large part of their populations. At the same time, the economies of migrant-sending countries become grossly and disproportionately dependent on the remittances of their overseas nationals.[1]

Central to the concerns of this chapter, migrants endure a spectrum of socio-economic and legal challenges to life not experienced by locals, more so if they are non-citizens. Some lack access to basic rights such as education, health care, employment and freedom of movement. Non-citizens can range from expatriate professionals and permanent residents to foreign students, migrant labourers, refugees, asylum-seekers, victims of trafficking, temporary visitors, as well as stateless people (Das and Hamoud, 2017, p. 17). Hence their experiences vary. Some migrants, such as the so-called expatriate high-earning professionals, enjoy lifestyles that are often the envy of the locals. However, most cross-border migrants are low-income workers who migrate to escape poverty in their home countries. These are the groups most easily exploited, and the challenges for them increase if they lack legal documents.

Migration is most traumatic when it is forced and people are displaced. The *World Migration Report 2020* highlights a marked intensification in 2018 and 2019. Conflicts such as those in Syria, Yemen and South Sudan have displaced millions, causing great hardship, suffering, trauma and loss of life. Extreme violence such as that being afflicted upon the Rohingya in Myanmar, and severe economic and political instability such as in Venezuela have forced millions of others to flee. Environmental and climate-related hazards also triggered large-scale displacements in many countries (IOM, 2019, p. 2). In total, the UNHCR reported 79.5 million forcibly displaced people worldwide at the end of 2019, consisting of 26 million refugees, 45.7 million internally displaced persons, 4.2 million asylum-seekers and 3.6 million Venezuelans displaced abroad.[2]

Migration flows are usually from the rural areas to the cities and that is where encounters involving migrants and the socio-cultural 'other' are likely to occur. Social diversity in the cities of developed countries is mainly due to international migration. However, for developing countries, internal migration is the more likely source. More disconcerting, migrants are disproportionately represented among the urban poor in developing countries where the urban growth rate is also fastest (IOM, 2015, pp. 2, 17). A major 'emerging challenge' identified in the United Nations' *World Cities Report 2016* is 'exclusion and rising inequality', which stems from the widening gap between the urban rich and the poor (2016, pp. 17–20). Case studies in Malaysia show that urban space is being increasingly carved out to accentuate the divides, particularly with respect to foreign migrant workers. 'Wide swathes of the city have become spaces of exclusion ... the structure of the city (re)produces structures of social inequality in the wider society' (Tedong et al., 2014, p. 1022).

Global migrations: the theological-biblical landscape

Roman Catholic thought on migration generally preceded that of other Christian traditions, but across the board, it has become a more prominent topic since the turn of the millennium.[3] For Catholics, pastoral concern for the welfare and faith life of migrants was a primary entry point (Ellis et al., 2010, pp. 23–6).[4] Daniel Groody and Gioacchino Campese's *A Promised Land, a Perilous Journey* exemplifies this, explicitly stating, 'foremost in our hearts and minds was our pastoral interest in the plight of immigrants' (2008, p. xix). The book addresses issues of social justice, human rights, the ethics of immigration controls, and the sustenance and integration of the migrants' faith into a foreign culture. This approach humanizes migrants as more than mere objects of ministry. 'Migrants are also the *subjects* of the church's mission. Christian migrants themselves have precious gifts to give to the Church itself – to form it more fully into the body of Christ in the world' (Groody and Campese, 2008, p. 90).

In the United States, Protestant reflections on migration came forth in debates on immigration policies. James Hoffmeier's *Immigration Crisis* (2009) examines the relevant biblical texts to address the ethical and legal questions surrounding illegal immigrants. M. Daniel Carroll's *Christians at the Border* exegetes biblical laws and teachings about sojourners and hospitality to argue for the welcome of immigrants (Carroll, 2013). However, neither Hoffmeier nor Carroll queries the assumption that the nation's immigration laws should be obeyed, unlike Catholic scholars such as William Cavanaugh (2011), who deconstructs assumptions about the development of the modern nation-state to argue that God's laws take precedence over the nation's immigration laws. In the UK, Catholic theologian Anna Rowlands highlights the 'worrying failings in moral judgement and basic humanitarian responsibility in UK asylum practice', arguing for theological reflection that leads to practices that challenge democracy's exclusionary tendencies (2011, p. 846).

A cluster of literature also emerged within the Lausanne Movement, with the fulfilment of the Great Commission as the main entry point. 'Diaspora Missiology' recognizes God's hand on global migrations and uses the transnational features in ethnic diasporas to formulate strategies in reaching them with the Christian gospel (Wan and Tira, 2009; Tira and Yamamori, 2016). However, this narrow focus runs the risk of objectivizing migrants, either as targets for evangelism or as means for mission (Krabill and Norton, 2015). It also has to guard against the tendency towards functionalism. To counterbalance, Samuel Escobar challenges churches to 'Christian compassion and sensitivity' and 'to take a prophetic stance in the face of society's unjust treatment of immigrants'. This is in addition to his challenge of migration being 'an avenue for the evangelistic dimension of mission' (Escobar, 2003, p. 19; Escobar, 2018).

In more recent years, a wealth of Christian reflections on migration have come forth around the globe. Elaine Padilla and Peter Phan edited a series of books that present theologies of migration from different faith traditions (Padilla and Phan, 2014), explore *Christianities in Migration* (Padilla and Phan, 2016) and analyse their theological implications for world Christianity (Phan, 2020). Scholars based in Asia add to the conversations in *God at the Borders* (Ringma et al., 2015). It is noteworthy that specific lacunas on migration issues are enriched by the contributions of non-White scholars. Tisha Rajendra (2017) develops a Christian ethic of immigration that builds on 'justice as responsibility to relationships'. Safwat Marzouk (2019) explains the ideals of the 'intercultural church' as the biblical way forward even as migrations cause Christians from diverse origins to meet and interact. In short, there is considerable Christian engagement with the diverse issues related to migration.

The pilgrim identity

Across the Christian traditions, the Christian existence is considered a pilgrimage, an image 'deep into the psyche of the early Church' (Padilla and Phan, 2014, p. 67), and the church a 'pilgrim church' (Paul VI, 1964).[5] Through the centuries, believers also practise different types of actual physical pilgrimages. These pilgrimages are journeys for purposes of faith (Padilla and Phan, 2014, p. 14). Some travel to locations where others have encountered God in hopes of similar personal impact. Others embark on journeys as a means to experience God, and for purposes of mission and evangelism. It is regrettable that after the Reformation, Protestant Christianity in the West tended to view pilgrimages purely in metaphorical terms (Boer, 2011, pp. 827–8). Significantly, even as church attendance in Europe has diminished, visits to pilgrimage sites there have increased dramatically. A revived interest in physical pilgrimages in Europe has led to fresh theologizing on both the physical and metaphorical aspects of the theme (Bartholomew and Hughes, 2004). A body of work emerged in the Scandinavian context, 'emphasising themes of journey toward the holy and an ecclesiology of provisionality and movement' (Bradley, 2011, p. 390).

The pilgrim identity may thus be viewed as a spirituality. It is not synonymous with the migrant identity. The migrant identity with its sense of unsettledness and search for new belongings naturally emerges when people migrate. Gemma Cruz's (2010) research on Filipino domestic workers in Hong Kong shows that migrant experiences may trigger and lead to the pilgrim identity. However, it should not be assumed that all migrants develop the pilgrim identity. I propose the pilgrim identity as an inner spiritual posture and perspective that is consciously embraced. It is a posture directed towards God that converts the impermanence and uncertainties of the earthly life into an inner journey with God. In grappling with the loss of past belongings, it finds a deeper belonging in God. It engenders dependence, faith, obedience and surrender to God and his purposes. It is a spirituality that views this temporal life on earth as a spiritual journey. These components in turn shape other aspects of life, altering perspectives and interactions with other people. The pilgrim identity thus goes beyond the migrant identity. At the same time, it is possible for non-migrants to embrace and develop the pilgrim identity as a spirituality and a paradigm for life.

Migration in the Bible: arena, means and identity

The larger canvas of the role that migration plays in the Bible sets the context for the pilgrim identity of all believers. Migration in the biblical narratives fulfils two broad functions. First, it serves as both arena and means through which God's purposes are worked out. Second, it imprints the migrant identity on to the biblical characters, be it through voluntary migration or forced displacement.

Migration as arena and means for God's purposes

In the Old Testament and 'down through biblical history the deepest experiences of Israel are marked by migration' (Groody and Campese, 2008, p. 22). The seed of the Abrahamic promise in Genesis 12.1–3 unfolded when Abraham obeyed God to embark on life as a migrant. It was through migration that Israel emerged as a people into the land of Canaan. Although some view this as a gradual process of different waves of migration and settlement (Boadt, 2012, pp. 157–60), the biblical narrative presents an Israel forging its collective identity as God's people in the course of their exodus from Egypt, desert wanderings and shared encounters with God. Later, it is through the ordeals of the Babylonian captivity and years in exile that Israel broke free from the propensity towards idolatry plaguing their earlier existence. Tchavdar Hadjiev surmises that 'the Hebrew Bible in its final canonical form presents biblical Israel essentially as a migrant people ... marked by the constant flow of exiles and exoduses, deportations and returns' (2018, p. 437).

In the New Testament, Phan portrays Jesus as the 'paradigmatic migrant', the 'perfect imago *Dei Migratoris* ... the "reflection of the glory" of God the Migrant ... a migrant and border-crosser at the very roots of his being, Jesus performed his ministry of announcing and ushering in the kingdom of God always at the places where borders meet' (Padilla and Phan, 2014, p. 100). Subsequently in the book of Acts, 'early Christian mission is closely related to migration and dislocation, voluntary or by force', with the Jewish Diaspora playing a major role in the spread of the gospel (Stenschke, 2016). Believers dispersed by persecution that was at times violent took the gospel to wherever they fled (Acts 8; 11). The gospel followed the routes that connected the centres of the Jewish Diaspora. Then in the general Epistles, we find the author of the first letter of Peter addressing the Christian communities in north and central Asia Minor as 'elect exiles of the Dispersion' (1 Peter 1.1) and the author of James addressing his pastoral letter to 'the twelve tribes in the Dispersion' (James 1.1).

Migrant identity in the Bible

The terms 'migrant' or 'migration' may not be used in the biblical narratives, but words such as 'exodus', 'exile' and 'dispersion' indicate the deep impact of migration. Migrations deeply shaped the consciousness and self-identity of God's people in both the Old and New Testaments. Donald Senior asserts that 'the wanderings of the patriarchs, the Exodus, the exile, the dispersion, and the return ... became embedded in the consciousness of the people of Israel and helped define their character as a people and the nature of their relationship to God' (Groody and Campese, 2008, p. 22). By the time of the New Testament, further dispersions under the Greeks and Romans have brought into being 'the Diaspora' – Jewish communities scattered throughout the Mediterranean world with a deep consciousness as a migrant people. The modern usage of 'diaspora' in fact has its origins and initial terms of reference in this Jewish experience (Dufoix, 2017, p. 1). In the New Testament, portrayals and reflections of migration experiences are integral to the understandings of Jesus and the Christian life. All of this implies that the 'idea of being migrants, pilgrims, and strangers is so foundational within Scripture that it defines how the people of God should live ... [It is] part of our theological, historical, and spiritual DNA' (Das and Hamoud, 2017, p. 6).

The pilgrim identity of God's people in the Bible

The concepts of the people of God either as migrants or pilgrims, and that of hospitality, come forth in virtually all Christian responses to the many complex issues related to migration. These two categorical themes are inextricably intertwined in the Bible. Herein, I will draw out from the biblical narratives the specific concept of the pilgrim identity and its connotations of inclusiveness. This is on the premise that the pilgrim identity is foundational to Christian responses to migration. When Christians and churches embrace this identity, it provides the basis and motivation for an authentic Christian hospitality that practises welcome and inclusiveness of the socio-cultural 'other'. It is also integral to our Christian identity because all of us are but pilgrims on earth.

The Old Testament 'alien': the pilgrim identity and inclusiveness

The word 'pilgrim' is not found in most English translations of the Bible. To tease out from the Old Testament the concepts of the pilgrim identity, spiritual pilgrimage and inclusiveness, we shall explore the Hebrew *gēr* that most commonly translates as 'alien' in English. *Gēr* is derived from the Hebrew root *gwr* (to sojourn) and is variously translated as 'sojourner', 'stranger', 'foreigner', 'non-Israelite', 'immigrant', 'temporary resident', 'resident alien', 'foreign resident', 'protected citizen' or 'client', depending on the contexts (Knauth, 2003, p. 27).

Gēr and its cognates are applied to the patriarchs in a number of passages but only three actually allude to notions of spiritual pilgrimage.[6] The first is in Genesis 17.7–8 where God reaffirms his promise to Abraham, 'I will give to you and to your offspring after you the land of your sojournings [*magwr*], all the land of Canaan.' Abraham had obeyed God's call 24 years earlier to migrate (Gen. 12.4). He is now 99 years old, still without an heir, and very much aware that he is not likely to take actual possession of the land in his lifetime. In this context, 'sojourning' evidently carries deeper connotations than his earthly status as an alien among the Canaanites. It is thus an encouragement for Abraham to trust God. God's promises will not fall to the ground but will be fulfilled, even beyond his lifetime. Meanwhile, he is to continue 'sojourning' with God.

In the second passage, Isaac looks in faith to God's promise to his father as he blesses his son Jacob, before the latter departs for Paddan-aram. He prays, 'May he give the blessing of Abraham ... that you may take possession of the land of your sojournings [*magwr*] that God gave to Abraham!' (Gen. 28.4). At this point, in his relative youth, Jacob's awareness of his own spiritual pilgrimage is debatable. However, Jacob's pilgrim identity is more than evident in the third passage. Here, introduced to Pharaoh in his old age, he says, 'The days of the years of my sojourning [*magwr*] are 130 years. Few and evil have been the days of the years of my life' (Gen. 47.9). After a lifetime of drivenness – conniving, triumphing, yet also failing, suffering loss, heartbreaks and brokenness – Jacob has clearly come to a place of faith. For all of his human schemes, abilities and frailties, he realizes that his fate and that of his family are in God's hands. His own life is a pilgrimage to a place of trust in God.

Thereafter in subsequent parts of the Old Testament, the use of *gēr* and its cognates as metaphors for spiritual pilgrimage and the pilgrim identity become more explicit. King David self-identifies in his prayer that 'we are strangers [*gēr*] before you and sojourners, as all our fathers were' (1 Chron. 29.15). This is echoed by the psalmist: 'For I am a sojourner with you, a guest [*gēr*], like all my fathers' (Ps. 39.12). The emphasis on the pilgrim identity is also seen in God self-identifying as *gēr*, placing himself alongside the Israelites, 'for the land is mine. For you are strangers [*gēr*] and sojourners with me' (Lev. 25.23). This verse is in the context of an extended passage that makes provisions for the poor in the Pentateuchal Law (Lev. 25.23–55). This, as will be made clear shortly, links the pilgrim identity with care for migrants and inclusivity.

In addition to the pilgrim identity and pilgrimage, *gēr* is closely linked to ideas of inclusiveness and care for the migrant.[7] The main use of *gēr* and its understanding within the Pentateuchal Law is for the non-Israelite foreigner. However, in addition to being a marker for ethnicity to differentiate the Israelite from the non-Israelite, Robin Knauth (2003) points out that *gēr* also denotes a 'dependent socioeconomic status'. This generally refers to persons not native to the locality and therefore likely to be bereft of family ties or landed property (Ex. 12.19; Lev. 24.16; Num. 15.30). In this respect, *gēr* can refer to both Israelites and non-Israelites in the context of the Pentateuchal Law. It designates a particularly vulnerable category who warrant special protection and provision. The Israelite brother who becomes poor is to be treated kindly and 'you shall support him as though he were a stranger [*gēr*] and a sojourner' (Lev. 25.35). The Levites who were not given a tribal inheritance of land (Josh. 13.14) are said to 'sojourn' (*gwr*) among the other tribes of Israel (Deut. 18.6; Judg. 17.7–9). Hence, by reason of their landlessness, they are conferred the special legal status and protections applied to foreigners. They are listed alongside aliens (*gēr*), as are the orphans and widows in the categories that qualified for the benefits from the tithe (Deut. 14.29; 26.12–13), and in joining the celebrations of the Feasts of Weeks and Tabernacles (Deut. 16.11, 14). The special status of provision for the landless is similarly implied of Ephraim, Manasseh and Simeon who are 'sojourning' (*gwr*) in Judah (2 Chron. 15.9) (Knauth, 2003, pp. 28–9).

The pilgrim identity: 'a wandering Aramean was my father' (Deut. 26.1–11)

The pilgrim identity is not obvious from a cursory reading because Deuteronomy 26.1–11 is essentially instructions and a creedal formula for the annual offering of firstfruits. The intimation of the pilgrim identity is in the opening phrase of the second and longer part of the creed: 'A wandering Aramean was my father. And he went down into Egypt and sojourned there' (verse 5). This liturgical ritual is, in my view, the closest equivalent to an explicit command that God's people should intentionally embrace the pilgrim identity. Anthropology informs us that community rituals and recitals of creeds are never mere actions and words void of significance. This is especially the case in ancient societies. Rather, they 'give expression to, and … communicate … information about the culture's cherished beliefs, feelings, and values, and provide a sense of personal and corporate identity' (Hiebert et al., 1999, p. 290). Hence, a divine command to repeat this ritual and recite the creed on an annual basis bespeaks God's intention. Deuteronomy 26 is widely understood as 'an oath of allegiance' whereby Israel accepts its identity as God's people and swears to abide by the statutes and ordinances given in the preceding chapters 12–25. The offering of firstfruits situates it 'as a pivotal liturgical opportunity to enact and declare Israel's peculiar identity as YHWH's people' (Brueggemann, 2001, p. 137).

The opening phrase of 'a wandering Aramean was my father' can appear incongruous when one considers the context of the worshippers. The initial generations of Israelites who settled in the land of Canaan were obviously able to identify with the phrase. They knew of no other way of life other than that as landless nomadic herdsmen on the fringes of Canaan or as a people under Joshua warring for ownership of a land that was never completely secured until the rise of the Davidic kingdom. However, one is wont to ask: how is the phrase significant for or experienced by the later generations (until the dispersions) who did not know life without landed homes and cultivating land that they also own? What does an offering of the produce of the land unto God have to do with a nomadic ancestor that it warrants a regular recital? I propose that the opening phrase of 'a wandering Aramean was my father' is a divine intention that goes beyond a mere reminder of the past. Integral to Israel's identity as God's people is their being in essence a migrant-pilgrim people. It is, in fact, central to a self-identity that is to be intentionally inculcated into every generation of God's people. In other words, the Israelites are not to forget their roots in this wandering Aramean because this defines who they are as God's people.

Many scholars agree with Gerhard von Rad that this creed in Deuteronomy 26.3–10 is 'probably the earliest and at the same time the most widely used ... confessional formulae' that preserve 'Israel's primal liturgical declaration of its identity as YHWH's people'. Thus, the people are to interpret their existence from the framework of salvation history of God's call upon their ancestors, deliverance from bondage, and gift of the land. As each generation of Israelites presents the offerings of first fruits and recite the creed, they become 'present tense' with the earlier generations (Green, 2016, pp. 242–3; Brueggemann, 2001, p. 137). Hendrik Bosman (2019) argues for a post-exilic formulation of the creed – the exiles returning from captivity seeking to 'recover a past' in an attempt to 'imagine a future'. This adds to the premise of the creed's intention. It fosters a pilgrim identity that brings God into their exilic and post-exilic travails. The first-person pronouns in the creed enable the worshipper to participate vicariously in the experiences of the past. It starts with the first-person singular pronoun (Deut. 26.3), but it is quickly dominated by first-person plural in the second part of the creed (Deut. 26.5–10). It now becomes 'our' faith as the worshipper is incorporated into the larger identity of God's people (Gerbrandt, 2015, p. 286).

Developments in Judaism: precursors to the pilgrim identity in the New Testament

By the time the New Testament letters were written, the pilgrim identity was probably already embedded in Jewish thought. Judaism is the soil from which the Christian faith sprouted. Its ideas undoubtedly influenced the New Testament authors, particularly the authors of James and 1 Peter. They addressed their readers respectively as 'the twelve tribes in the Dispersion' (James 1.1) and as 'the elect exiles of the Dispersion' (1 Peter 1.1). The Greek noun *diaspora* for 'dispersion' has a distinctively Jewish flavour because it originated as a neologism in the Septuagint, the third-century BC Greek translation of the Hebrew Bible. According to Stéphane Dufoix, *diaspora* was a previously non-existent noun (the verb *diaspeirō* was already in use), which the Jewish religious scholars coined with theological intent for the Septuagint (2017, pp. 30, 49).

Diaspora only appears 14 times in the Septuagint, but what makes it significant is that it is never used to translate the Hebrew *Galuth* (exile) and *golah* (exiled) of the Babylonian captivity despite their apparent associations. Neither does it translate a single Hebrew word, but rather several words with very different roots. Hence, it conveys a cluster of connotations. A large part of its essence is revealed in its first two occurrences – in Deuteronomy (see also Neh. 1.9; Ps. 147.2; Isa. 49.6). Deuteronomy 30.4 reads, 'If your outcasts [*diaspora*] are in the uttermost parts of heaven, from there the LORD your God will gather you.' However, in Deuteronomy 28.25, the term translates a completely different word, 'The LORD will cause you to be defeated ... You shall go out one way against them and flee seven ways before them. And you shall be a horror [*diaspora*] to all the kingdoms of the earth.' Dufoix therefore suggests that the intent of the Jewish translators in coining the term is primarily theological. It is to convey both threat and promise – God's chastisement through dispersion if the Jews do not heed God's laws, and God's restoration to the land upon repentance. It is God who disperses with all its attendant horrors, and it is also God who re-gathers (Dufoix, 2017, pp. 40–1, 46–9).

The theological framing of the *diaspora* is part of the developments in Jewish theology. The Jews needed to re-create a new existence centred in the dispersion. After the Babylonian captivity, more Jews lived outside Palestine than inside and by the first century AD, their numbers far exceeded those in the homeland (Baskin, 2011, p. 134; Trebilco and Evans, 2000, p. 286). At the same time, the Jews in Palestine lived under conditions of subjugation. How then do you interpret the Scripture passages about the exile? How do you practise the precepts of the Torah in which the land is central and the means and end of Jewish life? How do you reconcile the biblical longing for the homeland and the messianic longing for return, now that Jewish life is largely settled in foreign lands? (Schoenfeld, 2014, pp. 28–30).

Devorah Schoenfeld's review of influential Jewish texts from the second century AD onwards shows perspectives that reflect the pilgrim identity. Similar explications from earlier Judaism are yet to be retrieved, but the notions are well worth noting because the need to come to terms with life lived largely in dispersion was already present centuries earlier. The Jewish rabbis developed what she calls 'the cycle of exile and return'. It holds

> a tension between longing for the land of Israel and accepting the possibilities for finding God in places of exile ... Exile is not the end but the middle of the process ... Exile leads to suffering, suffering leads to calling out to God, and calling out to God begins the return of the Jewish people to their God and to their land. (Schoenfeld, 2014, pp. 27, 31)

Exile is a tragedy, but in that place one finds God.

The pilgrim identity: reflections from 1 Peter

The letter of 1 Peter represents the major New Testament themes on the pilgrim identity in ways that also encapsulate the threads from the Old Testament. Foremost, it explicitly uses the pilgrim metaphors of 'exile' and 'sojourn'. Unlike the Pauline writings, there is a marked absence of the divide between Israel and the church. The author 'has appropriated the language of Israel for the church in such a way that Israel as a totality has become for this letter the controlling metaphor in terms of which its theology is expressed' (Achtemeier, 1996, p. 69). The letter also addresses the problem of Christian suffering and persecution (1 Peter 3.8–22; 4.12–19). This makes the pilgrim identity highly relevant given that persecution is a lived reality for the readers located in the northern half of Asia Minor. The persecutions were likely to be localized in nature, often sparked by the unwillingness of Christians to take part in the religio-cultural activities of local communities. In the eyes of the general populace, this offends the gods and brings divine disfavour (Achtemeier, 1996, p. 35).[8] In these contexts, the pilgrim identity becomes a spiritual resource for the Christians in providing a sense of dignity (1 Peter 1.1), a perspective for holy living (1 Peter 1.17) and a higher earthly purpose (1 Peter 2.11).

1 Peter 1.1

The address, 'elect exiles [*parepidēmos*] of the dispersion [*diaspora*]' confers a dignity upon the readers living in difficult circumstances. It immediately connects them to God's call in the

Old Testament with its imageries of spiritual pilgrimage. 'Exiles' has a connotation of forced residence, but given the metaphorical intent, it is better rendered as 'those who reside as aliens' (NASB). This gives the idea of temporary residence away from the homeland (Grudem, 1988, p. 52). 'Exiles' coupled with *diaspora* unites them with other believers in a shared identity. As aliens, they are at times reviled and rejected because they do not share in the values deemed important to the societies they reside with. *Diaspora* inducts them into the larger community of God's people. It draws from the connotations of the term so that although scattered in the present, they are 'one people destined to return and reunion' (Senior, 2003, p. 39). 'Elect' as the qualifier cements their dignity as God's pilgrim people, indicating that their belonging to this *diaspora* is 'not a sociological accident', but a result of God's choice and intention (Achtemeier, 1996, p. 80).

1 Peter 1.17

Nested in the exhortation for holy living in 1 Peter 1.13–21, the pilgrim identity sets the context and perspective. The passage starts with the call to readers to prepare their minds for holy living by setting their hopes fully on the grace of God's reward that will be fully theirs on Christ's return (verse 13). They are to be holy, living in holy fear because it aligns with God's nature, God whom they also call 'Father' (verses 15–17). They are then exhorted to 'conduct [themselves] with fear throughout the time of [their] exile [*paroikia*]' (verse 17). From the context, the 'time of your exile' refers to this temporal present life. This temporariness is the context from which believers should view their earthly life. It is the right perspective for holy living amid the pressures to conform. The world they live in is characterized by passions they are no longer to conform to (verse 13), and marked by an emptiness, 'futile ways inherited from [their] forefathers', when viewed through the lens of their new-found faith (verse 18). Its temporariness stands in sharp contrast to the eternal nature of Christ who is now made known to them (verse 20), its richest wealth not even remotely comparable to the value of Christ's precious blood that ransomed them (verses 18–19).

1 Peter 2.11–12

The exhortation 'as sojourners and exiles to abstain from the passions of the flesh' (verse 11) follows the declarations in 1 Peter 2.4–10 of God choosing them as his people. That status as God's chosen people climaxes with the purpose that they 'may proclaim the excellencies of him who called [them]' (verse 9). This parallels the reason given in verse 11 on why they should keep their 'conduct among the Gentiles honourable'. It is so that the Gentiles 'may see [their] good deeds and glorify God' despite their verbal hostility. Read in this larger context, the passage points towards a missional purpose for them as God's pilgrim people – to make God known to others. The associations with Exodus 19.4–6 and Isaiah 43.21 in being God's chosen people, a royal priesthood, holy nation and God's own possession (1 Peter 2.9) further drives home this call and purpose for their earthly journey. The terms 'sojourners' (*paroikos* – someone away from home) and 'exiles' (*parepidēmos* – aliens residing temporarily) aptly portray the sense of disconnection often experienced by believers. It is a disconnection created by their conversion to a new way of life that stands in opposition to the values and practices of people around them. Yet, in the disconnection and earthly pain, God's people can live with a higher purpose – representing Christ, so that others may have their disconnections with God bridged.

Pilgrim identity, hospitality and inclusiveness

As noted earlier, the biblical concepts of God's people as migrants and pilgrims are entwined with the theme of hospitality. Hospitality is the bridge linking pilgrim identity with inclusiveness. The experiences of Israel as aliens (*gēr*) that form the basis for its pilgrim identity serve as the experiential framework by which they are to welcome and care for the alien (Pohl, 2003, p. 6). This is reflected in the remarkably strong language of inclusiveness used in the Pentateuchal Law with respect to the alien. Leviticus 19.34 reads, 'You shall treat the stranger [*gēr*] who sojourns with you *as the native among you*, and you shall *love him as yourself*, for you were strangers [*gēr*] in the land of Egypt' (emphasis added). Except for passages that warn or deal with the idolatrous practices associated with aliens, Old Testament references and instructions regarding them are generally positive. Aliens are conferred legal status and protections that elevate them to positions that are at times indistinguishable from the natives. They are listed alongside poor Israelites, orphans and widows for the benefit of the tithe (Deut. 14.29; 26.12–13). More telling, they are granted the privilege of joining in their religious feasts and festivals (Deut. 16.11, 14). The narratives of Rahab (Josh. 2) and Ruth, non-Israelites included in the ancestry of the Messiah, and the miracle of healing for Naaman, the Syrian general, in 2 Kings 5 are further indicators of inclusiveness.

Christine Pohl (2003) articulates the twin themes of the alien-migrant status and hospitality coming together in the life of Jesus in the New Testament. He was born in an unfamiliar town and, for a season, sojourned in a foreign land. A world created through him treated him as a stranger. Yet, he played host to huge crowds and befriended the unwanted. He taught believers to welcome 'the least' and those who seemed to have little to offer. This ties hospitality to God's welcome, making it akin to welcoming Jesus himself (Luke 14.12–14; Matt. 25.31–46) (Pohl, 2003, pp. 5–8). The twin ideas of the alien-migrant status and hospitality are also evident in the formation and growth of the early church. Believers opened their homes to persecuted Christians and to those travelling to spread the gospel. Shared meals and the practice of hospitality provided the liminal space for the formation of new identities and transformational relationships. It was the place where the early church wrestled to transcend socio-economic, cultural and ethnic boundaries. This extraordinary hospitality and inclusiveness of the church, especially to those on the fringes of society, was such that early Christian apologists used it as proof of the truth of Christianity (Pohl, 2003, pp. 8–9). Today, Lebanese Christians are in a similar manner offering hospitality to Syrian refugees (Gourlay et al., 2019, p. 46).

When embraced, the pilgrim identity motivates us to change the way we view migrants and the socio-cultural 'other'. When we live in the light of our own alien status and recognize that the world is not our home, migrants and people who are different become more than objects and recipients of charity and outreach. They become fellow pilgrims. In a world of ethnic tensions, injustices and vast socio-economic gaps, sharing meals and conversations with migrants make 'powerful statements to the world about who is interesting, valuable, and important for us' (Pohl,

2003, p. 10). Authentic hospitality creates spaces of liminality where we allow ourselves to be vulnerable and changed as we welcome migrants. The host role is a position of power. Thus, hosts may act as gracious providers, but that role can serve as a means to mask deep injustice and disrespect, reinforcing status distinctions and dependence. When one is in a place of privilege, there is also the trap of imagining a one-way flow of resources. In reality, there is much that we can receive from guests and strangers when we open ourselves (Pohl, 2003, pp. 9–12). The pilgrim identity is tied to biblical hospitality, a way of life that assumes inclusivity.

Concluding reflections

In this chapter, I have drawn from the Bible and its narratives to outline the key elements of the pilgrim identity and to show the relevance of that identity to the Christian experience and perspective.[9] I conclude this chapter as I started – with personal reflections. Growing up with migrant parents, listening to their stories (especially my mum's), and observing their attitudes, I glean important implications for the Christian pilgrim identity. For my parents, in their early years in what was then 'Malaya', where they lived was but a stopover point – their final destination was China. 'Real home' was in China – that is also where their hearts were. This resonates with the spiritual pilgrim's feel of Psalm 84.3–4 where 'even the sparrow finds a home ... blessed are those who dwell in your house' and the assertion of Philippians 3.20 that 'our citizenship is in heaven'.

Where they lived was a temporary place to accumulate for life back home. They came prepared for hard work and to rough it out: mobile, ready to pack up and move whenever required. They lived frugally, setting aside whatever they could. Yet, they were willing to give sacrificially when family in China needed help. This is etched into my childhood memories because it was a period of poverty for our family that coincided with China's worst years – the Cultural Revolution and its aftermath. These migrant perspectives parallel Matthew 6.20, 'lay up for yourselves treasures in heaven', and Paul's reflective response about death, 'If I am to go on living ... this will mean fruitful labour for me ... I desire to depart and be with Christ ... but it is more necessary for you that I remain' (Phil. 1.22–24, NIV). I also observed my mum's acceptance of and kindness to others. It did not matter that they were not Chinese. Be they Indians or Malays, she easily befriended them, conversing in her broken Malay. Perhaps it was because others had befriended her and helped her along the way as a migrant?

Despite taking on Malaysian citizenship, my dad also saw himself as representative of all things good from his land of origin. Christians are similarly representatives of God's kingdom to this world, bearing witness to the good news of Christ. Nonetheless, in my teenage years and early adulthood, I could not identify with my dad's migrant perspective. My dad's defence of all things Chinese was often to my dismay. I felt no affinity for China and at that time saw little virtue in the Confucian values he espoused. Without realizing it, I was deeply impacted by the perspectival biases of my English-language education. My parents could not speak English but, in view of what they foresaw, decided to send all but one of us siblings to English-speaking schools. By the time I was in my teens, I spoke English better than my mother-tongue. It was also in my teens that I came to faith in Christ through the witness of a friend who himself was a convert of a few months. The youngest of the siblings, but the first to become a Christian, this brought much displeasure, especially to my parents. Thankfully, my parents and most of my siblings also came to faith, but that was much later, over the next 15 to 25 years.

Regrettably, I never saw the connections between my parents' migrant identities with the biblical concept of pilgrim identity until very much later in my Christian journey. This is despite having gone to seminary, years of pastoring in cross-cultural contexts and serving Christians from diverse ethnic and country origins. It was only decades later, while doing my doctoral studies in a foreign land and researching migration concerns, that I reflected deeper on the formation of my own identity and made the connections. Identity and identity formation is indeed complex. It is the totality of a person's self-conception and it includes one's beliefs about oneself, one's roles and group belongings (McGill, 2016, p. 16). It also includes one's beliefs about God and others. The pilgrim identity is but one part in the totality of all that constitutes our human identity. I propose that as Christians, it should form a major part. It is a lens through which we know God, live life and treat others. It is not only integral to Christian spirituality. In a world of difference and exclusion, it is a resource to bridge the chasms.

Bibliography

Achtemeier, P. J., 1996, *1 Peter: A commentary on First Peter*, ed. E. J. Epp, Minneapolis, MN: Fortress Press.

Baggio, F. and A. M. Brazal (eds), 2008, *Faith on the Move: Toward a theology of migration in Asia*, Quezon City: Ateneo de Manila University Press.

Bartholomew, C. and F. Hughes (eds), 2004, *Explorations in a Christian Theology of Pilgrimage*, London: Routledge.

Baskin, J. R. (ed.), 2011, *The Cambridge Dictionary of Judaism and Jewish Culture*, Cambridge: Cambridge University Press.

Boadt, L., 2012, *Reading the Old Testament: An introduction*, 2nd edn, rev. by R. Clifford and D. Harrington, Marwah, NJ: Paulist Press.

Boer, A. P., 2011, 'Pilgrimage', in *Dictionary of Christian Spirituality*, ed. G. G. Scorgie, S. Chan, G. T. Smith and J. D. III Smith, Grand Rapids, MI: Zondervan, pp. 827–8.

Bosman, H. L., 2019, 'Reconsidering Deuteronomy 26:5–11 as a "Small Historical Creed": Overtures towards a "migrant reading" within the Persian period', *HTS Theological Studies* 75(3), pp. 1–8.

Bradley, I., 2011, 'Pilgrimage', in *The Cambridge Dictionary of Christian Theology*, ed. I. A. McFarland, D. A. S. Fergusson, K. Kilby and I. R. Torrance, Cambridge: Cambridge University Press, pp. 390–1.

Brueggemann, W., 2001, *Deuteronomy*, Abingdon Old Testament Commentaries, Nashville, TN: Abingdon Press.

Carroll R. M. D., 2013, *Christians at the Border: Immigration, the church, and the Bible*, 2nd edn, Grand Rapids, MI: Brazos Press.

Castles, S., H. de Haas and M. J. Miller, 2014, *The Age of Migration: International population movements in the modern world*, 5th edn, New York: Guilford Press.

Cavanaugh, W. T., 2011, *Migrations of the Holy: God, state, and the political meaning of the church*, Grand Rapids, MI: W.B. Eerdmans.

Chan, N.-C., 2018, 'When Migration Converges with Urbanization: Thinking and engaging Missionally', in *Urbanization: Impacts on the Church, Mission and Society Today*, ed. L.-S. Chen and W.-K. Cheong, Kota Kinabalu, Malaysia: Sabah Theological Seminary; The Asian Centre for Mission, pp. 47–74.

Cruz, G. T., 2010, *An Intercultural Theology of Migration: Pilgrims in the wilderness*, Leiden: Brill.

Das, R. and B. Hamoud, 2017, *Strangers in the Kingdom: Ministering to refugees, migrants and the stateless*, Carlisle: Langham Global Library.

Dufoix, S., 2017, *The Dispersion: A history of the word diaspora*, Leiden: Brill.

Ellis, A., S. de Lacalle and P. Santos, 2010, *The Phenomenon of Migration and the Magisterium of the Church: Notes for further development of Catholic social thought*, Madrid: Fundación Universitaria San Pablo CEU.

Escobar, S., 2003, 'Migration: Avenue and challenge to mission', *Missiology* 31(1), pp. 17–28.

Escobar, S., 2018, 'Refugees: A New Testament perspective', *Transformation* 35(2), pp. 102–8.

Gerbrandt, G., 2015, *Deuteronomy*, Believers Church Bible Commentary, Harrisonburg, VA: Herald Press.

Gourlay, M., M. Swamy and M. Daehnhardt, 2019, *How the Church Contributes to Well-Being in Conflict-Affected Fragile States: Voices from the local church*, Cambridge and Teddington: Cambridge Centre of Christianity Worldwide and Tearfund.

Green, S. G., 2016, *Deuteronomy: A commentary in the Wesleyan tradition*, New Beacon Bible Commentary, Kansas City, MO: Beacon Hill Press.

Groody, D. G. and G. Campese (eds), 2008, *A Promised Land, a Perilous Journey: Theological perspectives on migration*, Notre Dame, IN: University of Notre Dame Press.

Grudem, W. A., 1988, *1 Peter: An introduction and commentary*, 2009th edn, Tyndale New Testament Commentaries, vol. 17, Downers Grove, IL: Baker Academic.

Hadjiev, T. S., 2018, 'Introduction: Images of migration in the Hebrew Bible', *Biblical Interpretation* 26(4–5), pp. 435–8.

Hiebert, P. G., R. D. Shaw and T. Tiénou, 1999, *Understanding Folk Religion: A Christian response to popular beliefs and practices*, Grand Rapids, MI: Baker Books.

Hoffmeier, J. K., 2009, *The Immigration Crisis: Immigrants, aliens and the Bible*, Wheaton, IL: Crossway Books.

International Organization for Migration (IOM), 2015, *World Migration Report 2015 (Migrants and Cities: New Partnerships to Manage Mobility)*, Geneva: International Organization for Migration.

International Organization for Migration (IOM), 2019, *World Migration Report 2020*, Geneva: International Organization for Migration.

Knauth, R. J. D., 2003, 'Alien, Foreign Resident', in T. D. Alexander and D. W. Baker (eds), *Dictionary of the Old Testament: Pentateuch*, Downers Grove, IL: InterVarsity Press, pp. 26–33.

Krabill, M. and A. Norton, 2015, 'New Wine in Old Wineskins: A critical appraisal of diaspora missiology', *Missiology: An International Review* 43(4), pp. 442–55.

Marzouk, S., 2019, *Intercultural Church: A Biblical vision for an age of migration*, Minneapolis, MN: Fortress Press.

McCartney, D. G., 2009, *James*, Baker Exegetical Commentary on the New Testament, Grand Rapids, MI: Baker Academic.

McGill, J., 2016, *Religious Identity and Cultural Negotiation: Toward a theology of Christian identity in migration*, American Society of Missiology Monograph Series, Eugene, OR: Pickwick Publications.

Padilla, E. and P. C. Phan (eds), 2014, *Theology of Migration in the Abrahamic Religions*, New York: Palgrave Macmillan.

Padilla, E., and Phan, P. C. (eds), 2016, *Christianities in Migration: The global perspective*, Basingstoke: Palgrave Macmillan.

Paul VI, 1964, *Lumen Gentium*, Vatican II, www.vatican.va/archive/hist_councils/ii_vatican_council/documents/vat-ii_const_19641121_lumen-gentium_en.html, accessed 28.03.2021.

Phan, P. C. (ed.), 2020, *Christian Theology in the Age of Migration: Implications for World Christianity*, Lanham, MD: Lexington Books.

Pohl, C. D., 2003, 'Biblical Issues in Mission and Migration', *Missiology* 31(1), pp. 3–15.

Rajendra, T. M., 2017, *Migrants and Citizens: Justice and responsibility in the ethics of immigration*, Grand Rapids, MI: Eerdmans.

Ringma, C. R., K. Hollenback-Wuest and A. O. Gorospe (eds), 2015, *God at the Borders: Globalization, migration and diaspora*, Manila: OMF Literature and Asian Theological Seminary.

Rowlands, A., 2011, 'On the Temptations of Sovereignty: The task of Catholic social teaching and the challenge of UK asylum seeking', *Political Theology*, 12(6), pp. 843–69.

Schoenfeld, D., 2014, '"You Will Seek from There": The cycle of exile and return in classical Jewish theology', in E. Padilla and P.C. Phan (eds), *Theology of Migration in the Abrahamic Religions*, New York: Palgrave Macmillan, pp. 27–46.

Senior, D., 2003, *1 Peter*, Sacra Pagina Series, vol. 15, Collegeville, MN: Liturgical Press.

Stenschke, C., 2016, 'Migration and Mission: According to the book of Acts', *Missionalia* 44(2), pp. 129–51.

Sunquist, S. W., 2013, *Understanding Christian Mission: Participation in suffering and glory*, Grand Rapids, MI: Baker Academic.

Tedong, P. A., J. L. Grant, W. N. A. W. Abd Aziz, F. Ahmad and N. R. Hanif, 2014, 'Guarding the Neighbourhood: The new landscape of control in Malaysia', *Housing Studies* 29(8), pp. 1005–27.

Tira, S. J. and T. Yamamori (eds), 2016, *Scattered and Gathered: A global compendium of diaspora missiology*, Oxford: Regnum Books.

Trebilco, P. R. and C. A. Evans, 2000, 'Diaspora Judaism', in A. E. Evans and S. E. Porter (eds), *Dictionary of New Testament Background*, Downers Grove, IL: Baker Academic, pp. 281–96.

United Nations Human Settlements Programme (UN-Habitat), 2016, *World Cities Report 2016 – Urbanization and Development: Emerging futures*, Nairobi, Kenya.

Wan, E. Y.-N. and S. E. S. B. Tira (eds), 2009, *Missions Practice in the 21st Century*, Pasadena, CA: William Carey International University Press.

Notes

1 The dependence on migrant labour is not confined to low-paying labour-intensive economies. It is equally true of high-end economies that profit from new research, information technology and global financial flows, such as in Silicon Valley in the United States and global financial centres such as Singapore. The difference is in the labelling. Instead of 'migrant workers', they are referred to as 'expatriates'. Migration dramatically impacts the demographics of entire countries (IOM, 2019).

2 See www.unhcr.org/en-my/figures-at-a-glance.html.

3 Roman Catholics have an established tradition in dealing with modern migration dating from Pope Pius XII's *Exsul Familia* in 1952, which addressed forced migration and refugee concerns after World War Two. The opening of their Scalabrini International Migration Institute in 2000 reinforces this scholarship (Baggio and Brazal, 2008, p. x). The earliest document from the World Council of Churches (WCC) that focused on migration issues was a memorandum and recommendations entitled *Practising Hospitality in an Era of New Forms of Migration*, adopted by its Central Committee in 2005.

4 Pastoral concern sets the tone for *De Pastorali Migratorum Cura* (On the Pastoral Care of Migrants) issued by the congregation of Bishops in 1968, and the *Chiesa e Mobilita Umana* (Church and Human Mobility) from the Pontifical Commission for the Pastoral Care of Migrants and Itinerant People to the Episcopal Conferences in 1978 (Baggio and Brazal, 2008, p. x).

5 Kondothra M. George (Padilla and Phan, 2014, p. 67) writes from the Orthodox tradition. The Roman Catholic Vatican II document describes believers as 'pilgrims in a strange land, tracing in trial and in oppression the paths He [Jesus] trod' (Paul VI, 1964, p. 64). Scott Sunquist, a Protestant mission historian, views Christianity as a 'pilgrim faith' where 'Christians are not at home ... [but] pilgrims and refugees' (2013, p. 19).

6 It is applied to Abraham (Gen. 17.7–8; 20.1; 21.34; 23.4), Lot (Gen. 19.9), Isaac (Gen. 35.27), Jacob (Gen. 28.4; 32.4, 37.1) and Joseph and his brothers (Gen. 47.4).

7 It is noteworthy that *gēr*'s most common usage is for people displaced by famine (Gen. 12.10; 26.3; 47.4; Ruth 1.1; 1 Kings 17.20; 2 Kings 8.1) or war (2 Sam. 4.3; Isa. 16.4). On this basis, Knauth suggests 'refugee' as its closest modern equivalent (2003, p. 27). In view of the increased numbers of displaced peoples and refugees around the world in recent years, responses to current refugee concerns based on Old Testament perspectives and treatment of the *gēr* are especially relevant.

8 Both James and 1 Peter are circular letters probably intended for a mixture of Jewish and Gentile believers (McCartney, 2009, pp. 33, 36; Achtemeier, 1996, p. 57). For more detailed discussions about the scale, type and nature of the persecutions faced by the early church, see Achtemeier, 1996, pp. 28–36.

9 For an alternative approach, I highly recommend Jenny McGill's *Religious Identity and Cultural Negotiation* (2016).

6

Case Study: The Journey of the Latin American Campaign 'As Born Among Us'

LOIDA CARRIEL ESPINOZA AND
MARÍA ALEJANDRE ANDRADE VINUEZA

Introduction

Migration is as old as life on this planet. Everything that breathes, migrates: birds, mammals, humans, even plants. From the very beginning, people have moved and, in doing so, they have shared stories, cultures, ways of understanding the world; they have mixed with other cultures and created new ones. The world as we know it is the product of historic migrations. So, despite contemporary media narratives, migration is not new: it has always happened and always will. It is part of the history of humanity, right back to the Bible's account of Adam and Eve being banned from the Garden of Eden in Genesis 3.

The causes of migration in the Bible are very similar to those borne out in the stories of migrant people today: hunger, conflict, persecution, climatic events ... History has seen some peaks in terms of the frequency and the number of people being forced to flee their countries. Today, the world is facing one of these peaks and trends indicate that violence, socio-political conflict and climate change are likely to increase migration in some regions. In parallel, xenophobia is also increasing in both transit and destination countries – even in 'sending' countries – making the journey of displaced communities even harder.

How should 'receiving' societies react to the millions of migrant people arriving in their countries, when they are already struggling with their own economic, social, political and environmental crises? It seems that the choices are limited: deny that the crisis is happening, blame and actively reject migrant communities, or accept the new reality and embrace attitudes and practices of inclusion towards migrants, one of the world's most vulnerable populations. Existing research has shown that migration can be very positive if inclusive policies and practices are in place and implemented (Info Migrants, 2018; Andrade, 2017, p. 95). By contrast, exclusion of specific populations has proved to cause deep fractures in societies and complex problems in the immediate, medium and long term. Therefore, working towards inclusion of migrant communities seems to be not only an ethical obligation but also a strategic one. For Christian communities, inclusion as a call to radical hospitality is a biblical mandate from a God who always sits on the side of the marginalized. It is precisely here that churches can play a key role, providing alternative narratives to migration, becoming welcoming communities and speaking up against xenophobic policies.

The case study below is based on the experience of the Latin American campaign *Como nacido entre nosotros* ('As born among us'), which was launched on 21 June 2019, World Refugee Day. Its membership includes faith-based organizations (FBOs) from across the region collaborating on protection and integration of migrant communities and promoting their rights. This case study has four sections. The first section proposes that migration is the new face of exclusion in Latin America and the Caribbean. The second presents 'As born among us' as an initiative that responds to the biblical call to inclusion and radical hospitality (see also Chapter 5). The third section describes the campaign's key objectives and actions, and the fourth section shares some achievements and learnings. The conclusion provides some insights on the campaign's vision for the future.

Migration as the new face of exclusion in Latin America and the Caribbean

Over the past few decades, migration flows have changed very significantly in terms of size, direction, general characteristics and their overall impact in countries of origin and host countries alike. The Economic Commission for Latin America and the Caribbean (ECLAC) has identified three major migration patterns in Latin America and the Caribbean (ECLAC, 2001, p. 20):

- *Historical immigration* into Latin America from overseas between the mid-nineteenth and mid-twentieth centuries, with a strong European component
- *Intra-regional migration*, caused by socio-economic developments and structural factors, particularly during the period 1970–90, which saw the highest rates of migration within Latin America
- *'South–North' migration flows*, resulting in the loss of qualified workers in Latin America and the Caribbean, the emergence of immigrant communities, and the economic potential associated with the remittances sent by migrants to their countries of origin.

In recent years, the region has experienced a growing migratory wave, which has displaced millions of people. These movements follow historical patterns from the South to the North – from Latin American countries to the United States and Canada – but, today, they also reflect new intra-regional trends. Most of the current migrants come from Venezuela, Honduras, Guatemala, El Salvador, Nicaragua, Colombia and Haiti, and seek to move and stay in other Latin American countries or try to reach the US. In their journey, they face all kinds of threats including kidnapping, extortion, sexual abuse and exploitation, robbery, smuggling, trafficking and other types of rights violations, which are exacerbated by growing expressions of xenophobia, both in transit and destination countries (ACNUR, 2019; OIM, 2016).

People migrating from Central America to the US are escaping from criminal violence, poverty, disasters, political insecurity, lack of opportunity, climate change and food insecurity, and today they are also fleeing the Covid-19 pandemic (Brookings, 2021). El Salvador, Honduras and Guatemala – wrongly called the 'Northern Triangle' countries – have high rates of criminality and two of them (El Salvador and Honduras) are in the top ten countries for homicide rates (Index Mundi, 2019). The Migration Policy Institute (2019) affirmed that, in 2017, El Salvador, Guatemala and Honduras were the top three origin countries for migrants from Central America.

'Migrant caravans' are 'a way to describe the large groups of people moving by land across international borders' (IOM, 2021). These migrant caravans have increased in number and frequency since 2018, with thousands of people and families walking by road trying to reach Mexico and the US border and capture the 'American dream'. They choose to migrate in caravans because these offer them protection against the many types of violence they are exposed to, such as crime, kidnappings, disappearances, physical and sexual assault, trafficking and execution (IOM, 2020, p. 105).

In recent years, Venezuela has experienced a rapid deterioration in its economy as a result of political instability, violence and corruption. This has led to widespread unemployment and a lack of basic services, education, health care and, above all, opportunities (ACNUR, 2020). In search of a better life, millions of Venezuelans have migrated to neighbouring countries. However, these countries face their own challenges of poverty, inequality, endemic corruption and violence, so migration adds a lot of extra pressure on already stretched public resources.

According to the United Nations High Commissioner for Refugees (UNHCR) (ACNUR, 2020), it is estimated that in the last four years almost 6 million Venezuelans have left their country; 4 million of them have migrated to neighbouring countries such as Colombia, Ecuador, Peru, Chile, Argentina and Brazil. There, these migrant peoples experience high rates of discrimination and xenophobia and a severe lack of opportunities.

In Venezuela, an unthinkable situation has come upon us as a church in recent days. In 2015, we began to feel the immense movement of Venezuelans seeking better futures and opportunities. Since then, each Sunday, we pray for members of the Church who are in their migration journey, as we keep saying goodbye to others. We try to make the most of our networks, connecting them with other churches in other countries, hoping that there will be as little tension and trauma as possible in their difficult journey. There are thousands of 'walking migrants' on the highways of our neighboring countries. For those who depart, and for us who stay, there is one word that describes this feeling: pain. We see people with chronic illnesses, pregnant women and elderly adults walking in search of medications. We live a nightmare, which seems not to end any time soon. It is painful and it touches me very deeply. (Pastor César Mermejo, President of the Evangelical Council of Venezuela)[1]

'As born among us': a biblical call to inclusion and radical hospitality

In addition to the many risks and difficulties that migrant populations face in transit and destination countries, they also face discrimination and rejection in every stage of their journey. In fact, according to migrants themselves, xenophobia is perceived as the hardest part of migration. According to the UNHCR, xenophobia is defined as the 'attitudes, prejudices and behaviour that reject, exclude and often vilify persons, based on the perception that they are outsiders or foreigners to the community, society or national identity' (UNHCR, 2020). Xenophobia is based on perceptions – which are subjective – but has very concrete and serious consequences: attitudes, behaviours and actions that can provoke physical, mental, emotional harm, even death. Given that migratory flows will not cease, as long as there is poverty, violence and persecution, the only constructive response that transit and receiving societies can take is to accept their 'new neighbours' and look for the best ways to integrate them into society. The failure to integrate migrant communities effectively into society – through policies of inclusion that guarantee access to health services, education and work – is likely to cause deep social divides in the years to come. In other words, good integration of migrant communities into their new 'neighbourhood' can be very positive for society; bad integration processes can become a serious threat to it. Therefore, broad practices of inclusion of the migrant should be seen not only as an ethical mandate but also a strategic one. It is precisely around addressing xenophobia that faith communities can play a key and distinctive role.

Tearfund's work through the 'As born among us' campaign is built on the understanding that the phenomenon of migration is complex but that the biblical mandate compels Christian communities to receive foreigners as if they were receiving Jesus himself (Matt. 25.35): unconditionally and with open hearts. This means embracing radical hospitality and becoming inclusive communities.

The name of the campaign comes from the biblical text of Leviticus 19.33–34, which touches the heart of the problem around xenophobia:

Don't take advantage of any stranger who lives in your land. You must treat the outsider *as one of your native-born people*

– as a full citizen – and you are to love him in the same way you love yourself; for remember, you were once strangers living in Egypt. I am the Eternal One, your God. (Leviticus 19.33–34, *The Voice Bible*, emphasis added)

In this passage, Yavhé reminds the Israelites that their story is also one of pilgrimage, which should lead them to receive the strangers arriving in their lands with empathy and care. It is important to remember that the Israelites of the Old Testament distinguished themselves from other Ancient Orient nations because their own experience prompted them to develop a progressively more open, welcoming attitude of solidarity towards foreigners. Bible scholar José Ramírez Kidd proposes that the Israelites moved from an optional compassionate attitude towards foreigners (Deut. 10.17–19), to the establishment of policies to protect them from oppression (Deut. 24.17; Ex. 20.10; Lev. 19.9–10), to bringing down the barriers that keep them apart, including geographical, ethnic and cultural identities (Ramírez Kidd, 2003). So, Yavhé's call to treat the outsiders 'as one of your native-born people – as a full citizen' overrides all the existing reasons for discrimination towards foreigners among the Israelites, confers on them the very same legal status – full citizens – and affirms the most important ethical principle in relationships: love them in the same way you love yourself. In this way, effective inclusion does not rely any longer on anyone's willingness; nor is it dependent on the effective application of laws. It is based on the undeniable affirmation of all human beings having a God-given dignity and belonging. There is no stronger reason for loving the foreign-other than a shared humanity and being made in the same divine image. The pilgrim identity, as discussed in Chapter 5, becomes a 'spiritual resource' enabling Jesus' followers to welcome the outsider. 'As born among us' calls on Christian communities to embrace radical hospitality towards migrant communities, because it is an ethical mandate, because it has the potential to enrich both the people arriving and the welcoming societies, and because it responds to the Christian's imperative to love one's neighbours as oneself.

Key objectives and actions of the campaign

'As born among us' seeks to encourage Latin American evangelical churches to respond to the current migration crisis, inspired by the model of Jesus, in order to become a community that will welcome and defend the rights of migrant peoples. This is meant to be achieved through:

1 *Envisioning*: create awareness among churches and civil society with a strong theological framework on hospitality.
2 *Mobilizing*: encourage different expressions of the church to take concrete actions to respond to the needs of migrant communities.
3 *Advocacy*: call on national and regional authorities to create and implement laws that protect the rights of migrant populations.
4 *Integration*: promote fellowship between migrant populations and resident church communities.
5 *Accompaniment*: support left-behind populations (families of migrant people who stayed in their countries of origin).

In its first year and a half, the campaign had gathered 65 diverse FBOs operating at national and regional levels. These include local churches, theological institutions and Christian non-government organizations and movements. Each organization contributes their own capacities and resources, providing clothing, meals, shelter, medicines and holistic support to migrants, as well as advocating to the authorities in defence of migrants' rights. Together, they are currently responding to the needs of migrant populations in 12 countries: Mexico, Guatemala, Honduras, Colombia, Ecuador, Peru, Brazil, Chile, Argentina, Nicaragua, Panama and Venezuela (in many of which Tearfund does not currently have a presence). The mobilization of these organizations was made possible through a face-to-face event (prior to Covid-19) in Bogotá, in March 2020, where 60 leaders from FBOs (Evangelical, Catholic and Jewish) in ten countries developed a joint plan to respond to the migrant crisis in Venezuela. One of the concrete results from that meeting was the creation of a 'church-based humanitarian corridor' that provides a more joined-up and holistic response to the needs of migrant communities. The campaign's website and free app[2] provide information in Spanish and Portuguese on safe shelters, national and international legislation for migrant communities, and spiritual support – biblical 'pilgrim capsules' – for individuals who decide to migrate from Venezuela to neighbouring countries. Through regular online meetings, training and open events, the campaign has become a virtual interfaith space of collective action, support, learning and exchange of experiences, resources and contacts. In addition, the campaign has organized a number of contests to identify, feature and support successful and innovative actions from all over the region in support of migrant communities. These contests have articulated the anthropological phenomenon of migration through art, theology, youth projects, advocacy and innovation.[3]

FIGURE 1 *Semillas de Esperanza ('Seeds of Hope'), a photo that won the migration and art contest 'Migrant Expression' in 2019.*

The campaign has also reached out and influenced governments through public statements relating to events and specific laws that affect the rights of migrant communities. Faith communities in Latin America have called on governments to respect international treaties and learn from the experiences of other countries; the organizations affiliated to the campaign monitor actions and influence governments, international organizations and migrant collectives.

'As born among us' has become a wind of hope and life for the people of God. We have joined and we are filled with joy to

participate because our Biblical mandate is to save life, without regard for nationality. And this should be the priority of all, not only of governments, but of everyone.
(Prof. Rubén Ortiz, Latino Field Coordinator, Cooperative Baptist Fellowship, USA)

Successes and lessons learnt from the campaign

Although the 'As born among us' campaign is still relatively new, there are some achievements that are worth celebrating and sharing. First of all, the campaign has been well received by FBOs from all over the region, as a space for sharing, discussing current efforts and catalysing new joint actions. The campaign is currently recognized as a faith-based, prophetic voice that has boosted a diversity of concrete actions to facilitate the inclusion, good treatment and protection of migrant individuals and communities. Its impact is documented in internal monitoring reports as follows:

- 65 regional denominations and Christian organizations are currently part of the campaign.
- 300 Christian leaders and local churches from 12 countries in Latin America have taken concrete actions to welcome, promote, protect and integrate migrant populations.
- 55 faith leaders associated with the campaign participate in decision-making spaces at national and regional levels where they influence and advocate for new laws and practices in favour of migrant communities.
- 33 Christian institutions and/or movements from seven countries in the region have received public recognition for their work and for the way that faith moves them to action.

'As born among us' is a platform that permits us to reflect anew on the mandate of the Lord who said, 'I was a migrant and you welcomed me in.' The migrants come to us to evangelize us. They visit us and they tell us that hospitality and respect for people's lives are important to God.
(Prof. Alfredo Mosquera, Interfaith committee, Cali, Colombia[4])

Important lessons learnt from the campaign in its initial phases are shared here, in the hope they prove useful to similar initiatives:

- *A catalytic approach[5] expands the frontiers.* Not restricting the campaign to the countries where Tearfund has a presence allowed us to increase the number of allies and the FBOs reached, including in Argentina, Chile, Ecuador, Mexico, Venezuela, Costa Rica and the US. It also gave Tearfund the ability to act as a voice of authority in the faith and justice space. The tension between following global priorities, honouring country strategies and boosting this regional campaign requires constant management and intentional alignment, to prevent duplication of efforts, make the most of the limited resources and avoid contradictions between projects.
- *Diverse is good.* The campaign was aimed at evangelical organizations but, along the way, many Catholic and inter-faith platforms asked to join. Interfaith partners have been the most amazing allies in the care of migrant communities. The journey has been one of mutual respect, admiration and enrichment.
- *From owner to convener.* The role of convener – the one who brings together different organizations – is very much appreciated and well received by other FBOs. The organizations that are linked to this campaign are not asking for Tearfund's funding but for Tearfund to act as a convener. This role requires its bearer to have credibility, leadership, a collaborative spirit, the humility to listen and to learn, and a passion for the vision rather than a desire to push their organization's 'brand'.
- *Technology is a bridge-builder.* It allows organizations from different countries, languages and cultures to get closer and make the most of their efforts. It also brings people (migrants communities, in this case) closer to sources of information and support, which could mean the difference between life and death for them. Finally, technology keeps the migrant population connected to their countries of origin, their families and communities, which is fundamental for their well-being.
- *Catalysing a movement of FBOs is not cheap.* There was an assumption that movement-building requires less investment, but this experience has demonstrated that building a sustainable movement requires, above all, people and time.
- *Teamwork makes work holistic.* The contribution of all the Tearfund regional staff, with their particular expertise and

resources, has allowed the response to the migrant crisis to be holistic, as it includes humanitarian support, advocacy, church mobilization, theological reflection and spiritual nurture.

• *Non-traditional catalytic work cannot be done through a traditional approach: it calls for innovation.* Working with a catalytic approach is an invitation to migrate to a new spirit of networking, new dynamics, new models, new timings and new measuring and monitoring tools.

'As born among us' is a platform that helps us at a regional level to put into practice all of the realities that are affecting migrants and link our efforts to be a voice and hands for those who do not have a voice. I hope that this effort can gain a high level of influence with the authorities.
(Prof. César Mermejo, President of the Evangelical Council of Venezuela[6])

Conclusion: the journey ahead

The campaign 'As born among us' was born out of Tearfund's vision to inspire and bring together churches and other FBOs in Latin America to respond to the needs of migrant populations, in response to God's call that we should 'love our neighbour'. From the very beginning of this journey, Tearfund saw itself as a con-vener and catalyser of collective action; this is not 'Tearfund's campaign', as its growth, impact and sustainability rely strongly on its allies.

The campaign was launched with many expectations and hopes, knowing that the migrant communities face exclusion and that faith communities have a significant and distinctive role to play in facilitating migrant inclusion. The campaign started by putting the topic on the table, in order to create awareness and identify key stakeholders. Then it focused on identifying and catalysing joint actions between different stakeholders, including FBOs from different traditions, as well as governments and civil society. After almost two years, the campaign celebrates import-ant achievements and is committed to continuing, as migration is not likely to decrease in the immediate future. As a result, in 2021, while continuing the current actions with Venezuelan migrant communities, some of the additional initiatives of the campaign include catalysing a process similar to the one in South

America with Venezuelan migrant communities in Central America, Mexico and the US. The first meeting was scheduled for April 2021, and aimed to bring together FBOs in the northern part of the region that already support migrant communities and families in their decision to leave, in their journey, in their arrival at their destination and in their return home if they are deported. The second and longer-term key action is developing a diploma on church-based response to migration, in collaboration with Fuller Theological Seminary, which takes the best of each organization's expertise, content, resources and contacts on the topic.

The need is growing but so too is the hope that we can make a difference in the lives of migrant populations, treating them as if they were *born among us*. We conclude this chapter with reflections by Jared Diaz (2019):

I am a citizen of the world, I was born from a woman,
I filled my lungs with air and cried so hard for everyone to
    know it,
I remember my heart throbbing through this sky, and scraping
my knees on the same earth I'm leaving now,
    as I tried to work it but it's so dry I'm running out of food.

And I left my home, cleaning my shoes with every promise
    that everything would get better,
so I'd be able to walk a little further and get there.
Leaving behind all my feelings,
seeing the sun so unreachable on the horizon, cutting
    myself off
from my children's present so they can have a future.

But the birds do not pay tolls and the sky is not divided by
    nationality,
not even the sun is discriminated by where it is born;
tell me about the times that you have worked harder for your
    loved ones
and my feet will tell you in kilometers travelled.
I am a stork without wings, dragging my sentence far
    from home,
exchanging dignity for a plate of hope,
hope guarded by foreigners in their own land,

enduring the rough terrain so I don't have to rip my heart
    back home
and keeping smiles in my trouser pocket,
so I can send them as remittances when I get there.

And sailing the ocean of human cruelty,
I wonder, can anyone help me?
For even though the whole world boasts of having
    abolished slavery
and being free of racism,
my features make me worthy of rejection
and my poverty is inadmissible within your borders.

But in my journey the great surprise that Jesus would be
    waiting for me,
with a sip of water and a piece of bread,
with a frayed hat to keep the sun off me
and shelter for when the clouds kiss the earth.
And with these tears I thank you for these beans
that I still can't provide for my family
and pray that there are others along the way,
who will make this exodus less painful.

Because I am a citizen of the world and I am a criminal for
    wanting to live with dignity.
(Jared Diaz, winner of the migration and art contest 'Migrant
Expression', 2019[7])

Bibliography

ACNUR, 2019, 'Un estudio de ACNUR destaca los riesgos que enfren-
tan las personas venezolanas vulnerables en movimiento', Panamá:
UNHCR, www.acnur.org/noticias/briefing/2019/7/5d31abd74/un-estu
dio-de-acnur-destaca-los-riesgos-que-enfrentan-las-personas-venezola-
nas.html, accessed 16.03.2021.
ACNUR, 2020, 'Situación en Venezuela', *UNHCR*, www.acnur.org/situ
acion-en-venezuela.html, accessed 16.03.2021.
Andrade, M. A., 2017, '"We Don't Want Them Here": From the politics
of rejection to sustainable relationships with immigrants', *Journal of
Latin American Theology* 12(1).
Brookings Institution, 2021, 'The Imperative to Address the Root Causes
of Migration from Central America', *Brookings*, www.brookings.edu/

blog/order-from-chaos/2021/01/29/the-imperative-to-address-the-root-causes-of-migration-from-central-america/, accessed 16.03.2021.

Economic Commission for Latin America and the Caribbean (ECLAC)/ Population Division, Latin American and Caribbean Demographic Centre (CELADE), 2001, *International Migration and Development in the Americas*, Chile: ECLAC.

Index Mundi, 2019, 'Intentional homicides', *Index Mundi*, www.index mundi.com/facts/indicators/VC.IHR.PSRC.P5/rankings, accessed 16.03. 2021.

Info Migrants, 2018, 'Migrants have Positive Impact on Developing Countries', *Info Migrants*, www.infomigrants.net/en/post/7337/migrants-have-positive-impact-on-developing-countries, accessed 16.03.2021.

IOM, 2020, *World Migration Report 2020*, Geneva: IOM.

IOM, 2021, 'Migrant Caravans: Explained', San José: IOM, https://rosan jose.iom.int/SITE/en/blog/migrant-caravans-explained, accessed 16.03. 2021.

Migration Policy Institute, 2019, 'Central American Immigrants in the United States', *Migration Policy Institute*, www.migrationpolicy.org/ article/central-american-immigrants-united-states-2017, accessed 16.03. 2021.

OIM, 2016, 'Tráfico Ilícito de migrantes', San José: OIM, https://rosan jose.iom.int/SITE/es/trafico-ilicito-de-migrantes, accessed 16.03.2021.

Ramírez Kidd, J. E., 2003, *Paz y migraciones*, San José, Universidad Bíblica Latinoamericana.

UNHCR, 2020, *Guidance on Racism and Xenophobia*, Geneva: UNHCR.

Notes

1 Quote from an interview conducted by the Community Manager of 'As born among us' with the President of the Evangelical Council of Venezuela in Bogotá, Colombia, during a regional event for Christian churches supporting Venezuelan migrants in South America, 3 February 2020.

2 See www.comonacidoentrenosotros.org/.

3 More details on these contests can be found at www.comonacido entrenosotros.org.

4 Quote from a film interview conducted by the Community Manager of the 'As born among us' campaign in Bogotá, Colombia, during a regional event for Christian churches supporting Venezuelan migrants in South America, 3 February 2020.

5 For Tearfund, a 'catalytic approach' is about moving from a traditional 'donor' role to one that enables sustainable, locally grown, locally led solutions to poverty. From this perspective, the future of development is therefore increasingly about shared problems and working together on shared solutions.

6 Quote from an interview conducted by the Community Manager of the 'As born among us' campaign with the President of the Evangelical Council of Venezuela in Bogotá, Colombia, during a regional event for Christian churches supporting Venezuelan migrants in South America, 3 February 2020.

7 The original poem was written in Spanish and has been translated into English. Its title is 'Acheronte' (Acheron in English), which is the name of a river in Greece, known in ancient Greek mythology as the 'river of woe'.

PART 3

Inclusion as Requiring Change

7

Inclusion in a Networked Society: Digital Theological Perspectives

JONAS KURLBERG AND
REI LEMUEL CRIZALDO

Introduction

For years, Fr Benigno Beltran and his organization, Sandiwaan Center for Learning, have provided educational opportunities for out-of-school children in the slums in the Philippines. Realizing that even the people living by the garbage heaps of Manila have access to mobile phones, Sandiwaan developed online learning platforms to engage young people who are not in formal education (Handley MacMath, 2016). This is a brilliant example of the transformative potential of digital technology for those living in extreme poverty. Yet this success story can be contrasted with other examples that highlight the ways that the same technology can also amplify inequality. In the midst of the Covid-19 pandemic, state authorities in the Philippines mandated that schools should continue to provide classes by shifting to online learning. The result, however, has exposed glaring inequalities between rich and poor students, uneven access to good internet connection, and the inability of teachers to adapt to educational philosophies appropriate to digital technology. This was illustrated powerfully in the photo of a young boy that went viral on social media: it showed him working as a street vendor while trying his best to read 'learning modules' on his small mobile phone under a dim street lamp.

These examples illustrate why inclusion in the context of digital technologies is among the topics being debated within academia and more widely. On a positive note, digital technology has been hailed as an equalizer, promising greater participation in social, political, economic and religious life for those who have

JONAS KURLBERG AND REI LEMUEL CRIZALDO

previously been excluded or marginalized. Sceptics, however, have spoken of the 'digital divide', fearing that the internet will only deepen global inequalities between those with resources, power, knowledge and connectivity, and those who are unconnected, materially poor and marginalized. For churches, this question has surfaced during lockdown in the Covid-19 pandemic as a result of the move to online worship. While many churches have found that online services have attracted larger numbers than normal Sunday services, concerns have been raised that they exclude those lacking the financial means or know-how to participate (see Chow and Kurlberg, 2020).

Beyond the question of accessibility, digitalization marks a dramatic cultural shift that has a bearing on how we relate to one another. The emerging digital culture has far-reaching ramifications, not only for how we engage online: it also has a direct impact on offline cultural activity as it shapes our social imagination, or the lens through which we see the world and therefore engage within it. As digitality becomes more 'embedded, embodied and everyday' (Hine, 2015), the distinctions between online and offline are increasingly blurred. Digital culture, then, has a bearing on modes of being and relating, which in turn have an effect on practices and thought-patterns of inclusion, whether online or offline. For churches and faith-based, third-sector organizations, there are good reasons to pay attention to and reflect on the implications of the sometimes subtle, and at other times radical, changes transpiring under the forces of digitalization.

This chapter explores the possibilities and limitations of inclusion in a digital age. Employing the metaphor of the network, it does so through a theological lens, assessing practices and habits online that further or hinder the potential for inclusion. We build upon the basic premise of the theological framework for inclusion outlined in Chapter 2, which defines inclusion as needing to occur within a reconciliatory framework, and we seek to relay it to digital culture. One of the implications of this conceptualization is that it challenges the notion of inclusion as merely bringing those on the margins to the centre. Conceiving of inclusion primarily in relation to access ignores power asymmetries that inadvertently require the periphery to be transformed into the image of the powerful centre in order to participate. Neither does this definition of inclusion demand that the centre adjust in order to accommodate the marginalized. Thus, beyond accessibility, a relational understanding of inclusion suggests decentralization in which power is distributed and the centre undergoes a change in order to make space for the marginal other. Using this latter definition, we argue that digitality can enhance practices of inclusion by providing both the conceptual language and means to do so.

The network as a metaphor for a theology of inclusion

As a disruptive force, digitality can give cause to critically evaluate taken-for-granted beliefs and practices that enable us to see our faith with fresh eyes and innovate new ways of enacting it. For example, digital culture offers concepts and metaphors that can be used to illuminate and elucidate aspects of Christian faith and practice. One such use is Heidi Campbell and Stephen Garner's deployment of 'the network' as a metaphor for thinking and living faithfully in a digital age.

At its very core, the internet is a network. When the APRANET, as the internet was initially labelled, was launched by the US Defense Department's APRA team in 1969, their vision was to facilitate free and uncontrolled information- and resource-sharing between research communities (see Abbate, 1999, pp. 43–6). The repercussions of this network of connected devices have been such that it has reconfigured the structures of our societies. Manuel Castells, in his seminal *The Rise of the Networked Society*, argues that the digitalization of the world has resulted in a pervasive network logic that 'substantially modifies the operation and outcomes in processes of production, experience, power, and culture' (2010, p. 500). Campbell and Garner adopt this conception as an image to envisage faithful Christian living in an age demarcated by the expansion of digital communication technology. Referencing the dynamics of the tri-relational persons of the Trinity and the emphasis on relationality throughout Scripture, they argue that the use of this metaphor encourages us to theologically consider what it means to engage relationally in digital spaces (2016, pp. 80f.). In particular, they posit that conceiving of the church, or the kingdom of God, as a network 'can promote flattened rather than hierarchical structures, along with relationships that allow more dynamic interaction rather than being unresponsive and static' (2016, p. 14).

Naturally, the language of 'network', as Campbell and Garner submit, also chimes with Pauline imagery of the body of Christ. The apostle Paul subverted a well-established political metaphor and infused it with a distinctively Christian meaning (Keener, 1993, pp. 478–9), mentioning it in several of his epistles. Imperial Rome used the image of a well-functioning body to pacify the lower classes into accepting their position and respective roles in society (Wright, 2003, pp. 160, 163–4). Paul, on the other hand, adopts the imagery not only to stress the interconnectedness of the parts of the body but also to uphold the dignity of each part (cf. 1 Cor. 12.12–31; Col. 2.19). This provides a rich metaphor of how both diversity and inclusion come together beautifully within the internal logic of the kingdom of God. Furthermore, Christ being the head of the body powerfully communicates that no single part is to exercise dominion over another. With a common point of reference, all stand on an equal footing with one another. Even Christ's headship, in Pauline theology, by no means denotes hierarchical superiority but rather models humble service and sharing of authority. This is consistent with a perspective on inclusion that reorients the relationship between those at the centre and those kept at the margins. This string of 'kingdom values' can be captured in contemporary terms through the imagery of a digital network. It is a conceptualization of inclusion that also concurs with the theological framework for inclusion outlined in Chapter 2. As noted above, this suggests that inclusivity is not achieved through bringing the marginalized and excluded to the centre but through a decentralization in which power is distributed throughout the network.

This theology of inclusion further suggests affinity with Grace Ji-Sun Kim's pneumatology. Kim emphasizes the Spirit – through her omnipresence – as a decentralizing force that neither privileges the centre nor is controlled by it. Conversely, God's Spirit of 'shalom justice' moves towards and among the marginalized as a liberating force (Kim, 2015, pp. 115–26). The Pentecost moment, depicted in Acts 2, is a vivid display of this decentralizing impulse. Having declared that 'all authority in heaven and on earth' has been given to him by his Father (Matt. 28.18 NRSV), Jesus later promises that this power will be dispensed and dispersed across a diverse network of unlikely individuals (Acts 1.8). We subsequently see how in Luke's chronicle the descending power of the Spirit of God serves as an integrating force that includes even those who were excluded in the initial Jewish make-up of the early church: the Samaritans (Acts 8.14–17), the Gentiles (Acts 10.44–47), John the Baptist's disciples (19.1–6) and even Saul, at one time the fiercest enemy of the church (Acts

9.17). As the early church shifted its centre from Jerusalem to Antioch, and later towards various cities of the Roman Empire, Luke effectively describes the development of a new religious movement whose operations closely resemble the fundamental characteristics of digital networks today.

Borrowing again from the language of digital culture, 'the cloud' becomes a metaphor for the kind of charismatic inclusion advocated in this volume. As the Spirit does not reside at a centre and is not contained in one locality, so 'the cloud' through mobile networks is dispersed across the world, empowering, levelling, connecting and reconciling all. As Guillermo Hansen evocatively declares, the church is 'the expression of a swarm without a center, for Christ is mediated by a decentered and decentering network of charismata. The network, the body, is the center' (2012, p. 41).

In this chapter, the image of the digital network is discussed both as a metaphor for inclusion and as a practical means to achieving it. Beyond affording a language to articulate a theology of inclusion, the internet provides the structures within which practices of inclusion can flourish. This is not to idealize digitality: there are some real issues that demand careful consideration, some of which are explored below. Rather, it is to affirm that digital communication technology provides infrastructure that can enable greater inclusion. Arguably, such use of technology is not something novel in the history of the church. Whether through roads built by the Romans, letters handwritten by the apostles, the distribution of pamphlets enabled by the printing press, or digital communication technology in our own age, the church universal has always been sustained by networks enabled by technology. However, while the mechanisms of today's networked society are promising, today's digital culture has to be infused with the supernatural workings of God. As Filipino theologian Melba Maggay notes, 'The dream of a diverse society with a pluralised sense of identity can only happen under the impulse and power of the Spirit of God working in human cultures' (2017, p. 109). What technology makes possible, spirituality will have to render sustainable.

Access or digital divide?

According to the latest annual report by We Are Social – a global agency tracking the growth of digital social media since 2010 – nearly 60 per cent of the world's population is now connected online. Considering the sheer rate and penetration of global digitalization, the report suggests that digital connectivity has today become 'an indispensable part of everyday life for people all over the world' (We Are Social, 2020, slide 3). This connectedness has unequivocally afforded millions of people globally greater access to information, markets and financial transactions, social relations, religious communities and the public sphere.

As global markets increasingly depend upon digital technology, there are examples of how poorer segments of the majority world can benefit from this digitalization. In India, for instance, thousands of computers have been set up in villages across the nation through the e-Choupal initiative by ICT Limited, to give farmers access to real-time market prices of crops, competitively priced quality seeds and useful advice on farming practices (ICT Limited). In many parts of the world, the use of simple mobile devices for monetary exchanges, circumventing the difficult process of setting up bank accounts, has been shown to have a direct correlation with poverty alleviation (see Asongu and Odhiambo, 2019). Studies on the booming gig economies in the majority world suggest this both brings greater autonomy and flexibility, and leads to social isolation and overwork (Wood et al., 2019). During the Covid-19 pandemic, the use of simple mobile phones has permitted millions of small vendors to continue to sell their goods by advertising them on social media platforms such as Facebook. In the Philippines, which has seen one of the longest lockdowns in the world during this time, media outlets have widely reported that people who lost their jobs shifted to selling home-prepared meals online and found ways to take full advantage of opportunities to make a living using digital tools (e.g. Barreiro, 2020).

This accessibility extends to the ways in which digital communication technology has allowed many people living with disabilities (PWDs) to be more integrated in society. Multiple studies univocally affirm that digital access has positively contributed to social interaction, job-seeking, educational opportunities and self-determination among PWDs (Tsatsou, 2020, p. 997). Further, for those with disabilities that affect their physical mobility, church buildings are often inaccessible spaces that create barriers for participation. Even before the lockdowns during the Covid-19 pandemic and the mass migration to online worship, the internet offered a means of religious participation and community for PWDs.

Much can also be said with regard to access to public conversations. Rei Lemuel Crizaldo (2020) argues that the internet has permitted theologians from the majority world not only to access often expensive theological resources from prestigious theological institutions and publishers in the West, but also to disseminate their own work to a wider global audience. As digital platforms emerge as the main arena where theological issues are brought to the table and discussed, the space also opens up for perspectives from Africa, Asia and Latin America. Digital connectivity has created spaces for instant and regular interaction and exchange among and between theological 'superstars' and tech-savvy local theologians, moving today's theological discourse closer to becoming more inclusive and thereby more global. Thus, digital technology enables global interaction that was previously limited to those with resources. There are numerous examples of such interaction, particularly during the Covid-19 pandemic. These include Tearfund's experience with its virtual Global Forum on Migration (September 2020) and Micah Global's virtual Asia Regional Consultation (November 2020), both of which were able to attract delegates from different regions of the world.

Thus, as an inclusive form of communication technology, the internet has provided those previously excluded from public conversations with new platforms through which their voices can be heard. This can further be seen in the use of social media to mobilize campaigners and elevate causes that can lead to socio-political change. Marginalized voices that were either ignored or suppressed, for better or for worse, find a new channel of communication through social media. During the Arab Spring, for example, social media was widely touted as a tool for democratization through which suppressed political voices could be heard. An early academic article on the Arab Spring concludes: 'Social media have become the scaffolding upon which civil society can build' as they provide democratic activists with 'information networks not easily controlled by the state and coordination tools that are already embedded in trusted networks of family and friends' (Howard and Hussain, 2011, p. 48). This continues to be the case with the sustained civil unrest brought about by

JONAS KURLBERG AND REI LEMUEL CRIZALDO

protest movements in many parts of Asia with restive democratic spaces such as Hong Kong, the Philippines and Thailand. In the Philippines, for instance, social media emerged as a ready tool for the marginalized to assert their political choice of an alternative social vision. One of the factors that explains the rise of Rodrigo Duterte on the country's political scene is the legitimate anger released by the 'underclass' in Philippine society (Dressel and Bonoan, 2019). The pivotal role of social media in translating this populist protest into a populist presidency that has gained indefatigable popular support has been well established in sociological literature (Curato, 2017; Arguelles, 2019). Much attention has also been given to how intricate networks of digital architects producing fake news have weaponized social media to manipulate and perpetuate public support for a presidency that later morphed into an authoritarian regime (Ong and Cabanes, 2018). This unfortunate turn of events led Katie Harbath (2018), Facebook's global politics and government outreach director, to label the country 'patient zero' in the global fight against the rise of digital disinformation.

However, there is a need for nuance in any reading of the relationship between digital media, disinformation and a disgruntled but vulnerable digital public. Cabanes (2020) challenged the usual 'transmission paradigm' employed by studies on disinformation in social media and instead offered the use of a 'ritual view of communication' to highlight human agency in the entire process:

> central to the persuasive power of digital disinformation is that they engage with powerful social narratives that people hold onto ... Attending to social narratives allows us to recognise that digital media users actually play a crucial role in crafting, entrenching, and challenging the social views that circulate across the media. At the same time, it makes us cognizant of how disinformation can be pernicious because they tend to amplify people's shared stories, and especially those that diverge from established media narratives. (Cabanes, 2020, pp. 2–3)

Therefore, digital technology can be used as a platform to open up spaces for contested causes of justice, but at the same time it can cause those spaces to shrink further in an era of digital disinformation. The key seems to lie in the increased capacity of social media users to exercise control over their digital engagement and harness its potential to aid causes beneficial to the common good. This moves the discussion towards the issue of digital literacy and competency – to how well people, through the tools of digital technology, are able to identify and also engage the forces that work to perpetuate unequal and unjust social arrangements.

Further, in a world in which socio-economic access is to an increasing extent determined by one's digital connectedness, some scholars have also pointed out that a 'digital divide' persists, excluding poorer and other marginalized groups. This divide is anchored in several interlocking factors: availability of technology, its accessibility for the wider public (including affordability), the degree of literacy and competency required to utilize available technologies well, and, lastly, open spaces that leverage usage of such technologies towards opportunities for social mobility (cf. OECD, 2001, p. 5). In an early treatise, political scientist Pippa Norris explores the consequences of the digital age for global, social and democratic inequalities (2002, pp. 3–4). While submitting that there is cause for cautious optimism, Norris writes: 'Even if the basic digital divide shrinks gradually over time, it is naive to believe that the virtual world can overturn fundamental inequalities of social stratification that are endemic throughout postindustrial societies' (2002, p. 17). Indeed, two decades later, even though the digital divide is still closing and billions more individuals are connected, it still persists, as the Covid-19 pandemic has highlighted.

In a work seeking to identify the global challenges that the church of the future will have to face from a sociological perspective, Jayeel Cornelio highlights the persistent problem of global inequality. In particular, he notes that 'attempts to address inequality through science and technology are welcome but far too often they benefit the affluent first' (2018, p. 43). As more services move online, access becomes all the more pivotal for participation in a growing number of everyday tasks such as food shopping, banking, work, education, social relations, state-sponsored social services and even religious activities. Therefore, those who remain disconnected find themselves potentially pushed even further towards the margins of society. This is a sharp reminder with regard to how digital technologies, if left unchecked, can actually contribute to and reinforce society's present exclusionary character. For Christians and churches for whom liberation theologians' call for the 'preferential option for the poor' (Gutiérrez, 1996) resonates, these matters are deeply important. Inclusion starts with accessibility, and in a digital age access to the internet is pivotal to participation in the social, political, economic and even religious life of contemporary societies.

From leveller to consolidation of power?

Beyond access, any theology of inclusion that works towards reconciliation requires careful reflection on the power dynamics at play in all social relations, whether at the intrapersonal or institutional level. Wherever power dynamics persist, the excluded and powerless are forced to accept the terms of the powerful and cannot engage on their own terms. While to some degree power is necessary to provide structure for social interaction, the basic premise of the gospel, as manifested in the life and death of Christ, is the relinquishing of power for the benefit of others (e.g. Phil. 2.4–8). Returning to the networked pneumatology discussed above, Pentecost becomes the paradigm for the distribution of power from the centre of Jerusalem to the ends of the world by the work of the Spirit. This reconfiguration of power and authority arguably finds a parallel in digital technology and culture. This, since the networked structure of social media affords a means of power distribution.

An illustration of how digital technology positively contributes to such a notion of inclusivity can be found in the increased use of videoconferencing in workplaces during the Covid-19 pandemic. The Zoom meeting has an equalizing effect in several ways. For one, hierarchies are less visibly enforceable on screens in comparison to the often deliberate seating arrangements of the boardroom. But more significantly, digital meetings mean that employees residing far away from head offices are not disadvantaged from the informal interaction that often influences decision-making within organizations. Thus, rather than bringing the periphery to the centre, digital technology, and by extension digital culture, can decentralize existing power structures, levelling the direction of influence. A concrete example can be found in the move of Tearfund's weekly staff prayer meetings to online platforms during the pandemic. Previously held at the global office in south-west London, meetings were broadcast so international staff or those dispersed throughout the UK could watch them, although they had limited opportunities to participate and contribute. The move to digital platforms during the pandemic has permitted a greater number of voices from around the world to be heard and seen, no longer privileging those based in Teddington. Further, speaking at staff prayers from one's home, rather than from the global office, has been normalized, as everyone is working from home during the pandemic. These changes, brought about and enabled by technology, affect interaction between staff members, and have wider ramifications for organizational culture, both online and offline.

Nevertheless, power structures do persist online. We have already discussed new media technologies as powerful publishing platforms. However, the fact that everyone from anywhere can now publish blogs, share a meme or tweet and upload videos does not mean that everyone gets heard. It is true that, through the advent of digital technology, old authorities and hierarchies have been disrupted and dismantled, but new ones are also emerging. Long gone is the era during which Silicon Valley was a haven for geeky computer enthusiasts creating hardware and software in their garages. It is virtually impossible to launch successful mobile phone apps and digital platforms without the backing of wealthy venture capitalists now. Far from early ideals of open source and free sharing, the internet has seen the rise of what Shoshana Zuboff (2019) calls 'surveillance capitalism', in which user data is harvested and sold to marketeers and propagandists who in turn seek to manipulate individuals through micro-targeted ads. The shift towards greater control over our digital lives can also be seen in the move towards monitoring citizens' online activities by state actors (or foreign state actors), often with the good intention of reining in online abuses and misuses. Surveillance technology is already ubiquitous and a normalized aspect of our societal infrastructure. Whether for crime-prevention purposes or to monitor employees' productivity and citizens' political activities, surveillance is clearly a tool of control. In these ways, digital tools are increasingly becoming the instruments of empire-builders, powerful corporations, governments and propagandists.

Applications of digital technology sometimes also have unintended consequences that sustain systemic exclusion and injustice. Over the last few decades, predictive modelling – the use of data analysis to predict future outcomes – has been applied to a number of areas, from healthcare to marketing, to trading, insurance and policing. Some of the applications are clearly laudable; for instance, they allow health services to allocate resources appropriately in order to contain the spread of viruses, or controllers to regulate traffic flows to avert traffic jams. Nevertheless, critical voices point towards the risk of perpetuating and even amplifying existing biases in some applications of this technology. For instance, predictive modelling has been widely used to determine the allocation of policing resources, such as patrolling, in order to prevent crime. However, some of the data used in these analyses is mined from previous police activity. Thus, in the UK where Black men have been over-represented in stop-and-search interventions by the police in the past, this existing racial bias is in turn perpetuated by data-crunching algorithms, leading to further discrimination and inequality (cf. Babuta and Oswald, 2019).

Even within the sphere of online religion, we see this ambiguity regarding digital power dynamics. Pauline Hope Cheong (2012) notes that scholars of digital religion can be largely divided into two camps. On the one hand, there are those who understand the internet as a free space of communication that challenges traditional religious authority, flattening existing hierarchies. Religious leaders are less in control of theological conversations that transpire in online environments where anyone can contribute. When leaders choose to engage on interactive social media platforms, they risk being challenged or spoken back to. Furthermore, the internet is brimming with religious activity that circumvents or ignores traditional religious institutions. These activities are consistent with Grace Davie's thesis that, at least in the West, while large parts of populations are still to some extent 'religious' or 'spiritual', they are less interested in institutional forms of religion; they are 'believing without belonging' (1994). However, while the internet strengthens such trends by providing opportunities for spiritual engagement without submitting to traditional religious authorities, the communal aspect of these activities perhaps suggests a believing with a new kind of belonging.

On the other hand, while reconfiguring and challenging some existing authorities, the internet can also extend the power and authority of traditional institutions who are switched on to the potential of digital communications technology and deliberately harness the potential of social media. Through the sharing of content, churches can further their reach both with members and non-members. Using messaging services such as WhatsApp, clergy can communicate with members throughout the week providing pastoral care and advice. Automation can create powerful organizational tools that make administration more efficient at a lower cost. Further, just as the digital age has given rise to new corporate powerhouses, within the religious sphere new authorities are emerging driven by digital creatives (see Campbell, 2021). The YouVersion Bible app is a good example. Since its launch in 2008, by Life.Church in Oklahoma City, the app has been installed on more than 400 million devices around the world, making it one of the most downloaded apps, in all categories. Featuring the Bible in more than 1,300 languages and hosting hundreds of study guides submitted by individuals and organizations from across the world, YouVersion has made the Bible accessible in ways that the Reformers could hardly have dreamt of. On the other hand, however, backed by a wealthy donor the YouVersion app has achieved near monopoly on digital Bibles, dictating how millions of Christians engage with and read the Bible, not least through its use of persuasive design (see Hutchings, 2017). The priorities of the leadership team behind YouVersion are reflected in the design choices that have been made. For instance, on the assumption that more regular Bible engagement changes the habits of users in positive ways, they have incorporated a 'streak' function – a habit-inducing mechanism that gives users points for every day they read the Bible.

As we have seen, then, digital communication technologies perpetuate both trends of power consolidation and power distribution; access is not sufficient for digital inclusion to flourish. A networked theology of inclusion reminds us that Christ bids us to give power away. Such a notion of inclusion demands deliberate and sustained effort to use the inclusive possibilities of the internet. Clearly, digital tools can be mobilized towards different ends and yet they are not completely neutral. While it is possible to censor people online, it is much more difficult to do so in this very live sphere than it was in bygone ages of mass and print media. The dominant and powerful will continue to exert their power online, but anyone can challenge and speak back at them through the interactive logic of the network.

Localized diversity or global homogeneity?

A final area of investigation in this chapter relates to that of diversity and homogeneity. Inclusion as reconciliation affirms diversity as inherently positive, for reconciliation demands making space for the other. The metaphor of the network suggests a multitude of connected but distinct nodes dispersed across the cyberworld. However, the emergence of the internet is deeply intertwined with the forces of globalization. We now interact with global audiences, join Zoom meetings and webinars with people from across the world, consume the same pop culture on YouTube, and are subjected to the formative functions of devices and the persuasive technologies of digital platforms. Returning to the theme of Pentecost, does the internet allow for the kind of decentralization advanced by the work of the Spirit? Or, conversely, does it perpetuate the homogenizing forces of globalization?

Contrasting the story of Pentecost with the narrative of the Tower of Babel, Maggay describes the latter as a primordial metaphor of humanity's tendency to fall into the drive towards centralization (2017, p. 46). Discussing the issue of social integration amid globalization, she writes:

What does Scripture have to say about uniting diverse peoples? We have seen earlier, in the Tower of Babel project, one way of going about this: unity based on uniformity. A new technology and a common language made possible a large-scale project such as the building of a city with a tower that reaches to the heavens. We see people organizing themselves into a secure, solid society with no need for God. In contrast, we find the event of the Pentecost, a new kind of social integration: unity based on diversity, made possible by an interior experience of spiritual power. The Spirit coming down in tongues of fire enabled communication to the diaspora Jews and other religious people who had come to Jerusalem from every country in the known world. (2017, p. 108)

In other words, the Pentecost moment serves as a paradigm for movements in history that seek to reorient human imagination towards designing a kind of society that recognizes elements of diversity and decentralization as vital to human flourishing.

A good case to consider with regard to the interplay of homogenization and localization is how locally rooted theologians have been exploring the frontiers opened up by digital theology. Much has been said about how contextual theologizing and its more radical cousin, decolonization, will result in the mushrooming of context-specific religious ghettos that neither recognize nor understand each other (cf. Carson, 1984; Tennent, 2007).

INCLUSION IN A NETWORKED SOCIETY

Concerns have been raised that the development of local or indigenized theologies will lead to the further fragmentation of the global Christian community (cf. Vanhoozer, 2006). The proposed alternative is to work in the opposite direction wherein some form of universal faith expression is maintained across the board though 'translated' into the contours of different cultures to facilitate local understanding. But as the missiologist Andrew Walls (1996) reminds us, the gospel has an 'infinite translatability' which will refuse homogenous static formulations.

Between this tension of fragmentation and homogenization in the field of theology, online theologizing permits what Kewster Brewin calls 'a distributed network of knowledge and authority' with 'a capacity to assimilate multiple perspectives' where none has a monopoly on defining truth (2007, pp. 110–11). Digital spaces, as such, allow theologians to explore a diversity of global religious expressions with no clear centre or point of reference, while at the same time remaining connected and thereby enriching each other's theologizing. These kinds of networked communities will operate from an 'open source' model akin to the one being used in the IT industry. Software systems that are 'open source' have a code that is freely available to a huge network of people who will constantly tinker with it, update it and improve it. Systems as such become far more adaptable and flexible as they are open to suit the specific needs and contexts of end-users. Decolonizing theologies can tap into the idea behind the 'open source' model of the IT industry by embarking on an open-ended, sustained and collaborative project of theology-making. Fused with the opportunities for shared virtual spaces afforded by digital technology, the potential of exchanges enriched by the diversity brought by the interface with multiple others can be harnessed well.

A global online gathering organized by NAIITS, a learning community of indigenous people from the First Nations of North America to the Maori of New Zealand in the Pacific region, illustrates the merits of this approach. An event initially constrained by the restrictions of international travel during the Covid-19 pandemic provided an unprecedented opportunity to be a more inclusive international assembly. The gathering demonstrates that while each ethnic grouping has developed its own understanding of the Christian faith and spirituality, as informed by the specificities of culture and tradition, digital technology allows such a diverse group to be in open conversation and fellowship with one another. This is a vivid picture of a *network* of theological thinkers who have nothing to impose upon or claim from any-one, and yet at the same time are open to mutual reciprocity. The result is a glimpse of how, within the body of Christ, celebrating diversity in unity can dovetail nicely with the pursuit of unity in the midst of diversity. Perhaps now more than ever, technology is paving the way for a thoroughly decentralized global Christian-ity, which is not necessarily torn in fragments, here and there, for it is actually flourishing all the more as a closely interconnected community of faith spread across the globe.

While the internet does create the possibility for genuine and deeply transformative encounters between different voices, there are suggestions that social media has also led to filter bubbles and echo chambers that make it difficult to hear the cultural, religious and political other. This is a far cry from the vision to 'give people the power to build community and bring the world closer together' that Mark Zuckerberg (2017) articulated when Facebook hit 2 billion monthly users. It stems from a realization that it is not enough to connect the world – humanity has to be brought closer together. Zuckerberg, in fact, talked of a more inclusive global community: 'The most important thing we at Facebook can do is develop the social infrastructure to give people the power to build a global community that works for all of us.' This is a clear manifesto on how digital technology can reach its greatest positive impact for the common good. By strengthening the social fabric of communities that disintegrated as a result of the weakening of traditional institutions which have knitted people together in the past – for example, churches and social clubs – Facebook was positioning itself as a community-building space in their stead.

Not long after this, however, Facebook was accused of exactly the opposite. As more and more people witnessed a world deeply polarized, the company found itself at the centre of controversies over the acceleration of social divides that turned populations of people against each other. Critics have claimed that, together with other social networking platforms, Facebook has had its share of being weaponized to sow discord and inflict deep divisions in many parts of the world. This is rooted in efforts by actors in the digital sphere to promote a homogenizing narrative that excludes and invalidates the other. The sorry aftermath is a toxic digital landscape marked with filter bubbles and echo chambers spread across a landmine of 'cancel culture'. According to Cass Sunstein, the effects of this are devastating, as 'it seems plain that the Internet is serving for many, as a breeding ground for extremism, precisely because like-minded people are connected with greater ease and frequency with one another, and often without hearing opposing views' (2017, pp. 76–7).

There are those who seek to nuance this debate by pointing to empirical research that suggests that the causal impact of social media on polarization has been exaggerated (e.g. Dubois and Blank, 2018). Interestingly, another study found that the most partisan segments of American societies are also those who are least digitally connected (Boxell et al., 2017). Nevertheless, one still wonders if the biggest and most pervasive social networking platforms have showcased the potential consequences of 'digital networks' failing to confront the toxicities of homogenization and polarization.

It is at this point that the interdependence of technology, human agents and the broader social environment come to the fore. The bigger picture will have us look into the flesh and blood behind the pixels and the digital culture that they inhabit. Surely, agitated 'netizens' in a digital space shaped by 'cancel culture' and an infrastructure of disinformation in a post-truth era will showcase the worst of how digital technology can be used to promote a homogenizing agenda that leads only to further social fragmentation. But there is an equally compelling case to be made for how digital connectivity can also bring out the best in today's global digital landscape. As we have argued, positive outcomes transpire when digital technology is used to affirm plurality and multiplicity within a shared space. In addition, there needs to be an intentionality towards nurturing people's capacity to transcend tolerance and move into a hospitality that refuses hatred and hostility and is instead open to be changed by encounters with the other. From the vantage point of digital theology, social inclusion of this nature can be reinforced by the initial vision of the church as a network of communities wherein the identity of all are celebrated and hospitality is encouraged. In Paul's day, the body was a culturally relevant metaphor. Today, the metaphor that can serve as the icon of this kingdom vision for inclusion is that of a healthy functioning digital network. The perils of the network being 'hacked' by elements with homog-enizing intentions can be checked by emphasizing the contrast between the tower of Babel and the power of the Spirit. It is the decentralizing giving away of power which guarantees that the Spirit of Pentecost prevails.

Conclusion: developing a digital culture of inclusion

We have seen that digital communication tools are multifaceted and have often contradictory outcomes. They have the potential both for access and exclusion, for the distribution of power and consolidation of power, for a global homogeneity and local diversity. It is therefore tempting to deduce that technologies are mere tools that can be employed to different ends. In his list of 'laws' on technology, however, historian Melvin Kranzberg contends that 'technology is neither good nor bad; nor is it neutral' (1986, p. 545). He illustrates this by positing that technological inventions often have a broader social impact than their immediate intended use. He further argues that the effects of technological artefacts are also context specific. This suggests that, while the introduction of technology alters human actions and culture in sometimes unpredictable ways, its impact is conditioned by pre-existing environments or cultures.

Thus, for a networked culture of inclusion to be actualized, there needs to be a deliberate development of a culture of inclusion, for concerted efforts to act upon the God-given human 'agency' or duty to foster a humane civilization. In this case, we have demonstrated that there is a Christian mandate to participate in the creation of digital spaces that stimulate digital cultures of inclusion. In many ways, this requires the same habits and postures of inclusion as in the offline or pre-digital world. We have highlighted a few of these throughout the chapter, including deliberately inviting a plurality of voices to the table, providing greater access to (digital) goods and services for those living in poverty, and making concrete efforts towards decentralization. Building a culture of inclusion is an ongoing task that demands collaboration between the different nodes in the network. It is a participatory, open-source project created by multiple actors across the world, fuelled by the movement of the Spirit, of which the end result cannot be predicted at the outset.

The central argument in this chapter is that digital technology through its networking propensity does open up new possibilities for practices of inclusion. The networked society, fuelled by digital communication technology, has an organic capacity to strengthen cultures and practices of inclusion. Just as the structures of a patriarchal society perpetuate and sustain gender inequalities, so the design of the network creates a predisposition through which inclusionary practices can flourish. The digital network is both a metaphor that enables a theologically informed vision of inclusion and the means by which such inclusion can be realized.

Bibliography

Abbate, J., 1999, *Inventing the Internet*, Cambridge: MIT Press.

Arguelles, C., 2019, '"We are Rodrigo Duterte": Dimensions of the Philippine populist publics' vote', *Asian Politics and Policy* 11(3), pp. 417–37.

Asongu, S. A. and N. M. Odhiambo, 2019, 'Mobile Banking Usage, Quality of Growth, Inequality and Poverty in Developing Countries', *Information Development* 35(2), pp. 303–18.

Babuta, A. and M. Oswald, 2019, 'Data Analytics and Algorithmic Bias in Policing' on RUSI website, https://rusi.org/publication/briefing-papers/data-analytics-and-algorithmic-bias-policing, accessed 26.11.2020.

Barreiro, Jr., V., 2020, 'Lifeline during COVID-19: How Facebook buy and sell groups meet people's needs', www.rappler.com/technology/features/how-facebook-buy-sell-groups-meet-people-needs, accessed 17.11.2020.

Boxell, L., M. Gentzkow and J. M. Shapiro, 2017, 'Greater Internet Use Is Not Associated with Faster Growth in Political Polarization among Us Demographic Groups', *Proceedings of the National Academy of Sciences* 114(40), pp. 10612–17.

Brewin, K., 2007, *Signs of Emergence: A vision for church that is organic/networked/decentralized/bottom-up/always evolving*, Grand Rapids, MI: Baker Books.

Cabanes, J. V., 2020, 'Digital Disinformation and the Imaginative Dimension of Communication', *Journalism and Mass Communication Quarterly* 97(2), pp. 435–52.

Campbell, H., 2021, *Digital Creatives and the Rethinking of Religious Authority*, Abingdon: Routledge.

Campbell, H. and S. Garner, 2016, *Networked Theology: Negotiating faith in digital culture*, Grand Rapids, MI: Baker Academic.

Carson, D. A., 1984, 'Reflections on Contextualization: A critical appraisal of Daniel Von Allmen's birth of theology', *East African Journal of Evangelical Theology* 3(1), pp. 16–59.

Castells, M., 2010, *The Rise of the Network Society*, Chichester: Blackwell.

Chow, A. and J. Kurlberg, 2020, 'Two or Three Gathered Online: Asian and European responses to COVID-19 and the digital church', *Studies in World Christianity* 26(3).

Cornelio, J., 2018, 'The Global Challenges of the Church of the Future', *Concilium: International Journal of Theology* 14, pp. 37–46.

Crizaldo, R. L., 2020, 'Digital Theology: Practicing local theology in an age of global technology', in Jonas Kurlberg and Peter M. Phillips (eds), *Missio Dei in a Digital Age*, London: SCM Press.

Curato, N., 2017, *A Duterte Reader: Critical essays on Rodrigo Duterte's early presidency*, Ithaca, NY: Cornell University Press.

Davie, G., 1994, *Religion in Britain since 1945: Believing without belonging*, Oxford: Blackwell.

Dressel, B. and C. R. Bonoan, 2019, 'Southeast Asia's Troubling Elections: Duterte versus the rule of law', *Journal of Democracy* 30(4), pp. 134–48.

Dubois, E. and G. Blank, 2018, 'The Echo Chamber is Overstated: The moderating effect of political interest and diverse media', *Information, Communication & Society* 21(5), pp. 729–45.

Gutiérrez, G., 1996, 'Preferential Option for the Poor', in J. B. Nickoloff (ed.), *Gustavo Gutiérrez: Essential writings*, Minneapolis, MN: Fortress Press, pp. 144–6.

Handley MacMath, T., 2016, 'Interview: Fr Benigno Beltran SVD, "asset-based developer", author', *Church Times*, 19 August, www.churchtimes.co.uk/articles/2016/19-august/features/interviews/interview-fr-benigno-beltran-svd-asset-based-developer-author, accessed 11.05.2020.

Hansen, G., 2012, 'The Networking of Differences that Makes a Difference: Theology and the unity of the church', *Dialog: A Journal of Theology* 51(1), pp. 31–42.

Harbath, K., 2018, '360/OS: On Protecting Election Integrity', *YouTube*, uploaded by Rappler, 23 June 2018, www.youtube.com/watch?v=dJ1wcpsOtS4, accessed 25.11.2020.

Hine, C., 2015, *Ethnography for the Internet: Embedded, embodied and everyday*, London: Bloomsbury Academic.

Hope Cheong, P., 2012, 'Authority', in H. Campbell (ed.), *Digital Religion: Understanding religious practice in new media worlds*, London and New York: Routledge.

Horsley, R., 1997, *Paul and Empire: Religion and power in Roman imperial society*, Harrisburg, PA: Trinity Press International.

Howard, P. N. and M. Hussain, 2011, 'The Upheavals in Egypt and Tunisia: The role of social media', *Journal of Democracy* 22, pp. 35–48.

Hutchings, T., 2017, 'Design and the Digital Bible: Persuasive technology and religious reading', *Journal of Contemporary Religion* 32(2).

ICT Limited, n.d., 'E-Choupal', www.itcportal.com/businesses/agri-business/e-choupal.aspx, accessed 11.05.2020.

Keener, C., 1993, *The IVP Bible Background Commentary: New Testament*, Downers Grove, IL: InterVarsity Press.

Kim, G. J., 2015, *Embracing the Other: The transformative Spirit of love*, Grand Rapids, MI: Eerdmans.

Kranzberg, M., 1986, 'Technology and History: "Kranzberg's Laws"', *Technology and Culture* 27(3), pp. 544–60.

Maggay, M., 2017, *Global Kingdom, Global People: Living faithfully in a multicultural world*, Carlisle: Langham Global Library.

Norris, P., 2002, *Digital Divide: Civic engagement, information poverty, and the internet worldwide*, Cambridge: Cambridge University Press.

OECD, 2001, 'Understanding the Digital Divide', Paris: OECD.

Ong, J. C. and J. V. Cabanes, 2018, *Architects of Networked Disinformation: Behind the scenes of troll accounts and fake news production in the Philippines*, Leeds: University of Leeds.

Sunstein, C. R., 2017, *#Republic: Divided democracy in the age of social media*, Princeton, NJ: Princeton University Press.

Tennent, T., 2007, *Theology in the Context of World Christianity: How the global church is influencing the way we think about and discuss theology*, Grand Rapids, MI: Zondervan.

Tsatsou, P., 2020, 'Is Digital Inclusion Fighting Disability Stigma? Opportunities, barriers, and recommendations', *Disability & Society* 39(9), pp. 995–1010.

Vanhoozer, K., 2006, 'One Rule to Rule Them All', in Craig Ott and Harold Netland (eds), *Globalizing Theology: Belief and practice in an era of world Christianity*, Grand Rapids, MI: Baker Academic.

Walls, A., 1996, *The Missionary Movement in Christian History*, New York: Orbis Books.

We Are Social, 2020, *Digital 2020: Global digital overview*, https://wearesocial.com/digital-2020, accessed 20.10.2020.

Wood, A. J., M. Graham, V. Lehdonvirta and I. Hjorth, 2019, 'Good Gig, Bad Gig: Autonomy and algorithmic control in the global gig economy', *Work, Employment and Society* 33(1), pp. 56–75.

Wright, N. T., 2003, *Paul for Everyone: I Corinthians*, London: SPCK.

Zuboff, S., 2019, *The Age of Surveillance Capitalism: The fight for a human future at the new frontier of power*, London: Profile Books.

Zuckerberg, M., 2017, 'Bringing the World Closer Together', www.facebook.com/notes/393134628500376, accessed 26.11.2020.

8

Interrogating Gender, Faith and Masculinities: Tearfund's Transforming Masculinities Approach

PRABU DEEPAN AND NINA KURLBERG

Introduction

The world we live in is broken. Inequality within human relationships has led to systems and structures that perpetuate inequality within our societies, and this systemic injustice disproportionately affects women, girls and others who are marginalized and disenfranchised. This deeply rooted gender inequality and injustice finds expression in sexual and gender-based violence (SGBV) which has reached epidemic proportions. In fact, SGBV affects approximately one in three women in their lifetime according to the World Health Organization (WHO, 2019). As the WHO also highlights, SGBV 'has devastating costs and consequences on individuals, communities and societies. It is a major public health problem and a violation of human rights' (Peterman et al., 2019, n.p.). In communities where there are high levels of fragility and conflict, women and girls are extremely vulnerable to SGBV (Storkey, 2015).

Although it disproportionately affects women and girls, it is important to note that men and boys are often also affected by SGBV and can experience it directly themselves. Further, and of particular relevance for this chapter, while all women are at risk of SGBV, irrespective of social status, ethnicity or age, poverty increases this risk. Women living in poverty tend to have limited access to the resources and information that could protect them and their right to life. Moreover, they are often in contexts where there are high levels of cultural, social and legal impunity (see, for example, Lesjane, 2017). UN Women explains it in this way:

When women are poor, their rights are not protected. They face obstacles that may be extraordinarily difficult to overcome … They are likely to be the last to eat, the ones least likely to access healthcare, and routinely trapped in time-consuming, unpaid domestic tasks. They have more limited options to work or build businesses. Adequate education may lie out of reach. Some end up forced into sexual exploitation as part of a basic struggle to survive. And while women at large have not yet achieved an equal political voice, women in poverty face extra marginalization. (UN Women, 2015, n.p.)

This chapter focuses on Tearfund's Transforming Masculinities approach, developed in 2013. The approach seeks to challenge inequalities in power and status that lead to SGBV, by addressing gender inequality within relationships, social norms, systems and structures, and bringing to light harmful gender norms and masculinities. It does this by working with and within faith communities (Deepan, 2017). At the core of the programme's theology of gender is the belief that all humans are created equal and in the image of the triune God. Participation in God's redemptive work in the world implies a commitment to gender justice, to the dismantling of systems that perpetuate inequality, and to the restoration of all human relationships (Tearfund, 2021; see also Storkey, 2015). While, historically, the Transforming Masculinities programme has worked with Christian communities, in recent years it has expanded to include other faith communities, at their request after they have witnessed the approach in action. Thus, in its broadest sense the programme can be described as working towards gender justice through a gender transformative model founded on the principles and sacred texts of the world faiths that value the well-being and equality of all human beings (Deepan, 2017).

After briefly outlining key terms and concepts, the first section seeks to position the chapter in relation to recent academic literature on the topic, highlighting the main lines of debate and inquiry that intersect with Tearfund's work in this area. The second section then introduces the Transforming Masculinities approach, focusing particularly on its emergence and development. Finally, some of the key points of learning from the programme are highlighted with reference to findings from the various pieces of research commissioned by Tearfund over the past decade. This section also notes the ways in which the programme relates to the current academic debates noted earlier. The chapter speaks into one of the main lines of thought underlying the book, which is that for inclusion to be possible as far as human relationships are concerned, justice is required. An essential component of gender justice is systemic or structural change. The Transforming Masculinities programme seeks to achieve this change by creating spaces within communities for conceptions of masculinity and gender relations to be reimagined.

Defining 'masculinities'

Before exploring the literature of relevance to the Transforming Masculinities work, it is important to first outline what is meant by 'masculinities'. Masculinities encompass 'the characteristics that define what it means to be a man or to be masculine' (Smith, 2017, p. 1109). As stated in Tearfund's Transforming Masculinities 'toolkit':

> This term conveys the fact that there are many socially constructed ways of being a man and that these can change over time and from place to place. 'Masculinities' refers to perceived notions and ideals about how men should or are expected to behave in a given setting. Masculinity and femininity are relational concepts; they only have meaning in relation to each other. The word 'masculinities' (plural) is used as opposed to 'masculinity' (singular) to emphasise that different forms of masculinities exist – shaped by class, ethnicity, race, culture and sexual orientation. Also, within masculinities, there are hierarchies: some are dominant or 'hegemonic' while others are subordinated, marginalised or complicit. Masculinities are normative practices, structured and shaped by gender relations. They are inherently historical and their making and remaking is a political process affecting the balance of interests in society and the direction of social change. (Deepan, 2017, p. 10)

Since masculinities are therefore expressions of a combination of 'cultural expectations, historical needs, and communal standards', at any point in time, multiple types of masculinities are 'being cultivated and endorsed ... each with an ideology, norm, and script for men who endorse these ideals' (Ming Liu, 2017, p. 1112). As such, masculinities are also fluid and vary across time and space as they adapt and adjust to the cultural codes and expectations in each circumstance. All of us play a role in shaping masculinities, accepting societal narratives by living them out. It is very difficult to perform masculinity outside of expectations; it could have negative consequences, such as the loss of important relationships or social stigma. Yet these narratives regarding masculinity have consequences for society, men included:

> Scripts and ideologies may seem innocuous, yet when men endorse these scripts and attempt to fulfill the expectations, the consequence for men is largely negative. Rather than being helpful and fulfilling for many men, these ideologies and scripts tend to be mostly restricting and confining. Research, for instance, shows that boys want to show emotions and are full of feelings, but the scripts and ideologies for boys and men are just the opposite: be emotionless, stoic, and restrained. Boys learn quickly via bullying, teasing, or physical abuse that the expression of emotions is considered within their culture to be 'feminine' and therefore to be avoided. (Ming Liu, 2017, p. 1112)

Among the most prevalent ideas and behaviours that boys are being socialized into are 'avoiding weakness, limiting the range of emotions, instilling the importance of power and competition, and maintaining control at all cost' (Smith, 2017, p. 1110). Given the prevalence of violence and abuse within our societies, it is becoming increasingly evident that there is a need for dominant conceptions of masculinity within our societies to be reimagined, for the sake of all (Anderson, 2019).

SGBV within the existing literature: three important discussions

In this section, several strands of work from within the existing literature are briefly introduced. This is not an exhaustive review of every relevant piece of work, but instead points to key publications and debates that intersect with Tearfund's work in this area and are of significance for the argument developed through the chapter. The focus here is therefore primarily on the Development Studies literature, but within this broader academic field,

the primary areas of interest are gender, religion and SGBV –
which intersects with the literature on HIV and AIDS – as well
as the body of work on masculinities and, in particular, the work
on Conflict Studies within this.

More specifically, there are three main threads and debates
within the existing literature that are of particular relevance to
Tearfund's Transforming Masculinities approach: work that
explores the advantages and disadvantages of religion in relation
to SGBV; work that emphasizes the need to consider systemic
factors in addition to focusing on behavioural change at the individual level; and work that highlights the risk of perpetuating
a colonizing agenda by enforcing Western discourses on gender
norms in other contexts.

Religion: source of stigma or transformation?

The connection between SGBV and the transmission of HIV is
well documented (Haddad, 2002; Agardh et al., 2007; Chitando
and Chirongoma, 2012; Parpart, 2015). As noted by Agardh et
al., for example, forced sex, among other things, enables 'transmission of sexually transmitted infections including HIV. Sexual
violence may cause damage to vaginal tissues and also thereby
facilitate infection. Men hoping to avoid infection by sex with
younger, possibly virgin [females], might be already HIV positive
and infect the women' (Agardh et al., 2007, pp. 12–13). Due to
its connection with HIV, the vast majority of the work on SGBV
within the Development Studies literature to date has focused
on Africa. The significance of religion in this context cannot be
understated (see, for example, van Klinken and Chitando, 2015,
p. 130; Palm et al., 2019, p. 3). Yet in relation to SGBV, faith
groups and their leaders have not always been a positive force.
In her work on HIV in Africa, Beverley Haddad draws attention
to the role of faith-based organizations, highlighting the silence
of the church on inequality between men and women, which she
believes is a factor causing the 'death of women and children
through the HIV and AIDS pandemic' (Haddad, 2002, p. 93).
Haddad also notes that anecdotal evidence points towards FBOs
fuelling stigma and discrimination in relation to HIV and AIDS
(Haddad, 2006, pp. 81–2).

Also writing within the context of Africa, Ezra Chitando and
Sophie Chirongoma focus on the role of masculinities. They use

the concept of 'redemptive masculinities' as a means of characterizing and identifying 'masculinities that are life-giving in a world reeling from the effects of violence and the AIDS pandemic' (Chitando and Chirongoma, 2012, p. 1). They highlight the role that religion has played, and can play, in shaping masculinities and note the need to draw on 'religio-cultural resources' in this endeavour. In their view, the academic literature on sub-Saharan Africa tends to ignore the potential of such resources in transforming masculinities – something they believe needs to be rectified (Chitando and Chirongoma, 2012, p. 7).[1] Yet they also acknowledge that religion is a 'double-edged sword' in this regard: although it has the ability to transform masculinities, it can also endorse and perpetuate masculinities that cause harm (Chitando and Chirongoma, 2012, p. 17; see also van Klinken and Chitando, 2015, p. 130).

According to Tamsin Bradley and Nida Karmani, who write on Hinduism in the context of India, although 'religion may not sanction violence against women directly it does so covertly by rigidly projecting a narrow and ultimately misogynistic system' (Bradley and Karmani, 2015, p. 218). This is why it is important to engage with the sacred texts of the world faiths, which is something Chitando and Chirongoma argue for: it is 'crucial to engage sacred texts in deconstructing harmful masculinities and generating life-giving masculinities' (Chitando and Chirongoma, 2012, p. 17). Also on the theme of sacred texts, research carried out by Tearfund in the African Great Lakes region illustrates the interplay between these texts, culture and norms, and more specifically, how Scriptures can be used to reinforce and support harmful cultural and gender norms (Deepan and Loots, 2019).

The role of religion is also a prominent theme within the literature on gender and development, again in terms of its potential for both harm and transformation. However, positions here vary widely and tend to lack nuance: some take a largely negative view and others place greater emphasis on its positive aspects (see Tadros, 2010). With reference to debates about whether and to what extent faith-based development initiatives are more conservative than secular development initiatives, Elena Fiddian-Qasmiyeh (2015) notes the need to challenge 'assumptions': it is not tenable to assume, for example, that either are 'a priori "conservative" or "liberal" with regards to gender roles and relations', and therefore critical analysis is needed whose purpose must be 'to overcome the diverse hierarchies and structures of oppression which underpin the development industry as a whole', whichever organizations and initiatives they exist within (Fiddian-Qasmiyeh, 2015, p. 561). She writes:

> It is clear that more evidence is needed to assess whether *assumptions* held by secular actors about local faith communities [LFCs] and national and international FBOs can or cannot be maintained, and to what extent. These include *beliefs* that FBOs are *automatically* more 'conservative' and 'patriarchal' than their secular counterparts; that LFCs and faith leaders will *necessarily* hinder the participation of women and girls as decision-makers, as aid and service providers and as beneficiaries alike; and that FBOs will *undoubtedly* refuse to engage with individuals and social groups who do not comply with norms regarding gender and sexuality. (2015, p. 566, italics original)

Structural as well as individual-level change

While interventions addressing masculinities tend to focus at the level of individual behaviour, Chris Dolan notes that in order to bring change, there is a need to focus on the broader political context and to challenge 'the social and political forces that shape those behaviours' (Dolan, 2011, pp. 132–3). This sentiment is echoed by Jane Parpart who explains that there are 'many development projects confronting gender-based violence by addressing the role of masculinity as it impacts and shapes men on an individual psychological level, but broader structural practices also need to be considered' (Parpart, 2015, p. 19).

Also important to highlight in this regard is the role women play in shaping masculinities. This is not only about women and girls internalizing harmful gender norms, but also about the ways in which they maintain such norms through their interactions with men and boys. As Adriaan van Klinken and Ezra Chitando write, it is crucial to 'investigate the values and understandings of masculinity that (grand)mothers inculcate in boys from very early on, and to examine women's perception of masculinity and their role in (re)shaping male behaviour more broadly' (van Klinken and Chitando, 2015, p. 135). Nevertheless, they also add a word of caution, that the blame for harmful masculinities should not be placed on women. The point they want to emphasize is, rather, that due recognition should be given to the multiplicity of factors that help shape masculinity.[2]

A colonizing agenda?

The risk of perpetuating colonizing discourses is often mentioned within the literature. Van Klinken and Chitando highlight this as one of the potential dangers of programmes aimed at 'transformative masculinities' within Africa. They question the extent to which such programmes are 'informed by local issues and concerns' and ask: 'To what extent do such programmes, perhaps even subconsciously, perpetuate a colonial and colonising agenda that stereotypes African men as dangerous, backward and unproductive? Are there indigenous resources for the transformation of masculinities?' (van Klinken and Chitando, 2015, p. 134). In their view, the challenge remains of how to advocate for 'more responsible masculinities, without slipping into colonising discourses' (van Klinken and Chitando, 2015, p. 128).

In a similar vein, Charlotte Mertens and Henri Myrttinen emphasize the need to remember 'the colonial trajectory' when considering 'how contemporary interventions regulate gender norms and roles, no longer through coercion but through more bureaucratic practices such as workshops, trainings and programs' (Mertens and Myrttinen, 2019, p. 434). Their concern is that programmes can push Western norms regarding both gender and individual agency on participants, without paying attention to the societal constraints – both material and structural – of the contexts in which they are situated (Mertens and Myrttinen, 2019). Writing specifically in relation to Women, Peace and Security policies, Hannah Wright highlights the importance of challenging gender norms 'not only among marginalized communities but – perhaps especially – among those with race, class, and other privileges, and not only in "conflict-affected" contexts but also in economically and militarily powerful states, including among policymakers themselves' (Wright, 2020, p. 667). She sees this as one way in which the reproduction of 'colonial logics' in this context can be avoided.

The Transforming Masculinities programme: emergence and development

Tearfund's work in the area of SGBV emerged from its HIV and AIDS work in Africa that began in the early 2000s and was led by Veena O'Sullivan. This work centred on attitudinal and behavioural change within evangelical churches. In *Tearfund and the Quest for Faith-Based Development*, Dena Freeman explains why this was so important:

> The predominant view of the evangelical churches in Africa at that time was that HIV and AIDS was a problem that was 'out there' and not part of the church. They held conservative attitudes towards sex and towards gender and believed that HIV was associated with promiscuity and immorality; thus they refused to acknowledge it could be a problem within the Christian community. In many cases religious leaders were central in stigmatising and ignoring people living with HIV, and in some cases even punishing them (Marshall and Taylor, 2006). (Freeman, 2019, p. 94)

At the heart of Tearfund's approach to HIV and AIDS within churches, then, was the desire for the church to move 'from being part of the problem to becoming part of the solution' (Freeman, 2019, p. 123; see also Marshall and Taylor, 2006). Tearfund therefore started a pilot project to address HIV and AIDS that involved working with local organizations and churches. In many ways, the approach taken laid the groundwork for the Transforming Masculinities programme. It was holistic, not only discussing safe and healthy sex but also building relationship and parenting skills; biblically rooted – enabling couples to reflect on Scripture together, particularly those passages often used to perpetuate gender inequality – led by local communities, and situated within the local church and its structures (Freeman, 2019, p. 124).

Local partner organizations often held different theological positions on some matters. Yet, embedding activities within church structures and creating space within local churches for discussion on issues that might previously have been considered taboo allowed harmful beliefs and behaviours to come to light. One of the key learnings from the programme was that in order for behaviour to be transformed, it is essential to engage with people's beliefs – even those that are tacit. It is also important that this process is carried out via local churches rather than those external to communities (Freeman, 2019, p. 124).

Nevertheless, it became clear as work in this area progressed that underlying the issue of HIV was that of violence against women, a phenomenon that was largely hidden despite its prevalence. Research was therefore commissioned to gain deeper understanding of SGBV in three countries in Africa – Rwanda, Liberia and the Democratic Republic of Congo (DRC) – and more specifically, 'the current and potential role of the church within communities affected by sexual violence and conflict' (le Roux, 2011, p. 5). The findings from this research were published in the report *Silent No More* (le Roux, 2011). As well as highlighting the extent of SGBV in Africa, the research found that the church was not the safe space that many women wished it to be, with church leaders often either ignoring SGBV or compounding the stigma of those affected. In spite of this, however, the research found that people in all three countries desired a church-based response (le Roux, 2011, p. 8). Thus, the research highlighted a critical area of need: engagement with faith leaders.

The role that faith leaders play in societies such as these cannot be underestimated. As Selina Palm explains, they 'influence attitudes and cultural and social norms, including notions of masculinity, femininity and gender roles as they relate to [violence against women and girls (VAWG). They are key opinion leaders present over the long term in remote, conflict-affected communities and are often turned to in time of distress, including by survivors needing support' (Palm et al., 2019, p. 3). During the research for the *Silent No More* report, one survivor from the DRC stated: 'Although my church has never done anything for me, I still feel welcome in church. It is a positive space for me' (le Roux, 2011).

Tearfund's SGBV work, then, arose in response to a clearly identified need. Yet it soon became clear that men and boys needed to be engaged in the work as well. This was a point raised by survivors, but there was also a growing realization that without addressing broader gender dynamics and harmful expressions of masculinity that justify violence, SGBV would never be eradicated. Thus, the Transforming Masculinities programme was established in 2013 and began by engaging men, boys and faith leaders in a series of pilot workshops. As the work progressed, and as the findings from formative research conducted during the initial stages of the work began to emerge, it became evident that it was not possible to talk about men and masculinities, or even gender and masculinities, only with men and boys. It was apparent that men and boys were not the only norm-holders within society: women and girls both internalized norms and carried expectations based on these norms, which affected both the way women interacted with men and how they saw themselves in comparison to men (Deepan, 2014). Thus, the patriarchal gate-keepers in communities were both women and men.

Another realization that emerged in the early stages of the work was that a more structured approach was needed, encompassing different layers of intervention. For example, there was a need to facilitate dialogues on a weekly basis, with the aim that these would outlast the projects and become ongoing spaces for interaction and discussion within places of worship. Based on the pilots and various learnings from 2013 to early 2015, Tearfund designed the Transforming Masculinities approach to have three main components. First, national, provincial and community-level faith leaders attend workshops that use biblical texts to engage and equip them to provide leadership and support for the process. The aim of this first stage is to walk with faith leaders as they also embark on a journey to understand how harmful norms influence and shape their behaviours, their theological understanding, and therefore their teaching. In the second stage of the process, these leaders identify community members – men and women – to be trained as 'Gender Champions' to facilitate small-group discussions, or 'community dialogues'. Ground rules for these dialogues are established at the outset so that the space is protected and women feel safe. Finally, 'small groups of men and women meet weekly in their communities for six weeks for discussion led by Gender Champions. Weeks 1–5 are conducted in single sex groups and Week 6 in combined sex groups' (Deepan, 2017).

Thus, the Transforming Masculinities approach enables participants and their communities to embark on a journey of exploration and dialogue within a safe space, affording people the opportunity to examine their own biases, cultural scripts and prejudices in order to reimagine masculinity in their context. It is therefore these spaces created through the programme that enable the possibility for transformation. In essence, Transforming Masculinities is a gender transformative approach that explores harmful gender norms that affect both men and women, although women disproportionately. It challenges unequal values, power and status as part of a process to deconstruct unjust societal systems, structures and practices. In the early stages of the programme, men would frequently ask how they could be something they had never seen modelled to them before. Therefore, Jesus is used as the model in discussions. For example, participants – both men and women – are encouraged to explore what kind of person Jesus was, what kind of leader he was, and how he engaged with people, particularly those considered to be vulnerable (Deepan, 2017, pp. 56–7; Deepan, 2018, p. 15). In this way, the programme enables masculinity to be reimagined using the stories of Jesus Christ.

Finally, it is also important to mention the role that theology plays in the process. It is essential to engage with the Scriptures and participants' theological understanding, since texts are often interpreted and used to support the harmful norms and practices that result in SGBV. This is even the case when it comes to mixed-faith communities. For example, an Islamic version of the programme is now in use in Nigeria, since communities recognized the need to address SGBV and saw the value of the approach. As Prabu Deepan notes:

> The scriptures in the curriculum are primarily from the Bible, but in mixed faith communities we also have suggestions for similar Qur'anic verses that facilitators can suggest to the groups. In these situations the facilitators are advised to use inclusive language – they would talk about 'holy texts' instead of 'scripture', 'places of worship' instead of 'churches', and so on. When it's time to reflect on the texts they would say, 'This is what the Bible says, and we would like Islamic participants to share verses from the Qur'an or hadith that resonate with this message.' If no-one comes forward, then we say, 'This is what previous participants have shared with us, what do you think?' Then we read the texts and reflect together. (As quoted in Freeman, 2019, p. 125)

Key learning to date

In this final section, key learning from the Transforming Masculinities approach to date is explored, focusing in particular on the ways in which this relates to the three debates within the existing literature highlighted earlier. We draw both on the experiences Tearfund has gained through running the programme, as well as the findings of several pieces of research that have been commissioned since the work began in 2013. This research includes a series of studies carried out in Burundi, the Central African Republic (CAR), DRC, Liberia, Nigeria and Rwanda from 2013 to 2017, which was commissioned to explore existing social norms around gender, particularly masculinities, as well as attitudes towards and understandings of SGBV.

As noted in the first section of this chapter, communities' religious resources have the potential to be a source of harm or transformation, and therefore the importance of engaging with faith leaders and communities cannot be underestimated. A piece of research Tearfund commissioned in CAR in 2015 highlights the harm that faith leaders can cause (Lusey, 2016). Tearfund's work in CAR began in 2013, and focused on meeting emergency needs in response to the civil war. SGBV was prevalent in the country before, but increased as a result of the conflict, with rape frequently used as a weapon of war. In April and May 2015, research was carried out among survivors of sexual violence to better understand their experiences and what a 'survivor-centric' response might look like. Researchers spoke with 151 survivors, most of whom identified as belonging to a religion (Lusey, 2016, p. 13).

It was evident that most participants felt faith leaders were a source of harm rather than transformation, 'contributing to rigid norms of masculinities, grounded on selective reading and interpretation of sacred texts' (Lusey, 2016, p. 8). The predominant societal narratives regarding masculinity – often endorsed by faith teaching – were for the most part rooted in harmful conceptions of manhood and this was thought to be one of the key factors underlying and maintaining the prevalence of gender inequality and SGBV in CAR.[3] In spite of this, however, there were signs of hope as some participants did evidence more positive forms of masculinities, including 'caring, non-violent and responsible masculinities, which equated men with job holders and thus better providers for their families' (Lusey, 2016, p. 8). Nevertheless, it became clear that there was a need for faith leaders to challenge rather than uphold harmful narratives regarding masculinity and, in this way, become a source of transformation. The role of faith leaders in contexts such as CAR is particularly important since, 'in such a context of ongoing conflict and displacement where the state provision of services breaks down, faith groups remain' (Lusey, 2016, p. 13).

Two reports based on a project conducted in the DRC in 2015–17 demonstrate the potential for faith leaders to move from being a source of harm to transformation (le Roux et al., 2020; Palm et al., 2019). Over a period of 24 months, Tearfund collaborated with a Congolese partner organization, HEAL Africa, to work in 15 conflict-affected villages in Ituri province in the DRC. The baseline survey carried out at the outset in the 15 villages showed that approximately 69 per cent of women were subject to intimate partner violence (IPV) and 21 per cent to non-partner sexual violence (NPSV). Over 95 per cent of those surveyed identified as belonging to a religion, and for 83 per cent of these people their faith was important or very important. The focus of the project was therefore on first working with faith leaders, accompanying them 'on a journey of awareness and change', and then looking to those within their faith groups and wider communities (Palm et al., 2019, p. 4).

As Palm and colleagues explain, the purpose of the project was 'to reduce VAWG and facilitate sustained changes in social norms related to VAWG, so that violence becomes unacceptable, survivors are supported and men and women form gender-equitable, violence-free relationships' (Palm et al., 2019, p. 5). Over the 24-month period during which the programme was running, the research shows a reduction in harmful beliefs as well as in the incidence of violence. Further, there was an increase in willingness to challenge violence. It is worth highlighting some of the results from the research (Palm et al., 2019, p. 9):

- Among men, self-reported perpetration reduced from 68 per cent to 24 per cent.
- Among women, reported IPV reduced from 69 per cent to 29 per cent.
- NPSV reported by women reduced from 21 per cent to 4 per cent.
- Belief that men are superior to women has dropped from 90 per cent to 70 per cent.
- Belief that God created men and women equal increased by 20 per cent among men.
- Justification of physical violence dropped from 71 per cent to 55 per cent among men.

- Belief that women are not allowed to refuse sex dropped from 80 per cent to 55 per cent among men.
- Women's belief that disobedience of wives justified violence dropped from 53 per cent to 38 per cent.
- By endline, 40 per cent of IPV survivors sought assistance from faith leaders – an increase from 2 per cent.
- 74 per cent of endline respondents felt their faith institutions supported survivors.
- Faith leaders are effective change agents and have become [the] primary group approached by survivors for support.

Thus the research demonstrates how working with churches and faith leaders can be an effective way of challenging harmful social and gender norms that perpetuate inequality, and the forces and structures that shape behaviours. With regard to Dolan's and Parpart's arguments noted earlier, this is also an example of structural change, which is essential if gender equality is to be achieved. There are several factors that play a role in enabling faith leaders to become a positive force within their communities. Change is not a linear process – indeed, it is often messy – but the research has shown that what is important is to create spaces where it can occur, and also to accompany people on the journey of change.

There is a need to build common theological understanding among faith leaders, and in light of the interplay between theology, culture and norms, also to provide them with the time and space for deconstruction and reconstruction. Discussions often focus on the practical application of Scriptures, and this is one of the values of the approach: it provides spaces in which the application of Scripture can be understood, examined and reimagined. It is not possible to change or transform years of knowledge and conceptualization around gender and masculinities through one workshop or over a few weeks: this is a lifelong process. The Transforming Masculinities approach is about enabling people – both faith leaders and communities – to embark on the journey.

Another point of learning is that although violence against men exists, and it is important to create spaces for men to acknowledge, seek support and heal, this must be done without co-opting the experiences of women. It is important to acknowledge that women are systemically discriminated against, and experience violence simply because they are women, and therefore it is important to address power and unequal systems. The

Transforming Masculinities process is not about maintaining the status quo or teaching people how to use their power well: it is about dismantling unequal systems.

Finally, while there is a need to be conscious of the risk of perpetuating colonizing discourses and approaches, the Transforming Masculinities programme has been designed to guard against this. For example, rather than imposing norms on communities, discussion spaces are created where existing norms can be challenged and reimagined, with local faith leaders leading the process (Deepan, 2017). This is also evident in the fact that the approach has been adopted across multiple contexts globally, including among other faith communities. The Transforming Masculinities approach is therefore not about imposing Western views on gender within different contexts. Instead, it focuses on rooting gender equality within cultural and faith understandings, highlighting that gender equality is God's intention for humankind and creating the space for people to both understand that and decide what it means in their specific context.

This work is evolving, and the fact that it is being implemented in 12 countries at present demonstrates how needed it is. The aim is to scale up this work in the various countries where robust evidence exists. For example, through the Passages Project, Tearfund is scaling up its work using the existing networks of partner organization Église du Christ au Congo (ECC) using radio programmes and integration into existing ministries (IRH, 2020). The team is also keen to grow the network of trainers who lead this work and create a mentoring and coaching space, as this sensitive work requires deep commitment from potential leaders. External organizations are keen to replicate this model, and we are working out what this could look like. Tearfund is committed to exploring how to improve the content and process of this work to ensure that it remains meaningful, transformative and inclusive.

Conclusion

If we want to live in a world without SGBV, then all must actively work towards transforming the harmful norms, systems and structures that perpetuate gender inequality. A world free of violence for women and girls is also a world free of violence for men and boys. In order to work towards truly gender transformative outcomes, however, harmful expressions of masculinities and male violence need to be brought to light, understood and engaged with. Tearfund's work on Transforming Masculinities is not simply about preventing violence, but also about allowing people to express and live out their God-given potential. This means creating spaces where they can be inspired to be more like Jesus, to imagine and aspire to being empowering, life-giving, non-violent, compassionate, caring, social justice-minded individuals working together for restoration. Faith leaders have a critical role to play in this process, which is not about imposing Western norms on gender in other contexts, but seeks instead to accompany these leaders on the journey towards gender justice.

The focus of the Transforming Masculinities programme is ultimately on dismantling an unequal and unjust system by creating spaces for dialogue and reimagination. The programme does not prescribe a model for relationships, but by working towards dismantling systemic injustice, human relationships can be made new. This process is life-giving not only for women or those who are oppressed but also for men. This is salvation: challenging systemic injustice, recreating the system and restoring balance within human relationships. It is liberation from an unjust system towards the hope of shalom.

Inclusion requires the active interrogation of systems, processes, norms and attitudes in order to challenge unequal values, power and status. This is essential if we are to work towards an inclusive society where men, women, boys and girls can thrive and live out their God-given potential.

Acknowledgements

The authors would like to thank Madleina Daehnhardt for reviewing the chapter and Rachel Paton for her helpful additions.

Bibliography

Agardh, A., B. Egerö, N. Eriksson, M. Hammarskjöld, J. V. Lazarus, J. Liljestrand and D. Mårtensson, 2007, *Men matter! AIDS, Gender and masculinities*, Stockholm: Sida.

Anderson, H., 2019, *Jacob's Shadow: Reimagining masculinity*, Eugene, OR: Wipf and Stock.

Bradley, T. and N. Karmani, 2015, 'Religion, Development and Gender', in E. Tomalin (ed.), *The Routledge Handbook of Religions and Global Development*, Abingdon: Routledge.

Chitando, E. and S. Chirongoma (eds), 2012, *Redemptive Masculinities*, Geneva: World Council of Churches.

Costenbader, E., S. Zissette, A. Martinez, K. LeMasters, N. A. Dagadu, P. Deepan and B. Shaw, 2019, 'Getting to Intent: Are social norms influencing intentions to use modern contraception in the DRC?', *PloS One* 14(7).

Deepan, P., 2014, *Masculinities, Faith and Ending Sexual and Gender-Based Violence, Tearfund: Burundi Summary Report*, Teddington: Tearfund.

Deepan, P., 2017, *Transforming Masculinities*, Teddington: Tearfund.

Deepan, P., 2018, 'Transforming Masculinities: Tearfund's approach to ending SGBV', in *Footsteps* 106, Teddington: Tearfund, pp. 14–15.

Deepan, P. and L. Loots, 2019, 'Masculinities, Faith and Ending Gender-based Violence in the African Great Lakes Region, Africa', in M. Kulkarni and R. Jain (eds), *Global Masculinities: Interrogations and reconstructions*, Abingdon: Routledge.

Dolan, C., 2011, 'Militarized, Religious and Neo-Colonial: The triple bind confronting men in contemporary Uganda', in A. Cornwall, J. Edström and A. Greig (eds), *Men and Development: Politicizing Masculinities*, London: Zed Books.

Fiddian-Qasmiyeh, E., 2015, 'Engendering Understandings of Faith-Based Organizations', in A. Coles, L. Gray and J. Momsen (eds), *The Routledge Handbook of Gender and Development*, Abingdon: Routledge.

Freeman, D., 2019, *Tearfund and the Quest for Faith-Based Development*, Abingdon: Routledge.

Haddad, B., 2002, 'Gender Violence and HIV/AIDS: A deadly silence in the church', *Journal of Theology for Southern Africa* 114, pp. 93–106.

Haddad, B., 2006, '"We Pray but We Cannot Heal": Theological challenges posed by the HIV/AIDS crisis', *Journal of Theology for Southern Africa* 125, pp. 80–90.

Institute for Reproductive Health (IRH), 2020, *Transforming Masculinities/Masculinité, Famille, et Foi Intervention; Endline quantitative research report*, Washington, DC: IRH and Center for Child and Human Development, Georgetown University with the United States Agency for International Development (USAID).

le Roux, E., 2011, *Silent No More*, Teddington: Tearfund.

le Roux, E., J. Corboz, N. Scott, M. Sandilands, U. Lele, E. Bezzolato and R. Jewkes, 2020, 'Engaging with Faith Groups to Prevent VAWG in Conflict-affected Communities: Results from two community surveys in the DRC', *BMC International Health Human Rights* 20(27).

Lesjane, D., 2017, *Exploring the Linkages of Gender, Masculinities and faith*, Teddington: Tearfund.

Lusey, H., 2016, *Gender Norms, Violence and Concepts of Masculinity*, Teddington: Tearfund.

Marshall, M. and N. Taylor, 2006, 'Tackling HIV and AIDS with Faith-Based Communities', *Gender & Development* 14(3), pp. 363–74.

Mertens, C. and H. Myrttinen, 2019, '"A Real Woman Waits" – Heteronormative Respectability, Neo-Liberal Betterment and Echoes of Coloniality in SGBV Programming in Eastern DR Congo', *Journal of Intervention and Statebuilding* 13(4), pp. 418–39.

Ming Liu, W., 2017, 'Masculinity Gender Norms', in K. Nadal (ed.), *The SAGE Encyclopedia of Psychology and Gender*, Thousand Oaks, CA: SAGE.

Palm, S., E. le Roux, E. Bezzolato, P. Deepan, J. Corboz, U. Lele, V. O'Sullivan and R. Jewkes, 2019, 'Rethinking Relationships', Teddington: Tearfund.

Parpart, J., 2015, 'Men, Masculinities, and Development', in A. Coles, L. Gray and J. Momsen (eds), *The Routledge Handbook of Gender and Development*, Abingdon: Routledge.

Peterman, A., S. Roy and M. Ranganathan, 2019, 'How is Economic Security Linked to Gender-based Violence? New insights from the Sexual Violence Research Initiative Forum 2019', *IFPRI*, www.ifpri.org/blog/how-economic-security-linked-gender-based-violence-new-insights-sexual-violence-research, accessed 10.11.2020.

Smith, S., 2017, 'Masculinities', in K. Nadal (ed.), *The SAGE Encyclopedia of Psychology and Gender*, Thousand Oaks, CA: SAGE.

Storkey, E., 2015, *Scars Across Humanity*, London: SPCK.

Strang, A., O. O'Brien, M. Sandilands and R. Horn, 2020, 'Help-seeking, Trust and Intimate Partner Violence: Social connections amongst displaced and non-displaced Yezidi women and men in the Kurdistan region of northern Iraq', *Conflict and health* 14(1), pp. 1–61.

Tadros, M., 2010, *Faith-Based Organizations and Service Delivery: Some gender conundrums*, Geneva: UNRISD.

Tearfund, 2021, *Reflecting the Image of the Triune God*, internal document.

UN Women, 2015, 'Women and Poverty', *UN Women*, https://beijing20.unwomen.org/en/in-focus/poverty, accessed 10.11.2020.

Van Klinken, A. and E. Chitando, 2015, 'Masculinities, HIV and Religion in Africa', in E. Tomalin (ed.), *The Routledge Handbook of Religions and Global Development*, Abingdon: Routledge.

WHO, 2019, 'RESPECT Women: Preventing violence against women', *World Health Organization*, www.who.int/reproductivehealth/topics/violence/respect-women-framework/en/, accessed 10.11.2020.

Wright, H., 2020, '"Masculinities Perspectives": Advancing a radical Women, Peace and Security agenda?', *International Feminist Journal of Politics* 22(5), pp. 652–74.

Notes

1 Recent research commissioned by Tearfund in Ninewa, Iraq, made use of a social mapping methodology to learn whom crisis-affected communities turn to for help and support – and whom they trust. When it came to seeking help in relation to intimate partner violence (IPV), as compared to other issues, far fewer connections and resources were trusted to help. Trust was reserved for family members and religious leaders, and was certainly not extended to non-government organizations (Strang et al., 2020).

2 Costenbader et al. (2019) have recently made an important contribution to this strand of enquiry, albeit with a focus on family planning rather than SGBV, with their investigation into the different types of social norms that affect individuals' intention to use modern contraception. Their study is notable for its development of a methodology (structural equation modelling) for measuring the influence of social norms – something that has lagged behind the capacity to measure individual behaviour and attitudes, for example.

3 These harmful conceptions included viewing men as 'tough', 'intelligent', 'providers', 'masters' and 'superior' to women, as well as having 'natural and God-given power' over them (Lusey, 2016, pp. 8–9).

9

Case Study: Localization and Inclusion

OENONE CHADBURN

Scene setting

Typhoon Haiyan hit the Philippines in November 2013, causing the deaths of more than 7,350 people. Scores of coastal economies were severely impacted, including the destruction of 33 million coconut trees affecting 1 million farmers (FAO, 2014). Tearfund's preferred way of working is through funding local partners, such as nationally registered NGOs and strong church networks, and Tearfund's supporters gave generously to respond to the crisis. The UN system declared a Level 3 emergency, a classification that required all UN agencies to provide the highest level of support. This included giving precedence to the 'cluster system', an international coordination mechanism bringing global aid actors together to ensure the response was effective and efficient and adhered to international protocol and good practice.

As our local partner staff had never experienced the international cluster system before, Tearfund explained the processes to them and promised an introduction to the local UN 'pop-up' emergency coordination office. Arriving at the office, the Tearfund officer and the two local partner staff requested to see the most senior person for introductions. A gruff 'You need to talk to her' was relayed with the minimal of eye contact. At their desks in this small open-plan room, the three international aid workers never once looked up. Finally, when the Tearfund officer decided to break the silence, she approached the woman in question and explained she felt it was important to hear from these local partners as they were already doing work with the different communities, and did not want to duplicate international aid efforts. The international aid worker spoke directly back to Tearfund, without acknowledging the national counterparts. The resulting conversation established that it was not a priority or of high importance what the local organizations were doing due to the smaller scale of reach that this work was achieving.

Never once were any of the guests asked to sit down. Never once was there any sense of inquiry as to how these local counterparts could collaborate and add value to the international response. Never once were they asked if they had lost loved ones or been directly affected. The national staff of the local partner left having had their fears realized: their work was of lesser importance than that of an international aid worker, reinforcing what other national Filipino NGOs were already experiencing. The years of previous hard work establishing their own local community development and emergency preparedness initiatives did not count for anything: the international way of business was better.

While much has been researched, documented and learnt from the Typhoon Haiyan experience, this story of international exclusiveness to the detriment of local inclusiveness is a common theme, both past and present. Following most significant crises, new promises are made and new practices are formed. However, often they are procedural and fail to acknowledge that it is underlying behaviours that need to change, and that needs to come from international aid workers themselves. More importantly, it belies the reality that transformational change requires local ownership and transfer of power.

Case study synopsis

This case study is structured in three parts: the intersection of theological reflection on inclusion with global humanitarian practice, an analysis of partnerships and the evolution of Tearfund practice, and a review of lessons learnt from Tearfund's perspective.

The predominant narrative is framed around the word 'localization'. It is a comparatively new term, which is used regularly by humanitarian organizations but is often interchanged with the term 'locally led response'. The ICVA (International Council of Voluntary Agencies) has defined localization as

the process through which a diverse range of humanitarian actors are attempting, each in their own way, to ensure local and national actors are better engaged in the planning, delivery and accountability of humanitarian action, while still ensuring humanitarian needs can be met swiftly, effectively and in a principled manner. (ICVA and HLA, 2019, p. 3)

To put it another way, 'it can [also] be viewed as a way of reconceiving the humanitarian sector from the bottom up. It recognizes that the overwhelming majority of humanitarian assistance is already provided by local actors' (IFRC, 2018).

This tension between local and international is so deep-rooted that it was at the heart of the first World Humanitarian Summit in 2016, a UN-convened multi-stakeholder conference to develop a new 'Agenda for Humanity'. However, recognizing that Western bi-lateral funding is a central tenet of power for the aid system, the donors agreed that change needed to begin here, and an international set of commitments called the Grand Bargain was established. 'Under the Grand Bargain, the signatories have committed to "making principled humanitarian action as local as possible and as international as necessary", while continuing to recognize the vital role of international actors, in particular in situations of armed conflict' (IFRC, 2018). This included directly funding national partners wherever possible, or via one intermediary only. The Grand Bargain has been and continues to be a noble attempt at addressing international exclusion in humanitarian crises. However, it has not had the impact that local actors crave, and while Tearfund may advocate for local actors to have a stronger voice, we also must look at the 'plank in [our] own eye'.[1]

Tearfund's theological framework for inclusion states: 'Tearfund should intentionally seek out and listen to voices and perspectives that have been marginalised, allowing them to transform the shape and nature of the organisation' (Kurlberg, 2020, p. 17). It goes without saying that this speaks to the heart of localization and the current debate within the international community. Inclusion is not just about increasing access, but moving to the margins, like Jesus' encounter with the woman at the well, and with Zacchaeus at his own home. With this as a foundational value, it follows that Tearfund must model, systematically practise, effectively evidence and constantly promote localization as a core part of our humanitarian DNA.

However, this journey is far from simple, and Tearfund has to balance a series of internal tensions: accountability to the source of income against accountability to crisis-affected populations;

requirements of UK international regulations against the increasing sovereignty of the crisis-affected countries and their desire for control; international humanitarian principles of neutrality and protection against local cultural norms, religions and taboos; economies of scale and established international aid experience against small-scale, locally led responses with blind spots about their own biases. Navigating this journey of relinquishing power and ownership can occasionally feel like giving up your paddle in shark-infested waters.

In this case study, we will review how and where humanitarian exclusion has happened, examining this at different levels, from the individual up to the systemic level. We will then assess Tearfund's own experience of this exclusion and go on to examine our own findings of how and where change needs to begin, citing examples of success and failure, from both our programme work and the experience of other peer agencies.

Throughout, we will be referring to localization from the perspective of the humanitarian system and disaster response. However, the term 'localization' does not have exclusive rights on the definition of 'locally led'. Localization could (and should) be broadened to look at sustainable international development, and indeed, for decades, the voice of those living in poverty has been central to ensuring effective and transformational development practice. Nonetheless, to help give focus to this case study, we will specifically be looking at the international humanitarian system, as this provides an opportunity to dig a little deeper and uncover small steps that can be taken to dismantle exclusion and embrace inclusion.

The centre's move to the margins: where theology informs practice

In 2012, TV producer Ricardo Pollack shot a one-and-a-half-hour documentary called the *The Trouble with Aid*. It charted the history of the modern-day aid movement, citing the Biafra War as the launch of a new 'industry'. While not always accepted as a fair critique, it posed some insightful questions, such as whether humanitarian aid does more harm than good (Aaronson, 2012, para 1). Tearfund was born in response to the Biafra War, and since that time it also has faced the same dilemmas and self-examination as many other aid agencies currently.

There have been several defining moments of the modern humanitarian aid movement: Biafra War; Cambodia 'Killing Fields'; the 1984 Ethiopian famine; the 1994 Rwandan genocide; the Indian Ocean Tsunami of 2004; the World Humanitarian Summit in 2016; and now the Covid-19 pandemic. The early events saw the establishment of modern bi-lateral aid, fundraising from the general public in richer nations, and the rapid growth of large international charities. However, the latter events, from the Rwandan genocide onwards, led to the aid industry taking a self-critical look, often leading to new international standards or good practice norms. Despite these attempts at self-regulation, some fundamental issues stubbornly persist. *At the core of all these critiques is the need for a voice and power shift to marginalized crisis-affected populations, enabling communities to self-determine their own crisis response.*

This exclusion of communities has often come from a place of misplaced good intent, the perspective that intensive learning from international emergencies can be driven at scale and effectively transposed into new countries by internationals motivated by life-saving compassion. In reality, it struggles to take into account that locally co-led emergencies can increase the effectiveness, relevance, appropriateness and connectedness of any humanitarian response (Ramalingam et al., 2013). More importantly, communities and those affected by a disaster have the moral right to be heard and to lead or shape any response to an emergency that affects them, preferably supported by other citizens and nationals of their country or region.

The false divide of sacred and secular

For Tearfund, responding to disasters has always involved local partners. Different approaches have been prioritized during different decades, including directly responding to humanitarian need when there has been no appropriate partner to work with. Such decisions were based on protecting the human rights of excluded conflict-affected communities, but these ethical decisions in themselves set in motion a chain of actions that can lead to a 'perpetuation of existence': they can shut down the space, funding and opportunity for local national organizations to thrive and grow, as large INGOs become permanent fixtures in long protracted and complex emergencies such as South Sudan and DRC. Equally, large-scale, long-term crisis response has, for Tearfund, provided life-stabilizing interventions for millions of people across several continents, and protected the rights of thousands of marginalized and excluded populations. The moral dilemma is difficult to navigate.

Further complications arise from the fact that the international humanitarian system is not only split along the line of international versus national/local, but also along the line of secular versus faith-based. The international humanitarian system is, arguably, secular at heart, particularly because of its emphasis on neutrality (Wilkinson, 2018). There has been a recent opening up towards the importance of engaging with religion, termed the 'turn to religion' by some scholars (Tomalin et al., 2019). However, according to Emma Tomalin, 'although global development and humanitarian institutions are now taking religion more seriously, they predominantly and selectively partner with faith actors that are already visible and functional at the *international* level' (Tomalin, 2020, p. 325, emphasis added). Tearfund fits those criteria, not only being international in its operation, but also being a long-term signatory to the Red Cross Code of Conduct and aligned with the Humanitarian Principles. This positions Tearfund and other 'visible and functional' international FBOs as intermediaries between the international system and the host of *local* faith-based actors who are still left out. It represents another moral dilemma for Tearfund, who believe that such intermediaries should not be necessary at all.

Indeed, it is becoming increasingly apparent that the humanitarian system ignores local faith actors at its peril. When individuals who had been affected by Typhoon Haiyan were asked to what extent they had felt supported by responding organizations, they made a clear distinction between faith-based organizations – which were predominantly local – and secular ones (Wilkinson, 2018). The short timelines and shallow interactions of secular actors were contrasted with the fact that those who were local and 'faith-based' stayed for longer, made return visits and, crucially, offered encouragement in non-material ways: through 'blessings, counselling sessions, debriefings, prayers, spiritual formations, and other psychosocial activities' (Wilkinson, 2018, p. 464). It rings true, therefore, that

> trying to be 'fair' by being secular when working to support people who are often deeply religious, is likely to be much

less effective. When people interpret disasters in terms of their religion, it becomes difficult to engage with them in a meaningful way by pretending that religion is not significant. (Terry Cannon, endorsement of Wilkinson, 2020)

Exclusion of the individual by the system

The number of people affected by humanitarian crises is constantly rising. In 2017, there were 68.5 million people displaced by conflict alone, an increase of more than 10 million compared to 2014 (OCHA, 2018). While governments bear responsibility for their population, many developing countries lack resources, or decentralized and/or functioning governance structures. Often the international community are either requested or expected to respond in the interests of humanity. However, the international humanitarian way of operating has been the object of increasing discontent on the part of affected populations and national NGOs.

Tearfund has long acknowledged that the current aid architecture is not fit for purpose, and that 'the heavy footprint and attitudes of international agencies [are] ... obstacles to both national leadership and the building of strong and sustained national capacities' (Patel and Brabant, 2017, p. 7). Recognizing this, Tearfund and other agencies backed the launch of 'Charter4Change' in advance of the World Humanitarian Summit, an initiative wherein INGOs sign up to eight commitments to demonstrate practically their commitment to prioritize, respect, support and advocate for the rights of national NGOs, even if this is at their own expense (Charter4Change, 2021).[2] Nonetheless, it is important to note that the power of change does not exclusively rest at the door of the INGOs. Attitudes to shifting 'the centre to the margins', bringing local communities to the centre of decision-making, rest with international institutions, bi-lateral government positions, national government legislation, as well as independent INGOs.

The humanitarian system is largely in agreement that reform is necessary, but it has been stuck in cyclical debates, and power plays.

At the heart of the local humanitarian action debate, are questions of value: what is valued, why and by whom, with direct implications for where and how the sector invests its energies, activities and resources. Of equal importance is the role assigning value plays in defining the power relationships among international and local actors, confining resources to a small number of players and influencing how those resources are applied and – consequently – what gets done. (Fast and Bennett, 2020, p. 12)

Kathryn Kraft also alludes to the uneasy relationships between different players, including Tearfund partners in Lebanon:

While evangelical churches wrestled with applying impartiality, and did so in ways somewhat different from other humanitarian actors, they also had their own highly valued principles. In fact, some of the informants in this case study were somewhat critical of other, larger humanitarian actors for their poor respect of other guidelines that they considered essential to good humanitarian response. The 'principle' most emphasized was that of human dignity. [A 'volunteer team leader' is then quoted as saying:] 'We treat beneficiaries with respect. When they come into the centre, we stand up, shake their hands, offer them a seat. This is different from the UN and their partners, who even refer to the refugees as "animals".' (Kraft, 2016, p. 417)

Localization and inclusion is thus about both recognizing where systematic structures create social divides and also being cognizant of where individual bias exists.

The reality of local partnerships: where perceptions and power govern

Tearfund has developed different ways of delivering humanitarian support, and these include responding '*via the local church wherever possible, via local and national partners wherever appropriate, and directly with our own teams wherever necessary*' (Tearfund, 2019c, p. 1). Critically, partnerships with church networks and local and national NGOs are the priority model for response. Tearfund sees these networks and NGOs as essential equitable partners to achieving humanitarian objectives, being a voice and a representative for those in need, as well as being a central source of local knowledge and understanding often lacking in international responses.

Very often, in these high-profile international emergencies, there is no question about the moral imperative of the international community to respond, but it is through the methods chosen to address these needs that issues of power come into play. Tearfund has both directly channelled funding to national partners and been an intermediary for international bilateral aid; it has also directly established its own projects to respond to emergencies. For most aid agencies, when determining if and when an international response should happen, 'lack of national capacity' is often cited as one of the key factors. This factual basis can be determined by previous poor experience, evidence of corruption or, at worse, ethnic and societal tensions where negative bias is implicit, and would lead to a failure of protection and safeguarding for marginalized groups.

Nonetheless, naive perceptions of how communities are structured and local civil society is organized lead to misguided analysis, especially in the context of a fast-onset crisis. At worse, international humanitarians' behaviour, language and actions lack respect, and demonstrate a lack of belief in the ability of the local actors, in favour of their own higher ability to care for local communities. Inevitably, one behaviour breeds another, and 'local organisations [downplay] their own contributions, referring frequently to their capacity deficits and to "international" capacity as something they [need] and [want], including through training' (Fast and Bennett, 2020, p. 12). Lack of confidence, and confusion around how the humanitarian system works, leads to exclusion from decision-making, especially for those 'non-traditional' actors such as faith leaders.

Tearfund's own experience of partnerships has evolved iteratively and uniquely, navigating the space between formal humanitarian accompaniment and fellowship sojourners. The typology of partnerships in Figure 2 below helpfully categorizes the differences, yet in reality country context and local circumstances will strongly influence which approach is appropriate. As a result, Tearfund's own experience covers the range of types, and any attempts to ensure consistency by promoting one particular type is not helpful, as it fails to recognize the importance of a locally led decision-making process.

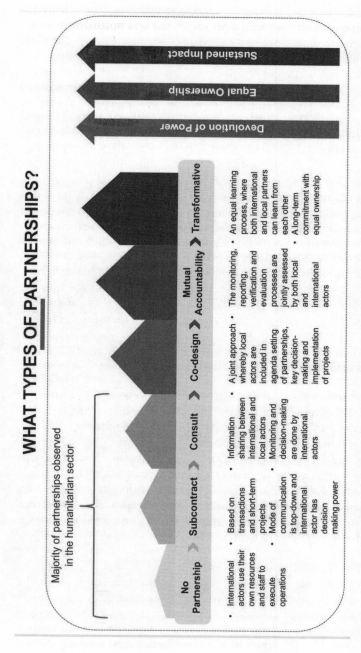

Figure 2: 'What types of partnerships?' Taken from Castillo, Maasbol and Yuan, 2018.

Instead, Tearfund focuses on national staff and their attitudes and perceptions of local partners as central to developing an appropriate country-level approach. Frameworks on 'Understanding Localisation for Tearfund' and 'Tearfund's Approaches to Localisation' capture both the values and behaviours that support localization, and provide evidence of Tearfund experiences as a way of giving strategic direction and sharing learning to staff globally (Tearfund, 2019d; Tearfund, 2020). This is supported by capacity-sharing and capacity-strengthening initiatives and programmes such as Tearfund's own Disaster Management Capacity Assessment tool – a self-assessment process that partners undertake against a benchmarking system developed by a series of international agencies (Tearfund, 2019a). This leads to the partner designing their own capacity-strengthening plan tailored to their own strengths and ambitions.

In analysing our own performance and effectiveness across a bespoke and broad-ranging set of approaches, Tearfund has been emphasizing a consistent set of themes and lessons learnt, many of which have direct and indirect implications for how we outwork our approach to inclusion in humanitarian settings. The final section of this chapter will discuss these themes.

Time and trust

By far the clearest lesson learnt is the importance of time and trust. Breaking down barriers and past historic structures and attitudes inevitably takes a heavy investment of time, much of this people-centred and relational. For Tearfund this ranges between seven and ten years, timeframes that the international humanitarian system rarely operates in. In north-east Nigeria, Tearfund has focused almost exclusively on strengthening the capacity of a local partner, CRUDAN, to address the humanitarian crisis from the conflict with Boko Haram. Tearfund conducted a study in which one participant explained:

> [The Tearfund model is] different because this is a long-term investment. It is led by the local organisation; Tearfund works as a facilitator for them to realise their capacities. The partnership is focused on finding solutions that are beyond a budget timeline or a donor timeline. It's about long-term sustainability. The fact that there's a technical person available to

work through the process with CRUDAN is very significant. People are able to be guided on a day-to-day basis rather than a get in/get out model. (Tearfund, 2019b, p. 2)

A review of other successes cited trust as central:

Trust was the most cited strength in the study. Stakeholders highlighted it as fundamental to the success of the approach undertaken in the CRUDAN–Tearfund partnership. Intense models of working (e.g. close accompaniment) and/or changes to pre-existing ways of working together can be challenging, putting a strain on relationships. Tearfund and CRUDAN's partnership was one founded on mutual respect and trust built over several years of working together in development contexts. This meant they were 'able to have tough conversations without the relationship falling apart', especially when there were frustrations along the way that both parties had to work through. (Tearfund, 2019b, p. 1)

Issues of trust are not just important to the relationship between one humanitarian agency and another: the trust factor also is central to the most local level of humanitarian response, the involvement of faith leaders. Tearfund's experience in Sierra Leone supported the notion that faith leaders are a central broker to including local perspectives in humanitarian decision-making. 'Because people trust them, when they started participating in the revised burial practices, people knew they could trust it and resistance ended. The participation of religious leaders was a game changer' (UN staff member, Sierra Leone, quoted in Featherstone, 2015, p. 8).

It would be wrong, however, to assume that Tearfund's experience of working with partners is without flaws. In an organization-wide assessment of different approaches to working with partners, Tearfund needed to 'redeem the nature of contracts, by keeping integrity, open communication and relationship at the heart' (staff member paraphrased in Tearfund, 2018, p. 24). One staff member helpfully likened the issue of time investment 'to the idea of the Kingdom of God: in responding to the emergency we must focus both on the "now and not yet"' (Tearfund, 2018, p. 24). The pressure to invest all funding in responding to humanitarian needs is great, but strengthening the power of the local must come with that long-term time investment.

Funding and finance

The pressure of funding and finance are also another two recurring themes in Tearfund's lived experience of 'moving to the margins'. Central to relinquishing power for INGOs is something at the very core of their business model. Many INGOs cannot operate unless they achieve a critical mass of operational funding which achieves economies of scale. In stark contrast, one of the central calls from the Charter4Change is for a larger proportion of international finance to go directly to local NGOs, bypassing INGOs altogether. Many international donors are struggling to achieve and justify this critical shift due to the increasing transaction and administration it would require, and yet without such a shift the long-term sustainability of local partners is in question. This is the lived experience of Tearfund's partners in Liberia where 'a shrinking funding pool for NGOs in general has meant agencies have "closed ranks" and are less willing to collaborate, instead competing for scarce resources. As a consequence, national actors such as Tearfund's partner, AEL, are being cold shouldered once more' (staff member, quoted in Tearfund, 2018, p. 15).

In Nigeria, Tearfund and its Dutch counterpart have advocated for flexible long-term funding for capacity strengthening. One of the successes of the CRUDAN case study was securing one such source, Dutch Relief Alliance funding. Consequently, CRUDAN was able to bolster its own reputation and has now started 'to diversify its donor funding portfolio in order to expand its humanitarian work. Thus far, it has obtained funding from the Nigeria Humanitarian Fund (the UN country-based pooled fund) and another INGO, independently of Tearfund' (Tearfund, 2019b, p. 3).

Nonetheless, such funding sources are few and far between. Tearfund has allocated some of its own internal funding on a regular basis to ensure investment in capacity strengthening, but the volumes allocated fall short of the need. Tearfund regularly consults with its partners on where improvements can be made. In one such consultation, there was a clear acknowledgement that although 'capacity transfer is a two-way process ... [there needs to be] ... a strong emphasis on capacity assessment and the inclusion of appropriate budget for capacity building into response programming' (Pritchard, 2020, p. 21). This reiterated the fundamental concern that to enable inclusion of locally led emergency response, the business model of local partners must clearly be addressed both on a case-by-case and a systematic level.

Dignity and delivery

In Haiti, after the 2010 earthquake there had been real concern about the exclusion of local NGOs in national and international decision-making. In an attempt to bridge the divide, Tearfund initiated the development of a local network called RIHPED.[3] To help address the issue of lack of access to funding, they pre-positioned a small local pool fund to support immediate response and needs assessment. However, this was not without challenges. In a survey to document the case study of RIHPED, one responder from a local organization explained, 'Members who contribute more money hold more weight in the decision making. The international organisations pay higher fees, and therefore have more influence than the local organisations.' Others worried a pattern of competition between the members affected their ability to collaborate. One INGO representative said, 'We felt there was too much competition among the members, [so] even when the rapid assessments were being done as a team, the results were not made available to all members at the same time' (Cerin, 2021). The research also found:

> Participation in the network is not without its challenges. One major issue is a power imbalance between the local NGOs with less resources and the INGOs. One member reports, 'Historically there has been a lack of confidence and capacity in the NNGOs.[4] They perceive they are inadequate against the larger skilled fully funded agencies.' To respond to this imbalance, RIHPED provides regular training and capacity building for local organizations. Where INGOs may get capacity strengthening from their home offices, many local organizations do not have that luxury. RIHPED provides international standard training on themes such as cash programming, logistics, monitoring and evaluation, etc. (Cerin, 2021)

It is also important to note that the research cited 100 per cent satisfaction from all those interviewed on their membership of RIHPED. The local NGOs saw their capacity and legitimacy strengthened, while the INGOs saw their knowledge of and legitimacy among local communities increase.

Another example is from South Sudan, where Tearfund as part of a consortium was funded by the Belgian government to innovate on ways to bring faith actors, faith leaders and humanitarian actors closer together. One concerning observation was on whether the identity of faith actors is in fact faith based or humanitarian based. It was found that power is described along 'the lines of both local/international and faith/secular divides, resulting in the reality that local faith actors can be doubly marginalised (alongside and adding to other marginalisation they may experience based on gender, race, age, ethnicity, etc.)' (Wilkinson et al., 2021, p. 3). This is also endorsed by Tearfund's experience in Liberia:

> Tearfund working in Liberia is a long term, subtle journey, the battle is still not yet won, we can't completely leave the partners to it. INGOs and the UN still have a vein of racism – early days information is usually only shared at expat parties … it is exclusive. (staff member, quoted in Tearfund, 2018, p. 15)

In evidence of how to overcome these challenges, it was clear from the above-mentioned CRUDAN experience that we needed to:

> Hire staff who 'walk the talk' in their approach to localisation and capacity strengthening. The partnership approach adopted in this case was intentional in enabling CRUDAN to take the lead while Tearfund undertook a hands-on advisory role, working side by side. Tearfund staff stepped back and allowed CRUDAN to lead on implementation as well as in humanitarian coordination forums. (Tearfund, 2019b, p. 1)

This was further evidenced from across the organization in our internal analysis of our models. One staff member said, 'Partners thrive when they are the organisation leading the project, they show interest in an area and Tearfund facilitate the training and support they need – building on the strengths of the partner' (quoted in Tearfund, 2018, p. 22).

Legitimacy and literacy

In the final two themes it has been clear that having legitimate identity, a common unifying language of understanding and a set of practices to support this are central to overcoming the international/national, as well as faith/secular, divide. This also applies at the level of disaster-affected communities, as evidenced in local faith leaders not accepting UN and government messaging in the West Africa Ebola outbreak, which sadly had disastrous consequences. Mainly due to lack of information and misinformation, the response of faith leaders was mixed: the measures that the UN and government were requesting people to take went against cultural values and religious practices. This resulted in denial of the disease by local communities and their hostility towards those seeking to contain it. It was found that 'many of those with Ebola chose to remain with their families and burials were undertaken in secret. As a consequence the disease continued to spread' (Featherstone, 2015, p. 8).

It is not only attitudes that affect legitimacy: it is also administration and bureaucracy. Lessons from Tearfund experiences in South Sudan show the importance of registration:

> Registration is a vital first foot in the door to enable participation in the formal humanitarian system for local faith actors. The effects of registration are then widespread such as the opportunity to receive training, the need for new bank accounts and the internal professionalisation that promotes their visibility in the eyes of other humanitarian actors and donors, and the legitimacy of registration that can aid in diminishing other forms of marginalisation. (Wilkinson et al., 2021)

Nonetheless, fears from the international community about the legitimacy of local partners are not without foundation. There is clear evidence of poor practice of bias from faith actors, such as in areas of gender inclusion:

> In Papua New Guinea, a church network involved in disasters and other activities, was almost entirely dominated by men, with women playing minor and peripheral roles. This was said to reflect the wider socio-cultural environment which tended to exclude women from all levels of the political system. (Twigg, 2019, p. 7)

Raising awareness on how to navigate inclusive theology and humanitarian principles in fast-onset situations are an area that needs constant monitoring, as a literature review on disaster reduction and the role of the local church shows:

> ... strong in-group social networks may prevent others from benefiting from assistance, as in parts of rural Tamil Nadu after the 2004 tsunami, where minorities, outcastes, and other non-members were often excluded from organized relief efforts due to discrimination and lack of connections. Parish priests and councils worked as intermediaries between villagers and relief organisations, and in some areas residents complained that only families active in Catholic Church activities and/or attending church-run schools benefited from the economic, social and educational opportunities made available. (Twigg, 2019, p. 7)

Nonetheless, we know that legitimacy and literacy can be overcome. One of the success points from CRUDAN was their gradual but significant acceptance:

> In cluster meetings, in sector meetings, people know CRUDAN staff and know that they will have something valuable to contribute. At the beginning, [the cluster meetings] were confusing. Over the years, we have become able to understand the humanitarian system, speak the same language, and integrate. (CRUDAN staff member, quoted in Tearfund, 2019b, p. 3)

Conclusion

Tearfund's theological framework for inclusion states: 'In a perfect world ... human relationships would be dynamic, characterised by interdependency and genuine, mutual openness ... Exclusion occurs when these boundaries are not respected. Relationships are then characterised by domination, elimination, assimilation and abandonment' (Chapter 2, quoted in Kurlberg, 2020, pp. 8-9). The evidence set out in this chapter has demonstrated that Tearfund's direct experience of the international humanitarian system has seen both the domination and abandonment of national NGOs and locally led responses.

This has been compounded further by the tensions between

faith-based approaches, humanitarian principles and human rights discourse. Perceptions that local faith-based partners have weaker capacity and a tendency towards bias are too dominant. While Tearfund's experience has seen some local partners dominate local power dynamics and fail to serve their local communities effectively, to abandon local actors totally and say they will never be capable or compete is to 'throw the baby out with the bath water'. Clear accompaniment can take local partners on a journey to play an equitable role in international humanitarian response, but this must also be met with the international community's desire to relinquish centralized power and move to the margins. This also goes for Tearfund.

Being intentional in listening to the voice of affected populations and local civil society will be essential to moving forward. Faith actors and national NGOs should not just be considered as trauma counsellors and a way to soak up smaller aspects of international response: they need to be central to the decision-making forums on disaster preparedness and risk reduction, as well as in humanitarian settings deciding on priorities. Climate change and the increase in national conflicts will also require the clear inclusion of local value-based approaches to address need, as well as those based on humanitarian principles and human rights discourse.

However, this does not mean that there is not an opportunity or place for Tearfund in the future – quite the opposite. As Tomalin, citing Bierschenk et al., argues, 'International Faith Based Organisations are "brokers of development" in the sense of "intermediaries who take advantage of their position at the interface between two social and cultural configurations"' (Tomalin, 2020, pp. 332–3). They navigate the thin space between the faith and secular divide, being able to provide the 'how to' on softer transactional aspects of aid and development, building trust and dignity, as well as modelling humility to transfer ownership of aid response to local actors wherever possible.

Undoubtedly, there will always be arguments for the international aid community's economies of scale, their ability to implement humanitarian standards and protocol effectively, and the systems and procedures needed to adhere to legislation and accountability. Nonetheless, at minimum, local partners should have an equitable voice at the table, challenging international perspectives and dominating personalities, demonstrating that effective humanitarian response does not need to be costly or have 'big boots'. Rather it can be barefoot, driven by local realities and locally led.

Acknowledgements

Many thanks to Rachel Paton for helping with the bibliography and citations, and for her input in the section on 'The false divide of sacred and secular'.

Bibliography

Aaronson, M., 2012, 'The Trouble with Aid', *E-International Relations*, 17 December, www.e-ir.info/2012/12/17/the-trouble-with-aid/, accessed 15.03.2021.
Castillo, A., M. Maasbol, Y. S. Yuan, 2018, *At the Crossroads*, HQAI.
Cerin, J. C., 2021, 'Lessons on Localisation from Haiti', *Humanitarian Exchange* 79, forthcoming.
Charter4Change, 2021, 'Localisation of Humanitarian Aid', *Charter-4Change*, https://charter4change.org/, accessed 15.03.2021.
FAO (Food and Agriculture Organization of the United Nations), 2014, 'Philippine Coconut Farmers Struggling to Recover from Typhoon', 27 January, *FAO News*, www.fao.org/news/story/en/item/212957/icode/, accessed 22.03.2021.
Fast, L. and C. Bennett, 2020, *From the Ground Up: It's about time for local humanitarian action*, London: Overseas Development Institute.
Featherstone, A., 2015, *Keeping the faith: The role of faith leaders in the Ebola response*, UK: Christian Aid/CAFOD/Tearfund/Islamic Relief Worldwide.
ICVA (International Council of Voluntary Agencies) and HLA (Humanitarian Leadership Academy), 2019, *Unpacking Localization*, London: HLA.
IFRC (International Federation of Red Cross and Red Crescent Societies), 2018, *The Grand Bargain Workstream 2: Localisation – FAQs*, http://gblocalisation.ifrc.org/grand-bargain-localisation-workstream-2/, accessed 15.03.2021.
Kraft, K., 2016, 'Faith and Impartiality in Humanitarian Response: Lessons from Lebanese evangelical churches providing food aid', *International Journal of the Red Cross* 897/898.
Kurlberg, N., 2020, 'Inclusion: A theological framework', Tearfund, internal unpublished document.
Miller, H., 2017, 'Rejecting "rights-based approaches" to Development: Alternative engagements with human rights', *Journal of Human Rights* 16(1), pp. 61–78.

OCHA (United Nations Office for the Coordination of Humanitarian Affairs), 2018, *Global Humanitarian Overview 2019*, New York: OCHA.

Patel, S. and K. Van Brabant, 2017, *The Start Fund and Localisation: Current situation-future directions – Executive summary*, Switzerland/UK: GMI (Global Mentoring Initiative)/The Start Network.

Pritchard, M., 2020, *Partner Listening Forums Report – Integral Alliance*, Watford: Integral Alliance.

Ramalingam, B., B. Gray and G. Cerruti, 2013, *Missed Opportunities: The case for strengthening national and local partnership-based humanitarian responses*, UK: ActionAid/CAFOD/Christian Aid/Oxfam GB/Tearfund.

Tearfund, 2018, 'No Size Fits All: Tearfund's response models and their impact on partner capacity', internal unpublished document.

Tearfund, 2019a, *Disaster Management Capacity Assessment (DMCA) Tool*, Teddington: Tearfund.

Tearfund, 2019b, *Shoulder to Shoulder: Approaches to strengthen local humanitarian leadership – Briefing paper*, Teddington: Tearfund.

Tearfund, 2019c, 'Tearfund's Humanitarian Identity', internal unpublished document.

Tearfund, 2019d, 'Understanding Localisation for Tearfund', internal unpublished document.

Tearfund, 2020, 'Tearfund's Approaches to Localisation', internal unpublished document.

Tomalin, E., J. Haustein and S. Kidy, 2019, 'Religion and the Sustainable Development Goals', *The Review of Faith & International Affairs* 17(2), pp. 102–18.

Tomalin, E., 2020, 'Global Aid and Faith Actors: The case for an actor-orientated approach to the "turn to religion"', *International affairs* 96(2), pp. 323–42.

Twigg, J., 2019, 'The Role of Local Churches in Resilience Building: A literature review for Tearfund', internal unpublished document.

Wilkinson, O., 2018, '"Faith can come in, but not religion": Secularity and its effects on the disaster response to Typhoon Haiyan', *Disasters* 42(3), pp. 459–74.

Wilkinson, O., 2020, *Secular and Religious Dynamics in Humanitarian Response*, Oxfordshire: Routledge.

Wilkinson, O., K. Logo, E. Tomalin, W. Laki Anthony, F. De Wolf and A. Kurien, 2021, 'Faith in Localisation? The experiences of local faith actors engaging with the international humanitarian system in South Sudan', *Journal of International Humanitarian Action*, manuscript submitted and under review.

Notes

1 Matthew 7.3, NIV.

2 Some INGOs directly implement projects and therefore they are not designed to work with partners. Other INGOs who receive international funding, which they then pass on to local partners, rely on the administration fee to maintain their financial buoyancy. The principle of Charter4Change fundamentally questions the business models of both these approaches.

3 Réseau Intégral Haïtien pour le Plaidoyer et l'Environnement Durable (Integrated Haitian Network to Advocate for a Sustainable Environment).

4 National NGOs.

PART 4

Inclusion as Belonging

10

Belonging to 'The House of the Lord': Ageing and Inclusion in the Rwandan Church

MADLEINA DAEHNHARDT AND
EMMANUEL MURANGIRA

Introduction

This chapter explores the lived experiences of older Rwandan Christians in the context of post-genocide Rwanda, and in light of the changing demographic and socio-economic contexts there. Taking a qualitative micro-perspective, we engage critically with the following questions: What do the narratives of older people and pastors tell us about ageing inclusion and exclusion in the church context? What is the role of churches as social institutions and informal networks in valuing and including older people in the life and mission of the Rwandan church? And what does this mean for faith-based organizations (FBOs) partnering with churches in their development programmes? The chapter draws from a substantial set of original interviews with older Rwandans (across the age range 60–100) and with pastors of different denominations. The interviews were conducted in 2019 as part of a study on *Ageing in Rwanda* in three districts in Rwanda where Tearfund works through its local church partners.[1]

The chapter is structured as follows: in the first section we set the study of older people, and the specific questions we raise, in the context of international development practice and faith-based programmes, and position Tearfund therein. We then elaborate on the Rwanda-specific socio-demographic context. In the second section we turn to the context of church and theology, before describing the methodology and literature we draw from. The third section presents the relevant findings from the empirical study and discusses how churches can be support networks, places of belonging, places of inclusion and places of exclusion. From a theological standpoint, inclusive communities are those where everyone can belong, and this experience of belonging is therefore a key component of inclusion. Since we understand belonging as a key to inclusion, our analysis focuses on different aspects of experienced belonging. Similarly, aspects of not belonging can be interpreted as signs of exclusion. Our fourth section discusses practical implications for churches and for FBO practice, and introduces Tearfund's recent work of intentionally including older people in programming.[2] To clarify our starting point, the chapter is built on the hypothesis that the Rwandan church – as a social institution – can play a role in old-age support through inclusion, and has great potential to expand in this area.

The international context: development practice, faith-based interventions and older people

Development practice overall focuses on the future – with participants in development programmes being mostly young and able to work in community development initiatives. Many international non-government organizations (INGOs) have an explicit focus on children in their approach, interventions and fundraising models. For example, Plan International and Save the Children are primarily child-focused in their approach, and so is the faith-based INGO World Vision, which works through child sponsorship in programmes and fundraising. This leads to an inherent bias that prioritizes younger people over older people in development practice. Faith-based (I)NGOs are not exempt from this trend. It is exemplified most starkly in the sectoral response to the current Covid-19 pandemic. A mapping exercise carried out by Tearfund in 2020 showed that neither international FBOs nor any of the leading global church networks had any guidance or material on how churches could support older people during the pandemic.[3] This is despite older people being among those most at risk when contracting the virus.

A discussion of faith groups and older people in some ways represents an overlap of two marginal spaces in mainstream development. Both religion and ageing seem to be at best a niche space in the current landscape of Development Studies. Putting the two together promises to make a valuable contribution to the field. What is more, there are implications for FBOs to reflect critically on theologies and practices of ageing – in their own internal recruitment, as well as in considering how to inspire faith actors to recognize older people's needs and their contributions, informing thinking, engagement and action. This is somewhat counter-cultural when set against the dominant 'growth' and 'youth' paradigms evident not only in mainstream development but also in church movements and FBO programming. In contrast, inclusive development and church programmes affirm the roles, contributions, reflections and 'sacredness' of older people, recognizing that older people are vital to the life of churches and communities worldwide.

Tearfund works through local churches to facilitate holistic development globally. In bringing together faith and ageing in constructive dialogue in international development, it is pioneering in a space characterized by multiple exclusions. In comparison to other chapters in this volume – on topics such as peacebuilding or gender which have been developed over years, both conceptually and programmatically – the question of ageing inclusion is really in its infancy within Tearfund at the time of writing and is largely being pioneered by the Rwanda country team. As a consequence, this chapter is more explorative and explicitly empirical, as there is neither a longer institutional history nor developed theological frameworks or internal position papers on age that we can draw on.[4]

The Rwandan context: growing old with changing social safety nets

Research on ageing in Rwanda is limited and therefore the literature on ageing is equally scarce. *The Fourth Rwanda Population and Housing Census 2012* report shows that about 5 per cent of the Rwandan population of 10.5 million is above the age of 60 (NISR, 2012). The majority of older people are found in rural areas in the north and south-west of the country (NISR, 2012). This means that many older people are dependent on subsistence agriculture that does not generate substantial income for them and therefore offers little prospect of a formal pension. The 2012 census report also shows that the numbers for outward migration in the last five years are very high for rural districts (except from Eastern Province districts). For example, in Gicumbi district of Northern Province, which has the highest number of older people according to the census, a total of 28,096 people left the district. Although the report does not break down the migration by age groups, it is likely that the majority of migrants are below the age of 60, and that they migrate mainly in search of paid employment (NISR, 2014). This has implications for ageing and old-age poverty and care, especially in rural areas, given that younger members of the population are traditionally providers of social safety nets and would naturally be those to provide for their ageing parents if they lose the ability to work and earn a living.

Rwanda has seen rapid improvements in life expectancy and population growth resulting from investments in social and health services (World Bank, 2020). But some of the positive changes may have negative implications for old age. While life expectancy improves, the increasing number of people above the age of 60 poses a great challenge to Rwanda's future development (Sabates-Wheeler et al., 2018). The effects on ageing trajectories of the 1994 genocide against the Tutsi, as well as the resulting deprivation and breakdown in social safety nets, present challenges peculiar to older people. These include loneliness and lack of informal social support systems that family relations and children would normally provide (Victor et al., 2005). One of the greatest effects of the 1994 genocide on old age was high mortality rates in the 25–45 age bracket, which means that the majority of genocide survivors were aged above 45 or below 25 at the time. This has implications for ageing, with the younger survivors becoming dependent on older people, and older people having to work past pension age to support themselves and their dependants (de Walque and Verwimp, 2010). An increase in migration for employment and education also means that older people are not only losing their support system but also finding themselves working into old age with no prospects of either formal pensions or informal support (Sabates-Wheeler et al., 2018).

While most of the scant literature on ageing in Rwanda and elsewhere in Africa has focused on the challenges of old age and social pensions, it has not examined the role of local social institutions in providing informal services in old age. Instead, the focus is on state social protection interventions and formal social pensions (Sabates-Wheeler et al., 2018). In the case of Rwanda, most of the literature has focused on the government-funded Vision 2020 Umurenge Programme (VUP) in selected administrative units.[5] The VUP addresses economic issues, but there are a number of social and psychological aspects intrinsic to old age which programmes such as the VUP have not generally been able to address (Victor et al., 2005). This chapter makes a contribution to the body of research that focuses on the psycho-social and spiritual dimensions of ageing, related constraints and the role of social-spiritual institutions. Often these psycho-social and spiritual issues are either the cause or consequence of the economic and social deficits in old age.

Context, methodology and approach

Background to the study: the context of church

Rwandan society – like any other on the African continent and indeed in other places where social systems are largely informal – has depended a great deal on informal social safety nets for social services. Recognizing the void in informal social networks for older people, due to changes in economic and demographic structures, the Tearfund Country Programme for Rwanda set out to investigate the situation of older people in Rwanda and address gaps in its church-based programming. The research study was carried out under the 'Empowerment for sustainable social intervention' component of its church and community transformation (CCT) programme.[6]

The church in Africa and in Rwanda in particular has not always kept up with the rapid social, economic and technological changes in the new millennium that have constrained people's abilities to live well in old age and thus has not particularly engaged with ageing in the recent past. The reasons for this could be manifold. Factors at play are: a lack of understanding, poor grasp and appraisal of changing social dynamics; the social-economic-spiritual mandate of the church which focuses primarily on youth; and/or simply a disconnect between the church and the social issues manifest in modern-day Rwanda. Whatever the reasons for this passivity, it is a gap with significant implications. Although the Christian faith and theology emphasize engagement with social issues in general, the most prevalent theology of ageing in the Rwandan church context seems to place the responsibility of care upon the biological family, almost at the exclusion of the church family (Murangira, 2018).[7]

Within the practices of the earliest church, there is, however, no distinction between the responsibility of the biological family and the family as a community of believers; they place the responsibility for those who are old and vulnerable upon the community of believers.[8] The book of Acts is a testimony to the early church's ministry and engagement with social vulnerability and mutual interdependence, reminiscent of Christ's teaching on what it means to obey the Mosaic law that required the people of God to honour their parents.[9] Pentateuchal texts on Mosaic family law put an emphasis on the relationships between parents and their children. A close examination of the biblical text, however, reveals an underlying principle, that of the wider responsibility of care for those who are unable to care for themselves.[10] Such a text would not have been intended for children still under the care of their parents, but for adult children and their ageing parents. In the New Testament, Jesus highlights the anomaly in scholars' application of the law based on cultural interpretation and preferences that put parents at a disadvantage.[11] In the apostolic letters, particularly in the Pauline text, there is an emphasis on the parent–child relationship as well as the care for the weak and those in need that would include older people, especially older widows.[12]

Despite the evident importance of caring for older people, only some churches seem to respond to the challenges and issues brought about by old age. Globally, the response of the church in the past has been to institutionalize the elderly, particularly its own clergy. Beyond institutions, the church has both a canonical and moral obligation to protect the aged, both socially and economically. The Bible sees older people not only as a source of social economic comfort but also as an important voice of wisdom.[13] No wonder then that the Bible sees leaders in the church as 'elders'. This is not just a simple label but a deliberate selection of people with authority and community experience brought into the role of spiritual leadership. The Bible sees age as a principal qualification for the office of spiritual leadership, both in the Mosaic era and in the New Testament church. This is because of the importance of lived experience in older people, which qualifies them to speak into complex spiritual and social issues in the community. Theologies of ageing inspire us to reflect on the multiple complexities involved in shaping the practical and spiritual valuing of age, which is often at odds with the lack of value that society attributes to age generally (SCOP, 2008).

Conceptual framework

There is a lack of contextual African studies on ageing and the church, and since most studies on pastoral care and theologies of ageing are situated in Anglo-American settings, this space is characterized by 'a clear Euro-bias' (Ayete-Nyampong, 2014, p. 17). An exception to this is Samuel Ayete-Nyampong's pioneering work in Ghana which developed a 'communal pastoral care model' emphasizing community as the context within which pastoral care can be effectively practised. In studying ageing inclusion in the Rwandan context, we draw from (African) theologies of disability and from Tearfund's theological framework for inclusion, which sees inclusion as reconciliation and highlights the importance of fostering inclusive community (Kurlberg, 2020). Within this framework, the practice of 'fostering inclusive community' has particular relevance to this chapter, and indeed speaks strongly into Ayete-Nyampong's aforementioned work. The Christian sense of community and communal responsibility applies to the care and inclusion of all people. Practically speaking, 'fostering inclusive communities' is especially important where the church lacks institutional resources and is solely dependent on voluntary member engagement in the community. Here, church becomes a grass-roots social institution stepping in for the service delivery of old-age care and support in informal settings where no formal social service structures exist.

Disability theologian John Swinton challenges the concept of inclusion and advocates for a move towards considering 'practices of belonging', instead of mere 'ideas of inclusion' (2012a, p. 183). Theologically speaking, inclusive communities are those in which all can experience 'belonging', which we therefore see as a key component of inclusion. Individuals being perceived as invaluable and crucial for the functioning of the community is one aspect of belonging; community members will notice and 'miss you when you are not there' (Swinton, 2015, p. 232).[14] We can learn from and draw parallels with African theologies of disability, in the development of scarce African theologies of ageing.[15] Disability is a social experience that is shaped by particular contexts in which a person's perceived difference is experienced.

While a person may have specific impairments, these need not be disabling; rather, it is the negative reactions of society to these differences that can be disabling (Swinton, 2012c, p. 444). The same can be said about ageing, and the experiences of ageing in society, which is why 'borrowing' concepts from disability theology is fruitful, especially the concept of interdependence.

For example, Paul Leshota through participatory research with people with disabilities in Lesotho, develops a practical theological paradigm of interdependence, which resonates with the New Testament notion of *koinonia*[16] and the African notions of *ubuntu* or *botho*.[17] Such notions depicting interdependence 'should be allowed to shape attitudes towards disability and people with disabilities' (Leshota, 2015, p. 8). Similarly, Fidelis Nkomazana, in the context of Botswana, argues that Christians are called into a community of belonging, where differently abled people have an essential part in a 'web of mutual dependence and common sharing' (2016, p. 59). Such a theology of interdependence should similarly shape attitudes towards ageing and older people, including attitudes of respect and 'honouring the elders'. Listening to the life stories of older people in Rwanda, we interpret these through evidence of practices of belonging (and not belonging) in the context of the church community, 'the body of Christ', where biblically speaking all parts are crucial and those perceived to be weaker parts are to be honoured.

Methods: a grounded qualitative research approach

This chapter is based on qualitative methods. It analyses 12 group interviews (with an average group size of eight) and 14 individual in-depth interviews (with five widows, three men and three older couples). The 12 group interviews contained three groups with older men, three with older women and three mixed-gender groups respectively, plus three groups comprising serving pastors who were largely middle-aged. Both individual and group interviews were semi-structured and were conducted in May 2019. In total, we draw from transcripts of interviews with more than 100 Rwandans.

The interviews were conducted in Bugesera, Gisagara and Kicukiro, that is, two rural and one urban district. We recorded the interviews in Kinyarwanda, and professional Kigali-based translators produced verbatim transcripts in English, from which we drew the verbatim quotes. In the qualitative research methods tradition, pursuing a grounded approach involved coding all interviews for main themes and assigning sub-codes. We used the qualitative software analysis tool Atlas.ti for coding and analysis. We re-coded relevant data segments asking the following questions: What can we learn from older Rwandans about fostering inclusive communities – theologically and practically? What do their lived experiences tell us about experienced inclusion/exclusion, and the importance of belonging, in the church?

Empirical findings from the interviews with older Rwandans

Churches as spaces of interdependence and support for older people

For genocide survivors, 'replacement families' generate a sense of belonging and a space for mutual interdependence. Such replacement families could be found both in churches and through raising orphans and taking in other genocide survivors. This in effect creates belonging for individuals in the form of loosely defined 'patchwork families' and house-sharing arrangements. The church as 'family in Christ' seems to facilitate such communities of belonging in the most profound ways over the life course of older genocide survivors, and sustains their sense of belonging into old age, irrespective of their nuclear family status, as a diverse range of older people indicate:

> After losing all my family in the genocide, I found myself in the church and there were parents, children, friends, and I found a family. That gave me joy. I don't feel alone. (FG2: Older widow in group interview, Bugesera, 2 May 2019)

> I found a new family, people who will stand by me and support me. This was new to me, because I had not had a biological family that supported me in times [when] I lost people. (FG18: Older woman in group interview, Kicukiro, 10 May 2019)

> The children are adults: they have left home. So we turn to the church … There we share our challenges, our burdens with the

brethren: they advise you on what to do or help you. (FG2: Older man in focus group interview, Bugesera, 2 May 2019)

These quotes indicate that the type of support network the church offers encompasses more than emotional-relational moral support: the local congregation at times acts as 'service provider' for older adults living in the community (Huber, 1995, p. 286). Historically, especially in rural areas, churches have been 'village centres' that provided community-based and neighbour-hood-serving facilities and a variety of health, social, recreational and educational services (Huber, 1995, p. 286). The importance of practical church-initiated support services in post-genocide rural Rwanda is especially profound for enabling older widows to cope. For example, church choirs take on the role of providing practical support to older widows:

Amahoro [peace] choir did something good for me ... They cleaned the house, they mowed the hedges, they built the pit latrine, they renovated the house and roofing where it was spoiled, and they did everything that you see [in this house]. (II9: Older widow in individual interview, Gisagara, 6 May 2019)

In our parish in the action plan, we have a programme to help the vulnerable, beginning with the elderly. Among the activities we do, we cultivate their lands, especially choirs that participate in this activity, a kind of outreach programme. (FG1: Pastor in group interview, Bugesera, 2 May 2019)

What is more, churches have the potential not only to serve their own congregations but, through outreach programmes, also to serve the wider community. A group of pastors discuss this matter in a group interview, giving examples from their own parishes:

Pastor 1: [The church helps] even others [from the community], not just those who come to church. It is our responsibility. [We address] the challenges they face. The church is structured in cell groups, and through those cells groups, advocacy is done for those who have problems. Now when a problem has been presented to the church by the cell group, the church works out a solution for that problem of the elderly.

Pastor 2: The church doesn't care for its members only; it also takes care of others in the community. For instance, the young ones in Sunday School, when they are sent to fetch water for an elderly person, they don't discriminate: they do it for parish members and even other elderly people in the community. (FG1: Pastors in group interview, Bugesera, 2 May 2019)

Churches and Scriptures as places of belonging and meaning-making

Theologies of ageing often emphasize that ageing is part of a spiritual journey, moving from 'a having and doing based life to a more spiritual one of integrity and wholeness' (SCOP, 2008, p. 2). Spirituality encompasses the search for meaningful relationships, interconnectedness and a sense of belonging. In the interview data, the theme of belonging appears in multiple shapes and forms, and the interview transcripts as such extend our understanding of belonging. In fact, a sense of belonging and meaning-making through Scriptures and being 'in the house of the Lord' was identified as one of four major faith-related coping mechanisms for older Rwandans (Daehnhardt, 2021).[18] The importance of belonging to 'the house of the Lord' emerges as a crucial theme in the interview narratives, which correlates with the concept of 'church as replacement family' discussed above. Research participants associate church with a profound sense of belonging, home and peace. The phrase 'in the house of the Lord' could be found more than a dozen times in interview transcripts and often overlapped with the sub-code 'source of happiness'. In the following quotes, respondents elaborate on this sense of belonging and relief experienced when 'in the house of the Lord':

He gave me peace in my heart. Even though I am a widow, having lost children, he gives me joy. I am happy to be in the house of God, which is the first thing for me. (FG5: Older woman in group interview, Bugesera, 3 May 2019)

What made me happy was to go to the house of the Lord. That is what I feel made me very happy because had I not gone to the house of the Lord, I would have been dead. But now, going in the house of the Lord is my life and that is what makes me happy: there is nothing else. That is what has made me still alive [laughs]. (II1: Older woman in individual interview, Bugesera, 2 May 2019)

Importantly, respondents sometimes mentioned 'the house of the Lord' in combination with Scripture reading, as sources of comfort, relief and mental well-being:

> I enter the house of the Lord: it is what makes me feel relieved. Otherwise, I would have had a mental breakdown. I thank God very much that he is healing my heart and the Word of God strengthens me. I have peace in my heart – and it is the only peace I have, because I have many health problems. The Word of God strengthens me; there is nothing else that strengthens me apart from the Word of God. (FG15: Older woman in group interview, Kicukiro, 9 May 2019)

> When I came to the house of the Lord and they would read the Word of God, I would feel relieved in my heart. (FG15: Older woman in group interview, Kicukiro, 9 May 2019)

The Scriptures were an important anchor in terms of belonging and identity for the older people interviewed, both as part of congregational worship, but also when they were recited and remembered at home. Passages mentioned as 'favourite Scriptures' by older people do tell us something about older people's inclusion in terms of their self-understanding and confidence in relation to God. A sense of belonging and peacemaking through reading the Bible, and a release from biographical pain through reciting comforting Scriptures about identity, God as a good shepherd and helper in times of need, emerged as theological themes. God as healer of the broken and disabled (Matthew 9), as restorer when calling in distress (Jeremiah 33.3) and as source of strength and help in fear (Isaiah 41.10) were cited as 'favourite Scriptures'. Respondents quoted passages from Job, who had lost everything and concluded that the fear of God was wisdom, and to shun evil was understanding (Job 28.28). Psalm 1 was mentioned, which describes God as just judge over evil, a very apt psalm for genocide survivors. A passage in John describing closeness to God as 'abiding' in him (John 15), and images of the good shepherd (Psalm 23) who cares and provides, were also referred to as favourite Scriptures.

Churches as places of inclusion? The challenge of continued belonging during houseboundedness

In this section, we discuss belonging during the last stage of life, what used to be described as 'the fourth age' in the literature, a stage past the active phase of 'the third age', characterized by diminishment, decline and frailty. Not all older people experience this life stage, but for those who do it has profound implications. Joan Erikson (1997), who still published on the topic aged 95, acknowledged that late life can be the hardest part of life to navigate effectively. Where the older person becomes frail (or develops dementia), a disconnect between the individual older person and others has been noted (MacKinlay, 2021).[19] This can have an acute impact on feelings of belonging, which can be eroded. Research on older people's lives in the UK shows that 'many older people talk of no longer feeling they really belong to their church' as stages of 'being known, valued, accepted and involved which were once strong are now diminished' due to sickness, disability or houseboundedness (SCOP, 2008, p. 5). From older people's life stories in the Rwandan context too, a stark difference in inclusion along the lines of physical mobility is apparent. Inclusion in the life of the church for older people who can walk to the church building, are mobile and able to participate in church activities is often in contrast to the exclusion of those who are at home and unable to attend church. Permanent or periodic houseboundedness is often due to physical disabilities and the inability to walk long distances, as in this example of a husband who is the carer of his severely disabled wife:

> Husband: As for her, she just stays in bed. The simple things I do are to sustain this family that God gave me.
> Wife: Sometimes when I manage to wake up, I just go to church.
> Translator: Oh, you [can] walk?
> Husband: Yeah, she walks [sometimes].
> Wife: Yes, I am able to walk with my stick and go to church [sometimes].
> Husband: They had agreed to give me crutches. (II4: Individual interview with husband and wife, Bugesera, 3 May 2019)

Others may simply be unable to walk to church as the nearest open churches are located too far away and they may be unable to get lifts or rides to attend. As one participant explains:

MADLEINA DAEHNHARDT AND EMMANUEL MURANGIRA

> Now that they closed our church, I cannot go because other churches are far. But they are building it. When they open it, I will be going to church. [Interviewer: So when it was still open, you used to walk there?] Yeah, or when I met someone with a bicycle, the person would drop me there. (II2: Older woman in individual interview, Bugesera, 3 May 2019)

Pastors in group interviews were sympathetic to older people's needs and recognized the difficulties of attending church, especially if they lived alone, as in the following example:

> There is one elderly woman who came to church yesterday morning. She told me that she woke up at 3am to get ready to come here. On Easter we had been busy: we didn't manage to get to see her ... She is very old, almost 100 years. She came here and arrived at church at 9:30am ... She told me no one could even give her a hand to help her get here. I almost cried, I felt so sad. They have different problems, but they love to come for services. (FG8: Pastor in group interview, Gisagara, 6 May 2019)

Pastors recognize the dilemma in the fact that pastoral care for older people is the responsibility of the church, but at the same time it tends only to extend to those who attend the church. As one pastor insightfully commented, those older people who are housebound may be reached on an individual basis, but not necessarily through organized church activities:

> Assisting the elderly is usually the responsibility of the church. However, among the elderly, some are not visible, we don't know where they live, the cause being that they don't attend church. The truth is the people who are assisted, cared for, are the ones who can come to church. Those who are unable to attend church, even in cases [where] one assists them, it is done individually, not on the church level. (FG1: Pastor in group interview, Bugesera, 2 May 2019)

On a number of occasions, pastors and older research participants mentioned the practice of bringing 'holy communion' to the homes of older people who were unable to participate in it in church, for example:

We have elderly men and women [in the congregation] who are like 100 years, who can no longer come to church ... There are some who are 75, 80, and you meet them in the early-morning prayers ... There is another one we have who is 90, who no longer comes to church. When we have holy communion, we take it to him at home and share it with him. (FG8: Pastor in group interview, Gisagara, 6 May 2019)

Regarding going to church, I am no longer able to go there. I can't even come down that hill. I just crawl to the veranda and sit there, in front of the house. However, the community communicated my problem to the church, and the church leaders always send me holy communion when they do that ritual and I take it from here. (II13: Older woman in individual couple interview, Kicukiro, 9 May 2019)

These insights pose big questions for practical theology and pastoral care. How do we include older people in the 'body of Christ' when they are no longer able to leave their homes and participate in services? What is the role of the home and home visitation? Could pastoral carers or church members conduct family services or small groups in the house of an older person so they can participate?

Churches as places of intergenerational encounter and exclusion: the youth focus

The church as an institution is consistently intergenerational, where quality of life for people of all ages is enhanced by intergenerational contacts and friendships (Huber, 1995, p. 290). Being known and involved and feeling accepted, valued and respected all lead to a sense of belonging (SCOP, 2008). The church context can be a space where intergenerational justice is experienced and mutual interdependence is lived out in practice. Older people have intrinsic value to church communities, as carriers of faith, history-bearers and a source of wisdom for younger generations. Older people's contributions are manifold in the Rwandan context (see Davis et al., 2019). As one pastor explained, when asked about older people's visibility in church, they are the stable pillars of the church:

Actually the elderly are the ones who are visible [chuckle]. It depends on churches, each church is different. We have the youth in the work of God, but when it comes to attending church service, the elderly don't miss the services. (FG8: Pastor in group interview, Gisagara, 6 May 2019)

However, the data reveals both areas of experienced inclusion and exclusion of older people in the church, and it is not possible to find homogeneity in what it means to grow old in church. One older man describes his experience as 'feeling welcomed', being visited and visiting others: 'We feel welcomed [when we go to worship]. They give us seats as elderly people: we are respected. [And] yes, we do get visitors, and we also visit each other' (FG11: Older man in group interview, Gisagara, 7 May 2019).

Yet, at the same time, older people interviewed had concerns regarding the youth, and uneasy feelings of some of the socio-cultural changes they witnessed in 'Young Rwanda'. Older people elaborated how the power of the youth can be destructive if not channelled appropriately within families: 'The power that destroyed this nation and which to this day still destroys the world is the power of the youth' (FG2: Older man in group interview, Bugesera, 2 May 2019).

When it comes to the question of intergenerational relations and respect, one older woman said: 'Some do [respect us]! Others can pass by you and do not even greet you' (II2: Older woman in individual interview, Bugesera, 2 May 2019). Such accounts point to a change in intergenerational contracts over time. Two older women respondents compared their experience of respect when younger with their experience now of disrespect in old age:

R1: I remember one time I saw an old woman with a walking stick, pulling the hoe behind her. It was a long distance: it was so sad because she couldn't carry her hoe. I feel bad when I remember her. That time I thought that old age where I was headed wasn't a pretty time.

R2: When I was young, I used to take with me a piece of fabric so that if I met an old woman carrying things, I would help them. If I met a mother carrying her child on the back, I would help her. Our parents had taught us such things. Unfortunately, we do not see it in this generation. Even when you meet them somewhere, they can't give you a seat they had. It can actually be the opposite.

African societies have traditionally valued older people, for their 'maturation, wisdom, integrity and experience which enable them to transmit to the younger generation the input necessary for the attainment of the social and moral ideal[s] which characterises the community's religious aspiration' (Ayete-Nyampong, 2014, p. 35). In the light of African elders' traditional roles of transmission of socially acceptable morals, customs and stories, being ignored or dismissed by the 'new generation' is particularly painful.

Multiple explanations for this manifest change in attitude and loss of respect were given – exemplified in ignoring the elders by not greeting them, which was traditionally unthinkable as well as contrary to Scripture.[20] Explanations were associated with loss of values, increase in self-centeredness and separation of extended families through migration, which contributed further to a change in intergenerational contracts:

> R1: I think that after the genocide, people lost their values and the young generations didn't receive those values. The genocide took the elders, the parents, the children everyone. Those who survived, they didn't have parents to teach them the right values; they had to raise themselves. For me, I think it is because of the genocide. Everyone started living a self-centered life. And love disappeared.
> R2: And the parents and children separated. They live separate lives trying to make a living and the mindsets changed. Because of that separation, the bond between parent and child broke. They would remember that there was a time they lived without parents and life continued. (FG12: Older women in group interview, Gisagara, 7 May 2019)

Swinton (2012b) points out the correlation between being missed and belonging. If younger people do not seem to care about or miss older people when they are absent from their community, then, Swinton would argue, older people do not fully belong to that community. Experienced exclusion can be connected to the changing socio-cultural context of intergenerational relations, but can also be explained by a lack of theological reflection that could speak helpfully into the experience of ageing in the Rwandan context. The church's own excessive focus on youth and growth seems to reflect contemporary narratives, where changing intergenerational relations in society and church are mirrored.

Societies do not, on the whole, value age when people are valued in monetary terms by what they earn, produce and consume; this creates an enormous gap between younger and older people and separates and alienates generations (SCOP, 2008, p. 1). Pastors reflected honestly on the exclusion of older people in church programmes, and a preference for active, income-generating younger church members, who are 'the future of the church':

> In general when we are talking about the churches in Rwanda, pastors, when we plan, we look at people who are productive, like the youth. To be honest, we really don't get to focus on the elderly, who do not do anything. Many of the old people we have do not have pensions. (FG14: Pastor in group interview, Kicukiro, 9 May 2019)

Pastors may feel a strong responsibility towards young people, and particularly towards the vast numbers of young people who are part of Rwandan churches. The wider predominant narrative of the future 'lying in the hands of the youth' leads to churches investing their resources in children and young people.

'Honouring the elders': the responsibility and challenge for the church

The notion of 'honouring the elders' is part of mutual respect and interdependence, for which reason we revisit now data segments coded under this sub-code. We found that just as it is not possible to find homogeneity in the experience of growing old in a church context, or to be definite in the analysis of intergenerational relations, so too views among clergy on whether older people are sufficiently honoured in churches or not differ widely. Pastors see and acknowledge the challenge of old-age inclusion to varying degrees, as shown in the wide range of answers to the question, 'Do you think your church honours its elders?'

> It is a good question, but difficult to answer ... the circumstances are different in each church. However, I can say that we honour the elders and help them in the little means we have. In the Rwandan culture, the young ones honour the elders. Even in church, the culture is taken into consideration; the church members try to honour the elderly. So I would say in church

the elderly are honoured. (FG8: Pastor in group interview, Gisagara, 8 May 2019)

Assisting the vulnerable and the elderly is the responsibility of the church. The CCT programme has helped us improve the way we do it, but it is the mandate of the church.[21]

No. Not as we should. Because there is no support for them. Only those who worked in the church and who get their pension from the government. But the other old people we preached to, who joined the church, they struggled. They are poor and we don't support them. (FG14: Pastors in group interview, Kicukiro, 9 May 2019)

Although the responsibility to help the vulnerable and poor in the church community is generally clear to pastors and congregations, reaching out to older people in the community seems to be more sporadic than organized, as pastors in a group interview suggest:

Pastor 1: Children can bring clothes or food to the parents, but they don't have someone like a house help to do the cleaning, cooking or even to keep them company. The help is inadequate because they need day-to-day assistance.
Pastor 2: People who are in old age, it is like they have no one to care for them. Their children, for those who have them, live far from them. By the time they are 80 years, 100 years, their children are grown and they have their own lives. And there is no system to help them that has been put in place by the church. Even when we help them, it is occasional. There is nothing regular, continuous. (FG8: Pastors in group interview, Gisagara, 6 May 2019)

In other words, the challenge for the church seems to be how to organize itself, in the light of changing socio-demographic rural contexts, to provide more regular social services reaching older people and find ways to mainstream these in its existing (outreach) work. It is to this subject that we turn next.

Implications for churches and FBOs: theologies and practices of ageing inclusion

Inclusion of older people in pastoral ministry and community outreach

From the data analysis, we have seen how the changes to social safety networks make the role of church as 'replacement family' and 'service provider' very prominent. We have interpreted those roles in the light of inclusion expressed in belonging and interdependence. These observations link to the concept of church as a 'social institution' that is socially accepted even by non-members in the community mainly because of its outreach and service to the community. The church can achieve credibility and create a sense of belonging as well as ownership by members of the community across generations. From this point of view, the church has influence in the Rwandan context and great credibility among members of the local community. What the church cares about is in effect what the community will come to care about too. If the church shows that it cares for the elderly, the community, irrespective of religious affiliations or belief, will tend to follow suit. One implication for churches in the Rwandan context is thus to think about their spheres of influence well beyond their own walls.

Globally, the types of services offered for older people vary from congregation to congregation. Elbert Cole (1991, cited by Huber, 1995) provides a simple schema that is conceptually useful to differentiate between the different types of outreach that exist or could be possible in the Rwandan context: life maintenance, life enrichment, life reconstruction and life transcendence. The practical help with chores and cultivation offered by choirs falls under 'life maintenance', and we have seen plenty of evidence in the data for such engagement. Counselling, bereavement and mental health support offered by or for older people fall under 'life reconstruction'. While this takes place informally among the older people interviewed, formal programmes are virtually non-existent. There is great potential for the Rwandan church to develop such programmes. As we have seen in the importance of meaning-making through Scriptures for older people, the biggest part the Rwandan church may play at present for older people is in 'life transcendence', through worship, prayer and Bible teaching. This is also where Dayle Friedman's (2001) pastoral roles of fostering a life of meaning and enabling a life of connection can primarily be located.[22]

Earlier work in the US context by Lucy Steinitz (1980) analysed different styles of ministry and theological persuasion in relation to church-provided social services for older people. The study of 40 churches found that conservative Protestant denominations, mostly medium-sized and small-sized with an emphasis on personal religious experiences and a spiritual/evangelistic persuasion – the US equivalent of the Rwandan churches in our sample – had few formally organized services for older people. These churches were characterized by reliance on informal social support networks generated according to patterns of friendship and a notion of religious duty within the church. In these types of churches, many opportunities for spiritual enrichment and the development of (intergenerational) friendships were found among parishioners (Huber, 1995, p. 289). These observations are relevant to the older people interviewed in our cohort. On the other hand, the gaps identified in intergenerational respect and lack of interdependence, and an overemphasis on 'youth' as the 'future of the church', require theological rethinking to bridge some of the divides between the generations as barriers to inclusion.

Often, pastoral care of older adults has not been a priority in the theological formation and pastoral education of (young) trainees (Kimble, 1995).[23] As a result, there are significant gaps, with consequences for practice, on which this chapter touches. The insights generated by the experience of houseboundedness in later life poses big questions for practical theology and pastoral care. Such questions are perhaps not asked often enough, or thought through by pastors and congregations in Rwanda (and elsewhere). How can older people be part of the 'body of Christ' when they are no longer able to leave their homes and participate in church activities?[24] What 'enabling actions' are necessary on the part of the congregation (Friedman, 2001) to create a stable sense of belonging? Swinton's work on dementia raises some similarly challenging questions for the church in the UK context, such as 'whether the act of welcoming people with dementia and their families has been central to the strategies of mission, evangelism, worship, and pastoral care' and 'if not [then] why not?' (2012a, p. 278). What Swinton calls 'a theology of welcome and belonging' in the context of dementia – which links in to 'a theology of visitation' – resonates strongly with the questions emerging from our interview material. For the church to include people with dementia and their carers, it requires them to take time and be with them and get to know them, and 'in order to know them, we need to visit them' (Swinton, 2012b, p. 280). We can extend this 'theology of visitation' from the context of dementia to all conditions which lead to gradual houseboundedness (and potential isolation) in later life. Houseboundedness clearly calls for inventiveness and creativity in pastoral care and congregational life.

Since Tearfund as an FBO works through and with the local church, we attempt to make a link between the theological mandate of the church and organized communities of practice. We now provide an example of Tearfund's most recent programmatic adaptations in Rwanda, intentionally making its CCT work more inclusive.

Tearfund as an example of an FBO including older people in programming

In examining the implications of inclusion of older people for FBO practice and programming, it is worth taking note of the attendant complexities and challenges relating to institutional identity. While all churches are inherently FBOs, not all FBOs are churches, and this has significant implications for practice and how organizations work and respond to issues of inclusion. Although FBOs and churches have faith as a common denominator, their modus operandi and their rules of operation differ greatly. However, our data analysis shows that the way the church and FBOs engage with older people is inherently determined by what they perceive to be their biblical mandate. Non-faith-based organizations may provide similar services but not out of reference to any strictly binding divine mandate.

That being said, research on ageing conducted by the Tearfund office in Rwanda found that national priorities had a focus on youth, with very little if any on older people (Davis et al., 2019). The research also found that most NGO programming focused on young and able-bodied beneficiaries, with very little social protection made available. It generated critical evidence that has informed different stakeholders in the development sphere in Rwanda, visibly influencing changes in both practice and services to older people. A number of churches, denominations, FBOs and even secular institutions that engaged with the research process have adopted more inclusive policies and strategies that ensure older people's needs are priorities. As part of this response to the research findings and recommendations, Tearfund in Rwanda started exploring ways of supporting partners and stakeholders to mainstream older people in existing programmes working through the local church.

1 *Advocacy and awareness-raising with the church.* Tearfund's work with churches now focuses on raising awareness of older people and their particular needs – not as a separate group, but as an inherent part of the congregation that needs special attention, spiritually, socially and economically. This work is inspired by the findings and recommendations of the research report, which included bringing to the attention of national denominational and church leaders actual elder abuse (see Davis et al., 2019). Churches, and national church leadership in particular, can use their position of influence to advocate for policies and practices that specifically address the needs of older people in Rwanda, given its unique history and the impact of the genocide on older people.[25] Churches are in a unique position to influence drastic changes in social norms that affect older people's welfare, as well as promote inter-ethnic and intergenerational peace. Working with the church therefore needs to go beyond simple awareness-raising, but seeks to build institutional partnerships to include ageing members of Rwandan society.

2 *Adapting programming to older people.* Although Tearfund's programmes have generally been thought to be inclusive in design, delivery and measuring impact, the intentionality of inclusion, particularly for older people, has not been a prominent feature. This is because, in the past, older people have not been seen through an inclusion lens, unlike other people groups, such as those with disabilities. The tendency has generally been to lump older people together with other vulnerable people groups, which means their specific challenges are not addressed. Integrating such challenges, but also recognizing the immense contribution older people make to projects and programmes, has meant re-evaluating social protection approaches, especially for projects and programmes that focus on empowerment. It requires critical examination of long-held views and conventions on how development is done and sustainability achieved where vulnerability is likely to persist far beyond a particular programme or project. Adapting and integrating the needs of older people in

projects and programmes, particularly in Tearfund's work in Rwanda, has necessitated retraining community development facilitators.[26] These trained facilitators mobilize communities and community groups to develop a community-led social protection and support mechanism for older citizens. It has also required retraining church leaders and partner staff, both in CCT programmes and in other projects, on how to include and integrate older people's needs in projects and programmes. This is particularly important in the Rwandan context, noting that the general, but mistaken, assumption has been that families take care of their old. In a country devastated by a genocide only a generation ago, there are few family members left for many ageing survivors, and the resources available to run an institutionalized support mechanism based on social protection models are inadequate.

3 *Making older people key beneficiaries in Covid-19 response work.* One of the benefits of awareness work with the churches was giving voice to older people during the coronavirus pandemic. The awareness work was able to highlight the plight of older people as a particularly vulnerable people group. Drawing from the recommendation of the *Ageing in Rwanda* report (Davis et al., 2019) and a new internal sector-wide mapping exercise, Tearfund developed tools and resources that enabled churches to consider and support older people during the pandemic, resulting in the publication of new guidelines (see Daehnhardt, 2020). The Tearfund guidelines for working with older people during the Covid-19 pandemic were adapted to the Rwandan context to ensure inclusion for older people was safe during the pandemic. In this context, the Rwanda team developed a project that specifically incentivizes communities and community groups to develop and sustainably manage home-grown systems that support older people. This came in the form of the Covid-19 recovery project where a stimulus package was made available to self-help groups to encourage community groups to provide long-term sustained support to older people, particularly those in greatest need. It helped bring the needs of older people to the fore, given their high levels of health, economic and social vulnerability to the pandemic and its knock-on effects.

4 *Internal capacity-building initiatives for staff on old-age inclusion.* Successful programming depends on staff capacity and their ability not only to deliver programme and project activities, but also to ensure activities generate the desired impact. Adapt-

ing programming approaches to ensure the needs of older people are adequately addressed by programmes and project activities requires retraining and equipping staff. They need to develop new skills in inclusive programme design, developing people-centred implementation approaches as well as constant information gathering to make sure needs are met. To ensure staff were equipped to support churches and para-church organizations in integrating care and support for old people, we adapted existing training materials (HelpAge, 2017). These had been designed by specialized agencies, and were slightly adapted to the operating context of Tearfund in Rwanda, as well as to its organizational culture and ethos. Although RedR's and ADCAP's 'Age and disability capacity programme' was initially designed for emergency settings, and thus based to a large extent on provision rather than enabling processes, it has informed change and innovations in practice in the use of training in Rwanda. The adapted training focuses not only on understanding the needs and capacities of older people, but also on critical knowledge for practitioners. It enables staff, churches and partners to adapt and contextualize resources, build stakeholder capacity and collect and analyse evidence to enable organizations and institutions to adapt their business process to inclusion of older people.

Conclusion

The plan to write this chapter preceded the coronavirus pandemic that began in 2020. Inevitably, the pandemic, ongoing as we write, has not only had an impact on our train of thought, but has also influenced the discourse on theologies and practices. To a greater extent, it has raised critical questions, particularly on how the church has adapted or should adapt the locus and target of its ministry in unusual circumstances that put older people at great disadvantage, as coronavirus has done. At the same time, lockdowns and restrictions have thrust many more of us into situations of houseboundedness and isolation, which perhaps makes some of the questions explored in this chapter more tangible. At the very least, it offers an opportunity to experience, and therefore empathize with, aspects of older people's lives more generally.

We have raised a number of theological questions, and questions regarding pastoral care and the faith-based development sector. We have tried to establish multiple links between empirical findings and implications for theology and practice, considering the role of the Rwandan church in 'honouring its elders' with a particular focus on 'fostering inclusive communities'. This chapter gives voice to a range of older Rwandans on different aspects of experienced inclusion, understood through the lens of belonging and mutual intergenerational interdependence. It makes a case for thinking about the church as a social institution, extending its mandate for inclusion beyond internal networks to wider community influence. It also highlights that the church's pastoral role can be extended more effectively for wider community impact through offering more mainstream social services for older people.

Our analysis has revealed areas of both inclusion and exclusion experienced by older people in the church, showing that the meaning of growing old in church is not homogenous but diverse. Churches, affectionately described by participants as 'the house of the Lord', are spaces for belonging, meaning-making, intergenerational friendship, support and interdependence. However, we have also highlighted the need for theological rethinking to bridge intergenerational divides that the research has highlighted, and the need for engagement if generations are to move towards mutual interdependence. We have called for inventiveness in a 'theology of visitation' in the face of houseboundedness. In some ways, this chapter raises more questions than answers. We hope these questions will spark further dialogue, reflection, research and action. Tearfund in Rwanda is on a journey of responding to the often ignored questions of inclusion of older people in development programming through local church partners. The initiatives of adaptation and innovation outlined here are only a snapshot taken in the early stages of what can be expected to be a longer-term trajectory. It is our hope that peer agencies and partner churches will join together in this endeavour, drawing inspiration from this pioneering work in twenty-first-century Rwanda.

Acknowledgements

We would like to thank our colleagues Nina Kurlberg, Rachel Paton, Marsha Setian and Sas Conradie for reviewing the chapter and for providing helpful feedback and comments. Thanks also to Rachel Paton for helping with part of the literature review.

Bibliography

Ayete-Nyampong, S., 2014, *A Study of Pastoral Care of the Elderly in Africa: An interdisciplinary approach with focus on Ghana*, Bloomington, IN: AuthorHouse.

Cole, E., 1991, 'Church and Community, Partners in Service', workshop at McKendree Village, Nashville, TN.

Daehnhardt, M., 2020, *Guidance for Churches on How to Support Older People during the Covid-19 Pandemic*, Teddington: Tearfund.

Daehnhardt, M., 2021, 'Belief and Belonging in Later Life – The lived experiences of coping among older Rwandans', *Journal of Religion, Spirituality and Aging* 33(1).

Davis, F., E. Murangira and M. Daehnhardt, 2019, *Ageing in Rwanda: Challenges and opportunities for church, state and nation*, Teddington and Birmingham: Tearfund and University of Birmingham.

de Walque, D. and P. Verwimp, 2010, 'The Demographic and Socio-Economic Distribution of Excess Mortality during the 1994 Genocide in Rwanda', *Journal of African Economies* 19, pp. 141–62.

Erikson, J., 1997, *The Life Cycle Completed: Extended version*, New York: W. W. Norton.

Friedman, D. A., 2001, 'Letting Their Faces Shine: Accompanying aging people and their families', in D. A. Friedman, *Jewish Pastoral Care: A practical handbook from traditional and contemporary sources*, Woodstock: Jewish Lights Publishing.

HelpAge, 2017, 'Age and Disability Capacity Programme (ADCAP)', *HelpAge International*, www.helpage.org/what-we-do/emergencies/adcap-age-and-disability-capacity-building-programme/, accessed 4.01.2021.

Huber, L. W., 1995, 'The Church in the Community', in M. A. Kimble, S. H. McFadden, J. W. Ellor and J. J. Seeber (eds), *Aging, Spirituality and Religion: A handbook*, Minneapolis, MN: Augsburg Fortress.

Kimble, M. A., 1995, 'Pastoral Care', in M. A. Kimble, S. H. McFadden, J. W. Ellor and J. J. Seeber (eds), *Aging, Spirituality and Religion: A handbook*, Minneapolis, MN: Augsburg Fortress.

Kurlberg, N., 2020, *Inclusion: A theological framework*, Teddington: Tearfund.

Leshota, P., 2015, 'From Dependence to Interdependence: Towards a practical theology of disability', *HTS Teologiese Studies/Theological Studies* 71(2), pp. 1–9.

Longman, T., 2010, *Christianity and Genocide in Rwanda*, Cambridge: Cambridge University Press.

MacKinlay, E., 2021, 'What Does it Mean to be Old and Frail? Implications for faith and the church', presentation given at the conference 'Theology, Ageing and the Life of the Church', hosted by Nazarene Theological College, Manchester, 30 January 2021.

Murangira, E., 2018, *'Honouring Our Elders'. Challenges and Opportunities for church intervention in promoting and facilitating sustainable old age care in Rwanda against the backdrop of the 1994 genocide against the Tutsi*, research proposal, Kigali: Tearfund.

NISR, 2008, 'Vision 2020 Umurenge Program (VUP) – Baseline survey', Kigali: National Institute of Statistics of Rwanda (NISR).

NISR, 2012, *The Fourth Population and Housing Census, Rwanda 2012. Main Indicators Report*, Kigali: National Institute of Statistics of Rwanda, Ministry of Finance and Economic Planning (NISR/MINECOFIN).

NISR, 2014, *Rwanda Poverty Profile Report. Integrated Household and Living Conditions Survey*, Kigali: NISR/MINECOFIN.

Njoroge, F., 2019, *Church and Community Mobilisation Process: Facilitator's manual*, Teddington: Tearfund.

Nkomazana, F., 2016, '"No One Who Has a Blemish Shall Draw Near": Pentecostals rising above a disabling hermeneutics', *Journal of Disability & Religion: Disability, Religion and Theology: African Perspectives* 20(1–2), pp. 77–83.

Sabates-Wheeler, R., E. Wylde, M. Ulrichs, I. Aboderin, J. Bayisenge and A. Irambeshya, 2018, *Population Aging in Rwanda: Current needs, future projections, and implications for policy*, University of Sussex: Institute of Development Studies.

SCOP, 2008, *A Theology of Ageing: Ageing well. Spiritual care for older people*, Oxford: Anglican Diocese of Oxford.

SDDirect, 2021, 'Who Are the "bottom billion" Older People?' Disability Inclusion Helpdesk, London: Social Development Direct.

Steinitz, L. Y., 1980, 'The Church within the Network of Social Services to the Elderly: Case study of Laketown', dissertation, School of Social Service Administration: University of Chicago.

Swinton, J., 2012a, 'From Inclusion to Belonging: A practical theology of community, disability and humanness', *Journal of Religion, Disability and Health* 16, pp. 172–83.

Swinton, J., 2012b, 'Hospitality among Strangers: Christian communities as places of belonging', in J. Swinton, *Dementia: Living in the memories of God*, Grand Rapids, MI: Eerdmans.

Swinton, J., 2012c, 'Disability, Ableism, and Disablism', in B. J. Miller-McLemore (ed.), *The Wiley-Blackwell Companion to Practical Theology*, Princeton NJ: Blackwell Publishing.

Swinton, J., 2015, 'Using Our Bodies Faithfully: Christian friendship and the life of worship', *Journal of Disability and Religion* 19, pp. 228–42.

Victor, R. C., J. S. Scrambler, A. Bowling and J. Bond, 2005, 'The Prevalence of, and Risk factors for, Loneliness in Later Life: A survey of older people in Great Britain', *Ageing and Society* 25(6), pp. 357–75.

World Bank, 2020, 'The World Bank in Rwanda – Overview', *The World Bank*, www.worldbank.org/en/country/rwanda/overview, accessed 14.10.2021.

Notes

1 The broader study on *Ageing in Rwanda* was published as Davis et al. 2019. The initial title of the research project proposal was 'honouring our elders' (Murangira, 2018), a title informed by verses in both the New and the Old Testaments in the Bible (Lev. 19.32; Prov. 23.22; Matt. 15.4).

2 Tearfund is both an FBO and an NGO (non-governmental organization) and we use these terms interchangeably. When referring to the wider mainstream international sector, we use the term INGOs.

3 Tearfund's mapping exercise 'Covid-19 hot-spotting: guides for older people' was conducted by Tearfund's Impact and Effectiveness team between March and May 2020. The aim of this exercise – combined with an analysis of rapidly documented emerging evidence of older people's experience of Covid-19 globally – was to produce a guidance document for churches (see Daehnhardt, 2020).

4 At the time of writing, Tearfund has developed a theology of peacebuilding, a theology of gender, a theology of inclusion and a theology of race and ethnicity. A theology of disability was being developed at the time of writing, but a theology of ageing has not yet been developed.

5 VUP is an Integrated Local Development Programme. This is an initiative by the government of Rwanda in collaboration with development partners and NGOs. The VUP aims 'to accelerate poverty eradication, rural growth, and social protection' (NISR, 2008).

6 As of 2021, CCT is one of three corporate priorities for Tearfund globally. Within CCT, the church and community mobilization process (CCMP) is regarded as Tearfund's flagship programme and faith-based approach to community development (see Njoroge, 2019). In Rwanda, Tearfund carries out CCT through church-based self-help groups.

7 See also research findings that seem to emphasize immediate family, and the focus of the ageing narrative on immediate family support (Davis et al., 2019, p. 11).

8 For example, see Acts 6.1–7, which is an account of the church appointing members to ensure all widows (many of whom could be assumed to be older) were included in the daily food distribution.

9 See Matthew 15.3–7 and Exodus 20.12. While these texts do not expressly mention the elderly, but rather speak of parents, hermeneutic

logic would suggest the parents would have been old and in need of help from their children. This particular text would be very relevant to the changing carescapes of older people and the biblical exigencies to honour older people in the community. The Mosaic law that Jesus was referencing would have been expected as a standard norm in community, family and individual expressions of piety.

10 Both the Old and the New Testaments put the onus on society, particularly the community of believers, *civitas dei*, to care for those who would not normally be able to care for themselves. What is more, in Psalm 41.1 the psalmist postulates that the care of those in need is a source of blessing.

11 See Matthew 15.3–6.

12 For example, Matthew 15.1–6, Exodus 20.12, Deuteronomy 5.16, Ephesians 6.1.

13 According to Job 12.12, wisdom is with the aged, and understanding in 'length of days'.

14 Swinton's work with people with dementia and their carers is an example, where he argues that '[they] need to be missed when they are absent. If they're not missed, they don't belong; and if they don't belong, there is no true community – for anyone' (2012b, p. 279).

15 Considerable overlap between disability and old age is visible in the higher disability prevalence among older people when compared with the general population, especially in low- and middle-income countries where disability prevalence is 43 per cent among people aged 60+ (in comparison to 29 per cent in high-income countries) (SDDirect, 2021).

16 Participants in the research, when asked about 'the meaning of church as people of God', spoke in nuanced ways of 'fellowship, communion, belonging, sharing and participation' (Leshota, 2015, p. 5).

17 The interconnection – and interdependence – of humans in *ubuntu* is well known (the literal translation of the Zulu term meaning 'I am, because you are'). Furthermore, *botho* is a Sesotho word that captures the essence of what it means to be human. The concept can be found in many forms in a number of societies throughout the African continent, in almost all of which it represents personhood or humanness (Leshota, 2015, p. 5).

18 This section draws from Daehnhardt (2021), who discusses in greater detail four coping mechanisms: first, the role of personal prayer and resilience; second, the impact of socio-spiritual capital in the form of other church members; third, the sense of belonging and meaning-making through Scriptures and being 'in the house of the Lord'; and fourth, healthy behaviours influenced by religious values which contribute to older people's well-being.

19 Frailty is likely to be characterized by low physical activity, few social interactions and several chronic diseases requiring medical care. Decreasing mobility, lack of control over one's own health and feeling isolated in residential care were mentioned as 'the hardest things now' by frail older people (MacKinlay, 2021).

20 Leviticus 19.32 provides an interesting parallel to the biblical association between respecting older people and respecting God: 'You shall stand up before the grey head and honour the face of an old man, and you shall fear your God: I am the LORD.'

21 The CCT programme refers to Tearfund's church and community transformation work, in which the interviewed pastor participated (see also n. 8).

22 Friedman outlines a compelling model for the role of pastoral care-giving addressing the three main spiritual challenges of the ageing process from late-midlife to life's end, that is, finding meaning, confronting empty time and counteracting disconnection (2001, p. 288).

23 Ayete-Nyampong, in response to a missing 'pastoral gerontology' in the context of Ghana, developed a course structure for the training of clergy at seminary level, which combines pastoral and biblical studies with gerontology. It involves sensitizing and equipping pastors to train volunteers in pastoral ministry with older people, facilitating greater engagement of the Christian church in Africa with the theology and praxis of its ageing members (see chapter 10 in Ayete-Nyampong, 2014).

24 Chapter 7 in this volume on digital inclusion offers some relevant points in the context of new church activities, although with limited application to rural Rwanda.

25 Churches were, and still are, powerful and influential institutions with the capacity to be constructive, destructive or passive actors. In this chapter, we do not analyse the history of Rwandan churches in the 1994 genocide against the Tutsi. See Longman (2010) for a detailed, critical account of the history of the Rwandan church.

26 Facilitators are community volunteers trained and equipped to facilitate, train and provide critical follow up and support to community members engaged in project or programme activities.

11

'Nothing wey no get cure for this world':[1] Interrogating Healing and the Miraculous for Women Living with Disability and HIV in Nigeria

JESSIE FUBARA-MANUEL

The quest for healing and well-being is central to humanity. Within Nigeria's Christianity and indigenous world views, healing and health are crucial aspects of the daily realities that connect individual progress to 'social development' (Obinna, 2012). Healing therefore has both personal and communal implications; it enables a person to engage in or restore 'relationships with family, friends, and community' (Oke, 2017). This communal element of healing is essential for people who, due to disability, disease and gender, face stigmatization that engenders discrimination and exclusion from social and religious spaces. This chapter draws on my field work researching the impact of faith for women living with both disability and HIV in Nigeria. The women in my study expressed their understanding of healing as holistic and encompassing all aspects of well-being. For these women, healing includes all that facilitates human flourishing, including social, mental, physical, economic and emotional well-being, transforming their identities, improving their physical conditions and enabling some degree of inclusion.

When women living with disability and HIV pray to Jesus Christ for healing, they display their belief that they can be healed of scientifically incurable conditions because of their personal relationship with him.[2] They believe that he can heal spiritual, emotional, psychological and physical diseases in a way they describe as miraculous. Their belief in the miraculous gives them the ability to cope with daily challenges and realities at the intersection of gender, disability and HIV.[3]

My focus in this chapter is to interrogate the claims of the women in my research through the lens of Micheline Kamba's scholarly and experiential understanding of healing. Kamba's views, born out of her personal experiences of disability, shape her theology of healing, which largely focuses on social, spiritual and emotional aspects of holistic healing rather than on the physical. Kamba's position, from the perspectives of my research participants, limits the concept of holistic healing, especially as she emphasizes her aversion to praying for physical healing. To Kamba, physical healing is 'seeing the person shifted to another level that was not expected, because many people with disabilities have been alienated by the culture and tradition of their context so that they cannot do anything in their lives because they are disabled' (2016, p. 274). Yet physical healing for my research participants means healing that results in specific visible physiological change in the body, which could lead to, but is different from, improvement in abilities which Kamba alludes to in her description of physical healing.

In arguing for a broader understanding of healing, this chapter explores two distinct ways that the women in my research appropriate healing and how this appropriation impacts their experiences of living with disability and HIV. First, that healing is transformation of identity that is liberating and affirming of their Christian faith; and second, that healing involves physical change or curing of a disease or disability.

Although there are differing perceptions of healing, for the women in my research, their understanding of healing is informed by their Christian faith and life's challenges. As such, any theological articulations of healing for disability should include such divergent perceptions to avoid imposing one's experiential realities on others. I argue, therefore, that because experiences of disability are personal, theological reflections about disability and healing should be holistic and open to other interpretations.

Research methodology

Findings for this chapter draw on six months of ethnographic research including participant-observation, interviews and focus group discussions (FGDs) which generated insightful conversations. Much of the data for this writing was gathered from four different FGD activities with 12 women living with both a disability and HIV.[4] Unlike one-to-one interviews, FGDs provide space for group participation to facilitate discussions on agreed themes or focuses while introducing varied perspectives and challenging normative practices (Kitzinger, 1994).

The 12 women who took part in these FGDs were living with different types of disabilities, among which were visual, hearing and physical impairments. All the women were within the age range of 28 and 56, and from various church backgrounds such as Catholic, Pentecostal and Charismatic denominations. Among them were single, married, divorced and widowed women living in the towns of Uyo and Port Harcourt, Nigeria. Due to the sensitive nature of this research and in line with best-practice research ethics, pseudonyms are used in writing up the research findings (Lee, 1993).

The main objective of this research was to investigate the extent to which faith impacts women living with disabilities and HIV within their cultural and religious contexts. My first intention was therefore to explore these women's understanding of Christian faith, what faith means for them and how faith is experienced by them. The women spoke of their faith as a personal relationship with Jesus Christ, the healer. Consequently, discussions about how women articulated health and healing from their lived experiences became a recurring theme in our conversations. These women's narratives, recorded and transcribed verbatim, will feature strongly in this chapter. A sign language interpreter assisted in some interviews.

This chapter engages with Kamba's lived experience and scholarly understanding of healing to interrogate these women's divergent articulations of miraculous healing. As such, I will attempt a qualitative textual analysis of selected written works by Kamba.[5] Particular focus will be on Kamba's PhD thesis, 'Developing a holistic educational programme through contextual Bible study with people with disabilities in Kinshasa, Democratic Republic of Congo: IMAN'ENDA as case study' (2013). I will also examine her article on 'holistic healing' (2016). An interview with Kamba offers her experiential insight on healing (Tearfund, 2019). Then, I will bring the analysis of Kamba's work into dialogue with the expectations of healing among the women I interviewed in Nigeria. I conclude by arguing that articulations of holistic healing must take seriously all aspects of healing. De-emphasizing any aspect limits the comprehensive nature of healing.

Understanding Kamba's theology of healing

Kamba's PhD thesis is grounded in a liberation theology of disability as expounded by Nancy Eiesland in her book, *The Disabled God* (1994). Kamba affirms Eiesland's opinion of a liberation theology of disability as expressing a 'lifelong struggle that people with disabilities have to face against widespread discrimination within church and society for their liberation' (Kamba, 2013, p. 10). Consequently, Kamba adopts a liberation theology of disability that involves the 'recognition and acceptance of the body's limits and the transcendence of these by means of interpersonal relations to effect social transformation' (2013, p. 12). It is from this understanding that Kamba articulates a 'theology of healing from disability perspective ... as a theology of hope and discovery' (2013, pp. 216–20). Kamba does not emphasize physical healing, but rather liberation from oppressive systems, inclusion, restoration of people broken by communities and the journey towards stability. Kamba came to this position from an autobiographical criticism which is inserting her disability experience principally in her interpretation of biblical verses that speak about healing (2013, p. 12).

In her writings, Kamba narrates her experience 'as a person with disability who has experienced failed physical healing' and who found it difficult to accept herself as a creation of God because of her disability and who therefore resorted to attempted suicides (2016, p. 274). Within Kenya's religious spirituality, as in much of Africa, people with disabilities are often perceived as needing physical healing and therefore often made to submit to being prayed for by pastors and church leaders (Kamba, 2019). In the midst of her trauma and frustration with her disability and lack of physical healing, Kamba said she 'prayed, cried, implored God to teach me the meaning of my life'. Following this encounter with God, which she refers to as a 'healing time', she never prayed to God to heal her physically but 'accepted' herself as a woman with disability. Consequently, Kamba said she reached her understanding of physical healing (visible change) from a liberation theology of disability perspective as the 'improvement of the abilities', which is possible when a 'person has experienced an emotional and spiritual healing' (2016, pp. 274f.). I have provided this narrative to explain the basis of Kamba's theology of healing, since this will be interrogated against the perspective on healing offered by the women in my study within a Nigerian context.

Disability and HIV in Nigeria

Nigeria is a nation of more than 200 million people with a significant number facing disability and HIV (UNAIDS, 2019). Fifteen per cent of the population live with a disability, the majority of whom are women.[6] Nigeria is the country with the second-highest burden of HIV, with more than 2 million people infected. Women make up about 60 per cent of this number. It has been noted that women disproportionately bear the burden of HIV due to their vulnerabilities within patriarchal systems (Attanasi, 2015). In Africa, women with disabilities appear to be at increased risk of HIV because of their vulnerability to rape and other sexual and gender-based violence (Grimes, 2012). A United Nations Population Fund study (2018) found that women living with a disability are up to ten times more likely to face gender-based violence than women who do not have disabilities.

Consequently, women with disabilities are more at risk of HIV infection due to poor education, gender-based violence or the inability to negotiate safe sex (UNAIDS, WHO and OHCHR, 2009). The health and social consequences of the combination of disability and HIV are enormous, leading to marginalization, inequality and reversals of development, especially for women (Kelly, 2010, p. 12). The intersection of disability and HIV shapes the life experiences of women already discriminated against due to gender dynamics in a patriarchal society such as Nigeria.

Nigeria is a 'multi-religious, multi-ethnic, and multi-cultural society', and predictably this creates tensions between religious, ethnic and cultural ideologies and beliefs (Obinna, 2017). In Nigeria, as in much of Africa, religion and culture provide a basis for the marginalization of women, especially those considered different due to disability or their HIV status. Many of the women in my study shared their experiences of exclusion from social and religious spaces due to popular stereotypes. These included the idea that disability is a curse from God or evil spirits and that HIV, especially for women, is transmitted through immoral sex. For the women in my research, their Christian faith was essential to countering the stereotypes that produced stigma and enabling them to find the support they needed to cope with the attendant challenges.

It was not surprising to observe how conversations that centred on the Christian faith, women's complex identities, about the ways in which women cope with the challenges of disability and HIV, always tended to include discussions about healing. As such, when women in my study spoke of healing, it touched on every aspect of their lives: their identities, their relationships, their bodies and their aspirations. Many of these women claim the experience of a personal relationship with Jesus Christ is essential to their capacity to cope with the challenges of disability and HIV. These women often testified that healing is their 'portion' because of their relationship with Jesus Christ.[7] I will argue that because healing is not limited to any one sphere of well-being, claims of healing can be articulated based on one's personal experiences with the healer.

Healing as transformed identity

Drawing from my interviews with women living with disability and HIV in Nigeria, it could be argued that the extent to which one appropriates or experiences healing is often dependent on an individual's perspectives, beliefs and relationship with the source of healing. The first experience of healing that women in my study talked about was a transformed identity. These women explained how Jesus makes them feel, how Jesus is the friend on their journey with disability and HIV, and how this relationship with Jesus gives them a sense of self-worth.

This transformed identity facilitated by their relationship with Jesus Christ is, for them, a form of healing. It enables them to see themselves as having value and worth when the stigma of society suggests otherwise. Transformed identity for these women means they can engage in affirming human relationships as friend, mother, wife, daughter and so on. They speak of relationships as necessary for mutual support and a crucial aspect of healing for women's flourishing. Transformed identity also means they can engage in economically beneficial ventures for women who live within the context of poverty and oppressive systems. These points were illustrated with Ula's narration of her understanding and experience of the Christian faith:

> My faith is about Jesus. I think of Jesus as my best friend. Jesus means a lot to me. I was nothing, nothing at all. I used to pray to God. I would say, 'Lord, please take away these crutches so that I can walk normally.' I was not born like this. I was walking until I was seven years old and started having problems. I

would cry, 'Lord, please take away this disease (HIV).' I wanted to kill myself. A neighbour witnessed to me about the love,
grace and mercy of God and asked me to give my life to Christ.
My life was so rotten, sad and bad. How could I give that to
Jesus? But by God's grace I did, and I received strength. Then,
Jesus came into my life and gave me strength, real strength. I
started small, I started treatment. Now, I have my own house,
even though it is small. I have a business [so I can feed my
family] better than those with legs. All because of Jesus.

Ula begins her narrative by linking her faith relationship directly
to Jesus and continues to make him the centre of her struggle,
survival and victory over the challenges of disability and HIV.[8]
Furthermore, Ula mentions the 'strength' that she receives
despite living with disability and HIV: she can now do things
she could not do before she 'gave' her life to Jesus Christ.[9] It is
also interesting to note from Ula's story that while she prayed
for her 'crutches' and 'disease' to be taken away, she felt content
that when Jesus came into her life, that was the 'strength' that
she received to start treatment for HIV, get a house and have a
business. It does appear that her identity as a 'nobody' has been
transformed into that of one who is a 'friend of Jesus', 'a house
owner' and 'an entrepreneur'.

Ula's description of herself as a 'nobody' is common among
many Nigerian women whose identities are shaped by patriarchal
relationships that can make women feel less than or inferior to
men (Oduyoye, 1986, p. 123). It is a picture of women whose
place in church or society is often ignored or overlooked so their
self-worth is diminished.[10] It is a picture of women whose identities are defined by the stigma of disability and HIV.[11] Psychology
literature recognizes that trauma that results from rejection and
abuse is capable of evoking self-stigma and poor self-esteem
(Moyo, 2019). This provides further insight into Ula's description of her feelings of 'rottenness' and 'nothingness'. According
to her, it was therefore her transformed identity in Jesus that
gave her the 'strength' to live and cope with the challenges of life,
an experience she describes as healing.

It is important to note that, as a researcher, I did not ask questions about healing at the FGDs or interviews. Stories of healing
came forth naturally. Maryann's story, which she says is about
the 'healing mercies of God', is somewhat like Ula's:

God has done the impossible with me before. People thought with disability, I cannot marry, I cannot give birth. By the grace of God, I have given birth, even though it was through operation, in spite of disability. I thank God my children are negative, even though I am positive. Everything they said I couldn't do with disability, I have done.

When Maryann says, 'Everything they said I couldn't do with disability, I have done,' she is referring to limitations that stigma placed on her due to her physical disability. But 'by the grace of God', she has proved 'them' wrong. She is not only a wife and mother: she is also a college-trained teacher working at a government school in Port Harcourt.

People with disabilities and/or HIV are often subject to paternalistic attitudes, and more so women. Women suffer more from paternalism because of the myth that women are helpless or weak, which then leads to women's oppression through a denial of their intrinsic capacity for or interest in engaging with and successfully carrying out responsibilities (Charlton, 2000, pp. 54–5). Consequently, when women with disabilities perform acts such as having babies or having a career, they are praised disproportionately, as they were never considered fit for such achievements. This is not unrelated to the assumptions present in many African cultures that people living with disability are 'inferior and an embodiment of bad luck' and also casts women as the epitome of 'shame and pity' (Charlton, 2000, pp. 54–5). Therefore, women with disabilities and HIV in my study claim that a relationship with Jesus Christ provides them with a sense of value of their personhood and identity, which enables them to cope with the stigma associated with disability and HIV.

Added to their perception of healing as transforming identity, the women in my study maintained a belief in physical healing that is accompanied by physiological change, something over which Kamba has reservations. Kamba applies the methodology of rereading scriptural texts.[12] In rereading Acts 3.1–10, Kamba interprets holistic healing as healing which does not focus on 'either physical or spiritual healing only' (2016, p. 268). She states that her objective with this interpretation is to highlight the inclusive nature of the healing of the man with disability at the temple. In so doing, she hopes to offer a 'new biblical understanding on the text ... that people with disabilities, like any human being, deserve to be in fellowship with God and with other people for the sake of social transformation' (2016, p. 270). Consequently, she restricts the idea of physical healing to the concept of 'seeing a person shifted to another level that was not expected' or the 'ability to act and do things differently' that allows for liberation of the person with disability (2016, p. 273). Undoubtedly, Kamba's effort to provide a new understanding of the concept of physical healing diverges somewhat from the general understanding of the physical body and seems to ignore the theological significance of the body.

It is safe to assume that, when related to the human body, the idea of 'physical' refers to tangible, concrete substance as opposed to intangible ability or inability to perform an act. Interestingly, Kamba begins her discourse about physical healing by noting how the man sitting at the temple 'jumped on his feet ... his feet and ankles were strengthened, and the man walked and leaped, living proof of the power of Jesus'. She regards this healing as 'a miracle ... instantaneous'. However, she chooses to concentrate only on the 'fact that the man moves forward to his life' in the community of church and society as the distinguishing aspect of the story.

This act of inclusion for Kamba is crucial for people with disabilities who are often excluded from society and church spaces. Interpreting Acts 3.1–10, Kamba says it is this liberative inclusion that ensures that the identity of the man who had been unable to walk is changed (or transformed) and recognized in such a way that he is now able to re-establish his relationship with God and the people (Kamba, 2013, p. 152). The man is no longer a beggar at the temple gate, but a worshipper and one who reconnects, thus allowing for spiritual healing to take place.[13] Here she emphasizes the inclusive nature of the healing as what is empowering and not necessarily the physical healing by which the man got up and walked.

When White (2017) uses the Acts 3.1–10 verses to discuss healing, he comments that the healing that the once-disabled man received was both physical and spiritual. Here, White differentiates between the physical and spiritual healing and places both in proper context as part of a holistic healing experience. Joseph Cromwell (2019) confirms that he prays for physical healing of his disability, as he does for the transforming power of Jesus that enables Christian believers to have self-worth through Jesus Christ. The positions of White and Cromwell accord with those of the women with disabilities and HIV whom I interviewed.

I hesitate to align myself with Kamba's explanations for physical healing as transformed identity that results in improved capacities, but I will attempt to highlight the reasons put forward by Kamba for her position in her PhD thesis. She downplays physical healing to highlight other forms of healing in the Gospels and to stop the Christian church from excluding people with disabilities on account of their physically visible disabilities. When people with physical disabilities are seen in church, it is often assumed by pastors that they are there for physical healing. This means their other needs may be ignored, which often leaves them hurt by humiliating experiences such as failed prayer.

Also, according to Kamba, when the church concentrates on physical healing, it is indicative of the failure of the church to acknowledge and accept that God created us all different, each with different gifts and resources with which to bless the church and society. Furthermore, there are people with disabilities who do not see their disability as needing to be changed or healed, but as evidence of God's glory and a solidarity with the suffering of Jesus Christ.[14] Many of the women in my research acknowledged some of Kamba's reasons for her position on physical healing. However, they did not seem to share her aversion for praying about or acknowledging the need for physiological-change healing for disability and HIV, as we shall see in the next section. For many of the women in my study, the miraculous exists in all healings as well as in the everyday ability to live and cope with disability and HIV.

One participant, referring to her struggle with HIV, said, 'Every day that I wake up, every day that this medicine works, it is healing for me, it is a miracle. This one is different.' Much like Kamba, the women in my research agree that healing is transformative and enables social inclusion. Unlike Kamba, these women claim that there is a distinction between physical healing and social or spiritual healing, and that all reflect the holistic nature of Jesus' healing. It is also clear that, for the women in my study, their relationship with Jesus Christ is central to this healing experience: they draw strength from him for communal relationships. Kamba does not emphasize the centrality of a relationship with Jesus Christ although her call for spiritual healing implies reconnection with the divine.

I argue that there is a place for considering healing to be as much about transformed identities as about physical healing bringing about physiological change. Kamba downplays physical healing to promote transformed identities because she wants to make a case for inclusion. I would argue that it would be worthwhile to reconsider this position on physical healing. Inclusion is adequately enabled by the various aspects of healing whether social, emotional, physical or spiritual.

Healing as physical healing

Physical healing has been described as 'the complete and successful functioning of every part of the human body in harmonious relationship with every other part of that body and with its particular and relevant environment' (Moyo, 2006). This description fits only partly with how the women with disability and HIV in my research talked about the kind of physical healing that they pray for and which they anticipate that Jesus as healer is able to perform for them. Speaking from their lived experiences of praying for healing, many of the women would argue that physical healing can take different forms across varying time frames, from instantaneous healing to progressive healing. It is interesting that, although these women still live with disabilities and HIV, they cheerfully testify about being healed from illnesses such as stroke, malaria, typhoid and so on. They would often refer to the healing miracles of Jesus as recorded in the gospel narratives and smilingly say that they believe such miracles are still possible today.

It is noteworthy that the women in this study did not try to minimize the effects of their struggles or underestimate their resilience in coping with the challenges of their daily lives because of the imposed stereotypes on gender, disability and HIV. They shared stories of being emotionally and verbally abused. They talked about feeling shamed by regular visits to the hospital to receive antiretroviral treatment. Others told of unpleasant experiences with partners, family and church members. So, when they pray for physical healing, they claim that because nothing is impossible with Jesus, they could be healed. While the women in my study know the realities of living with ill health, they are unwilling to relinquish the possibility of physical healing. Far from being an oppressive expectation as Kamba suggests, the anticipation of physical healing fills them with hope and determination.

As part of my participant-observation activity, I met with Esther at an HIV clinic in Port Harcourt. During our conversations, Esther told me she was tired of repeated visits to the HIV clinic because of the shame and stigma she experiences. Then her face brightened as she said that one day she would no longer make these visits because Jesus would heal her. I do not know if she was trying to convince me or herself because she suddenly burst out in pidgin English: 'Dem dey hoard the cure for this disease. Nothing wey no get cure for this world. Dat one na impossicant. Wetin Jesus no fit do?' Interpreted in English, Esther was saying that there is a cure for HIV which is being hoarded. To say that anything is without cure is impossible because there is nothing Jesus cannot do. Esther's comments demonstrate her utter dependence on Jesus to do the impossible concerning healing and beyond. I brought up this conversation with Esther at the FGD later that month and many of the women readily agreed with Esther. They asserted that to believe otherwise would be limiting the power of God in Jesus Christ who has already done many impossible things for them.

Maryann says:

I believe strongly in God. My faith is anchored in the work of Jesus on the cross for me. That is why I believe that one day I will be healed. God has done the impossible with me before. So, nothing is impossible with God. He can heal me of HIV.

When asked why she believes this so 'strongly', she responds:

Because the Bible says, by his stripes we are healed. I believe it. Jesus healed all manner of diseases and infections in the Bible. What is HIV before him? Nothing. What is disability before him? Nothing. The Bible says nothing is impossible with God.

The women's belief in Jesus' ability to do the impossible is not only grounded in the work of Jesus but, they argue, confirmed in the Bible. This practical approach to contextualizing sacred texts is not something that is peculiar to the women in this study. It has been noted that 'Christian women read the Bible as a source of inspiration in their daily lives' (Nadar, 2006). Often, they apply the text directly to their experiences without recourse to theological or hermeneutical arguments (Jenkins, 2008, p. 159). However, as the discussion progressed, there was a consensus among the women on two issues relating to their belief in physical healing with physical change.

The first was their commitment to continue adherence to HIV antiretroviral treatment because, for them, the medication is part of God's miraculous healing process. This is what Grace said in pidgin English:

I dey gidigbam. Since I start to take the medicine, my body don dey better. This medicine na God give us ohh, na miracle the medicine be. Before I bin dey sick well but no bi so again. I thank God.[15]

At this point, the women began to share their experiences of physical change following adherence to HIV medication, and were quick to add that it is through Jesus' help that the medication is effective.

The second reason that many of the women gave as to why they would continue to pray for physical healing is because they do not know the source of what they described as 'their troubles'. The complication with the problems of life in Africa is that it is often explained as being both physical and spiritual.[16] In both Port Harcourt and Uyo where these women reside, a belief persists in malevolent spirits such as water spirits or witches, with the ability to cause misfortune, sickness or disability (Fubara-Manuel, 2018). The Nollywood movie industry in Nigeria frequently dramatizes this belief in the presence of evil. Benebo Fubara-Manuel, a Nigerian theologian and pastor, has called for careful nuancing of the question of evil powers on the one hand as being responsible for disability or disease, and the sovereignty of God on the other hand. Yet the reality is that this question informs much of Nigerian and in fact African Christian spirituality.[17] Kwame Bediako therefore argues that 'in this setting of ubiquitous forces and mysterious powers, the Christian who has understood that Jesus is a living reality, can be at home, assured in the faith that Jesus alone is Lord, Protector, Provider, and Enabler' (2004, p. 9). For these women, therefore, relying on their relationship with Jesus means handing over every aspect of their disability and HIV to him as the miraculous healer.

Kamba believes that God can heal. She says: 'I know that nothing is impossible for God. If he told me today to leave my crutches and walk, I would not be surprised' (2019, p. 24). However, Kamba warns about the guilt factor when healing does not result in a change in physical condition as expected, especially when one has prayed for such healing. Often, one is accused of lacking faith and this can demoralize a person who is already stigmatized and excluded. Consequently, Kamba advocates that healing for people with disability should start from the soul, to help them negotiate their identities and restore relationships with God and humanity, instead of seeking physical healing. She promotes a 'theology of acceptance', which is acceptance of a person's current condition, whatever it may be, despite its limitations.[18] This means accepting disability to accept one's personal value and worth.

Klaus Fiedler and Samuel Kabue share Kamba's hesitations about praying for physical healing. For Fiedler, while he is 'convinced that God can and does heal people', he believes that this is rare for people living with HIV. This, he says, often leads to 'God's name being misused by those who serve him and instead of healing, in too many cases, death has resulted' (Fiedler, 2016, p. 26). For Kabue, 'an emphasis on physical healing has at times worked out very negatively on the faith of many persons with disabilities … if no healing takes place, one is presumed to have no faith' (2006, p. 113). The majority of the women I interviewed seem not to have allowed these fears or guilt to deter them from praying for and expecting physical healing.

They regarded their survival with HIV as a sign that they can receive healing from Jesus, insisting that not to expect a cure for disability or HIV is, in fact, a sign of inadequate faith. Furthermore, they did not mention any experience of guilt if physical healing failed to occur. Cromwell's view resonates with that of the women in this research:

> My philosophy is that it is God who heals and not human persons, not pastors or acclaimed miracle workers. I pray about my situation and leave the rest to God. In fact, I have been praying to God. If it happens while on earth I will be very glad. If it does not happen, I am still grateful to God, because it is God's grace and strength that is helping me to cope.[19]

Cromwell recognizes that the reason for many of the fears about whether to pray for physical healing is due to the false application of miraculous healing by pastors and faith healers. The women in my study acknowledge that there are pastors who make claims of a cure for disability or HIV but insist 'it is not God that is to be blamed but the pastors who speak when God has not spoken'.[20] This is why they continue to believe in and expect physical healing. It could be argued that these women's determined sense of confidence is part of their self-understanding or faith-understanding, flowing from the deep connection they experience through their relationship with and faith in Jesus Christ.

Musa Dube cautions that, while the church may interpret disability 'metaphorically to include a spiritual' dimension, 'we must remember that an integral point of the gospel of Christ was actual physical healing of the sick' (2008, p. 132). Dube does not deny the crucial place of a holistic healing that integrates and impacts social, emotional, spiritual and mental well-being, but she is also careful to mention that physical healing is integral to the gospel narratives.[21] As stated earlier, there is room for all spheres of healing, especially considering that the act of healing is assumed to be within the supernatural realms, which are removed from the natural. According to Fulata Moyo, 'it seems in the disappointment in prayer, that we should remember that God is wiser than any human person' (2006, p. 252). While Kamba's concerns are valid, they seem to go against the grain of Nigerian African spirituality where members and pastors pray for and believe in healing from physical and spiritual forces as the norm.

Conclusion

In this chapter, I have discussed how women with disabilities and HIV in Nigeria speak about healing from their lived experiences and realities. Without engaging in theological arguments or scholarly reasoning, they reject the idea of the incurability or hopelessness of their disability and HIV status. Instead, these women claim a transformed identity with which they can do and be what would otherwise be thought impossible for women with disabilities and HIV.

The Christian faith of the majority of the women in my study centred around a personal relationship with Jesus Christ as healer. This relationship changes the identities of these women, gives them greater confidence in themselves and provides the tools they need to live with disability and HIV, and to counter stigma and exclusion. This they perceive as positive holistic healing.

Unlike Kamba, who thought that an emphasis on physical healing was damaging for women with disabilities such as herself, the women in my research claim that prayer for and expectation of physical healing are important to their faith experience. It should not be minimized because of the potential for abuse by pastors and churches. Consequently, they argue for the acknowledgement of every aspect of holistic healing as distinctive, whether physical, social, emotional, spiritual or psychological; all healing comes from a personal relationship with Jesus and is not dependent on people.

As shown, the women in my study appropriate the healing of Jesus as a daily experience affecting all areas of their lives. They express that their healing is manifested through economic empowerment, self-confidence or transformed identities and affirming relationships. Finally, for the women in this study, healing is perceived as miraculous when it transcends the popular categories, and includes transformation of identities and physical change, which is often adequate to overcome the effects of stigma so people can engage in community.

In doing so, the women in my study promote, within the Nigerian-African context, an experience of healing that takes seriously all its transforming aspects and that provides a tool to challenge stigma and exclusion. I argue that because people's experiences and realities are different, it is expedient to exercise due recognition and respect for the divergent views on healing. This approach would enable, in the emerging discourse on disability theology in Africa, an openness to the possibilities that are informed by the lived faith of people with disabilities.

Bibliography

Attanasi, K., 2015, 'Pentecostal Theologies of Healing, HIV/AIDS, and Women's Agency in South Africa', *Pneuma* 37(1), pp. 7–20.

Bediako, K., 2004, *Jesus and the Gospel in Africa: History and experience*, New York: Orbis Books.

Charlton, J. I., 2000, *Nothing about Us without Us: Disability oppression and empowerment*, Berkeley, CA: University of California Press.

Cromwell, J. A., 2019, *Worthy: Society in search of the courage to accept disability through the lens of grace*, Houston, TX: InterCity Press.

Dube Shomanah, M. W., 2002, 'Healing Where There Is No Healing: Reading the miracles of healing in an AIDS context', in G. Allen Phillips and N. Wilkinson Duran (eds), *Reading Communities Reading Scripture: Essays in honor of Daniel Patte*, Harrisburg, PA: Trinity Press International, pp. 121–33.

Dube Shomanah, M. W., 2008, *The HIV & AIDS Bible: Selected essays*, Chicago IL: University of Scranton Press.

Eiesland, N. L., 1994, *The Disabled God: Toward a liberatory theology of disability*, Nashville, TN: Abingdon Press.

Fiedler, K., 2016, *Fake Healing Claims for HIV and AIDS in Malawi: Traditional, Christian and scientific*, Mzuni Texts, no. 5, Mzuzu, Malawi: Mzuni Press.

Fox, B. McKinney, 2019, *Disability and the Way of Jesus: Holistic healing in the Gospels and the church*, Downers Grove, IL: IVP Academic.

Fubara-Manuel, B., 2016, 'Speaking Meaningfully about Disability and Evil Powers', in S. Kabue, H. Ishola-Esan and I. Deji (eds), *Perspectives on Disability: A resource for theological and religious studies in Africa*, Ibadan: Baptist Press (Nig.) Ltd, pp. 275–98.

Fubara-Manuel, J., 2014, *Giver of Life, Hear Our Cries!* Geneva, Switzerland: World Council of Churches.

Fubara-Manuel, J., 2018, 'Together with All the Saints: Journeying with persons with disabilities', in S. Durber and F. Enns (eds), *Walking Together: Theological reflections on the ecumenical pilgrimage of justice and peace*, Geneva: World Council of Churches, pp. 101–10.

Grimes, P. S., 2012, 'HIV/AIDS and Women with Disabilities in Zimbabwe', thesis, Eugene, OR: University of Oregon.

Guijuan, L., 2009, 'Higher Education Research Methodology: Literature method', *International Education Studies* 2(4), pp. 179–81.

Hennink, M. M. and P. Leavy, 2014, *Focus Group Discussions*, Cary: Oxford University Press.

Jenkins, P., 2008, *The New Faces of Christianity: Believing the Bible in the Global South*, Oxford: Oxford University Press.

Kabue, S., 2006, 'Disability and the Healing Mission of the Church', *International Review of Mission* 95(376–377), pp. 112–16.

Kamba, M., 2016, 'Holistic Healing in Acts 3:1–10', *International Review of Mission* 105(2), pp. 268–79.

Kamba Kasongo, M., 2013, 'Developing a holistic educational programme through contextual Bible study with people with disabilities in Kinshasa, Democratic Republic of Congo: IMAN'ENDA as case study', PhD, Pietermaritzburg, South Africa: College of Humanities, University of KwaZulu-Natal.

Kamba Kasongo, M., 2019, 'Mission to Persons with Disabilities', *International Review of Mission* 108(1), pp. 18–24.

Kelly, M. J., 2010, *HIV and AIDS: A social justice perspective*, Nairobi: Paulines Publications Africa.

Kitzinger, J., 1994, 'Focus Groups: Method or Madness?', in M. Boulton (ed.), *Challenge and Innovation: Methodological Advances in Social Research on HIV/AIDS*, London: Taylor & Francis Ltd, pp. 157–76.

Lee, R. M., 1993, *Doing Research on Sensitive Topics*, London: Sage.

Moyo, F. L., 2006, 'Navigating Experiences of Healing: A narrative theology of eschatological hope as healing', in I. Apawo Phiri and S. Nadar (eds), *African Women, Religion, and Health: Essays in honor* of *Mercy Amba Ewudziwa Oduyoye*, Maryknoll, NY: Orbis Books, pp. 243–60.

Moyo, F. L., 2019, *Healing Together: A facilitator's resource for ecumenical faith and community-based counselling*, Geneva: World Council of Churches.

Nadar, S., 2006, '"Texts of Terror": The conspiracy of rape in the Bible, church, and society: The case of Esther 2:1–8', in I. Apawo Phiri and S. Nadar (eds), *African Women, Religion, and Health: Essays in honor of Mercy Amba Ewudziwa Oduyoye*, Maryknoll, NY: Orbis Books, pp. 77–89.

Obinna, E., 2012, '"Life is Superior to Wealth?": Indigenous healers in an African community, Amasiri, Nigeria', in E. Chitando and A. Adogame (eds), *African Traditions in the Study of Religion in Africa: Emerging trends, indigenous spirituality and the interface with other world religions*, Farnham: Routledge.

Obinna, E., 2017, 'Nigeria', in K. R. Ross, J. K. Asamoah-Gyadu and T. M. Johnson (eds), *Christianity in Sub-Saharan Africa*, Edinburgh: Edinburgh University Press, pp. 189–200.

Oduyoye, M. A., 1986. *Hearing and Knowing: Theological Reflections on Christianity in Africa*, Maryknoll, NY: Orbis Books.

Oke, R. O., 2017, 'Healing of the Haemorrhaging Woman as a Model for Checkmating Stigma of People Living with HIV', *Verbum et Ecclesia* 38(1), pp. 1–12.

Parsons, J. A., V. A. Bond and S. A. Nixon, 2015. '"Are We Not Human?" Stories of stigma, disability and HIV from Lusaka, Zambia and their implications for access to health services', Report, *PLoS ONE* 10(6).

Ross, K. R., 2002, *Following Jesus and Fighting HIV/AIDS: A call to discipleship*, Edinburgh: Saint Andrew Press.

Stinton, D. B., 2004, *Jesus of Africa: Voices of contemporary African Christology*, Faith and Cultures Series, Maryknoll, NY: Orbis Books.

Tada, J. E., 2018, *Place of Healing: Wrestling with the mysteries of suffering, pain, and God's sovereignty*, Colorado Springs, CO: David C. Cook Publishing.

Tearfund Learn, 2019, 'Interview: I Am Not Sick', Interview with Micheline Kamba, *Tearfund*, https://learn.tearfund.org/en/resources/publications/footsteps/footsteps_101-110/footsteps_108/interview_i_am_not_sick/, accessed 09.12.2020.

UNAIDS, 2019, 'Nigeria', *UNAids*, www.unaids.org/en/regionscountries/countries/nigeria, accessed 19.10.2020.

UNAIDS, WHO and OHCHR, 2009, 'Policy Brief: Disability and HIV', p. 8.

United Nations Population Fund, 2018, *Women and Young Persons with Disabilities: Guidelines for providing rights-based and gender-responsive services to address gender-based violence and sexual and reproductive health and rights*, New York: UNFPA.

White, P., 2017, 'The Biblical View of Humanity and the Promotion of the

Rights of Persons with Disabilities: The call and mission of the church',
Acta Theologica 37(11), pp. 120–34.
WHO, 2011, *WHO World Report on Disability*, Geneva: WHO.

Notes

1 Translation from Pidgin English: 'There is nothing without cure in
this world.'

2 Elijah Obinna (2012) mentions the often-contested claims in Nigeria
that the prayers of some 'men of God' are capable of healing HIV.

3 Bethany McKinney Fox states that the belief that Jesus heals, which
is 'beyond mere human power and effort', serves as inspiration for people
today (2019, pp. 46–7).

4 FGDs have been described as involving 'a *focus* on specific issues,
with a predetermined *group* of people, participating in an interactive *discussion*' (Hennink, 2014).

5 Guijuan Lin highlights the role of qualitative textual analysis as the
reading and analysis of literature to ascertain its essential elements. This
is what informed my choice of texts by Kamba, to concentrate on those
directly concerned with healing within Christian contexts (Guijuan, 2009).

6 WHO (2011) estimates that 15 per cent of any given population are
people who live with a form of disability.

7 Katharine Attanasi (2015) notes that 'Pentecostals connect healing
to the atoning work of Christ on the cross'.

8 Kenneth Ross notes how, in the gospel narratives, 'women found
Jesus approachable' as Jesus often 'spent time with women ... showed
understanding of the issues that concerned them ... and how women
engage directly with Jesus' (2002, p. 53).

9 Diane Stinton quotes John Mbiti as saying that in Africa people
affirm that 'divine healing is an extension of the saving benefits of God and
Jesus Christ' (2004, pp. 174–5).

10 Mercy Oduyoye (1986, p. 125) has acknowledged that 'women are
very much concerned about the church, but the church is not so much
concerned about women'.

11 See Parsons et al., 2015. Also, in Jessie Fubara-Manuel (2014,
pp. 57–60), I discussed how people with disabilities lose their identities,
are nameless and are often defined or described by their visible disabilities.

12 Kamba (2013) explains that the act of rereading the Acts 3 text was
'to explore aspects of healing other than those that become apparent in an
initial reading of the text'. Consequently, she claims to broaden the concept of physical healing for the sake of social transformation for people
with disabilities.

13 Kamba describes spiritual healing as the man's 'ability to enter the
temple, approach the throne of God and give thanks' and also, for the

people in the temple, 'their minds were opened to know that before God, everything is possible' (2013, p. 172).

14 Eiesland's concept of the 'disabled God' affirms that physical healing is not necessarily what people with disabilities need as Jesus himself went to heaven with a disabled body. Joni Tada (2018) does not agree with the idea of a disabled God, and sees her disability as suffering sufficient to embrace the image of God so does not pray for physical healing. But she hopes for healing in eternity, in accordance with what Musa Dube (2002, pp. 212–33) says: 'There is healing, for when we finally die, we are healed from our pains.' Within the deaf community, many do not perceive their inability to hear sounds as a disability; instead it is just another means of communication as sign language is another.

15 Translation from Pidgin English: 'I am very well. Since I started taking my medication, I feel well. The medication is given by God and it is a miracle. Before the medication, I was often sick but not again. For that, I thank God.'

16 Obinna (2017) observes 'how many Pentecostal and Charismatic churches devote much time to deliverance from the satanic forces that are believed to oppose Christians and are held to cause material and psychic problems in the sphere of health and wealth'.

17 See Fubara-Manuel (2016) for a detailed conversation on causation for disability within the Nigerian context.

18 Kamba's theology of acceptance follows on from her theology of suffering which she claims would 'create a sense of happiness and build self-confidence' because suffering is the life of disability (2013, pp. 211–14). Here she refers to Tada as saying that among the benefits of suffering is the fact that it 'heightens quest for Christ and restores a costly beauty in Christ'. The women in my research did not agree that they should suffer much more because of their disability or that they will feel closer to Jesus if they suffer. They felt Jesus has done all the suffering and therefore they should no longer suffer. Besides, they felt the challenges of being disabled and having HIV presented enough suffering in themselves.

19 Interview with Cromwell, 11 December 2020.

20 In Fubara-Manuel, I noted that sometimes when pastors pray and want physical healing for people with disabilities, it is because the church feels the lack of physical healing is an embarrassment to the church and the pastor's ministry (2014, p. 69).

21 This view appears to be a slight shift from Dube's earlier position when she spoke of healing in the context of HIV as belonging to the eschatological sphere (2002, p. 132).

12

Disability-inclusive Self-help Groups: Lessons from Tearfund in Ethiopia

SISAY MAMMO SIME AND

BARNABÉ ANZURUNI MSABAH

Introduction

Tearfund in Ethiopia has pioneered disability inclusion in its programming for over a decade. This chapter reflects on the challenges and achievements of this work, considering the wider impact of the inclusion of persons with disabilities (PWDs) in faith-based self-help groups (SHGs) within Tearfund's church and community transformation (CCT) programming.

In developing this chapter, we have consulted both primary and secondary sources and conducted interviews with programme coordinators of partner organizations. We have also referred to notes we took in different field visits made in order to learn from SHGs, and we have also reviewed reports of partner organizations. Added to this, we used the personal reflections of one of the writers of this chapter (who himself is engaged in implementing disability-inclusive SHGs and related programmes) as a reference. We have also consulted theological papers and research reports produced regarding SHGs in Ethiopia as secondary-source materials.

The chapter is organized into four parts. In the first part, the concept of disability and disability inclusion is discussed within the context of Christian theology and international development. The second part provides an overview of Tearfund in Ethiopia's SHG approach. The third section is the core of this chapter where we recount the journey of Tearfund in Ethiopia and its partners towards creating disability-inclusive SHGs. The fourth part highlights some practical lessons learnt from Tearfund and its partners' journey towards forming disability-inclusive SHGs. As the chapter concludes, recommendations offer a way forward.

Positioning disability and disability inclusion within the context of Christian theology and international development

Background

There is a tendency to associate those who appear different from what we call 'the normal ones' in their physical, sensorial, or mental or intellectual body structure and functions in a category identified as 'persons with disabilities' (PWDs) (Picard and Habets, 2016; Grue, 2016; Davis, 2017; Barclay, 2019). It seems that sharing an experience of injustice and discrimination, as well as being considered to be 'abnormal', has served as a common denominator around which to associate PWDs (Picard and Habets, 2016; Barclay, 2019).

As Deborah Creamer (2003) puts it, these groups of people have been identified primarily by their impairment rather than by their identity as full human beings. Particularly in religious contexts, people with physical, sensorial or intellectual body impairments are 'portrayed as suffering personified (to be pitied), images of saintliness (to be admired), and symbols of sin (to be avoided) or signs of God's limited power or capriciousness (to be pondered)' (Creamer, 2003, p. 59).

Such a perspective seems to have also influenced the way the church engages with disability (Shrout, 2007; Epperly, 2003). In fact, to a large extent, the church has tended to treat disability according to theological assumptions based on harmful interpretations, misunderstandings and misapplications of God's intended message (Allen, 2010; White, 2017; Pressler, 2017).

Defining disability and disability inclusion

Although the literal interpretation of the term 'disability' implies the absence or negation of ability (Grue, 2016), in this context, the term is meant to be descriptive of the physical, psycho-social, as well as political and economic, situation of those with atypical physical, sensorial or intellectual body function and structure. By assessing society's beliefs and reflective descriptions on the origin and nature of this group's situation, scholars and disability rights activists have attempted to derive different descriptive models or frameworks of understanding for the concept of disability. It seems possible to put these into two broad categories: that is, traditional frameworks or models of understanding disability, and human rights-based ones.

The traditional models or frameworks understand disability as biological impairment within an individual and according to how such impairment is perceived in a socio-cultural context (SBL, 2009; Melcher, 2011; Grue, 2016; Davis, 2017; Creamer, 2003, 2009; Cobley, 2018), whereas the human rights-based models of understanding disability consider PWDs first and foremost as human beings. According to these models, disability is associated with activity or participation limitations that human beings face due to challenges that fail to accommodate their special needs, arising mainly from their impairments (Moss and Schipper, 2011; Burke, 2013; Cobley, 2018).

In view of this, contemporary scholars and disability rights activists have established a number of definitions and concepts to explain what disability is:

- *Disability as a bio-psycho-social condition.* Disability is viewed as an umbrella term for bodily impairment, functional limitation and limitation on the ability to participate in socio-economic and political activities due to environmental and social barriers (WHO, 2001, as quoted by Cobley, 2018; WHO and World Bank, 2011; UN, 2006).
- *Disability as a component of diversity.* Here, disability refers to various kinds of limitations that human beings experience in their body (Creamer, 2009); Freeman, n. d.).
- *Disability as a violence against human rights.* Disability is described as a violation of the rights of persons with physical, sensorial and intellectual or mental impairments, in relation to being able to participate equally within society (UN, 2006; Della Fina et al., 2017).
- *Disability in terms of human development.* This concept considers disability as a deprivation in terms of capability or functioning due to problems related to shortage of resources, structural barriers and the personal characteristics of those with impairment or health conditions (Mitra, 2018).

- *A theological understanding of disability.* In this perspective, disability can be seen as a means to seek God's grace in order to achieve recovery or efficiency in relation to living a dignified and flourishing life so people can fulfil the purpose for which they were created.[1]

Disability inclusion is therefore a concept that is about ensuring the full engagement of people with disabilities in all aspects of life in society. It is a human rights approach, upholding the right of PWDs to participate equally in society (UN, 2006). The notion behind disability inclusion is the fact that persons with physical, sensorial, intellectual or mental impairments are inhibited or disabled and cannot operate fully as human beings as a result of dehumanizing attitudes, physical and socio-economic infrastructures that are inaccessible, and exclusionary institutional practices.

Disability inclusion is carried out with a rationale of promoting basic human rights, sustainable development and economic prosperity. It is a change in approach and relationship towards and with persons who have disabilities. The change takes place within individuals, families, community groups such as SHGs, business and development organizations, governments and the whole of society. And the change should be made in recognition of the fact that all of us might experience disability personally or in our family or close neighbour at least once in our lifetime (Creamer, 2009).

This change should not be regarded as a one-off action. Rather, it is a process that requires determination and continuous commitment. The main focus of the change is to remove disabling barriers that prevent people with impairments and health conditions from participating equally in society. Mike Oliver asserts that these barriers are 'all the things that impose restrictions on disabled people; ranging from individual prejudice to institutional discrimination, from inaccessible buildings to unusable transport systems, from segregated education to excluding work arrangements' (as quoted by Cobley, 2018, p. 12).

Approaches and principles of disability inclusion in international development

Scholars and disability rights activists recommend that disability inclusion should be implemented through two interrelated approaches known as the twin-track approach (Bruijn et al., 2012). On the one hand, it mainstreams disability in all activities of life. And alongside this, it makes specific interventions that enhance the capabilities of people with disabilities who are deprived due to the specific nature of their impairments or functional difficulties and other related challenges. In addition, the fact that disability is closely related to issues such as poverty, gender inequality and child labour abuses highlights the intersectionality of disability inclusion. This justifies the mainstreaming of disability inclusion in all forms of development activities such as addressing poverty, promoting gender equality, promoting justice or human rights, and so on.

Disability inclusion has four main characteristics, which all apply to contexts of both local and international development (van Ek and Schot, 2017):

- *An inclusive attitude*: one that shows due recognition to and respect for personhood and the dignity of all, rather than magnifying the impairment and health condition of human beings as a means of identifying a person (UN, 2006; Della Fina et al., 2017).
- *Inclusive communication*: one that recognizes diversity and is always made using alternative approaches (Light for the World, 2017). Nurturing two-way communication on an equal basis and providing alternative forms of communication (plain text, sign language and non-verbal communication, audio messages, tactile codes, etc.) are the main features of inclusive communication (van Ek and Schot, 2017).
- *Accessibility*: making sure that all persons, irrespective of their impairment or health conditions, can access products and services, as well as physical and social environmental arrangements (UN, 2006, Article 9).
- *Participation*: persons with disabilities should be the main actors in their own affairs rather than being considered as needing support (van Ek and Schot, 2017). The principle of participation is always propagated by PWDs in the maxim: 'Nothing about us without us' (Charlton, 1998).

On the other hand, as stated in Article 3 of the United Nations Convention on the Rights of Persons with Disabilities (UN, 2006), disability inclusion in both local and international development needs to be implemented according to the following principles:

1 Respect for inherent dignity, individual autonomy including the freedom to make one's own choices, and independence of persons.
2 Non-discrimination.
3 Full and effective participation and inclusion in society.
4 Respect for difference and acceptance of persons with disabilities as part of human diversity and humanity.
5 Equality of opportunity.
6 Accessibility.
7 Equality between men and women.
8 Respect for the evolving capacities of children with disabilities and respect for the right of children with disabilities to preserve their identities.

A biblical understanding of disability inclusion

The biblical understanding of disability inclusion may be described as relational, intersectional, missional, justice-oriented and worship in action, as well as inward-looking and empathetic. Here, we attempt to describe briefly these five aspects of a biblical understanding of disability inclusion.

The relational aspect of disability inclusion in the Bible can be explained by the teaching of the apostle Paul regarding spiritual gifts and the body of Christ. Paul tells us that we are all part of the body of Christ, and each of us lives for the sake of other parts of our body (1 Cor. 12.12–27; Eph. 4.7–16). With this 'one body' mentality, no one will be left behind as unworthy or as unreachable. All have equal value, and even more care is given to those parts of our body that we normally consider of less value (1 Cor. 12.22–23).

When we look at both the healing acts and the crucifixion of Jesus, we can see that he followed an intersectional approach to break barriers of exclusion that isolate people with disabilities and other vulnerable groups. For example, we see that Jesus in many cases had to violate norms, rules and regulations (what we

SISAY MAMMO SIME AND BARNABÉ ANZURUNI MSABAH

identify today as institutional barriers) in order to enable PWDs and other isolated groups in society, such as women, children, Gentiles, and so on, to gain access to his redemptive work.

According to the Gospel of Luke, we see how Jesus began his ministry by declaring his mission in his home town, quoting what is written about him in the book of Isaiah (Isa. 61.1–2). Thus he declares that God has anointed him to preach the gospel for the poor and the prisoners, to make those who cannot see regain their sight, to liberate those who are treated badly, and to set his people free (Luke 4.18–20).

In the Bible, God strongly warns believers to act justly and indiscriminately as well as to be a voice for the voiceless, sight for those who cannot see, and to break the yoke of oppression (see, for example, Isaiah 58). In his confrontational letter to 'the twelve tribes scattered among the nations', the apostle James challenges his audience to reconsider what true worship of God means. According to James, true worship includes taking care of widows and orphans or those who are vulnerable (James 1.27).

A biblical understanding of disability inclusion first and foremost pinpoints that we should all first look into our infirmities and weaknesses if we are to serve others (Matt. 7.5). As Creamer (2009) argues, we all have our limitations. In spiritual terms, we have all lost the glory of God and are spiritually disabled (Rom. 3.23). This makes us realize that we serve others, particularly those whom we consider as weak and vulnerable, not because we are in a better position than them. Rather, we ourselves had been vulnerable and would have been objects of God's wrath, had not God's grace delivered us (Eph. 2.1–8). Hence, we became recreated or born-again Christians to 'do good works. Long ago God prepared these works for us to do' (Eph. 2.10 NIRV).

Self-help group approach and Tearfund in Ethiopia

Tearfund has been working in Ethiopia since the 1970s, focusing on resilience, emergency response and food security. It pioneered the self-help group (SHG) approach in Ethiopia in 2002 through establishing five such groups with 100 women living in poverty in Adama town in Oromia regional state, 55 miles (88 km) to the east of Addis Ababa. The initiative for Tearfund's SHG approach is taken from an India-based development agency called MYRADA (the Mysore Resettlement and Development

Agency) that was established initially to resettle Tibetan refugees. This agency promoted the approach of SHGs to contribute towards the social and economic transformation of communities living in poverty (Weingartner and Pichon, 2017; Cromie et al., 2017).

Since 2002, Tearfund in Ethiopia has been promoting SHGs in collaboration with the development wings of six faith-based organizations (FBOs). So far, more than 20,000 SHGs have been established across 50 locations throughout the country, with 300,000 group members or direct beneficiaries and about 1.5 million family members or indirect beneficiaries. The plan is to grow this work by about 50 per cent by 2026 (Hillgrove and Smith, 2020).

An SHG is a group created to solve shared problems and fight household poverty through the mechanisms of saving and loans, as well as learning and working together (Kumaran, 2011; de Hoop et al., 2019). Evidence from Ethiopia reveals that SHGs are both social and business community groups which enable the poor to deal with their economic difficulties and socio-political and cultural disadvantages (Elias, 2014; Dessiye, 2014; Haile, 2014; Data and Paulos, 2017; Yohannes, 2014; Maru, 2016).

Gebre Deko and colleagues describe how SHGs work in Ethiopia:

> A total of 15–20 individuals who know each other from the same neighborhood and on a similar socio-economic level form one SHG and develop their own by-laws. Approximately 8–12 similar SHGs living in close proximity establish a Cluster Level Association (CLA), which represents its members to lower levels of local government (Kebele and Woreda) and undertakes numerous other activities. A number of CLAs in a given area form a Federation Level Association (FLA) to represent membership to higher levels of local government (City, Zone, and Region) besides playing many other roles (2014, p. 8).[2]

The literature shows that in Ethiopia SHGs serve as grass-roots social protection, enhancing their members' ability to cope with chronic stresses and unexpected shocks through the provision of more flexible and alternative financial resources in a relatively cost-effective manner (Weingartner and Pichon, 2017; Meehan and Mengistu, 2016; Cabot Venton et al., 2013). As is well stated in Tearfund in Ethiopia's SHG learning resource, an SHG 'focuses on each individual's potential and facilitates a process of change that helps the individual to discover more about themselves. People are able to change at their own pace' (Carter, 2013, p. 7). Based on their assessment of the psycho-social well-being of sample SHG members established by Tearfund in Ethiopia and its partner organizations, Sam Cromie and colleagues (2017) assert that SHG members, particularly those who had spent a relatively longer period of time in an SHG, attested that their lives had been transformed, moving from being receiver to provider, from social isolation to participation and from dependent to independent.

Each member of the SHG is expected to save regularly, however small the amount. As Isabel Carter (2013) and Gebre Deko and colleagues (2014) note, there are three kinds of savings that SHG members are engaged in. The first is what we call regular saving, which is compulsory for members of SHGs: each is expected to save an equal amount of money. The second type of saving is optional saving, in which SHG members save as they wish, which is considered to be their capital. And the third kind of saving is saving for social purpose, which enables them to solve social problems that each member of SHGs faces in their day-to-day life (Carter, 2013; Deko et al., 2014).

SHGs are proven to be a hub of informal learning. Many members are able to change behaviour as a result of their involvement. Our experience in Ethiopia shows, for example, that husbands stopped beating and abusing their wives after they were challenged by the weekly learning discussions. Many have also acquired new life skills through SHG learning opportunities. And many women, in particular, developed their self-esteem and learnt to lead and manage their own family as well as community groups. Isabel Carter (2013) summarizes the learning potential for SHGs in Ethiopia, where participation has led to enhanced gender awareness, family planning, HIV awareness, environmental protection and functional adult literacy.

Connecting the practice of SHGs to biblical principles, two aspects stand out. First, the biblical text indicates that for human beings work is a standard way of helping oneself to combat poverty and live a dignified life (Prov. 6.6–11; 10.3–4; 14.23; 1 Thess. 4.12; 2 Thess. 3.6–12; Eph. 4.28). Second, it seems worth underlining that the uniqueness of SHGs comes from the fact that they are based on special group relationships relating to both the economic and social interactions of their members. Such kinds of group relationships are well rooted in Scripture (Eccles. 4.9–12). As Craig Blomberg (2013) notes, the first Christian communities lived a communal life, and even had a common treasury of funds, which enabled them to witness that there were no needy among them (Acts 4.34).

Towards disability-inclusive self-help groups: Tearfund in Ethiopia's journey

Background

Among Tearfund's country programmes, Ethiopia is one of the pioneers in disability inclusion, which has not yet been mainstreamed across every country where Tearfund as a global organization is working. The journey of Tearfund in Ethiopia towards disability inclusion began in 2007, when it met people from Light for the World, and began to feel challenged about promoting disability inclusion within its projects.[3] In 2009, Tearfund identified Ethiopia as a pilot for its disability mainstreaming programme. As a result it started to mainstream disability inclusion in some of the programmes, such as HIV, education and WASH (water, sanitation and hygiene), which it was implementing in collaboration with some partners (Tsegay, 2019).

At the same time, Tearfund also began to work with local disability-inclusive development organizations such as Ethiopian Center for Disability and Development (ECDD). The WASH programme that has been implemented through the collaboration of Tearfund and the Ethiopian Kale Hiwet Church Development Commission (EKHCDC) has been particularly successful in mainstreaming disability inclusion (Tsegay, 2019).

The most important success of Tearfund in Ethiopia in relation to promoting disability inclusion is in the area of creating SHGs that accommodate people with disabilities. In the following sections, we present four different initiatives around disability-inclusive SHGs that Tearfund has developed in collaboration with its partners, and point out some of the best practice and challenges involved.

Intersectional approach towards inclusion: the case of Meta Welkite SHG

Through the support of Tearfund UK and Tearfund Netherlands, Tearfund in Ethiopia in partnership with Meserete Kristos Relief and Development Association (MKCRDA) introduced the SHG approach to what is now called Meta Welkite *woreda*[4] in the West Shewa zone of Oromia regional state as early as 2006.[5] Geremew Terfa, now Programme Coordinator of MKCRDA, used to work in the *woreda* as teacher and later as project officer of MKCRDA. He notes that SHGs in Meta Welkite transformed the lives of PWDs and women in an intersectional approach by challenging unscientific beliefs that kept both PWDs and women in total isolation. Terfa recounts:

> Some fifteen years ago, before this project came to this *woreda*, persons with disabilities were counted to be hopeless. Even women used to live in a culture that put them in a far inferior position. Ignorance had prevailed in the area, and education was a very rare opportunity.[6]

Mulu Mammo is one of the women with disabilities whose lives have been transformed and who have become fully included in their communities as a result of this SHG approach. Mammo is a resident of Goro Mako *kebele*, Meta Welkite *woreda*.[7] She is 45 years old and a mother of four children. She narrates how she acquired her disability and suffered many socio-economic challenges:

> I became partially blind because my father hit me on one of my eyes while I was a child. In our community culture, no one is ready to marry people like me. Luckily, however, I got a man who became willing to be my husband. But one day, my husband quarrelled with someone and became injured: that made him incapable of engaging in activities that demand physical labour such as farming. This incident meant I had to shoulder our family household and farming responsibilities. Until I became a member of the SHG in 2006, life was too hard for me to manage ...
>
> After receiving training on how to make a business by the SHG, I took a loan from the SHG and purchased goats. When the goats became fattened, I sold them for a good price and

bought other goats to increase my income. This was the first step that I took to bring remarkable change in my life ...

Now I am engaged in rearing goats. I also engage in different income-generating activities such as farming, pumpkin production and compost preparation to increase my productivity and reduce my expense of purchasing chemical fertiliser. Now I am able to feed my whole family and manage the difficulties of life. I sent my children to school. Two of my sons have already got married and my remaining two sons are Grade 11 students.[8]

According to Terfa, programme coordinator of MKCRDA, Mammo is a very respected woman in her community. 'By her initiation, she has organised four SHGs in her village – and she has been supporting the groups to bring significant change in their lives as well as the lives of their children.'[9]

The story of Mammo is only one example of how SHGs transform lives in an intersectional approach. Currently, there are 117 SHGs in Meta Welkite, with 1,182 female members and 628 males, or 1,810 members in total. Of these, 30 are people living with disabilities (12 females and 18 males).[10]

However, given that it is a relatively long time since the disability-inclusive SHG was introduced in Meta Welkite *woreda*, the achievement of the joint Tearfund–MKCRDA project accommodating PWDs into SHGs may not seem hugely impressive. But the programme coordinator of MKCRDA notes that the project was interrupted for some time for various reasons and the growth of SHGs lost momentum; the SHGs in Meta Welkite would otherwise have involved larger number of PWDs and created more impact, he said.[11]

Breaking barriers of inclusion: the case of SHGs in Offa and Kindo Koysha

Tearfund in Ethiopia has also partnered with Terepeza Development Association (TDA) in promoting SHGs since 2006 (Carter, 2013). TDA is the development wing of Walayta Kalehiwet Church (WKHC). Since 2017, the joint TDA–Tearfund project has been engaged in promoting disability inclusion in selected SHGs and their cluster-level associations (CLAs) which operate in *woredas* called Offa and Kindo Koysha, within the Walayta zone of the South Nations Nationalities and Peoples Region

(SNNPR). Thus, 20 CLAs (ten CLA from each *woreda*), with each CLA containing about ten SHGs, were selected to become part of this journey. The initiative arose from the joint project's engagement in a consortium that came to be known as the Civic Engagement Alliance (CEA).[12]

Disability exclusion is one of the key development problems identified within the communities of Offa and Kindo Koysha *woredas*. On the one hand, PWDs face stigma and isolation. On the other, the various physical/environmental factors become barriers to the resources and services they need to access. This is aggravated by the fact that the two *woredas* are situated in difficult topography (hills, gullies, gorges and mountains of differing altitude), which creates issues for those with physical and visual impairments in moving from place to place (TDA, 2020).

Between 2018 and 2020, the joint Tearfund–TDA project in Offa and Kindo Koysha has been able to empower 585 PWDs (358 females and 227 males) through their involvement with SHGs so that they can begin to lead more independent lives. And this is mainly the impact of SHGs and their CLAs' efforts in breaking barriers of inclusion using locally available resources (TDA, 2020).

According to Tilahun Tadesse, Senior Programme Manager for Livelihoods and Food Security in TDA, the SHGs in Offa and Kindo Koysha often cover the membership fees of PWDs. This has encouraged many PWDs to join. Likewise, in many cases CLAs also cover the medical expenses of PWDs and other poorer members of SHGs.[13]

CLAs and SHGs are also covering school and related costs of 15 orphans (six in Offa and nine in Kindo Koysha). In a *kebele* called Sere Esho, Offa *woreda*, the CLA has provided chickens to five PWDs (two for each) so that they can engage in income-generation activities. (TDA, 2020)

Tadesse further notes that within just five months, between January and June 2020:

SHGs collected 400kg of grain food and distributed it to 40 (30 female and ten male) needy members of the community. Six homes have been constructed for homeless persons with disabilities who live in both *woredas*. And six others are under construction. Moreover, SHGs provided ten SHG members with disabilities with clothes. (TDA, 2020)

Almaz Kutaye, a mother of five who lives with disability and who is a member of one of the SHGs, had had her home confiscated in Bale, the capital town of Kindo Koysha *woreda*. She says:

> I and my five children became homeless for seven years. Thanks to my CLA leaders, they advocated for my cause. They went with me to the court and spoke to judges and local government officials on my behalf. Now I have got back my home, and received certificate of my ownership of the land where my home is built. (TDA, 2020)

A 30-year-old man, Meskele Lemma, is one of the PWDs who are organized into SHGs through the support of the joint TDA–Tearfund project. Lemma lives in a *kebele* called Tepa, Kindo Koysha *woreda*. Tepa is situated in very rugged topography, completely inaccessible by vehicular transport. Lemma has a physical disability which means he cannot move his legs and is forced to crawl using his hands. He says: 'My life completely changed after I joined SHG. I try to do many business activities now. My wish is to go to Bele and live there by constructing my own home.'[14]

The success of the projects in Offa and Kindo Koysha is astounding, as SHGs are breaking down barriers to inclusion that hinder PWDs and prevent them from living a dignified life. And yet this initiative is in its infancy. Unfortunately, at the end of 2020, the CEA consortium project was phased out. Therefore, time will tell how sustainable this initiative proves to be.

Associations of persons with disabilities introduced to the SHG concept: the case of SHGs in Adama Town

Associations of persons with disabilities (APDs) are associations that are established by and for PWDs in order to uphold their human rights through an organized approach. In many parts of Ethiopia, PWDs organize themselves into APDs and struggle to ensure their rights get respected. Nonetheless, to a large extent, APDs do not succeed in enabling their members to become empowered in socio-economic terms.

Sew Mehon Alebin is one of the APDs in Adama town, 55 miles east of Addis Ababa. The Amharic name 'Sew Mehon Alebin' may be translated as 'We need to reach the level of manhood'.

Amiha Worku, the chairperson of Sew Mehon Alebin, says:

> Our association is created aiming that we should also live
> and act like other people without disabilities. But most of our
> association's members are uneducated. We do not know how
> to work. But we are sure that we can be transformed if we are
> able to work. And yet we do not know how to reach there. I
> believe that if you can help us, [we can live as you do].[15]

The Adama SHG project is one of the first that Tearfund established in Ethiopia in 2002, in collaboration with its partner,
the Ethiopian Kale Hiwet Church Development Commission
(EKHCDC) (Carter, 2013). However, until 2018, the Adama
SHG project had not engaged deliberately in promoting disability
inclusion, except in so far as a few PWDs had joined the SHGs
incidentally.[16]

On this matter, Nigat Mekonin, the coordinator of the Adama
SHG project, admits:

> We were not aware that persons with disabilities can be able
> to work. When we got any person with disability, we used to
> consider the person as a permanent recipient of help, and refer
> the person to a safety net programme.[17]

In August 2018, leaders of the Adama SHG federation-level
association (FLA) and CLA received training on how to promote
disability inclusion. This training was the result of Tearfund in
Ethiopia and its partner EKHCDC's engagement in the CEA
consortium.[18]

The training gave an opportunity for the CLA and FLA leaders
to meet representatives of the town's APDs. Mekonin notes how
the training was a turning point for her and the whole Adama
SHG project:

> This training was an eye-opener for us in reconsidering our
> approach towards persons with disabilities, and we began to
> discuss among ourselves what can we do to ensure the inclu-
> sion of persons with disabilities in our SHGs.[19]

As a result, the Adama SHG project seems to be engaged in helping the Adama APDs to become platforms for SHGs. According
to Mekonin, five SHGs for people with disabilities have been
established so far. She says: 'So far we are able to organise 100

persons with disabilities in five SHGs. Since October 2019, they are able to save a good deal of money, and their capital has reached 60,000 ETB [Ethiopian Birr].'[20] She also adds:

> The challenge is that many of them do not have their own jobs. Many of them save in SHGs by begging. Some of them use begging as habit. They drink alcohol by the money that they collected through begging. It is very hard to convince persons who develop this habit to quit begging easily and change their behaviour. And this is aggravated by the fact that the socio-economic environment of Adama town is not conducive to create employment opportunities for PWDs. But it is encouraging to see some persons with disabilities becoming resilient and trying to engage in income-generation activities. We saw, for example, that some people are trying to be engaged in petty-trade activities.[21]

Clearly, the initiative of the Adama SHG approach to collaborating with APDs to promote the economic empowerment of PWDs is a new approach and has helped conventional APDs to become platforms for fostering a culture of self-help among PWDs. In many parts of Ethiopia and low-income countries, there is a tendency to consider PWDs as objects of charity. By contrast, this initiative is trying to make PWDs become agents of their own change, by helping them to save what they have, and at least create seed money for their business that will undoubtedly evolve by exploiting their hidden potential. But it is very difficult to sustain the initiative unless innovative strategies are designed that enable PWDs to engage in livelihood activities in accordance with their talents and capacity. This is not an easy task. It requires a strong sense of partnership and collaboration between the different stakeholders.

Holistic model of inclusion: the case of SHGs in the Flourishing with Disability project

Flourishing with Disability Ethiopia (FDE) is an ongoing project run and implemented by Tearfund in Ethiopia in collaboration with the Ethiopian Mulu Wongel Amagnoch Church Development Commission (EMWACDC) since April 2019. Its overall objective is to help create more inclusive spaces for PWDs and

SISAY MAMMO SIME AND BARNABÉ ANZURUNI MSABAH

address the barriers that may prevent inclusion so that they are empowered to pursue their vocational, educational and spiritual goals and see whole-life transformation for themselves and their families.[22]

To this end, the project has come up with a holistic model of inclusion, integrating different tasks and mechanisms to tackle challenges that hinder the equal participation of persons with disabilities in socio-economic, political and spiritual activities. Accordingly, FDE has set the following goals:

- *Creating evidence-based understanding* of existing knowledge, attitudes and practice at national (the legislative environment), organizational (Tearfund in Ethiopia and EMWACDC) and local (Debremarkos and Injibara towns) levels in relation to promoting disability inclusion. Accordingly, the project has made an audit of disability inclusion, both of Tearfund and EMWACDC. The country's legal and policy environment for disability inclusion is also being audited in the same way. Moreover, an assessment of the knowledge, attitudes and practice regarding disability inclusion has been made in the two project sites. Audits of selected government offices, self-help groups and churches in the two project sites have also been made. This was accompanied by social mapping exercises by community representatives in the same areas, to identify the living conditions of local PWDs.
- *Strengthening the disability-inclusive initiative* that was begun by Tearfund's programme in collaboration with EMWACDC in Debremarkos and Injibara towns, in the East Gojam and Awi zones of Amhara regional state. Since 2015, the church and community mobilization (CCM) project has managed to establish SHGs within the church and the local community. It was also able to establish some SHGs that enabled PWDs to be more independent and self-sufficient.[23] FDE has been engaged in promoting community dialogues so that existing SHGs established by the CCM programme could accommodate more PWDs. Moreover, it has been making efforts to facilitate market linkage for those PWDs who began running their own businesses as a result of involvement with these SHGs.
- *Establishing 40 new disability-inclusive SHGs* that work in the context of urban communities, churches and schools. So far, two SHGs have been created by parents of students with disabilities in Negus Teklehaymanot and Kosober primary

schools in Debremarkos and Injibara towns respectively. Of the 40 new disability-inclusive SHGs planned, 31 have already been set up (19 in Debremarkos and 12 in Injibara).[24]

- *Helping churches* (in Debremarkos and Injibara towns) to become disability-inclusive in their ministry. This is done by: raising church leaders' awareness of issues of disability inclusion; equipping them with biblical understanding of disability; helping them mainstream issues of disability in their annual and strategic plans, as well as in their day-to-day operations; helping churches to modify their physical and communication infrastructure; and helping church leaders adapt their services, such as worship programmes and Sunday school, to accommodate PWDs.

- *Enhancing the capacity of the education sector* to promote disability inclusion. This is done by providing educational assistive devices and strengthening the educational resource centres of two primary schools in the two towns, training special needs education teachers and key management staff at the schools, and providing training on the special educational needs of children with disabilities, as well as collaborating with local government in the two project sites with a view to establishing a town-level core team of inclusive education ambassadors.[25] This team is made up of representatives of educational stakeholders including PWD associations; its main purpose is to mobilize resources and standardize best practice in accommodating the special needs of children with disabilities across all government-owned schools in the two towns.

- *Building up networks* of stakeholders that can create positive synergy to promote disability inclusion and break down barriers of exclusion. To this end, associations of PWDs, universities and colleges, community-based organizations such as *eders* and religious institutions, relevant local government offices, and relevant international and local non-government organizations (NGOs) in the two project sites are part of the network.[26]

Project implementation was scheduled to take place in two 18-month phases, between April 2019 and March 2022. However, FDE is still in its first phase. Sporadic unrest around the project sites and the Covid-19 pandemic have negatively affected both the performance and impact of the project. Yet it is hoped that FDE will achieve its objective in its second phase, using the strategy of a holistic model of inclusion.

Lessons learnt

In this section we draw lessons from Tearfund in Ethiopia's journey towards creating disability-inclusive SHGs over more than ten years.

First, SHG is an ideal community platform to empower PWDs and other vulnerable groups in society, in an intersectional approach. In this regard, for instance, we have witnessed how SHGs have served as an instrument of outreach in Meta Welkite *woreda* in Oromia. Since the formation of SHGs, 80 per cent of the population in the local area have engaged with Christianity, and PWDs are engaging in activities that are boosting their resilience. For example, some blind people have become prominent farmers.[27] This suggests that SHGs can be used further to promote inclusive education, inclusive health and inclusive livelihoods, and so on.

Second, SHGs demonstrate that a scarcity of resources does not have to be a hindrance in promoting inclusion. One of the lessons learnt from the SHGs in Offa and Kindo Koysha *woredas* is how the cause of PWDs, older people and poorer women is upheld through SHG advocacy. This has resulted in their helping PWDs and other vulnerable groups to engage in income-generating activities, and enabling them to benefit from government safety-net programmes, see unjust and discriminatory practices being challenged and enjoy the solidarity of the community. Therefore, if SHGs are well equipped with the appropriate knowledge and practical skills for leading and managing inclusion, resources from donor organizations can be used more strategically and more effectively.

Third, SHGs can be potential assets to build the capacity of APDs. While APDs help PWDs become organized to make their voice heard, disability-inclusive SHGs give economic strength to PWDs and their associations in working to ensure their rights are respected. In this regard, we should work on creating platforms that enable SHGs to engage their members with disabilities in active learning conversations with a view to exploring ways to break down barriers that bar them from having an independent and dignified life.

Fourth, inclusion is more successful when there is a holistic approach to removing barriers. There are many disability-focused international and local NGOs working on issues relating to education, rehabilitation, employment, health and advocacy, often duplicating one another's efforts. What seems to be lacking among these organizations' efforts is complementarity and a holistic approach to disability inclusion. Hence, disability projects are phased out before showing permanent and tangible changes in the lives of PWDs. So there is both a limitation in the scale-up of projects during the programme cycle, and in their sustainability after the programme cycle. Lack of sustainability remains a challenge for many inspiring initiatives of disability inclusion in different parts of the world. What we have learnt from the Flourishing with Disability Ethiopia project in Debremarkos and Injibara towns, Amhara, is that a holistic approach to disability inclusion has the potential to create links between different entities such as churches, SHGs and other community-based organizations, APDs, schools and higher educational institutions, relevant local government offices and NGOs. If such stakeholders can join their hands, the issue of sustainability, scale-up and impact should not be a problem.

Recommendations

Disability has not yet been mainstreamed across Tearfund at corporate level and a theology of disability is in development at the time of writing. There is a need for Tearfund's definition of the concept of disability to reflect our faith, vision and mission. On the one hand, its definition should be made in recognition of the similarities and differences that exist between the concepts of impairment and disability. And on the other hand, the definition should reflect the different facets of disability.

So first and foremost, Tearfund is, and needs to be, on a journey towards disability inclusion. We should see disability inclusion as part of creating a social climate and infrastructure that can accommodate all sorts of vulnerable groups, enabling us to address issues of disability with an intersectional approach. For us, disability inclusion in particular, and social inclusion in general, should be a way of exercising our humanity in its fullest sense. As a faith-based INGO working through local churches, we need to understand that inclusion is also a means of living out our reverence to God in practical terms, and fulfilling our mission.

We should also realize that in our approach to disability inclusion we need to be empathetic and inward-looking, for we all have our own disabilities. It is only through God's grace that we can achieve recovery or efficiency in relation to living a dignified and flourishing life in order to fulfil the purpose for which we are created. Further, we need to recognize that it is our responsibility to spread God's grace by promoting the inclusion of those who are currently excluded.

Conclusion

In this chapter we have seen that SHGs complement Christian development practice and create a positive synergy so that people can act against poverty, exclusion, disability, ignorance, injustice and discrimination. At the core of this chapter, we have drawn from the experience of Tearfund in Ethiopia in collaboration with its partners, who have been engaged for more than ten years in promoting SHGs that are disability-inclusive. Accordingly, we have seen the lives of PWDs and other vulnerable groups being transformed using intersectional approaches. We have also realized that SHGs are strongly effective in enabling PWDs to release themselves from poverty and promoting solidarity within the community, particularly in resource-poor settings. We have also witnessed that SHGs can be a potential opportunity to enhance the capacity of APDs: they offer fertile ground for helping APDs become effective agents in upholding the rights of PWDs and ensuring their development, thereby ensuring disability inclusion becomes sustainable. To this end, the presence of a network of stakeholders such as SHGs, FBOs, development agencies, relevant government institutions, educational institutions and APDs is essential.

As seen throughout this chapter, systems and structural barriers are doing an injustice to PWDs, by promoting unhelpful norms, beliefs and cultural practices that increase the isolation of vulnerable groups. Disability-inclusive SHGs in the church context are uniquely positioned to address such injustices.

To a great extent, in Ethiopia and many other low-income countries, issues of disability have been managed through charity or approaches involving cash provision. By contrast, the SHG approach makes PWDs agents of their own change, by enabling them to save what they have and create seed funding for businesses that will undoubtedly evolve by exploiting their hidden potential. This is not an easy task. It requires an innovative approach and the involvement of many different stakeholders. The positive grass-roots examples given here show that even relatively small, low-cost initiatives can model disability inclusion approaches with the potential for much wider scale-up and replicability.

Acknowledgements

First and foremost, we would like to thank Almighty God for helping us generate ideas, gain strength and accomplish this work, despite technological challenges and a pandemic. A disability-inclusive SHG is in itself a relatively new concept so we're grateful to Tearfund's Theology of Inclusion working group for their patient support in helping us devise this concept paper.

Bibliography

Allen, R., 2010, 'Faith and Disability: Comfort, confusion or conflict? how does the adoption of Christian faith influence the lives of people who identify as "disabled" in Britain in the 21st century?', unpublished MA dissertation, University of Leeds.

Barclay, L., 2019, *Disability with Dignity: Justice, human rights and equal status*, New York and Abingdon: Routledge.

Beates, M. S., 2012, *Disability and the Gospel: How God uses our brokenness to display his grace*, Wheaton, IL: Crossway Books.

Blomberg, C. L., 2013, *Christians in an Age of Wealth : A biblical theology of stewardship*, E-pub edn, Grand Rapids, MI: Zondervan.

Bruijn, P., et al., 2012, *Count Me In: Include people with disabilities in development projects. A practical guide for organizations in Global South and North*, AR Veenendaal, the Netherlands: Stichting, Light for the World.

Burke, P., 2013, *Disability and Impairment Working with Children and Families*, digital edn, London and Philadelphia: Jessica Kingsley Publishers.

Cabot Venton, C., et al., 2013, *Partnership for Change: A Cost Benefit Analysis of Self Help Groups in Ethiopia*, Teddington: Tearfund.

Carter, I., 2013, *Releasing Potential: A facilitator's learning resource material for self-help groups*, s.l.: Tearfund Ethiopia.

CBM, 2012, *Inclusion Made Easy: A quick program guide to disability in development*, s.l.: CBM.

CBM, 2015, *Dialogues on Sustainable Development: A disability-inclusive perspective*, s.l.: CBM.

Charlton, J. I., 1998, *Nothing About Us Without Us: disability oppression and empowerment*, Berkeley, Los Angeles, and London: University of California Press.

Cobley, D., 2018, *Disability and International Development: A guide for students and practitioners*, Abingdon and New York: Routledge.

Creamer, D. B., 2003, 'Toward a Theology that Includes the Human Experience of Disability', in R. C. Anderson (ed.), *Graduate Theological Education and the Human Experience of Disability*, Binghamton, NY: The Haworth Pastoral Press, electronic copy.

Creamer, D. B., 2009, *Disability and Christian Theology: Embodied limits and constructive possibilities*, New York: Oxford University Press.

Cromie, S. D., H. Quinn-Gates, P. Fagan and M. Rebsso, 2017, *Psychosocial Outcomes and Mechanisms of Self-help Groups in Ethiopia*, July 2017, Dublin.

Data, M. and Z. Paulos, 2017, 'Factors Affecting Income Improvement of Women in Self Help Groups: The case of Damot Gale Woreda Wolaita Zone Ethiopia', *Journal of Economic Sustainable Development* 8(15), pp. 53–60.

Davis, L. J., 2017, 'Introduction: Disability, normality, and power', in L. J. Davis (ed.), *The Disability Studies Reader*, 5th edn, New York and Abingdon: Routledge, electronic copy.

de Hoop, T., C. Brody, S. Tripathi, M. Vojtkova, R. Warnock, 2019, *Economic Self-help Group Programmes for Improving Women's Empowerment*, London: International Initiative for Impact Evaluation.

Deko, Y. G., D. Shibiru and T. Chibsa, 2014, *Self Help Groups in Ethiopia: Activities, opportunities and constraints*, s.l.: Development Assistance Group (DAG).

Della Fina, V., R. Cera and G. Palmisano, 2017, *The United Nations Convention on the Rights of Persons with Disabilities: A commentary*, Geneva: Springer.

Dessiye, S., 2014, 'The Success and Challenges of Self Help Groups/SHGs in Addis Ababa: The case of "Addis Zemen" SHG in Wereda 6 and 7, Addis Ketema Sub-City', unpublished MA thesis, Addis Ababa.

Elias, T., 2014, 'The Role of Self-Help Groups in Empowering Commercial Sex Workers' Livelihood in Addis Ababa: Implication to social work practice', unpublished MA thesis, Addis Ababa.

Epperly, B. G., 2003, 'Healing and Hospitality in Jesus' Ministry', in R. C. Anderson (ed.), *Graduate Theological Education and the Human Experience of Disability*, Binghamton, NY: The Haworth Pastoral Press, electronic copy.

Freeman, A. J. (n. d.), *Some Theological Perspectives on Disability*, Moravian Theological Seminary.

Grue, J., 2016, *Disability and Discourse Analysis*, Abingdon and New York: Ashgate Publishing and Routledge.

Haile, T., 2014, 'Role of Self Help Groups Assessment of SHGs on Livelihood Diversification and Women Empowerment: A case to children's home society and family service; Hossana Program', unpublished MA thesis, s.l.

Hillgrove, T. and K. Smith, 2020, *Tearfund UK and Tear NL – Disability Review Final Report*, January 2020, Teddington.

Kumaran, K. P., 2011, 'Role of Self-Help Groups in Promoting Inclusion and Rights of Persons with Disabilities', *DESAI* 22(1), pp. 105–13.

Light for the World, 2017, *Resource Book on Disability Inclusion*, s.l.: Light for the World.

Maru, A. G., 2016, 'Evaluation of the Self-help Development Approaches in Promoting Women Empowerment in Ethiopia: The case of Debremarkos Districts of Amhara Region of Ethiopia', unpublished MA thesis, University of South Africa.

Meehan, F. and E. Mengistu, 2016, *Drought, Resilience, and Self-Help in Ethiopia: A review of Tearfund self help groups following El Niño*, Addis Ababa: USAID.

Melcher, S. J., 2011, 'A Tale of Two Eunuchs: Isaiah 56:1–8 and Acts 8:26–40', in J. Schipper and C. R. Moss (eds), *Disability Studies and Biblical Literature*, New York: Palgrave Macmillan, electronic copy.

Mitra, S., 2018, 'Disability Health and Human Development', in S. Grech, N. Groce and S. Mitra (eds), *Palgrave Studies in Disability and International Development*, New York, USA: Springer Nature.

Moss, C. R. and J. Schipper, 2011, 'Introduction', in J. Schipper and C. R. Moss (eds), *Disability Studies and Biblical Literature*, New York: Palgrave Macmillan, electronic copy.

Picard, A., 2016, 'No Longer Strangers: Disabled ontology and the church as meaningful community in liquid modernity', in A. Picard and M. Habets (eds), *Theology and the Experience of Disability: Interdisciplinary perspectives from voices down under*, Abingdon and New York: Routledge, electronic copy.

Pressler, C., 2017, 'Numbers', in P. D. Miller (ed.), *Abingdon Old Testament Commentaries*, Nashville, TN: Abingdon Press.

SBL (Society of Biblical Literature), 2009, *Disability in the Hebrew Bible: Interpreting mental and physical differences*, Cambridge: Cambridge University Press.

Shrout, J. R., 2007, 'A Strategy for Educating the Church Concerning Those with Special Needs', unpublished PhD thesis, Lynchburg, VA.

TDA (Terepeza Development Association), 2020, *SPCC-CEA Progress Update on PWDs Inclusion in Offa and Kindo Koysha (WKHC-TDA)*, 27 June, Soddo.

Tsegay, E., 2019, *Ten Years of Journey to Disability Inclusion in Ethiopia: Tear/Fund and partners*, Teddington: Tearfund.

UN (United Nations), 2006, *Convention on the Rights of Persons with Disabilities*, Geneva: UN.

van Ek, V. and S. Schot, 2017, *Towards Inclusion: A guide for organizations and practitioners*, s.l.: Light for the World.

Weingartner, L. and F. Pichon, 2017, *How Self-help Groups Strengthen Resilience: A Study of Tearfund's approach to tackling food insecurity in protracted crisis in Ethiopia*, London: ODI UK.

White, P., 2017, 'The Biblical View of Humanity and the Promotion of the Rights of Persons with Disabilities: The call and mission of the church', *Acta Theologica* 137(1), pp. 120–34.

WHO, 2001, *International Classification of Functioning, Disability and Health*, Geneva: WHO.

WHO and the World Bank, 2011, *World Disability Report*, Geneva: WHO.

Yohannes M., 2014, 'Challenges and Contributions of Self Help Groups in Empowering Poor Women: The case of Ethiopian Kale Heywet Church, Addis Ababa Integrated Urban Development Project', unpublished MA thesis, Addis Ababa.

Notes

1 As Michael Beates (2012) asserts, 'Brokenness seems to be a prerequisite that God demands before doing lasting work through a person.' The story of Jacob that we read in Genesis 32.24–30, for instance, clearly shows how the final physical impairment of Jacob has become a sign of the beginning of his real salvation that is based on Jacob's complete trust on God and no more on his might (Gen. 32.28–30).

2 *Kebele* and *woreda* are the first- and the second-lowest levels of government units in Ethiopia, respectively. Accordingly, in Ethiopia government structure is hierarchically organized at *kebele*, *woreda*, zone, region and federal levels. Towns and cities may serve as capitals of *woreda* or zone. Normally, cities are highly advanced and developed towns and will serve as capitals to regional or federal government levels.

3 Light for the World is a disability-focused international non-governmental organization, working in Ethiopia and many other low-income countries. It mainly promotes disability inclusion using the twin-track approach (mainstreaming disability in existing development programmes and designing specific intervention strategies to enhance capability of PWDs).

4 The term *woreda* may be equivalent to a county or district, depending on a nation's geographical arrangement. Meta Welkite *woreda* was formerly part of Metarobi *woreda*. For more information, see note 2.

5 Project profile of MKCRDA Meta Welkite Project provided by MKCRDA programme coordinator (28 July 2020).

6 Phone interview with Geremew Terfa, programme coordinator of MKCRDA, 28 July 2020, Addis Ababa.

7 A *kebele* is the lowest local government administrative unit, smaller than a *woreda*. For more information, see note 2.

8 Mulu Mammo, as quoted in a MKCRDA project profile for Meta Welkite, provided on 28 August 2020.

9 Phone interview with Geremew Terfa, programme coordinator of MKCRDA, 28 July 2020, Addis Ababa.

10 MKCRDA project profile for Meta Welkite, provided on 28 July 2020.

11 Phone interview with Geremew Terfa, programme coordinator of MKCRDA, 28 July 2020, Addis Ababa.

12 CEA is a consortium of different international and local NGOs including Tearfund in Ethiopia and TDA, aiming at enhancing the lobbying and advocacy of civic society organizations, which include SHGs. One of the writers of this chapter has served as disability inclusion adviser within the CEA consortium (May 2018 to August 2019). As a result, he was in a position to gather information on how disability-inclusive SHGs are created among consortium members, and how consortium members (including Tearfund) journeyed towards disability inclusion.

13 Phone interview with Tilahun Tadesse, 24 July 2020.

14 We met Meskele Lemma, who was 28 at the time, on a visit to the Offa-Kindo Koysha SHG project to document best practice examples of disability-inclusive SHGs, as part of the CEA project, in December 2018.

15 Amiha Worku made this statement as the Adama APDs shared experiences from the Adama SHGs on 1 August 2019, at one of the SHG gathering places in Adama town. We facilitated this experience-sharing as part of a CEA initiative to promote disability inclusion among consortium members.

16 Brief interview with former EKHCDC focal person of the CEA consortium, 26 July 2020.

17 Nigat Mekonin made this statement on a visit arranged with Tearfund partner the Ethiopian Mulu Wongel Amagnoch Church Development Commission (EMWACDC) to the Adama SHG programme, 9 November 2019.

18 See note 12. This training was organized and facilitated by one of the writers of this paper, while he was working for the CEA consortium as disability inclusion adviser. The training was held on 13–14 August 2018.

19 Nigat Mekonin made this statement during refresher training on promoting disability-inclusive SHGs to Adama FLA and CLA leaders led by the CEA disability inclusion adviser, 31 July 2019.

20 Brief interview with Negat Mekonin to gain project updates on disability-inclusive SHGs in Adama town, 1 August 2020.

21 Interview with Negat Mekonin, 1 August 2020.

22 One of the writers of this paper is serving as Tearfund in Ethiopia's focal person for this project, and as an adviser to EMWACDC.

23 In our audit of existing practices of disability inclusion in SHGs, conducted as a baseline assessment for FDE, we found that the CCM programme of Debremarkos and Injibara managed to establish three SHGs (1 in Debremarkos and 2 in Injibara) which are owned and operated by PWDs. The CCM project has also enabled mainstream SHGs to include PWDs as members. In some cases, we have even seen PWDs assuming leadership positions.

24 EMWACDC FDE annual project reports of Debremarkos and Injibara sites (2020).

25 Negus Teklehaymanot Primary School, Debremarkos town and Kosober Primary School, Injibara town.

26 *Eders* are community-based organizations established to serve as a traditional scheme of social insurance. Accordingly, people make small payments on a regular basis. When a member of an *eder* loses a loved one, all *eder* members will come to their home and comfort them. Nowadays, *eders* are also engaged in supporting vulnerable people such as older people and PWDs in severe need.

27 Phone interview with the programme coordinator of MKCRDA, 28 July 2020, Addis Ababa.

13

Abya Yala: 'A house that sings for all nations'[1]

JOCABED REINA SOLANO MISELIS
AND JUANA LUIZA CONDORI QUISPE

I looked at myself in the river, I saw my eyes and water came out.
  I am Water.
When I spoke and breathed, air came from my mouth.
  I am Wind.
I ate and my body was fed by the earth. I am Earth.
I felt my skin was hot and cold. I am Fire.
I realized that I am Water, Wind, Fire and Earth.
We are Earth.

From times long past, this land, Abya Yala, has been home to our ancestors. She is home to many daughter nations organized into small communities – *comarcas*, *tentas*, *ayllus*[2] – embracing diversity in all their different cultural manifestations, social struggles and calls for justice. Like threads being woven together to form a whole, we live and work with our gaze fixed on the firmament, the stars, the celestial bodies, the direction of the wind, the comings and goings of the sun, and the changing light of the moon.

The inclination towards oneness in our communities enables us to see the value of unity and the living interrelatedness of all of creation. All life, whether on the economic, social, political or spiritual plane, exists and develops in a vital space, the land. We sprout from the very roots of these lands: we feel and we see from her perspective, the sacred territory that bestows life. Keeping a sense of spirituality under the conditions we find ourselves in today is more challenging yet profound. The life of our society incorporates more than humankind, going beyond the barriers of what is known and penetrating the mysteries of creation in its manifest diversity.

The faces and voices of Abya Yala weave a sense of community and a collective imagination. They reveal and give a glimpse of the transformative values, visions and feelings that are embedded in the spirals of our pathways. We are committed to a dialogue of responses and solutions based on ancestral wisdom that involves humanity, land and animal and plant life, and promotes respect for diversity. Our intent is to overcome egoisms and ethnocentrisms, which always threaten ways of coexisting that are able to overcome barriers.

If one immerses oneself in the daily life of our peoples, one can truly understand full social harmony. This way of conceiving of harmonious coexistence guides a continual dialogue that is a real strength in a world that is visibly fragmented in all areas of knowledge, spirituality and life-building because of Eurocentric development. Paradoxically, the recognition of full harmonious coexistence as a paradigm for life does not have its origin in the church or educational institutions or even among the non-profit organizations that work for life and serve the poor.

A church committed to the gospel is just when it is aligned with the Creator's salvific plan for the whole of humanity. Our desire is for the gospel to be truly 'good news' for the descendants of the men and women who witnessed the cross and the sword together come ashore on to their lands with the *conquistadores* more than 500 years ago in Abya Yala. The gospel imparted in the conquest and the colonies in these lands took on and still takes on a foreign, disconnected, theological and pastoral perspective. Historically, it has had very little regard for indigenous nations and peoples as bearers of messages, revelations and paradigms of coexistence that might be worthy of consideration.

Yet, if the history of the church is the sum of the lives and paths we all walk, then ours are vital histories that the church as the body of Christ must not forget: 'Let us therefore make every effort to do what leads to peace and to mutual edification' (Rom. 14.19, NIV). As a living part of this body, we are called to express our experience. In this way, we enrich the work of the church with the powerful testimony that pours from the multiplicity and plurality of our peoples, nations and ethnic groups, in all their manifestations in full coexistence. Peoples and nations move forward following Jesus' footsteps in unity with their story.

This chapter explores the potential of narratives, ancient and ancestral stories, as valuable resources for enriching theological reflection on the key concepts that shape our understandings of 'ethnic' and 'ethnicity' in Abya Yala. While these terms originate outside indigenous contexts, indigenous peoples have appropriated them in order to manage their position in society and in all spaces of coexistence. We are plural, and we are Gunadule, Aymara, Wiwa, Embera, Misak, when we identify ourselves in one way or another with the narratives that sustain our lives.

Exploring 'ethnicity' in the context of Abya Yala

Ethnic identity and 'plurinational coexistence'

The emergence of the idea of 'ethnic' in Abya Yala in the last two decades has given rise to different ways of understanding and articulating the concept of 'ethnicity'. It is presented in diverse ways, invigorated by its interactions, demands and resistances, rather than being narrowly determined only by cultural manifestations or acts (Oré Rocca, 2010, p. 4). The existence of records showing the cultural creation of 'ethnic groups', or drawing attention to their social realities, reaches its full importance when we consider what makes each people who they are. The articulation of different social practices and cultural characteristics, expressed and displayed in the collective imagination, shapes the ethnic characteristics that ascribe a certain particularity in relation to others, formulating our identity. These particularities both feed our sense of belonging and differentiate us from others, and this ends up reaffirming in ourselves who we think we are and how others perceive us.

Our peoples are considered indigenous because they descend from populations that inhabited a geographic territory before the establishment of other people groups. These groups later structured the country according to how it most suited them while ignoring the land's first inhabitants (natives, aboriginals). In other words, being descendants of (pre-hispanic) peoples who existed here before the Conquest is what makes us indigenous ethnic groups.

Indigenous communities are part of a pluricultural community that is consolidated in dominant monocultural institutions with European roots. Yet, in order for coexistence to be possible, pluralism must be embraced: that is, 'the acceptance of the "other" or several distinct "others", considering that differences complement and enrich us all, more than obstruct us' (Albó and Barrios, 2006, pp. 36–54). We could also speak of 'otherness', being equals yet different, and the obligations that implies. Understanding the principles of pluralism and otherness will be key for understanding religious, judicial, economic and political pluralism in the plural space.

Indigenous peoples in different countries recognize how important their ethnic identity is for them. Many of them also call themselves nations, as distinct from the nation-state. For example, in Canada many call themselves First Nations. Furthermore, in many parts of Abya Yala, people propose that the state of which they form a part should be defined as a plurinational state out of respect for indigenous peoples. Unlike other uses of the term 'nation', viewing indigenous peoples as nations introduces an element of ethnic consciousness and a political project.

'Multi-' and 'pluri-' are widely used prefixes in many countries in Abya Yala where both mean 'many'. It has been posited that the difference is that the former has a more quantitative sense while the latter is qualitative. However, many states declare themselves 'pluricultural' by law yet they perpetuate negative intercultural relations of a colonial nature between different peoples and cultural groups. Thus, we are presented with the challenge of learning to structure intercultural relations with positive principles of plurality that include the collective rights of ethnic communities. From our ethnic perspective, the ideal is no longer a total homogenization of national society, but rather a pluri- and intercultural society in which different identities and cultures can be sustained and can coexist. While many cultural patterns might be shared, cultural pluralism is a strength. Yet, in order for true interculturality to be realized, we must confront the inequalities between ethno-cultural groups that we find in our plurinational coexistences.

Epistemicide in Abya Yala

It is also important to point out the stories of death in our contexts, both in general society and in the church in Abya Yala. We must denounce colonialities,[3] epistemicides,[4] globalization and homogenization as expressions of death that threaten full harmonious coexistence. These are systems that try to kill the spirit of the peoples and nations that do not live under the dominant categories. Here, perhaps, we could also include the hegemonic powers that suppress the other in all their expressions.

Epistemicide continues to wound the hearts of the peoples of Abya Yala. Furthermore, what we have already mentioned about the faces of violence against minorities is once again expressed in the proposals that we find in 'development' models. Nicolás Panotto (2015) states:

[W]hen Western societies speak of development, generally they are referring to urbanisation, capitalist economic systems, new technologies and globalisation. Development and underdevelopment become two opposing poles. Development implies conditions found in the nations of the 'centre' being reproduced in the Third World. In this sense, the idea of development becomes a sociocultural concept that not only means difference between two parts but in that moment also creates a dynamic of submission, one to the other. In geopolitical and sociocultural terms, we see the same concepts of domination and underdevelopment applied to indigenous groups. The geopolitical position of the smallest nations within the largest nation-state is one of inferiority in the widest sense of the word.

These proposed models 'benefit' some and oppress others. They widen the gap between the privileged and the vulnerable in our societies, with economic models sustained by the labour of those who do not reap the benefits of all their hard work. Furthermore, these are models that exploit and do violence to the earth, causing the death of animals, forests, the biodiversity found in the jungles, and destroying knowledge of the plants that many indigenous peoples know well and that do not exist in other places. But it also brings death to humanity, affecting the most vulnerable most immediately. And the vulnerable are vulnerable because of this system, even though they are the ones doing the least damage to this *nega* (home) that we call earth.

In the midst of all this, we must recognize that there exist age-old models of living in harmony with the earth among the indigenous nations in Abya Yala. It is vital for society to know, appreciate and learn from the wisdom of indigenous peoples, who offer a valuable contribution to humanity. We should do this not just in an effort to include people traditionally discriminated against, as is the current trend, but rather including them as legitimate models offering hope-filled proposals for the world. If we do not urgently work on these proposals with serious intent, we as a society will lose a great deal. With the disappearance of indigenous languages, knowledge of medicinal plants and indigenous peoples' wisdom, the collective memory of humanity and different perceptions about the relationship of humanity with the earth are all lost. This loss affects us all.

Theologies that are nourished by the dynamics of hegemony and homogenization are not born out of good living, of shalom. In contrast, such theologies are divorced from the founding principles of the good news: they create ways of life identifying with social systems and with cultural patterns such as consumerism, extractivism and the globalization and homogenization of knowledge. These, in turn, generate their own subcultures and have other social and economic consequences. The biblical narratives, however, are a rich resource for theological reflection on ethnicity and have the power to shape and transform our understanding and our practice. These narratives are explored in the following section.

'Ethnicity' and the biblical narratives

Old Testament

Ethnic identities are not finished and determined constructs. Rather, they are subjectively constructed or modified in time and space, including and excluding, demarcating human groups. This was how the ancient Hebrew communities who lacked a specific ethnic identity were consolidated. Elamites, Akkadians, Arameans, Hittites, Amorites, Jebusites, even Philistines, fused and came together to form part of the northern and southern Israelite kingdoms. These latter had to reconstruct their nations over and over again as they were invaded by Assyria and Babylon, contending with cultural assimilation yet persisting in their identity. Their ritual animal sacrifices, dietary restrictions, rules and social norms distinguished them from the other nations around them.

Distinct narratives that reference the multi-ethnic character of the area they inhabited in those days speak of ethnicity as a gift from God. In the Genesis narratives, God wanted the land to be filled, but human groups insisted on trying to group together to outwork their own idea of God's will to populate the earth. The story of the Tower of Babel (Gen. 11.1–9) presents God as the author of the linguistic and ethnic confusion of the builders: they thought that the elimination of diversity found in the different ethnic groups would represent a way out, according to their own human will. We see in this narrative how in this confusion God's real multicultural and multi-ethnic proposal for humanity is an act of grace, separating them from the threats that human diasporas represented to the fulfilment of the Creator's will.

God's salvific project would continue with one person who responded to his call, Abraham. In the story, all nations would be blessed through this servant of God. The biblical term for 'nation' is very similar to our term 'ethnic group'. Isaiah 2.2–5 foresees many ethnic groups marching towards the city of God, multitudes moving towards a pluricultural community life in one space and in one mind. They move in the light of the divine host to whom they give their fragrant gifts, which help promote relationships, alliances and bonds of peace. He presents all ethnicities in a house of prayer, collective spiritual development in a common space recognizing the differences of its protagonists (Isa. 56.7). In Jeremiah 31, the author alludes to a scene of what is to come, shared by different social classes, where all are assumed to be equal. Jeremiah felt he was sent not only to the chosen people but to all nations. For his part, Amos recognizes that there is one universal God of justice, leading to fellowship and communion among all peoples.

Yet, after the covenant that Yahweh makes at Sinai with God's people, they internalize the notion of chosen people. This event marks the start of an ethnocentric posture which creates a tempting artifice to justify their rejection of other ethnic groups, who just like Israel, were consolidating their collective identity around a common ancestor. Being God's chosen people was interpreted by the Israelites in terms of exclusivity, causing them to abandon their responsibility towards other nations and to instead build a supposed intra- and inter-ethnic security. It caused them to reject others to the point of promoting extreme self-seclusion, as can be seen in the books of Ezra and Nehemiah.

The Gospels

Jesus, the Saviour of all, came to his own and his own did not receive him. Yet his dialogical essence reached beyond his ethno-cultural borders. One demonstration of this is found in the parable of the great banquet in Luke 14, when the invited guests find all kinds of excuses not to attend. In the end, it is those who are excluded and disregarded by society who take part in the feast.

Jesus was recognized and visited by magi, astrologers and priests from a different latitude who held different beliefs. In the Gospel of Matthew (chapter 2), a book whose audience was the Jewish community, we are told of these wise men searching for Jesus. Their capacity to see the light fulfils God's covenant promise and gives to the non-Jewish peoples the task of announcing the birth of the Messiah. Isaiah (60.3–6, NIV) had prophesied: 'Nations will come to your light, and kings to the brightness of your dawn.' This speaks of nations, peoples and ethnic groups who pursue the light, human powers that surrender to hope, and a kingdom that is open to and fully inclusive of all people.

In the story of Jesus' healing of the centurion's servant (Matt. 8.5–13), neither the Roman official nor his servant was considered worthy of a Jew's attention. Yet Jesus recognizes their faith and shows his love for all by healing the servant and then declaring that many from the East and West will be in the kingdom of heaven. Jesus opens the possibility for people of all origins, from all the peoples of the earth, to be part of the kingdom of God. The ideas of inclusion and exclusion are part of the discourse of the kingdom of God.

A Canaanite woman begs Jesus to heal her daughter in Matthew 15.21–28. For generations, the Canaanites had been considered people who used trickery and fraud to obtain goods and riches, and people who served many gods. In the dialogue that Jesus has with the Canaanite woman, the prejudices that the Jews held against the Canaanites at the time are reflected in Jesus' words: 'It is not right to take the children's bread and toss it to the dogs' (Matt. 15.26, NIV). Although Jesus uses this phrase, it is unclear whether he is merely restating the Jews' beliefs or voicing his own. In any case, the story invites us to reflect on how the influence of his people, culture and ethnicity caused Jesus to have to question his own identity. It highlights the tension between who he was in relation to his own people and who he was in relation to other peoples and, furthermore, who he was in relation to the kingdom of God.

In his body, all these elements are present. How do we listen to the background music in order to see the other from God's perspective when we are full of so many mixed influences that permeate how we see the other? From this point of view, we can consider the importance of the Canaanite woman's response to Jesus' disquieting words, which opens up a space for dialogue about the unknown. Her answer gets Jesus' attention and he stops to listen to the voice of the insistent woman, in whom he does not expect to find hope. The humility and wisdom of the woman's response amaze Jesus, who anticipates the so-called pagans' entrance into the kingdom of his Father. And so the daughter of the woman of another ethnicity, whose boundaries were not to be crossed from the exclusive Jewish perspective, is healed.

In the multi-ethnic space in which Samaritans, Canaanites, Greeks, Jewish converts and Jews lived, the Jews established rigid boundaries to define their differences and interests. The Jews considered the Samaritans, for example, as inferior to them. Jesus built bridges and dialogue, surpassing the limits of their imagination, because he found a hunger for his teaching among the people. It was often those excluded from Jewish society who saw hope in Jesus (John 12.20).

Samaritans appear in more than one parable in Jesus' teaching as a living example of selfless love for the other. In a way, the Samaritan was much more prepared to see the face of God in the people who suffered pain and abandonment (Matt. 25.31). The image of God that Jesus offers is that of a God who above all invites, loves and offers forgiveness. Jesus' understanding of the people of God is inclusion par excellence. Here we sense his strength and optimism in the future becoming of humanity among the nations, peoples and ethnic groups in the last days. Here we have a Jesus fighting to break through barriers built by Israel. Jesus was the living example of the role of bridge between ourselves, others and otherness.

Pentecost

At the outpouring of the Holy Spirit, God invites the nations to be reconciled with one another, and in and with God (Acts 2.1–12). At Pentecost, a multitude of nations hear a common message about all God has done, and God initiates a deeper involvement in all nations and peoples, including all ethnicities. Cultures are an effective way of establishing the church as a pluralistic space for working on just, multi-ethnic community life together. In Acts 2.11, the Holy Spirit descends on the saints, the pagans and those of Jewish origin. In this event God rejoices and reveals Godself, affirming different languages and cultures as valuable tools for communicating and for engaging with the kingdom.

The mix of Jewish and Greek elements and the cultural and ethnic features from the provinces in Paul's day were all reflected in the churches themselves. The combination of Judaism, Christianity and Gnosticism, which Paul referred to as hollow and deceptive philosophy (Col. 2), was an almost natural assimilation. The results of the multi-ethnic religious climate pulsed in the mind and imagination of the believers.

Paul's words in Galatians 3.28 (NIV) highlight the existing walls and inequalities: 'There is neither Jew nor Gentile, neither slave nor free, nor is there male and female, for you are all one in Christ Jesus.' His background observation here relates to the search for equality when the combination of ethnic oppression, social class and gender inequality are so evident in the community, supported by narratives of power rather than by the shalom of God. 'There is no longer ...' is not a call for homogenization. What Christ creates is unity in diversity: beyond that which differentiates us is a bond between oneself and the other in Jesus that transcends other identities. In other words, diversity runs through the essence of Jesus and in essence we in our diversity are one in him. Therefore, we continue to propose diverse ways to build community. Our identity in Jesus is not uniform; rather, we have a connection in Christ, whatever our ethnicity or ancestry, which leads to a new way of life, in whom we continue to be, whether Gunadule, Aymara, Wiwa, Embera, Maya, or Mapuche. Jesus is the connection that identifies us and gives us an identity that is transversal to our own identities, rather than being the only way of coming close to, discovering and knowing the revelation of the mystery of God. This manifestation is poured out through grace on cultures and each people group responds in the way that is unique and specific to their culture. In Jesus Christ we find the one who liberates us from the discriminating and exclusive boundaries humanity has built, in order to show us the light of love that embraces and rejoices in diversity.

Revelation

The book of Revelation emphasizes the huge variety of cultures and ethnicities on the earth. The lion of the tribe of Judah, the offspring of David, has with his blood 'purchased for God persons from every tribe and language and people and nation' (Rev. 5.9, NIV). The multitude of the redeemed will be 'from every nation, tribe, people and language' (Rev. 7.9, NIV). When the prophetic call of John is renewed, between the sixth and seventh trumpets, he is ordered to 'prophesy again about many peoples, nations, languages and kings' (Rev. 10.11, NIV). According to Revelation 14.6, an angel proclaims the gospel 'to those who live on the earth – to every nation, tribe, language and people'.

This vision allows us to question ourselves about the responsibility we all share to preserve the identity of every lineage, people group and nation. As we see clearly in the creation account of Genesis 1.1, in the beginning God created the heavens and the earth, including human beings who received the breath of *Ruah* and who were made in the image and likeness of God. Therefore, before God, all human beings have the same standing because we carry the essence of God's breath. So the creative capacity to organize ourselves in different ways, even before the Lamb, preserves the essence of who we are in all our diversity because of God's breath.

Before the Lamb, the good purposes of God that have been present from the beginning are manifest in creation, in all its fullness. This is in contrast to the reality of the seven churches to which the book of Revelation is directed, and which are under death's dominion. One of the characteristics of hegemonic power is to kill and homogenize identities. The backdrop against which the Genesis and Revelation accounts are written is one of power.

And it is in this context that justice as good news is expressed when we acknowledge and appreciate one another, when we learn and fight to preserve the knowledge and wisdom of people groups different from our own, and when we value and recognize the dignity of the life of each person as an individual.

Woman and man both reflect the image and likeness of God. In the Gunadule and Aymara cultures, as well as others, complementarity is important. For this reason, in Gunadule theology, God is referred to as Mother and Father. God cannot exist only as Father. And this way of understanding the Creator leaves its mark on social life and relationships in the community.

In the same way, the good news also values diversity in collectivity, diversity within ethnicities. When we embrace this principle of the justice of God, we take care not to lose that part of the image and likeness of God that is present in each people group. Only when each people group lives out of its diversity do we fully reflect the image and likeness of God in humanity because the *Ruah* has breathed the breath of life in all of creation. The body of Christ made manifest in his church cannot be complete without the presence of all nations. As Costa Rican theologian Juan Stam writes (2012):

> The importance that John obviously gives to this formula can be seen as an indication of the meaning of ethnic, social and linguistic realities for him. Beyond a simple abstract concept of 'universal', these expressions indicate the eschatological preservation of the diversities that mark our history; John seems to conceive of 'enduring life' as characterised by the same cultural identities as now.

The theme continues until the end of the book. In 21.3 John makes a radical and significant change in the language of God's old covenant with Israel. The old covenant, according to its nature and purpose, said 'I will be your God and you will be my people', in the singular. But the Greek of 21.3 transforms it in a plurinationalist sense: 'and they will be your peoples' (plural). Such an apparently 'heretical' change could not be a coincidence.[5]

In the following section, we briefly introduce two narratives – from the Aymara and Gunadule people – to show how they sustain and bring life to our communities, and why it is vital to preserve them.

'Ethnicity' and indigenous narratives

Aymara narrative

Aymara[6] communities' way of living in solidarity and harmony (*suma qamaña*[7]) is fundamental as a principle of justice, a principle that is promoted by our elders and authorities (*mallkus/t'allas*). But every so often, a community member experiences a time of darkness, causing sadness, abandonment and desolation in the family, and as a consequence the balance of the community is thrust into crisis. Fathers and mothers who are ill-treated, children who are abandoned, women who are beaten, and neighbours who are victims of robbery, all these demand corrective sanctions or punishments, and communities have an intriguing way of ensuring restoration.

The person who abandons, beats, mistreats or even robs remains in the community to restore the balance, returning that which was stolen, putting right his or her mistakes through hard labour for the whole community. Like any other Aymara community member who eats from the land, they must continue to meet their family's needs, overseen by the entire community. Even without having been transformed completely in their behaviour, they are still considered a member of the community, with all the rights and obligations that implies.

It is well known that Aymara communities do not isolate social offenders; rather, they keep them in the community to do work that aims towards restitution for the damages caused both to the family and the community. The person is not imprisoned because imprisonment would mean no recompense: he or she would not be working or supporting anyone. The idea is that, at the very least, they must earn their daily bread and demonstrate to the community that they are willing to continue living under and respecting the community's way of life.

This story is so rich and complex. It establishes tolerance under the premise that isolation and separation are not wise measures in our time; rather, wisdom suggests that the Aymara offender remains and continues to be included. At one point in time, they were under the influence of darkness but now in community they are emerging into the light under the diligent oversight of the *mallku* judges who will over time settle what the person's real intentions are as long as they stay in the community voluntarily.

The re-emergence of ancestral wisdom calls us to reflect on

our ancestral outlook alongside our church practices, for our own edification. It is essential that we grow closer to our communities as generative, life-giving tools to help organize human time, space, territories and community so that there is a continual dialogue with that which is contradictory and divergent. This relationship of initial resistance, moderated by acceptance, brings freedom: this gives sense to our values, which aim to reflect the life of Jesus Christ, who never hesitated to listen to and favour those who were neglected by a system that discriminated against them on the grounds of class and ideas of purity. If we do not follow the example of the teacher of teachers, our interactions become unfair and intolerant and our ways of receiving one another become as ambiguous as our understanding.

Gunadule narrative

It is a day like any other. The inhabitants of the Gunadule[8] nation get out of bed very early in the morning before the sun rises to start their daily activities. You hear Grandfather get up to go to the field to work the land. You hear the voices of other brothers who are preparing to go fishing. There is a murmur coming from the kitchen where Grandmother is preparing breakfast. It is still dark, but everyone in the house knows they must get up early to get the day's work done. They have heard from generation to generation that it is important to get up before *Dad Ibe* (Grandfather Sun) rises, so that his energy gives us energy and finds us ready to start our work. Because if you are not found ready, Grandmother says, laziness will get you.

There are narratives that shape or misshape a nation. And the Gunadule have many stories, symbols, dances and songs that give shape to the people to help them live out one of the greatest ethical principles of the Gunadule people: the meaning of life in community. However, things were not always harmonious in the Gunadule community, our grandparents tell us. There was a time when chaos reigned in our communities, where we did not desire to live in community with one another, which is why God taught us through the earth to live in community as Gunadule brothers and sisters. Gunadale stories also speak of how we have resisted several waves of violence, such as the Spanish conquest of Abya Yala that caused the largest genocide in human history, and the colonialities that still exist today in many different forms.

Gunadule stories are full of characters that represent Gunadule life and how it has been organized over time. The Gunadule people have many stories that challenge and invite the community to live in harmony. Furthermore, in their search for abundant life the Gunadule have created stories that demonstrate their experience of their relationship with God, the land, the Gunadule community and, more recently, with other peoples. In turn, the Bible presents narratives that challenge us to live the abundant life found in God's shalom. Jubilee, the Sabbath year and Sabbath days are all intended to show humanity how to live abundantly.

When we connect one of the Gunadule stories of *Balu Wala*[9] and the biblical text of Exodus 23.10–11,[10] we can see they have some things in common. Both stories have their origin in God. The story of *Balu Wala* mentions that *Ibeler*[11] knew that all that *Baba Nana* (God) had created was not just for one group but for all the children of Mother Earth. In the biblical text on the Sabbath year and jubilee, everything comes from God. Both narratives mention that the fruit of the earth is for all creatures. In *Balu Wala*, the idea is to protect humanity: in the jubilee and Sabbath years it is to protect the clan. In *Balu Wala*, the land is not the property of anyone. The jubilee and Sabbath year remind us that the land and people belong to God, in contrast to the royal tax system where the land and people were considered the king's property. In the jubilee year they enact agrarian reform so that all families who have had economic problems can return to work their ancestral lands.

The jubilee keeps alive the original utopia over and against the tax system of kings and empires to which the Israelites were subject. When they heard the Lamb, there was *iubileaus*, celebration of restitution, liberation and a general restoration of order. In *Balu Wala* the pain of the earth is expressed when people appropriate it for themselves. In the jubilee the joy of the land, the slave and the exploited is expressed. In *Balu Wala*, the cutting down of the tree was a disgrace for those who had possession or riches (material, mineral, spiritual), but for those who cut it down it was a celebration. It brought justice and equity for all. Jubilee and the Sabbath year demonstrate the good purposes of God for all.

Concluding remarks

In the memories of the peoples and nations of Abya Yala, there have been dynamic processes of encounter and mis-encounter. Throughout this journey the construction of identities has changed. The ethnic groups of 500 years ago are not the same as the ethnic groups of today. Being from Abya Yala leads us to ask ourselves who is speaking and from where. In some cases, identities have been imposed or taken on from elsewhere. One could speak of the 'indigenous being' in an intermittent way, of the multiple identities of the indigenous person, expressions that perhaps we do not consciously think of as indigenous people in our own contexts but which influence us in some cases because of our blood heritage. But beyond lineage, what other elements of our cultural heritage identify us?

Perhaps beyond defining concepts, we can say that we are Gunadule, Aymara, Wiwa, Embera, Misak, among other peoples, when we identify ourselves with the narratives that sustain our lives. And these narratives are ultimately tied to the memory of the earth as a special gift granted by God to each of our peoples, even though we may look very similar to one another through the legacy of having learnt from the voice of the earth, which in Gunadule is known as *Nabgwana* (Mother Earth). It is very important that each people group acknowledges and appreciates the particular gift that they have and that makes them unique on this earth. It is in this mystery that the good news of God for this particular people may lie and should be shared with others.

The identification with the land, the territory, the language, the symbols of a place, ways of communicating, their symbolic universe, their understanding of God, cultural and theological assumptions made when trying to understand life and the presence of God in life, these are all part of the indigenous face of God that speaks of the gift that each people group has been given. When we understand that the interpretation of the revelation of God is specific to a people, we conclude that when a people group with their own specific culture dies, something of God dies. And those of us who say we wish to know God must recognize that we cannot know God fully without our brother or sister who brings us that special gift of God from their people. For this reason, it is imperative that we develop theologies in our churches and Christian organizations that promote, preserve and listen to the peoples of the world, because there too we find the good news of God.

Acknowledgements

This chapter was translated from Spanish to English by Andrew Jennings.

Bibliography

Albó, X. and F. Barrios, 2006, *Por una Bolivia plurinacional e intercultural, Informe sobre Desarrollo Humano* (Proyecto, BOL/02/008), accessed 29 March 2021: www.bivica.org, accessed 29.03.21.

de Sousa Santos, B., 2010, *Descolonizar el saber, reinventar el poder*, Montevideo: Ediciones Trilce.

Oré Rocca, C. A., 2010, 'La etnicidad y sus usos: Reflexiones acerca de la difusión de la etnicidad', *e-cadernos CES, 07/2010*, https://journals.openedition.org/eces/423, accessed 29.03.2021.

Panotto, N., 2015, 'Posdesarrollo, diferencia e identidades socio-culturales: "lo divino entre-medio" como aporte a una epistemología de la eco-teología', Taller de Oikotree sobre Educación Transformadora, 3–9 February 2015, Matanzas, Cuba, pp. 197–208.

Stam, J., 2012, 'Evangelio, cultura y religiones: misión y pluralismo', *Lupa Protestante*, www.lupaprotestante.com/blog/evangelio-cultura-y-religiones-mision-y-pluralismo/, accessed 29.03.2021.

Wagua, A., 2011, *En defensa de la vida y su armonía*, Panamá: Proyecto EBI Guna/Fondo Mixto Hispano Panameño.

Notes

1 The name the Gunadule people have for the continent that the majority know as America. When indigenous peoples sing, we are lifting up our prayers to the Creator. Song is a very deep expression in indigenous spirituality, expressing as it does the connection of the human being with God and the cosmos.

2 These do not have a direct translation into English. They are different terms used by different indigenous peoples, each with its own local context and connotations for which in English we would most closely use the general word 'community'.

3 'Coloniality' represents a large variety of phenomena, from the psychological and existential to the economic and military, but all have a common characteristic: the determination and domination of one culture, world view, philosophy, faith or way of living over another. In an economic and political sense, coloniality is the reflection of the dominance of the extractive, productive, commercial and financial sectors of the 'neo-colonised' states and sectors (mostly found in the majority

world) by the industrialized countries of the minority world. This leads to dependence and the 'development of sub-development', the subordination and marginalizing of the 'neo-colonies' by the dominant empires of today (Panotto, 2015).

4 Western knowledge has imposed a world view based on the impossibility of imagining another world distinct from the capitalist world. Boaventura de Sousa Santos (2010) speaks of 'epistemicide' to define how this Western perspective has subjugated the knowledge and wisdom of other cultures and peoples.

5 Original text in Spanish.

6 The Aymara people have their origins in the ancient Aymara territories that stretched out across the Andes around Lake Titicaca, occupying the high Andean plains of what is today Bolivia, Peru, Chile and the north of Argentina.

7 This term in Aymara can roughly be translated 'living well'. Aymara is a language spoken by the people of the same name. It is an agglutinative language whose structure is built on suffixes.

8 An indigenous people group that has existed in Abya Yala since time immemorial. They are currently located in Panama and Colombia.

9 The Gunadule narrative of the salt tree speaks about the system of oppression under which the marginalized and poor suffer. Their liberation comes from the dispossessed cutting down the tree in order to live in harmony, sharing with everyone the riches found in the tree.

10 'For six years you are to sow your fields and harvest the crops, but during the seventh year let the land lie unploughed and unused. Then the poor among your people may get food from it, and the wild animals may eat what is left. Do the same with your vineyard and your olive grove' (Ex. 23.10–11, NIV).

11 The central character in Gunadule stories who represents goodness and the liberation of the land, including for humans.

Afterword

As I write this in April 2021, in the midst of the Covid-19 pandemic, Tearfund's commitments to diversity, equality and inclusion remain strong and grow increasingly stronger. The year 2020 was significant for our diversity and inclusion work as we lamented, and responded to, racial injustice experienced in the US, UK and around the world. We published our 'Anti-racism statement' setting out our commitments to learn, grow and improve.

At Tearfund we believe that every person on the earth was created in the image of God. Within that belief lie the values of love, compassion, patience, peace, truth and acceptance; we acknowledge that these are fundamental to the ways we interact with each other and all of those we serve, regardless of their diverse backgrounds or beliefs. We are committed to working towards an inclusive organizational culture where there is equity and where, irrespective of identity or background, there is equal access to opportunities. We want to create an environment where all staff feel valued and accepted and where everyone belongs. We are also committed to helping our staff, partners and other stakeholders develop an understanding of how they can more effectively serve and engage with others in ways that take individual needs and experiences into account and reflect our Christian values. We will pursue justice and reconciliation where misunderstanding has caused broken relationships. We will provide safe spaces and clear channels where issues can be discussed openly and courageously.

These are ambitious commitments that require a long-term journey of change and transformation for us as a collective body. And that journey has to start with us as individuals. Based on Tearfund's experience and learning, some of which has been shared through this book, this is not an easy journey. It is one that requires great courage, vulnerability and faith. A journey that requires us to continue to ask the big and difficult questions, to remain curious and, in doing so, to walk alongside and be guided by communities, individuals, our staff and our partners, the church and others.

Covid-19 and the global wake-up call on racial injustice has meant that sitting by and watching is not an option. We must all put diversity and inclusion at the heart of everything we do – societies, governments, faith groups and other civil society actors – if we are truly to see the transformational change and impact the world so needs. This book was collated in the hope that it will inspire action, and that through sharing the good and the not so good, it will enrich and further the dialogue on diversity and inclusion within our faith communities and beyond. Thank you for joining us on this journey.

Catriona Dejean
Director of Strategy and Impact

Index of Names and Subjects

Local vs Expat?
No in regional offices
Pay at each level (Rv)
P 166 Zoom is an equaliser